I0885334

Transforming the Financial Landscape With ICTs

Dharmendra Singh
Modern College of Business and Science, Oman

Garima Malik
Birla Institute of Technology Management, Greater Noida, India

Shalini Aggarwal
Chandigarh University, India

A volume in the Advances in Finance, Accounting, and Economics (AFAE) Book Series

IGI Global
PUBLISHER of TIMELY KNOWLEDGE

Published in the United States of America by
IGI Global
Business Science Reference (an imprint of IGI Global)
701 E. Chocolate Avenue
Hershey PA, USA 17033
Tel: 717-533-8845
Fax: 717-533-8661
E-mail: cust@igi-global.com
Web site: http://www.igi-global.com

Library of Congress Cataloging-in-Publication Data

Names: Singh, Dharmendra, 1974- editor. | Malik, Garima, 1980- editor. | Aggarwal, Shalini, editor.
Title: Transforming the financial landscape with ICTs / edited by Dharmendra Singh, Garima Malik, Shalini Aggarwal.
Description: Hershey, PA : Business Science Reference, [2024] | Includes bibliographical references and index. | Summary: "This book is to explore various issues and ideas about the application of information communication technology (ICT) in the finance sector through the lens of theoretical, practical, and empirical research. This book explores the difficulties and dangers associated with this technological revolution, including cybersecurity threats, privacy concerns, and ethical considerations"-- Provided by publisher.
Identifiers: LCCN 2023049432 (print) | LCCN 2023049433 (ebook) | ISBN 9798369315033 (hardcover) | ISBN 9798369315040 (ebook)
Subjects: LCSH: Finance--Technological innovations. | Information technology--Economic aspects.
Classification: LCC HG173 .T744 2024 (print) | LCC HG173 (ebook) | DDC 332--dc23/eng/20231027
LC record available at https://lccn.loc.gov/2023049432
LC ebook record available at https://lccn.loc.gov/2023049433

This book is published in the IGI Global book series Advances in Finance, Accounting, and Economics (AFAE) (ISSN: 2327-5677; eISSN: 2327-5685)

British Cataloguing in Publication Data
A Cataloguing in Publication record for this book is available from the British Library.

For electronic access to this publication, please contact: eresources@igi-global.com.

Advances in Finance, Accounting, and Economics (AFAE) Book Series

ISSN:2327-5677
EISSN:2327-5685

Editor-in-Chief: Ahmed Driouchi, Al Akhawayn University, Morocco

MISSION

In our changing economic and business environment, it is important to consider the financial changes occurring internationally as well as within individual organizations and business environments. Understanding these changes as well as the factors that influence them is crucial in preparing for our financial future and ensuring economic sustainability and growth.

The **Advances in Finance, Accounting, and Economics (AFAE)** book series aims to publish comprehensive and informative titles in all areas of economics and economic theory, finance, and accounting to assist in advancing the available knowledge and providing for further research development in these dynamic fields.

COVERAGE

- Taxes
- Development Economics
- Statistical Analysis
- Investments and Derivatives
- Health Economics
- Public Finance
- Stock Market
- Labor Economics
- Economics of Risks, Uncertainty, Ambiguity, and Insurance
- Environmental And Social Accounting

IGI Global is currently accepting manuscripts for publication within this series. To submit a proposal for a volume in this series, please contact our Acquisition Editors at Acquisitions@igi-global.com or visit: http://www.igi-global.com/publish/.

The Advances in Finance, Accounting, and Economics (AFAE) Book Series (ISSN 2327-5677) is published by IGI Global, 701 E. Chocolate Avenue, Hershey, PA 17033-1240, USA, www.igi-global.com. This series is composed of titles available for purchase individually; each title is edited to be contextually exclusive from any other title within the series. For pricing and ordering information please visit http://www.igi-global.com/book-series/advances-finance-accounting-economics/73685. Postmaster: Send all address changes to above address.

Titles in this Series

For a list of additional titles in this series, please visit:
http://www.igi-global.com/book-series/advances-finance-accounting-economics/73685

Digital Technologies for a Resource Efficient Economy
Patricia Ordóñez de Pablos (University of Oviedo, Spain)
Business Science Reference • copyright 2024 • 326pp • H/C (ISBN: 9798369327500) • US $345.00 (our price)

Intelligent Methods and Alternative Economic Models for Sustainability
Latifa Dekhici (University of Sciences and Technology of Oran Mohamed-Boudiaf, Algeria) Khaled Guerraiche (LDREI Laboratory, Higher School of Electrical Engineering and Energy of Oran, Algeria) Rabia Azzemou (University of Sciences and Technology of Oran Mohamed-Boudiaf, Algeria) and Jihène Jlassi (Higher Institute of Industrial Management of Sfax, University of Sfax, Tunisia)
Business Science Reference • copyright 2024 • 332pp • H/C (ISBN: 9798369314180) • US $285.00 (our price)

Social and Ethical Implications of AI in Finance for Sustainability
Abdelkader Mohamed Sghaier Derbali (Taibah University, Saudi Arabia)
Engineering Science Reference • copyright 2024 • 368pp • H/C (ISBN: 9798369328811) • US $325.00 (our price)

Revolutionizing the Global Stock Market Harnessing Blockchain for Enhanced Adaptability
Nuno Geada (ISCTE, University Institute of Lisbon, Portugal) Rohit Sood (Lovely Professional University, India) and Ajay Sidana (Amity International Business School, Amity University, Noida, India)
Business Science Reference • copyright 2024 • 285pp • H/C (ISBN: 9798369317587) • US $295.00 (our price)

Six Sigma DMAIC and Markov Chain Monte Carlo Applications to Financial Risk Management
Vojo Bubevski (Vojo Bubevski Consulting, UK)
Business Science Reference • copyright 2024 • 299pp • H/C (ISBN: 9798369337875) • US $255.00 (our price)

IGI Global
PUBLISHER of TIMELY KNOWLEDGE

701 East Chocolate Avenue, Hershey, PA 17033, USA
Tel: 717-533-8845 x100 • Fax: 717-533-8661
E-Mail: cust@igi-global.com • www.igi-global.com

Table of Contents

Detailed Table of Contents

The COVID-19 pandemic is altering the ways in which we connect with one another, communicate with one another, and work together. The economic crisis brought about a fast transformation in both the "what" and the "how" of businesses. There has been a shift in recent years towards conducting business online. This shift includes selling things, generating leads, and establishing connections with clients. The emergence of the chatbot as a trend is one that is contributing to the reduction of the social distance that exists between customers and businesses. A chatbot is a software programme that is created for conversations that are meant to sound human. This study seeks to determine the extent to which many businesses have implemented the tool into their communication strategy. Additionally, the chapter attempts to put forward an understanding of chatbots marketing and the usage of chatbots in the process of online purchasing. In addition to this, the chapter makes an effort to discuss at length the design in such a manner that it will operate at its highest possible level in terms of user acquisition.

Artificial intelligence (AI) has emerged as a catalyst for change in numerous sectors. AI chatbots have been shown to be able to enhance customer engagements and loyalty. This research endeavor aims to explore the nuanced facets of AI-chatbot service quality dimensions and their substantial impact on favorable customer behavioural outcomes such as their attitudes, satisfaction, and loyalty. The study utilized data collected from people in Delhi-NCR region of India who have used AI-powered chatbot services previously. Results showed that every dimension of service quality has a positive association on satisfaction. However, only three dimensions impacted customer attitude significantly. In addition, the outcome of analysis showed that customer loyalty was positively and significantly impacted by user satisfaction towards AI-chatbots and attitude. This study offers a novel and impactful strategy to enhance our understanding of chatbot's potential to significantly alter the way online companies interact with and market to their customer base.

The emergence of Industry 4.0 has transformed the financial landscape by integrating unconventional technologies and artificial intelligence (AI) into consumer interactions. This chapter explores the evolving paradigm of human-centric AI-thinking in the context of emerging customer interactions in making financial decisions. The review analyses the opportunities and the challenges that arise from the integration of AI tools and human-centric approaches in addressing the diverse needs and behaviours of consumers within emerging financial markets. More specifically, the review critically examines the utilization of AI-driven technologies, such as predictive analytics, natural language processing (NLP), and machine learning algorithms, in customising the financial services to cater the emerging-market consumers. Moreover, the current study explicates how AI enables personalized customer interactions, risk assessments, and ethical decision making and financial inclusion strategies while considering the socioeconomic and cultural landscapes. The study has focussed on addressing the concerns related to data privacy, risk assessment, and transparency towards AI-powered financial solutions with ethical standards. Through an exhaustive

In today's digital age, the importance of cybersecurity cannot be overstated, as it directly affects an individual's or organization's ability to protect themselves from various types of fraud. Organizations and individuals must stay vigilant, continuously update their security practices, and invest in cybersecurity technologies to minimize the risk of falling victim to fraudsters. Cybersecurity is the proactive defense against digital threats, while fraud prevention involves safeguarding against deceptive and dishonest activities. To effectively combat fraud, individuals and organizations must implement robust cybersecurity measures, stay informed about emerging threats, and educate themselves and their employees about the tactics used by fraudsters. Fraud and cyber security are two closely related topics that revolve around protecting sensitive information, assets, and systems from unauthorized access, manipulation, or theft.

Software defect classification must be automated in order to ensure software dependability, as the use of automatic software-based applications grows. This chapter suggests an automatic software defect classification approach that is expert-based. The technique of grouping defects into predetermined categories is known as defect report categorization. Recently, numerous machine learning (ML) techniques have been introduced to classify defects into different categories. This study suggests a classification model that creates new word embeddings from defect reports using deep learning (DL) models, specifically the long short-term memory (LSTM) network, recurrent neural network (RNN), convolution neural network (CNN), and multilayer perceptron (MLP). The outcomes are compared to pre-trained word embedding using Google's word2vec in terms of recall, accuracy, and precision. The experimental results show that LSTM outperforms the other models used in the investigation. The maximum accuracy that LSTM can attain on the redmine dataset is 70%.

It is crucial to assess the impact of digital transformations on the financial sector given the rapid emergence of digitalisation. As such, the study aims at identifying the extent to which digitalization has impacted on financial sector development in a sample of small island developing states, over the period 2000 to 2020. Additionally, given the crucial importance of institutional quality in reducing banking sector risk, and therefore enhancing the level of development in the financial sector, the study investigates the nexus between digitisation and financial development through the moderating impact of institutional quality. The study adopts the PVECM framework to investigate the link. The results demonstrate digitalization is important to boost financial development and digitalization coupled with good quality institutions will further promote financial development. More so, FDI and trade openness are also determinants of financial development for the case of the small island economies considered in the present study.

The integration of e-payment systems in digital microfinance marks a pivotal intersection between financial inclusion and fintech innovation. This chapter traces the evolutionary trajectory of e-payment methods, from their origins to contemporary tools like mobile wallets. It underscores the profound benefits of these platforms, emphasizing unparalleled accessibility, efficiency, and benefits for underserved regions. However, merging technology with finance presents challenges, including limited adoption, technological barriers, and regulatory complexities. The chapter highlights the RBI's regulatory role, showcasing how e-payment platforms are reshaping the microfinance sector through real-world examples. Ultimately, it advocates for these platforms as essential drivers for achieving comprehensive financial inclusion.

Mobile banking is a new form of payment service that aims to acquire the underserved market of prospective mobile banking consumers. Social media influencers are used as a means of disseminating ideas through social media. However, the influence of financial literacy is still not known. This study aims to examine the impact of influencer credentials on mobile banking acceptance. The results demonstrate that influencer reliability has a significant favourable impact on m-banking acceptability as evaluated by attention, interest, desire, and action depicting the cognitive stages of

Preface

Welcome to *Transforming the Financial Landscape With ICTs*. In this dynamic and rapidly evolving world, Information and Communication Technology (ICT) has become a cornerstone of innovation and progress, especially within the financial sector. As editors, it is our pleasure to present this compilation of research papers and case studies that delve into the profound impact of ICT on reshaping how we perceive, engage with, and manage financial activities.

The financial sector is undergoing a monumental transformation driven by technological advancements. From the rise of online and mobile banking to the disruptive potential of blockchain and cryptocurrencies, from the integration of artificial intelligence and chatbots to the utilization of big data analytics, the possibilities are vast and transformative. This book serves as a comprehensive exploration of these technologies and their implications for financial institutions, regulators, businesses, and consumers alike.

Our aim with this edited volume is to provide a platform for scholarly discourse, practical insights, and empirical research on the intersection of ICT and finance. We delve into the opportunities and challenges presented by this digital revolution, addressing critical topics such as cybersecurity threats, privacy concerns, regulatory frameworks, and ethical considerations. Through a combination of theoretical discussions and real-world case studies, readers will gain a deeper understanding of how ICT is shaping the future of finance.

This book is designed to be a valuable resource for a diverse audience, including students, researchers, academicians, practitioners, and policymakers. Whether you are exploring the potential of fintech startups, delving into the complexities of AI-powered risk management, or examining the nuances of blockchain governance, you will find relevant and engaging content within these pages.

CHAPTER OVERVIEW

- **Chapter 1 - The Impact of COVID-19 on Operational Strategies and Online Business:** This chapter delves into the profound transformations brought about by the COVID-19 pandemic, particularly in how organizations operate and engage in online business. It explores the rise of internet-based commerce, the integration of chatbots into marketing and online transactions, and the critical role of design in optimizing user acquisition strategies.
- **Chapter 2 - Exploring AI-Chatbot Service Quality in Customer Engagement:** This chapter investigates how AI-powered chatbots are enhancing customer engagements and loyalty. It explores dimensions of service quality and their impact on customer attitudes, satisfaction, and loyalty, offering insights into how online companies can leverage chatbots to improve customer interactions and market effectively.
- **Chapter 3 - Human-Centric AI-Thinking in Financial Decision-Making:** Focused on Industry 4.0's impact on finance, this chapter emphasizes the evolving paradigm of human-centric AI in financial decision-making. It discusses the importance of empathy, ethical considerations, and human values in AI-driven financial solutions, offering recommendations for stakeholders to navigate the complexities of emerging financial ecosystems.
- **Chapter 4 - Digital Financial Inclusion and Poverty Alleviation:** This chapter examines the role of digital financial inclusion in poverty alleviation and economic growth. It assesses the current status of digital financial inclusion, influential studies and authors in the field, and collaborative trends among researchers, providing valuable insights into strategies for fostering financial independence and sustainable development.
- **Chapter 5 - Central Bank Digital Currency (CBDC) and Its Implications:** Delving into the potential of CBDCs, this chapter evaluates their impact on monetary policy, financial inclusion, digital literacy, and economic development in African countries. It explores the opportunities and limitations of CBDC adoption, shedding light on its role in addressing key challenges while outlining realistic expectations.
- **Chapter 6 - AI-Driven Solutions in Higher Education:** Focused on AI's impact on student interactions and academic support, this chapter explores how universities are leveraging AI-driven solutions like chatbots and predictive analytics. It highlights the benefits for students, especially international ones, in overcoming language barriers and adapting to cross-cultural learning environments.
- **Chapter 7 - AI in Insurance Fraud Detection and Prevention:** This chapter investigates the role of AI in detecting and preventing insurance

fraud. It discusses the limitations of traditional fraud prevention methods, emphasizes the importance of clear legal frameworks, and explores AI's potential as a powerful tool in safeguarding the insurance industry's integrity and protecting policyholders.

- **Chapter 8 - Cybersecurity and Fraud Prevention in the Digital Age:** Focusing on the critical intersection of cybersecurity and fraud prevention, this chapter emphasizes the importance of robust cybersecurity measures in combating digital threats. It highlights the proactive defense against fraudsters and the need for continuous vigilance and education in safeguarding sensitive information and assets.
- **Chapter 9 - Automatic Software Defect Classification Using Deep Learning:** This chapter presents an innovative approach to automating software defect classification using deep learning models. It discusses the methodology, compares different ML techniques, and highlights the potential of LSTM networks in accurately classifying software defects, contributing to enhanced software dependability.
- **Chapter 10 - Digitization's Impact on Financial Sector Development:** This chapter assesses the impact of digitization on financial sector development, particularly in small island developing states. It explores the nexus between digitization, institutional quality, foreign direct investment (FDI), and trade openness, offering insights into how digitalization can promote financial development and stability.
- **Chapter 11 - E-Payment Systems in Microfinance:** Examining the evolution of e-payment systems in microfinance, this chapter discusses their benefits, challenges, and regulatory implications. It highlights the transformative potential of e-payment platforms in promoting financial inclusion, particularly in underserved regions, while addressing technological and regulatory hurdles.
- **Chapter 12 - Buy Now, Pay Later (BNPL) Services:** This chapter investigates the rise of BNPL services and their impact on consumer finance. It analyzes the costs and risks associated with BNPL, including customer charges and vulnerabilities, providing a comprehensive overview of this emerging payment method's benefits and challenges.
- **Chapter 13 - Digital Lending and Buy Now, Pay Later (BNPL) Services: Assessing Costs and Risks:** This chapter delves into the disruptive impact of digital lending and BNPL services in the financial industry. It explores how these services have revolutionized credit access and management for customers, particularly the younger generation, by offering ease of use and flexibility in online purchasing. However, despite their popularity, the chapter critically evaluates the potential costs and risks faced by BNPL

consumers. The study reveals that while BNPL products offer interest-free installments, consumers may incur financial charges comparable to credit card fees. Moreover, loopholes in customer protection expose consumers to unfavorable risks, leading to varying expenses and annual percentage rates (APR) ranging from 0% to 36%. This chapter provides a comprehensive analysis of the benefits and pitfalls of BNPL services, highlighting the need for transparent disclosure and consumer awareness in navigating these innovative yet potentially costly financial solutions.

CONCLUSION

As editors of *Transforming the Financial Landscape With ICTs*, we are thrilled to present this comprehensive exploration of the intersection between Information and Communication Technology (ICT) and the financial sector. Our aim with this edited volume was to provide a platform for in-depth scholarly discourse, practical insights, and empirical research on how ICT is reshaping finance.

Throughout the chapters, we have delved into transformative topics such as the impact of COVID-19 on operational strategies, the evolution of AI-powered chatbots in customer engagement, and the emergence of human-centric AI in financial decision-making. We have also examined crucial aspects like digital financial inclusion, central bank digital currencies, and the disruptive forces of digital lending and Buy Now, Pay Later (BNPL) services.

Each chapter offers valuable insights and perspectives, from exploring the potential benefits and risks of new financial technologies to discussing the challenges of cybersecurity and fraud prevention in the digital age. Readers will find a wealth of knowledge and analysis that will deepen their understanding of how ICT is shaping the future of finance.

We believe this book serves as a valuable resource for a diverse audience, including students, researchers, academicians, practitioners, and policymakers. Whether you are delving into the complexities of AI-driven solutions, examining the impact of digitization on financial sector development, or exploring the transformative potential of e-payment systems, you will find relevant and engaging content within these pages.

We extend our gratitude to the contributors who have shared their expertise and insights, making this book a reflection of collective knowledge and innovative thinking. We hope that *Transforming the Financial Landscape With ICTs* sparks discussions, inspires further research, and contributes to the ongoing evolution of the financial industry.

Dharmendra Singh
Modern College of Business and Science, Oman

Garima Malik
Birla Institute of Technology Management, Greater Noida, India

Shalini Aggarwal
Chandigarh University, India

Chapter 1
Elevating Business Experiences:
AI-Powered Chatbots Reforming Marketing and E-Commerce

Mehul Waghambare
Symbiosis Institute of Digital and Telecom Management, India

Sandeep Prabhu
https://orcid.org/0000-0002-2146-1960
Symbiosis Institute of Digital and Telecom Management, India

P. Ashok
Symbiosis Institute of Digital and Telecom Management, India

N. A. Natraj
https://orcid.org/0000-0002-8726-5284
Symbiosis International University, India

ABSTRACT

The COVID-19 pandemic is altering the ways in which we connect with one another, communicate with one another, and work together. The economic crisis brought about a fast transformation in both the "what" and the "how" of businesses. There has been a shift in recent years towards conducting business online. This shift includes selling things, generating leads, and establishing connections with clients. The emergence of the chatbot as a trend is one that is contributing to the reduction of the social distance that exists between customers and businesses. A chatbot is a software programme that is created for conversations that are meant to sound

DOI: 10.4018/979-8-3693-1503-3.ch001

human. This study seeks to determine the extent to which many businesses have implemented the tool into their communication strategy. Additionally, the chapter attempts to put forward an understanding of chatbots marketing and the usage of chatbots in the process of online purchasing. In addition to this, the chapter makes an effort to discuss at length the design in such a manner that it will operate at its highest possible level in terms of user acquisition.

INTRODUCTION

Evolving Customer Experience in Era of Digitalization

IoT and AI will have the greatest impact on the rate of economic development in many countries (Kasey Panetta, 2016). The increasing functionality of these technologies' devices, systems, applications and equipment is surely one aspect that enables their adoption in corporate, consumer, and societal dimensions. On the one hand, they serve as a catalyst to developing emerging solutions as a result of their presence, and on the other hand, they serve as the digital economy's unique DNA code, subjected to ongoing processes that increase their potential (Kaczorowska-Spychalska, 2019). Digital change is unavoidable, and it contributes to the current culture and technology system, which fosters new social behaviours while also accelerating the creation of new, impossible things. Computers and other digital innovations rely on our brains' ability to comprehend and modify our surroundings. Digital technologies are currently thought to expand the functionality of implemented solutions, increase operational effectiveness, and improve and optimise existing processes and tools in an individual organisation. The "digital revolution" has radically changed the customer experience over the last 20 years. Consumer preferences have evolved, technology has advanced, and communication is no longer constrained by distance or time. The convenience and speed of this transaction also contribute to the growth of online businesses all over the globe. Digital technologies have lowered the cost of entering some markets, even across borders. For new entrants, digitalization has also lowered the burden of scaling up production, advertising, and distribution (OECD, 2018). The ease of starting a business online has resulted in the growth of thousands of businesses in every industry online (Avis, 2015). This possibly could create a market full of perfect competition. Businesses hence are looking into different marketplaces, exploring ways to market their services differently in order achieve competitive differentiation. In a fast-paced market that is full of competition, it becomes almost essential for businesses to cater to their consumers efficiently and well in time. Customers are demanding 24-hour service for everything from banking and finance to healthcare. In this century, quick and efficient technology

Figure 1. Digital customer experience areas

has become the norm and consumers have high expectations. If a business does not address a consumer's needs, the individual has enough options to let go and turn to a competitor business. Hence, it has become imperative for companies to put into place an enhanced digital system to cater to their consumers. Fig.1 shows the Digital Customer Experience Areas.

EFFECT OF COVID-19 ON CUSTOMER BEHAVIOUR AND SHOPPING

COVID-19 has had a huge and immediate impact on customer behaviour. Spending is down across most industries, purchases are changing from physical to the online platform, and consumer well-being has become a primary consideration for businesses. Companies have acknowledged that customer experience would be shaped by current behaviours in the upcoming years. They should next make sure these opportunities are compatible with their firm's objectives and capabilities. Dynamic customer data, Safe and contactless engagements and Digital excellence will define the post-pandemic customer experience. Each organisation will pursue these priorities in their own way, depending on its industry competitive landscape as well as the starting point. Some organisations have begun to demonstrated their awareness of what customers value as well as have innovated strategies to fulfil both their previous and new expectations. These early adopters provide a useful guide for how to proceed (Elevating Customer Experience Excellence in the next Normal | McKinsey, n.d.).

While financial flexibility is becoming more limited, many customers now have more time on their hands. Physical and in-person activities are increasingly being replaced or supplemented by digital alternatives as a result of shelter-in-place requirements, as a result, internet and digital channels have seen unprecedented levels of participation. Globally, businesses have quickly responded to the tremendous transition to digital platforms. From education to fitness, from meals and groceries to money, every potential activity now has a digital or online equivalent, and many of them have seen a surge in usership.

COVID-19's impact on customer behaviour has resulted in boosting of projected trends, formation of new preference, and the full reversal of some pre-existing behaviours. As a whole, this combination will keep developing, laying the groundwork for the future normal. Businesses can use nudging to not only influence future customer behaviour that will likely persist after the pandemic, but also in the post-pandemic age, they are establishing themselves at the forefront of influencing client experience.

The Commerce industry has been hit the hardest by the economic downturn. Consumers who have never purchased products from an e-commerce website are now more inclined to do so. They have been forced to start browsing e-commerce sites, and some of them may become accustomed to it even after the crises have passed. With the increase in the number of consumers, many businesses have begun to place a greater emphasis on their online portals in order to generate more leads and sales. However, as more businesses began to focus on e-commerce markets, competition has increased, as everyone is attempting to capture as many potential leads as possible.

Because fierce competition necessitates new strategies and planning, the question is: what is the best strategy for businesses to employ in this situation?

CHATBOTS AS A LATEST TREND

Chatbots, as an emerging technology, will eventually become an essential part of an organization's process more so in pandemic and post-pandemic era. In recent years, there has been a tremendous increase in on-demand messaging, which has changed how customers communicate with brands. To deliver superior client service, over the last decade, chat services have surpassed telephone help as the primary method of accessing customer service (Charlton, 2013). Chatbots are a type of intelligent, conversational software program that responds to natural language input in the form of text, voice or both. (Nicole Radziwill and Morgan Benton, 2017) Personalization has become a key trend in the market's shifting paradigm and companies have identified chatbots as an excellent opportunity to exploit social network and set up streams of human-to-computer communication that will provide a personalized experience and boost relationship marketing in the digital environment (Zumstein & Hundertmark, 2018). One of the modern technology advancements for client communication is chatbots. (Letheren & Glavas, 2017). Moreover, chatbots also assist businesses in reducing customer service costs by reducing response time and answering common routine questions. The existence of chatbots first came into being in 1966 and the first chatbot was called ELIZA (Pereira et al., 2019). Joseph Weizenbaum's creation, ELIZA, was capable of conversing with humans and responding as one. The very first conversational agent's success was attributed to the fact that humans were unable to discern if they were conversing with a robot or another human (Pereira et al., 2019). ELIZA was soon enough followed by several different chatbot models that were invented to further explore the fascinating world of artificial intelligence and tap into this new technology. Chatbots have drastically evolved since then, becoming much easier to train and implement.

In today's world, chatbots are becoming increasingly popular among businesses and consumers. In fact, In March 2016, Microsoft CEO Satya Nadella said that chatbots would be the next big thing, alongside the graphical user interface, web browser, and touch screen. (Dale, 2016) From 2015 to 2017, nearly half of all online conversations have been aided by chatbots (Tsvetkova et al., 2016). The magnitude of this can be gauged by looking at the massive increase in Facebook Messenger chatbots which increased from 30,000 in 2016 to over 100,000 in 2017 (Zumstein & Hundertmark, 2018). Along with the number, the variety of chatbots have also skyrocketed and there is a new type of chatbot for every business - right from ordering food to shopping, from finding like-minded people to booking flights, and from reading the news to chit-chatting. Chatbot transactions are projected to produce up to 32 billion US dollars in yearly revenue globally (Zumstein & Hundertmark, 2018).

Despite their widespread use, chatbots frequently fail to meet consumer expectations due to a lack of understanding of user input. Facebook's Project M (a text-based virtual assistant) is said to have failed in more than 70% of interactions (Weinberg, 2017). Even the most advanced chatbots make mistakes. In this paper Web-based conversational agents will be discussed, chatbots in particular, with a focus on their significance in online purchasing and user acquisition.

THEORETICAL BACKGROUND

Traditional Application of Chatbots

Many people prefer to shop in physical stores. Every week, a large number of people visit supermarkets and they are introduced to a wide range of product options. To add to the experience, customer service representatives (CSRs) are employed in many shopping centres to answer questions from customers about products. The CSRs also play a huge role in influencing and consulting their potential customers and leading them to make their purchasing decisions. According to one study (Froehle, 2006), CSRs can influence customer satisfaction by their thoroughness, knowledge, and preparedness, hence they are also trained accordingly. However, if all CSRs are busy interacting with other customers, a customer may have to wait a long time for assistance. This could be a downside to retail industry as they would have a stream of customers coming in but less employees to deal with them, further straining on expenses of hiring and training. For services providing businesses, it is very important to strike a balance between service efficiency and quality. The businesses that are able to maintain this in a long run are likely to find success in their respective ventures (Meuter et al., 2005). In Addition, customers today expect quick, convenient, and personalised service, thus, businesses are under increasing pressure to innovate (Kasey Panetta, 2016). The large proportion of customer service expenses spent to training and labour can be dramatically be lowered by employing automated solutions. Retailers are increasingly using data and evolving technology to improve the customer experience both online and offline. The four pillars of this technology-driven retail revolution are speed, immersion, automation, and convenience.

Conversational AI is the one consumer-friendly tool that retailers use today to deliver on these tenet (Analytics, 2020). These humanised interfaces enable brands to provide support 24 hours a day, seven days a week while automating key aspects of customer service. Thousands of brands are using chatbots effectively leveraging artificial intelligence technology. What is the relation of personalization and chatbots? AI-powered or Machine Learning Chatbots can provide answers to ambiguous questions. In other words, you don't have to be specific when asking these chatbots questions. Natural language processing is used by the chatbots to generate responses from scratch. Artificial intelligence will be the foundation for a level of customer personalisation that will not only be recognised, but also demanded by fickle customers all over the world (Pearson, 2019). In the course of resolving any of the customer's issues, a human personnel spends 33% of their time understanding the nature of the inquiry and 25% of their time finding the correct information for the customer (Reddy, 2017), chatbots become smarter over time as they learn from previous questions and answers. That means, Chatbots have the potentiality to create a personalized experience while carrying out the programmed task. According to (Schumaker et al., 2007) a chatbot is a system that "seeks to mimic conversation rather than understand it". Whereas (Schumaker et al., 2007) place a greater emphasis on mimicry and simulation than on comprehension, Mauldin (Pereira et al., 2019) described chatbots as systems with the goal of "thinking". According to (Michiels, 2017), chatbots are available to provide service at any time and in any location.

Chatbots have mostly been employed in messenger apps, rather than computer programs, since the emergence of smartphones and mobile applications (Letheren & Glavas, 2017). We shall take a closer look at how chatbots are used on social media. Chatbots are increasingly widely used in electronic marketplaces and customer service across a wide range of websites, social media platforms, and messaging apps. Customers can, for example, turn to CAs that are available 24/7 to ask a question or make a complaint instead of contacting a call centre or sending an e-mail. Consider the number of Facebook chatbots, Facebook Messenger, for example, is reported to have had more than 1.2 billion active users per month in 2017. In 2019, the platform was being used by approximately 300,000 developers, and people and businesses exchanging over 20 billion messages each month (Business, 2019).

The biggest advantages a CA can bring to any business is the enhanced customer experience (Gnewuch et al., 2017; LUCIA et al., 2003). CSRs can be burdened with the overwhelming amount of customers' requests coming in at each hour, bot can easily handle all of them at once without becoming overworked. According to studies, each year, 265 billion customer support calls cost $1.3 trillion to businesses. Chatbots can save organisations money on customer service by reducing response times, allowing contact center employees to take their time and deliver better service by freeing up human agents to answer more difficult enquiries, while catering to up to 80% of common questions (Ai, n.d.; Reddy, 2017). Annual salary savings of $23 billion might be achieved by businesses using chatbots (Business Insider Intelligence, 2016).

TYPES OF CHATBOTS

The convergence of two enabling technologies has fueled recent growth in conversational agents. First, the Internet became a universal communication medium. Web-based conversational agents are scalable corporate solutions that use the internet to provide big groups of people with simultaneous chat-based services. Secondly, substantial progress has been made in computational linguistics, an area of artificial intelligence concerned with natural language software. For example, the ability to comprehend natural language has substantially improved because for parsing technology advancements. Chatbots are of two types: Rule-Based Chatbots (Linguistic Based) and Natural Language Processing (Artificial Intelligence-Based) Chatbots.

- *Rule-Based Chatbots*

The communication of rule-based chatbots is based on pre-defined rules. In order to receive an answer, user input must follow these pre-defined rules. Often, only buttons are used with such bots. They are also referred to as decision-tree bots, as they only follow a series of defined rules based on recognizing the lexical form of the input text without creating any new text answers (Adamopoulou & Moussiades, 2020). The chatbot's knowledge is hand-coded by humans and organised and presented using conversational patterns (Adamopoulou & Moussiades, 2020). These types are most applicable to customer support functions, ideally suited for common inquiries such as business enquiries, delivery status, or tracking information and a larger rule-database will allow the bot to respond to a wider range of user input. Consumers see chatbots as a faster way to connect humans. 34% of all consumers see chatbots helping in finding a human service assistance (Salesforce UK, 2018). This type of model, on the other hand, is not resistant to grammatical and spelling errors in user input (Adamopoulou & Moussiades, 2020).

- *AI-Based Chatbots*

The AI based chatbots, unlike rule-based bots, process natural language using algorithms (neural networks). This is done using Machine Learning, a feature of AI that makes bots smarter over time and with use. NLP and Machine Learning are two major elements of AI chatbots and they go hand in hand. During bot training, the chatbot uses machine learning to learn from user requests and data. When a query is received, machine learning helps the bot monitor the prior discussion it had with the user before responding appropriately (Ai, n.d.). Natural Language Processing, or NLP, is a type of artificial intelligence that helps a bot understand and interpret information. Because of natural language processing (NLP), you can train your chatbot with numerous intentions that the user would input during the interaction. These intents will simplify the response to the query (Ai, n.d.). AI Based chatbots come with major benefits and scope that is yet to be completely explored.

In the retail industry, the popularity rise of chatbots has been fueled by recent advancements in natural language processing, as well as a shift toward messaging as a primary mode of communication (Gnewuch et al., 2017). One important scope this paper tries to explore is the use of these chatbots in customer acquisition and purchasing initiation. This can be powered by personalized marketing, a process of using data to deliver targeted and individual brand messages, also known as one-to-one marketing. Customers can receive personalised offers from AI-based chatbots based on their life events or profile data. Chatbots can qualify leads by asking pertinent questions before directing them to a sales representative or an appointment scheduler.

This reduces the amount of time the sales team spends searching for qualified leads. It speeds up the lead generation process and makes it more profitable. As a result, companies across a wide range of industries are eager to use intelligent bots to optimise operations, automate procedures, boost productivity, improve customer acquisition and retention, and raise employee and client engagement (Toader et al., 2020). These bots can also completely be transformed into selling agents to add another touchpoint for new users and to explore and provide a peculiar yet potentially very personal shopping experience to customers. They have a lot of potential for lead generation and can be integrated in sales funnel to streamline sales cycle.

DESIGN OF THE CHATBOT

(Medhi Thies et al., 2017) to determine which chatbot personalities are the most appealing to India's youthful, urban users. They experimented with three different chatbots, each with a different personality. Participants desired a chatbot that could bring value to their lives by making valuable recommendations, as well as being reassuring, empathetic, and non-judgmental. As a result, the paper demonstrates that people who use the chatbots have a higher expectation with its output, It does not, however, include insights on how well current chatbots meet these expectations. (Liao et al., 2016) observed incorporation of a chatbot into a Human Resource Management System (HRMS) in the workplace. They discovered that, in addition to being functional, participants were interacting with the chatbot in a playful manner, which can be interpreted as a positive experience and promising signs for future research. Another study (Jain et al., 2018) carried about by IBM researchers in which they made 16 participants of different demographics interact with 8 chatbots (chatShopper, CNN, Call of Duty, Pandorabots, Alterra, Hi Poncho, Trivia Blast, Swelly) to counteract order effects, in a randomised order. Post the experiment the participants showed disappointment and even frustration with the chatbots' "mediocre natural language capabilities". They believed that the chatbots at some moments, failed to comprehend or understand their text inputs, and that chatbots were unable to engage or respond to them efficiently.

As a result of the feedback, in the research it was concluded that chatbots will need to evolve quickly with respect to its core competencies for effectively engaging and retaining users. Moreover, during the study A few chatbots received positive feedback. Pandorabots' witty human-like conversational skills were particularly popular with participants. It appeared to be able to comprehend the user's input and respond in a timely and intelligent manner. Hi Poncho bot was thought to have a pleasant and enjoying personality. Participants also liked Trivia Blast, which despite having a non-chatty and click-based interface, within a messaging interface, delivered an entertaining quiz experience.

These three top-rated bots highlight the crucial takeaways for future chatbots: chatbots must either deliver natural language-driven functionality with adequate conversational joy, or an engaging app-like experience specifically developed for the familiar turn-based messaging interface. The higher the users' positive appraisals of the agents and the better the emotional and social relationships they build with them, the more emotions they communicate and the more empathy and sympathy they show.

PERSONALITY

Personality can provide a consistent pattern for how chatbots are perceived, resulting in a more consistent user experience. The bot personality chosen, determines the type of interactions the audience will have with it. It is important for the personality of the chatbot to be consistent with the brand. In a study (Ruane et al., 2021) noted, qualities of personality can be reliably reproduced via text and without the usage of extra audio or visual cues can still be viewed as the users intend, also that the user experience is influenced by the personality of a chatbot and is thus a significant design concern. A chatbot can appear empty and cold without a persona. Creating an identity based on the brand fosters user empathy and reflects the personalised service they receive from the team.

Design bot to be cheeky if the company is a cheeky retailer. A brand with target audience as young urban teenagers can design a chatbot's personality to be trendy and witty. Since humour is still too hard to generate automatically, (Medhi Thies et al., 2017) suggest including a variety of jokes in response to frequent inquiries. A chatbot is a virtual representation of a person, and represents the company ideas and image, so it should have a personality that reflects that. Bots with strong personalities and well-named names are more likely to be remembered, whereas bots with weak names are more likely to be forgotten. A bot that performs poorly and bears a company's brand name will be forever linked to the company. In a study done by (Medhi Thies et al., 2017) users of experimental chatbots have stated that they want the bot to be comforting, empathic, and nonjudgmental, while also not being overly caring. Other research have looked into whether a personality match between the agent and the user improves the user experience. (Land et al., 2013) studied In a low-stakes discussion activity, how an agent's perceived extraversion/introversion affects user experience. They found Users appreciate consistency in both verbal and nonverbal personality indications, as well as a personality that is complementary to their own rather than identical. User engagement can be measured by lexical features such as in every turn the amount of characters or words used being used, however, these characteristics may express the chatbot's personality qualities and be linked to the effectiveness and informativeness of the agent from the user's perspective. Emoticons and expressive punctuation are examples of syntactic features that can be used to express feelings or emotions. Finally, reaction time and duration of each turn will vary substantially based on the chatbot and user interaction.

(Horzyk et al., 2009) proposed the Human Personality Traits (HPT) model. It identifies various demands connected to a particular personality and describes particular human behaviors and activities in relation to their personality. Each HPT has its own unique vocabulary. Additionally, HPT can help companies decide how to address each customer uniquely and manage them so that they are happier while interacting with an intelligent chatbot system. The 11 human personality types indicated by this psycholinguistic paradigm are dominant, maximalist, inspirational, discovering, verifying, systematic, Assurant, harmonious, emphatic, task-oriented, and balancing. Chatbots that can recognize HPTs and their demands can utilize the right algorithms to negotiate with clients, persuade them, and reinforce their activities. Words and phrases are used to help identify HPTs, and consumers are handled properly to evoke favorable reactions. The incorporation of a chatbot engine into an e-commerce system enables a business to understand the thought processes of its clients, which may result in novel e-commerce prospects.

Figure 2. Chatbot engine recognizing a customer personality
Source: Horzyk et al. (2009)

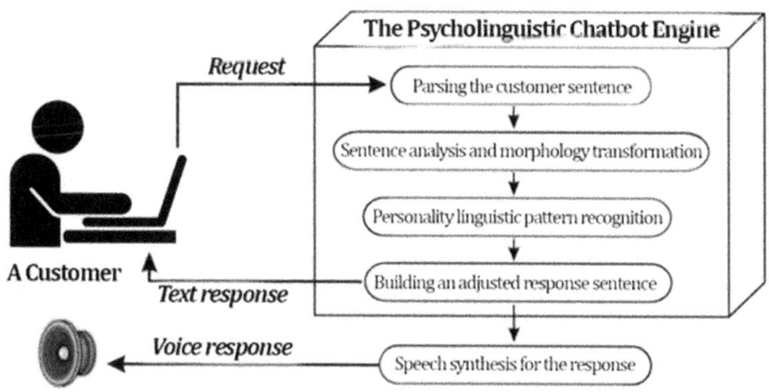

PERSONALISATION

People are constantly bombarded with information these days, whether it's billboard ads, TV commercials, emails, social media, or hundreds of brands vying for their attention. So, it's natural for consumers to tune out most of that, especially what isn't personally relevant to them. That means, the businesses that reach out to their customers with content that is generic and impersonal, are missing out on a huge opportunity of engaging them into their brand. It's not just initial communication that matters in this case, but also the approach taken by businesses. Personalization of chatbots, in particular, is gaining traction. Users like chatbots that have human-like personality qualities, according to studies by (Pearson, 2019).

Personalization can range from simply naming a chatbot or inserting an image into the conversation to reacting to user emotions. Marketing personalization, in a nutshell, means interacting with your audience and customers in a way that feels personal and human, taking into account their likes, preferences, and interests. Advertisers use personalization to personalise advertisements to a person's preferences and attributes (Sundar & Marathe, 2010). Chatbots are also referred to as "digital assistants" that are aware of human capabilities. Bots decipher the user's intent, process their requests, and respond quickly with relevant information. Chatbots are a new type of service encounter made possible by artificial intelligence and natural language processing advancements (Um et al., 2020).

Bots' strength lies in their ability to have personalised conversations, provide personalised offers, and make quick purchases. They can analyse patterns in our speech using data and serious computing to determine when and what to advertise They can also increase engagement and bring your brand personality to life (Letheren & Glavas, 2017). Facebook has even added the ability to send audio, video, GIFs, and other types of responses in addition to text. This has only added more personalization capabilities to the chatbots technology. In this era, where Internet is not only a place to seek for information but also a place for humour, chatbots interface can be personalized with respect to the type of audience the business hopes to cater to. For example, a hyper casual Business that caters to a young audience can add a fun quotient to their chatbot's chatting style Chatbot advertising is the next stage in personalised advertising, and because advertising and support are so closely related, chatbots are well-suited to perform both (Letheren & Glavas, 2017). Facebook, on its Messenger platfrom has begun to offer advertising via chatbots, which they define as "sponsored messages" to the customers that have already been reached out to be the advertisers, either through a Messenger bot or live chat assistance (Weinberg, 2017).

Figure 3. The inbound marketing framework
Source: Talking the Talk: The Beginner's Guide to Designing a Chatbot Conversation (2017)

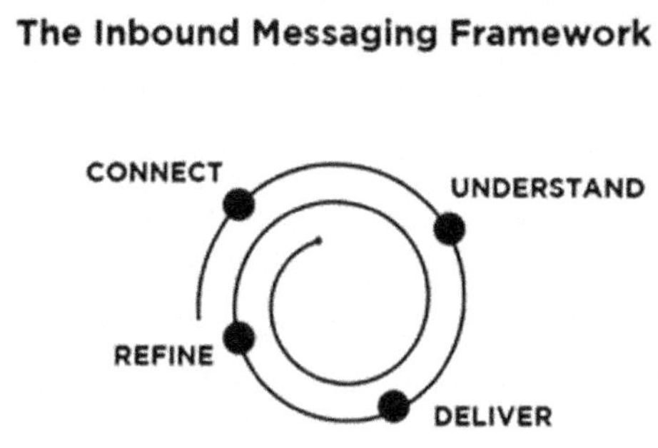

THE INBOUND MESSAGING FRAMEWORK

The Inbound Messaging Framework designed by Hubspot, provides a guide into designing an effective marketing chatbot.

- *Connect*

Connecting with the audience is the first step in the Inbound Messaging Framework. A chatbot must be able to respond to any customer request sent through a messaging app. Use a conversational tone and add context by referring to the existing contact record. Chatbot frameworks enable developers to create a single bot that responds to people in the same way across multiple channels, including web chat, Facebook Messenger, Skype, and others.

- *Design*

Create a conversation with filtering questions to gain a better understanding of the user's intent. Highly chatty chatbot can deviate the user from the actual intent. A conversationally engaging yet straight-forward approach could prove beneficial.

- *Deliver*

Provide a rich media solution without forcing users to leave the messaging app. Developers should provide chatbots with as much information as possible about the company, its products, and services. Facebook Messenger users will soon be able to make payments directly from the app while chatting. These users may receive different responses from your bot than those who communicate through your website's chat window. Users of the website can be sent to a standard checkout page, but Facebook Messenger users never have to leave the app and can pay right there.

- *Refine*

Continue to improve your conversational strategy based on user feedback to provide more value and encourage users to use the bot on a regular basis. A chatbot designed to increase engagements could surprise customers with its highly engaging responses, boosting remarketing potential even more.

CHATBOT SHOPPING EXPERIENCE

Attitude Towards E-Commerce Bots

Because of its ability to have automated conversations with consumers using human language, prompting them to create content (via questions) and apply brand and customer-specific content, chatbot messaging lays the groundwork for greater customer engagement (through tailored automated responses based on data previously obtained from users). Customer Perceptions of Chatbots Cognitive factors like perceived usefulness, perceived ease-of-use, and perceived helpfulness are linked to customers' attitudes toward technology adoption, in accordance with the Customer Acceptance of Technology Model, which is a unified theory of technology acceptance. It also claims that consumer attitudes have an effect on adoption intentions (Ting Yan Chan & Hong Leung, 2021). Same way, (Brandtzaeg & Følstad, 2017) underlined the relevance of chatbot service quality in the literature, for the adoption of chatbots and their attitude towards them, perceived helpfulness and usefulness were found to play a crucial role were also found to be two important determinant of chatbot experience which is frequently the goal of commercial chatbots. When chatbots help people save time or find information more quickly, they are perceived as very helpful (Brandtzaeg & Følstad, 2017). (Gefen & Straub, 2003) study explicates, a stronger priority should be placed on detecting conversational cues that increase users' impressions of social presence. Perceived Intrusiveness was found to be a negative factor which could cause irritation and have a negative impact on message acceptance in social media advertising (Van den Broeck et al., 2019) and chatbot interactions. Changing the linguistic style of an e-commerce chatbot can affect overall customer satisfaction, service engagement, product interest and the perceived value of the product. Chatbots could be used to develop prediction models that improve

Figure 4. The customer engagement cycle
Source: Sashi (2012)

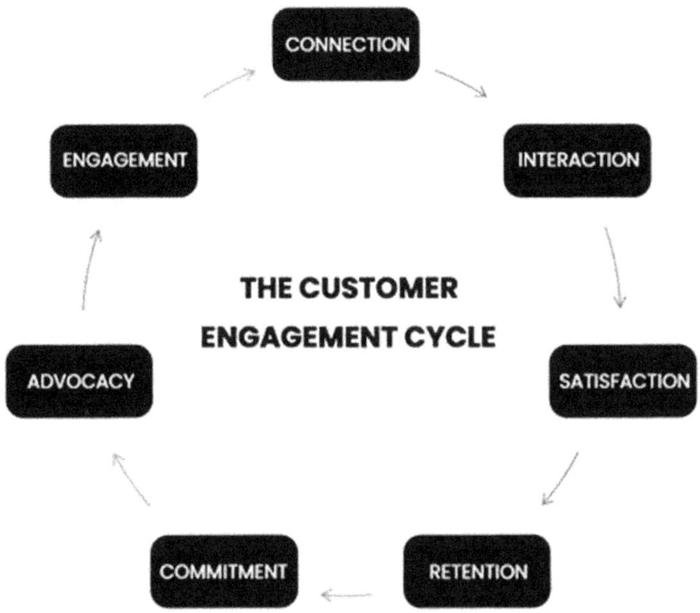

client commitment and loyalty by combining transaction information and customer profiles., resulting in a long-term relationship.

Customer Engagement Cycle

The process of constructing customer engagement for a corporation is described by the proposed customer engagement cycle by (Sashi, 2012). The client passes through seven phases in this model: engagement, connection, interaction, satisfaction, retention, commitment, and advocacy. Chatbots have a part to play in each of these stages thanks to its functionality, personality, conversational intelligence, and UI components. Client engagement, in the opinion of (Sashi, 2012), should be concentrated on gaining long-term customer loyalty by offering value that is superior to that of competitors.

- *Connection*

To create customer engagement, you must first establish contact with potential customers. Traditional offline methods as well as digital technologies such as chatbots can be used to make these connections (Sashi, 2012). A Chatbot can be designed as a sales assistant and be used in marketing programs to establish interactive engagement session with potential leads and customers.

- *Interaction*

The tools that enable more frequent, richer, and quicker interactions with leads and potential consumers include texting, instant messaging, blogging, social networking, and, in especially, chatbots. By communicating with customers more regularly, businesses may get more information about their wants. Chatbots can be a key component of engagement if user experience is elevated because the design and responses will reflect the brand's personality.

- *Satisfaction*

A satisfied consumer is more likely to be loyal to the business and will express their satisfaction with the interaction. As in this context, chatbots are the starting point of contact with the customers, they must be designed in such a way that it able to assist all requests in a way that pleases the outcome. Customer satisfaction is important for creating customer engagement, but it isn't enough because it doesn't guarantee a customer's repurchase. Because of its ability, it can handle the emotions of a disgruntled customer, that will directly improve the user experience. Customers are always pleased when their issues are resolved quickly, which improves the overall experience.

- *Retention*

Customer retention, which can result in a long-term consumer-seller connection, is a result of customer happiness and general positive attitudes toward a brand. A chatbot designed to increase engagements might astound clients with its incredibly engaging response and increase the possibilities for retargeting.

- *Commitment*

Chatbots have the potential to develop Affective commitment. Customers who have an affective commitment to a brand are more likely to be emotionally invested in the company that makes the products they enjoy. They identify with the brand on a personal level, and consider it to be a close friend or an extension of themselves at times. This can be triggered when customers are able to relate with the brand's personality.

- *Advocacy*

When a consumer is content with a service, business, or product, they can tell others about it to spread the word about their experiences (Sashi, 2012). In the linked world of today, people talk about brands and share their experiences on social media. If the service offered is satisfactory, customers can easily be directed to utilize a chatbot by way of a link or a few clicks.

- *Engagement*

A customer is more engaged with a brand if they are both satisfied with it and feel some loyalty to it (Sashi, 2012). Consumer engagement demands both an effective and calculative commitment, as it calls for a solid link and better value for the customer. Through word-of-mouth and technical channels like social media, engaged customers can become brand ambassadors and attract new interested potential customers (Sashi, 2012).

Purchasing Behaviour

Since marketing encompasses everything a company does to sell products to clients and influence their purchasing behaviour, it is crucial for firms to understand what their needs are and how to meet them (TODOR, 2016). As a result of the increased access to information, consumers have become less reliant on sales and marketing. Instead, today's consumers are more likely to rely on the recommendations of other customers via online reviews and word-of-mouth referrals.

Environmental cues have also been proven to influence impulse buying, with people feeling compelled to buy impulsively when aroused by particular situational elements during a shopping interaction (e.g., ambient elements such as music, lighting, etc.) (Youn and Faber, 2000). The environmental psychology model provides a more thorough conceptualization of emotional and behavioural responses. Several researchers have looked into the aspects of the internet environment that lead to impulse buying in an online context (Adelaar et al., 2003). In chatbots' context, we can associate the environment with the chatting style of the bot and the interface. Behavioral cues and social signals are part of conversational language, and they transmit additional information and have a significant impact on conversational engagement (McTear et al., 2016). Functionality, personality, conversational intelligence and interface are the 4 main aspects of a chatbot's design. Functionality focuses on how well the chatbot carries out the requested tasks. An interaction without error could incline the customers to make a purchase (Toader et al., 2020). For a chatbot to be successful, its functionality must be up to par. Numerous human sensory modalities, such as taste, touch, smell, kinesthesia, vision, and hearing, can be represented by various media content representations. Individual processing of verbal or visual information can influence how people perceive environmental stimuli, as well as how they react emotionally and behaviorally. Businesses may provide consumers with specific types of media experiences that are used to set the stage or create a context in which related products and/or services are promoted or sold (Rifkin, 2001). (Gefen & Straub, 2003) study explicates, Texts convey personal presence in the same way that Personal photographs and pictures do. The intention to buy a specific product or service distinguishes behavioural intent to purchase from actual purchasing behaviour. To put it another way, a consumer's actual purchasing behaviour is based on the assumption that a consumer may decide to buy a product or service spontaneously. Shopping assistant oriented chatbots have the power to evoke a spontaneous purchasing behaviour triggering impulse buying behaviour.

Conversational intelligence, personality and interface can be tweaked in a way to maximize personalization potential. As covered above in this literature, The personality of a chatbot has a big influence on the consumer experience, and plays a big part in how the user views the conversation (Ruane et al., 2021). Several elements, such as the company's brand identity, the activities, the tasks of the chatbots, and target audience preferences, all play a part in building a chatbot personality that matches the business. During the study done by (Jain et al., 2018) chatbots with distinct personalities were popular among the participants. They expected the chatbot's personality to match its domain; for example, a news chatbot should be serious, whereas a shopping chatbot can be humorous and casual. Users are more likely to connect with a chatbot that has a consistent personality (Jain et al., 2018). Across all disciple, researchers have suggested that CAs should emulate human communication traits to be more natural and engaging (Gnewuch et al., 2017). (Schumaker et al., 2007) posited that the conversational knowledge assists users in their decision making skills. Furthermore, the experiment conducted by (Toader et al., 2020) indicated that Gender signals are crucial in eliciting favourable responses from customers. Study participants who interacted with an virtual assistant posing as a female displayed higher readiness to share personal information, showed increasingly higher level of patronage intentions, were more forgiving to the chatting errors, and were just happy and intrigued to interact.

USE OF CHATBOTS IN SALES FUNNEL

A sales funnel is a consumer-focused marketing model that depicts the journey consumers take as they move toward purchasing a product or service, for those who are unfamiliar with the term. Chatbots can direct users to the next step in the sales process.

Chatbots as Marketing Agents

Chatbots allow companies to contact their target audience using messaging applications such as WeChat Messenger, WhatsApp Messenger, Facebook Messenger as they are looked at as a new information, communication, and transaction channel. The essential beauty of an artificially intelligent bot is that it can work on an endless number of channels. Bot frameworks allow developers to create a single A bot that reacts to users in the same way across many platforms, including web chat, Facebook Messenger, Skype, and others. Artificial Intelligence (AI) has the potential to significantly advance the methods used by businesses to address a variety of marketing issues. The latest advancements in chatbots in customer service and sales are impressive and AI chatbots can be located among the most recent technological advancements in customer communication (Letheren & Glavas, 2017; Van den Broeck et al., 2019). Customers' demands for personalised services are becoming increasingly sophisticated. Companies must adopt new technologies that allow for humanlike communication in real time in order to make customers happy. However, the use of intelligent conversational agents, or Chatbots-AI, for personalised marketing is still in its early stages around the world (Ai, n.d.).

Chatbots can be used to promote more intimate consumer-brand relationships, greater trust, and can be incorporated into customers' shopping process. With the power of personalization, businesses can witness chatbots' upselling potential. The majority of customers in the instant gratification era seek service speed. Chatbots can assist in cross-selling a company's services or products while keeping customers engaged by providing solutions to their problems. The more a customer is engaged, the more profitable an organisation becomes as a result of increased customer satisfaction. To keep customers interested, many chatbots use visual content such as images and videos. A character-driven experience has also aided in better customer engagement on occasion. On a single platform, chatbots educate, inform, and entertain users. As a result, any company with a social media account should make sure that its potential customers can have a useful conversation with them. According to recent reports, chatbots' strength lies on their capacity to obfuscate the distinction between aid and advertising (Letheren & Glavas, 2017; Van den Broeck et al., 2019). When a chatbot offers pertinent clothing options that are tailored to the customers' interests and past purchasing behaviour, users feel more like they are being served by the brand rather than being sold to. This is an example that could illustrate the aforementioned assertion (Van den Broeck et al., 2019). (Toader et al., 2020) believes, despite the complexities of consumers' psychological and behavioural responses to virtual assistants, further blurring this barrier, companies may be able to compensate for the loss of human connection in online environments while simultaneously increasing their willingness to trust technology and participate in positive consumer engagement. As it was mentioned in this literature, tweaking three(personality, interface and conversational intelligence) of the four functionality of a chatbot, organizations can explore chatbot's customer acquisition potential. Chatbots must either deliver natural language capabilities with sufficient conversational joy, or an entertaining app-like experience tailored to the familiar turn-based messaging interface (Jain et al., 2018). At its best potential with respect to its functionality, A chatbot can possibly facilitate the following: Making it easy for customers to find information and make a purchase anywhere and anytime, offering customers personalised products, recommendations and content more likely to meet their needs, providing agent decision-support with next best offer suggestions, rapidly scaling up and down to always serve new customers in a cost-efficient manner (Ai, n.d.). These services' use of natural language in online interactions makes automated marketing and communication services viable candidates for new business growth (Brandtzaeg & Følstad, 2017). In order to be more natural and engaging, CAs should take on the qualities of human communication. Moreover, When CAs become orchestrators of consumer interactions and engagements, they might provide a point of difference and a competitive advantage, not just within the company, but across other companies as well (Thomaz et al., 2020).

Chatbots as Shopping Assistant

Consumer buying behaviour is expected to change as a result of the increased use of chat applications. Companies are starting to identify chatbots as an excellent opportunity to better exploit social networks while also gaining competitive differentiation. Chatbots suggest a potential change in how people interact with internet businesses (Brandtzaeg & Følstad, 2017). The survey's findings indicate that users favour chatbots because they are convenient, easy to use, and may help with online purchases. Nevertheless, respondents expected the chatbot's performance to improve with time. In addition to making chatbots easy to use, marketers are expected to increase the perception of human-like dialogue and enhance the entertainment features of chatbots (Ting Yan Chan & Hong Leung, 2021). The results of the survey also suggested that respondents favoured natural language chatbot communication (Ting Yan Chan & Hong Leung, 2021). While some Conversational Agents may offer an impersonal or cold experience, the most effective agents will be built to personalize and engage the users (Thomaz et al., 2020). Consumers expect a Chatbot's demeanour to fit its domain; for example, a news chatbot should be serious, but a retail chatbot might be lighthearted (Jain et al., 2018). CAs must develop social signals (e.g., appearance or language) which are both also consistent with these service agent characteristics and appropriate for the context in which they are used (Gnewuch et al., 2017). In terms of the user experience, chatbots can mimic an interpersonal conversation, both in terms of communication and prospective offers to consumers, with a high level of personalisation (Letheren & Glavas, 2017). Maintaining context improves user input efficiency by reducing required amount of user inputs. This capability can range from keeping context within a single chat to keeping context across numerous conversations. Context resolution is interpreted by users as a feature of a personalized, empathetic, and intelligent chatbot (Jain et al., 2018). The secret to designing a successful shopping assistant bot is personalization. Chatbots can provide specialised customer service conversations, individualised information, and ideas (Zumstein & Hundertmark, 2018). Additionally, chatbots can save user preferences based on past purchases, requests, and other behaviours (Zumstein & Hundertmark, 2018) and offer suggestions for future purchases and keep delivery information current (Brandtzaeg & Følstad, 2017). When a chatbot presents clients with relevant clothing options that are tailored to their interests and past purchasing history, this clearly demonstrates the usefulness of chatbots. Users are more likely to feel supported by the business than like they are being sold to (Van den Broeck et al., 2019). A virtual assistant can help your customers wherever they need information, guidance, or buying ideas. When speaking with a bot via a messenger app or a physical installation in a store, airports, or customer service desks, the functionality of the bot is easily provided.

By putting a chatbot in charge of capturing customers, the company can spend less money per customer to persuade them to complete their purchase than if it used traditional conversion methods. CAs can use the collected personal data in future contacts to further personalise dialogues with people on a large scale (Thomaz et al., 2020). CAs have the potential to voluntarily encourage the users to share personal information by providing a sense of companionship a an entertaining chatting experiences (Brandtzaeg & Følstad, 2017). The perceived benefits of CAs will be amplified to the degree that they are regarded as more engaging, pleasurable, and useful, while the perceived privacy dangers will be reduced to the extent that they are perceived as more trustworthy (Thomaz et al., 2020). Designers should use humour and a wide variety of chatbot responses to diversify the conversation. Positive characteristics include wit, sarcasm, and playfulness. Excessive politeness, on the other hand, is regarded as a negative trait (Jain et al., 2018). Chat applications will be able to accept payments in the future, allowing for a seamless shopping experience without having to leave the interface (Braveen Kumar, 2016). The messaging app can handle the order, billing, and delivery while the bot evolves into a personal assistant capable of performing a variety of consumer-focused tasks. WeChat, a popular Asian messaging app, already offers a number of services within the app.

Some of the integrated functionalities include money transfers, food ordering, movie ticket purchases, and flight booking. Furthermore, search engines may be linked into chatbots to find, select, and provide the best alternatives to the user based on past choices, preferences, and online interactions.

DISCUSSIONS

The Coronavirus outbreak has forced businesses to rethink how they reach their customers, continue deliver relevant customer experiences, and how to use digital channels to stay in business during the crisis and beyond. Businesses need to evolve the way they provide their services and can leverage on the AI technology to test the chatbot trends. When leveraged properly, features of chatbots not only can not only help the e-commerce industry to overcome the challenges, but can also help provide a superior online shopping experience. Companies must provide an omnichannel approach to customer engagement. However, from a data retention and engagement standpoint, it's also critical to ensure that these various channels intersect. Companies that are already operating on the digital landscape can capitalize by experimenting on chatbots and integrate it in their online sales funnel. Chatbots have become popular among businesses as a way to better leverage social media and gain a competitive advantage on the Internet over competitors who do not use them. Personalization has been identified as one of the most effective ways for businesses to build relationships. Chatbots are a new technology that is expected to take over mobile commerce and shopping apps in the near future. Companies who identify its application with the help of this study, could build bots best suited for shopping. Integration of chatbots in sales funnel could help business online explore an unchartered opportunity, provided that the development of the bot is aligned and built to the best of its ability with respect to its scope of customisable functions i.e. personality, interface and conversational intelligence as elaborated in this literature.

REFERENCES

Adamopoulou, E., & Moussiades, L. (2020). An Overview of Chatbot Technology. In IFIP Advances in Information and Communication Technology: Vol. 584 IFIP. Springer International Publishing. doi:10.1007/978-3-030-49186-4_31

Adelaar, T., Chang, S., Lancendorfer, K. M., Lee, B., & Morimoto, M. (2003). Effects of media formats on emotions and impulse buying intent. *Journal of Information Technology*, *18*(4), 247–266. doi:10.1080/0268396032000150799

Ai, C. (n.d.). *The New wave of customer and employee experiences.* Deloitte Digital.

Analytics, C. (2020). *Key Factors Driving the Growth of Conversational AI in Retail.* Uniphore. https://www.uniphore.com/key-factors-driving-the-growth-of-conversational-ai-in-retail/

Avis, E. (2015). The Rise of Digital Challengers. *Independent Banker, 65*(11), 28–30. http://search.ebscohost.com/login.aspx?direct=true%7B&%7Ddb=bth%7B&%7DAN=111109565%7B&%7Dsite=ehost-live

Brandtzaeg, P. B., & Følstad, A. (2017). Why people use chatbots. Lecture Notes in Computer Science (Including Subseries Lecture Notes in Artificial Intelligence and Lecture Notes in Bioinformatics), 10673 LNCS, 377–392. doi:10.1007/978-3-319-70284-1_30

Braveen Kumar. (2016). *How Conversational Commerce Is Forever Changing the Way We Shop.* Shopify. https://www.shopify.in/blog/113660229-how-conversational-commerce-is-forever-changing-the-way-we-shop

Business, F. (2019). *F8 2019: Making It Easier for Businesses to Connect with Customers on Messenger.* https://www.facebook.com/business/news/f8-2019-making-it-easier-for-businesses-to-connect-with-customers-on-messenger

Business Insider Intelligence. (2016). *80% of Businesses Want Chatbots By 2020.* https://www.businessinsider.com/80-of-businesses-want-chatbots-by-2020-2016-12?r=DE&IR=T

Charlton, G. (2013). *Consumers Prefer Live Chat For Customer Service: Stats.* Econsultancy. https://econsultancy.com/blog/63867-consumers-prefer-live-chat-for-customer-service-stats#i.1nockyz1cffd8a

Dale, R. (2016). The return of the chatbots. *Natural Language Engineering, 22*(5), 811–817. doi:10.1017/S1351324916000243

Elevating customer experience excellence in the next normal | McKinsey. (n.d.). Retrieved August 5, 2021, from https://www.mckinsey.com/business-functions/operations/our-insights/elevating-customer-experience-excellence-in-the-next-normal# doi:10.1111/j.1540-5414.2006.00108.x

Gefen & Straub. (2003). Managing User Trust in B2C e-Services. *E-Service Journal, 2*(2), 7. doi:10.2979/esj.2003.2.2.7

Gnewuch, U., Morana, S., Adam, M., & Maedche, A. (2017). This is the author ' s version of a work that was published in the following source Please note : Copyright is owned by the author and / or the publisher. Commercial use is not allowed. Institute of Information Systems and Marketing (IISM) The psychop. *Thirty Eighth International Conference on Information Systems.*

Horzyk, A., Magierski, S., & Miklaszewski, G. (2009). An Intelligent Internet Shop-Assistant Recognizing a Customer Personality for Improving Man-Machine Interactions. *Recent Advances in Intelligent Information Systems*, 13–26.

Jain, M., Kumar, P., Kota, R., & Patel, S. N. (2018). Evaluating and informing the design of chatbots. *DIS 2018 - Proceedings of the 2018 Designing Interactive Systems Conference*, 895–906. 10.1145/3196709.3196735

Kaczorowska-Spychalska, D. (2019). How chatbots influence marketing. *Management, 23*(1), 251–270. doi:10.2478/manment-2019-0015

Kasey Panetta. (2016). *Artificial intelligence, machine learning, and smart things promise an intelligent future.* Gartner. https://www.gartner.com/smarterwithgartner/gartners-top-10-technology-trends-2017/

Land, R., Beetham, H., Sharpe, R., DeNoyelles, A., Zydney, J., Chen, B., Sendall, P., Shaw, R., Round, K., Larkin, J., Barczyk, C. C., Duncan, D. G., Abes, E. S., Jones, S. R., McEwen, M. K., Boon, S., Sinclair, C., Borup, J., West, R. E., ... Tu, C.-H. (2013). Social Presence and Cognitive Engagement in Online Learning Environments. *Language Learning & Technology, 10*(1), 1–22. doi:10.1111/j.1467-8527.2008.00397_1.x

Letheren, K., & Glavas, C. (2017). Embracing the bots: How direct to consumer advertising is about to change forever. *QUT Business School*, 11–13. https://eprints.qut.edu.au/107945/

Liao, Q. V., Davis, M., Geyer, W., Muller, M., & Shami, N. S. (2016). What can you do? Studying social-agent orientation and agent proactive interactions with an agent for employees. *DIS 2016 - Proceedings of the 2016 ACM Conference on Designing Interactive Systems: Fuse*, 264–275. 10.1145/2901790.2901842

Lucia, P., Schmid, B. F., Wolfgang, M., & Müller, J. P. (2003). Editorial: Software Agents. *Electronic Markets, 13*(1), 1–2. doi:10.1080/1019678032000062195

McTear, M., Callejas, Z., & Griol, D. (2016). The conversational interface: Past and. *The Conversational Interface: Talking to Smart Devices.*

Medhi Thies, I., Menon, N., Magapu, S., Subramony, M., & O'Neill, J. (2017). How do you want your chatbot? An exploratory Wizard-of-Oz study with young, Urban Indians. Lecture Notes in Computer Science (Including Subseries Lecture Notes in Artificial Intelligence and Lecture Notes in Bioinformatics), 10513 LNCS, 441–459. doi:10.1007/978-3-319-67744-6_28

Meuter, M. L., Bitner, M. J., Ostrom, A. L., & Brown, S. W. (2005). Choosing among alternative service delivery modes: An investigation of customer trial of self-service technologies. *Journal of Marketing*, *69*(2), 61–83. doi:10.1509/jmkg.69.2.61.60759

Michiels, E. (2017). Modelling Chatbots with a cognitive system allows for a differentiating user experience. *CEUR Workshop Proceedings*, *2027*, 70–78.

Nicole & Benton. (2017). Evaluating Quality of Chatbots and Intelligent Conversational Agents. *Arxiv.Org*.

OECD. (2018). *Maintaining competitive conditions in the era of digitalisation*. https://www.oecd.org/g20/Maintaining-competitive-conditions-in-era-of-digitalisation-OECD.pdf

Pearson, A. (2019). Personalisation the artificial intelligence way. *Journal of Digital and Social Media Marketing*, *7*(3), 245–269.

Pereira, M. J., Coheur, L., Fialho, P., & Ribeiro, R. (2019). Chatbots' greetings to human-computer communication. *CEUR Workshop Proceedings*, *2390*(1994), 61–66.

Reddy, T. (2017). *How chatbots can help reduce customer service costs by 30% - Watson Blog*. Ibm.Com. https://www.ibm.com/blogs/watson/2017/10/how-chatbots-reduce-customer-service-costs-by-30-percent/

Rifkin, J. (2001). *The Age of Access: The New Culture of Hypercapitalism, Where all of Life is a Paid-For Experience. 2*, 320. https://www.amazon.com/The-Age-Access-Hypercapitalism-Experience/dp/1585420824

Ruane, E., Farrell, S., & Ventresque, A. (2021). User Perception of Text-Based Chatbot Personality. Lecture Notes in Computer Science (Including Subseries Lecture Notes in Artificial Intelligence and Lecture Notes in Bioinformatics), 12604 LNCS(February), 32–47. doi:10.1007/978-3-030-68288-0_3

Sashi, C. M. (2012). Customer engagement, buyer-seller relationships, and social media. *Management Decision*, *50*(2), 253–272. doi:10.1108/00251741211203551

Schumaker, R. P., Ginsburg, M., Chen, H., & Liu, Y. (2007). An evaluation of the chat and knowledge delivery components of a low-level dialog system:The AZ-ALICE experiment. *Decision Support Systems*, *42*(4), 2236–2246. doi:10.1016/j.dss.2006.07.001

Seounmi Youn and Ronald J. Faber. (2000). *Impulse Buying: Its Relation to Personality Traits and Cues*. The Association for Consumer Research. https://www.acrwebsite.org/volumes/8383/volumes/v27/NA-27/full

Sundar, S. S., & Marathe, S. S. (2010). Personalization versus customization: The importance of agency, privacy, and power usage. *Human Communication Research*, *36*(3), 298–322. doi:10.1111/j.1468-2958.2010.01377.x

Talking the Talk: The Beginner's Guide to Designing a Chatbot Conversation. (2017). Hubspot. https://blog.hubspot.com/marketing/beginners-guide-to-designing-a-chatbot-conversation

Thomaz, F., Salge, C., Karahanna, E., & Hulland, J. (2020). Learning from the Dark Web: Leveraging conversational agents in the era of hyper-privacy to enhance marketing. *Journal of the Academy of Marketing Science*, *48*(1), 43–63. doi:10.1007/s11747-019-00704-3

Ting Yan Chan, W., & Hong Leung, C. (2021). Mind the Gap: Discrepancy Between Customer Expectation and Perception on Commercial Chatbots Usage. *Asian Journal of Empirical Research*, *11*(1), 1–10. doi:10.18488/journal.1007.2021.111.1.10

Toader, D. C., Boca, G., Toader, R., Măcelaru, M., Toader, C., Ighian, D., & Rădulescu, A. T. (2020). The effect of social presence and chatbot errors on trust. *Sustainability (Basel)*, *12*(1), 1–24. doi:10.3390/su12010256

Todor, R. D. (2016). Blending traditional and digital marketing. *Bulletin of the Transilvania University of Brasov, Series I: Engineering Sciences*, *9*(1), 51–56. http://ezproxy.leedsbeckett.ac.uk/login?url=http://search.ebscohost.com/login.aspx?direct=true&db=a9h&AN=116699220&site=eds-live&scope=site

TsvetkovaM.García-GavilanesR.FloridiL.YasseriT. (2016). *Even Good Bots Fight. December*. http://arxiv.org/abs/1609.04285

UK. (2018). *How Chatbots Can Redefine Your Sales Process*. https://www.salesforce.com/uk/blog/2018/09/how-chatbots-can-redefine-your-sales-process.html

Um, T., Kim, T., & Chung, N. (2020). How does an intelligence chatbot affect customers compared with self-service technology for sustainable services? *Sustainability (Basel)*, *12*(12), 5119. Advance online publication. doi:10.3390/su12125119

Van den Broeck, E., Zarouali, B., & Poels, K. (2019). Chatbot advertising effectiveness: When does the message get through? *Computers in Human Behavior*, *98*, 150–157. doi:10.1016/j.chb.2019.04.009

Weinberg, C. (2017). *How Messenger and "M" Are Shifting Gears*. The Information. https://www.theinformation.com/articles/how-messenger-and-m-are-shifting-gears

Zumstein, D., & Hundertmark, S. (2018). Chatbots: An interactive technology for personalized communication and transaction. *IADIS International Journal on Www/Internet, 15*(1), 96–109.

Chapter 2
Does AI Chatbot Service Quality Impact Customer Loyalty?
Examining Satisfaction and Attitudes

Rupali
https://orcid.org/0000-0003-0527-9365
Amity Business School, Amity University, Noida, India

Natasha Sharma
Amity Business School, Amity University, Noida, India

Prerna Arora
Amity Business School, Amity University, Noida, India

Paritosh Mishra
Amity Business School, Amity University, Noida, India

ABSTRACT

Artificial intelligence (AI) has emerged as a catalyst for change in numerous sectors. AI chatbots have been shown to be able to enhance customer engagements and loyalty. This research endeavor aims to explore the nuanced facets of AI-chatbot service quality dimensions and their substantial impact on favorable customer behavioural outcomes such as their attitudes, satisfaction, and loyalty. The study utilized data collected from people in Delhi-NCR region of India who have used AI-powered chatbot services previously. Results showed that every dimension of service quality has a positive association on satisfaction. However, only three dimensions impacted customer attitude significantly. In addition, the outcome of analysis showed that customer loyalty was positively and significantly impacted by user satisfaction

DOI: 10.4018/979-8-3693-1503-3.ch002

towards AI-chatbots and attitude. This study offers a novel and impactful strategy to enhance our understanding of chatbot's potential to significantly alter the way online companies interact with and market to their customer base.

INTRODUCTION

In a time characterized by swift technological progress, Artificial Intelligence (AI) has arisen as a catalyst for change in numerous sectors. Among its standout applications, AI-powered chatbots have redefined the landscape of customer service and engagement. As businesses progressively embrace AI-driven chatbots to engage with their clientele, it becomes crucial to evaluate how these digital assistants affect customer loyalty, contentment, and perception (Rios-Campos et al., 2023). The origin of chatbots traces back to as early as 1921, coinciding with the introduction of robotics. However, it was in the year 2000 that the significance of chatbots became more apparent, particularly highlighted by the emergence of the SmarterChild intelligent agent on AOL Instant Messenger, which notably facilitated searches for stock information and weather updates (Agarwal & Wadhwa, 2020). Over time, the acceptance of this idea increased notably in 2011 with the introduction of Apple's Siri, a voice assistant (VA) incorporating chatbot technology. Subsequently, these voice assistants have swiftly found widespread adoption across various domains (Johnson et al., 2012). The enthusiasm surrounding chatbots has grown, primarily driven by the notable advancements in artificial intelligence (AI) (Rahman et al., 2017).

In the contemporary age, where consumers increasingly dedicate their time to digital environments, businesses prioritize maintaining an online presence at all times and across various platforms to stay connected with their customers. Owing to advancements in digital technology and the escalating competition, companies are consistently striving to attract and retain customers. The 'modern customer in 2021' seeks to minimize the time spent and anticipates the ability to contact a company at any time and from any location, irrespective of the time, place, or communication channel (McLean & Wilson, 2016). Through the utilization of a chatbot, a customer develops increased trust in an organization, resulting in enhanced customer loyalty (Ameen et al., 2021).

The level of service excellence delivered by AI chatbots stands as a pivotal factor influencing customer loyalty (Ismail & Yunan, 2016). With increasing reliance on these digital representatives for customer engagements and loyalty, gaining insights into how various dimensions of service quality, including responsiveness, precision, and personalization, can offer invaluable guidance to businesses seeking to elevate their customer relations. The dynamics of consumer behavior and customer loyalty are intricate processes influenced by various factors. Among these factors, satisfaction and attitude are two key components that play a pivotal role (Sivadas & Baker-Prewitt, 2000). As consumers navigate a marketplace saturated with choices, their decisions are not solely driven by product features or pricing. Instead, their satisfaction with a product or service, coupled with their overall attitude towards a brand, becomes a powerful force shaping their preferences and repeat business (Akbar & Parvez, 2009). Furthermore, the development of favorable perceptions towards products, services, or brands is identified as a crucial factor preceding positive consumer behavior. Attitudes assume a pivotal role in shaping purchase intentions, decision-making processes, and the perceived value of offerings. The emotional and cognitive aspects of attitudes contribute to the complex network of consumer perceptions that ultimately steer their choices within the marketplace (Rizky & Hariasih, 2023). The attitude of customers play a pivotal role in molding their consumer behavior. Examining the ways in which service quality dimensions of AI chatbots influence satisfaction and attitudes can provide insights into the mechanisms by which these digital tools shape customer perceptions and emotions. This comprehension is essential for organizations aiming to refine their AI chatbot systems and cultivate favorable customer experiences (Cheng & Jiang, 2020). The interplay between user satisfaction and attitude, and customer loyalty stands as a foundational element of understanding how to make the best use of AI chatbots. Through an examination of the interrelationships among these factors, this research endeavor aims to clarify whether a customer base is more prone to display loyalty to a brand utilizing AI chatbots customer service. These insights can serve as a compass for organizations in formulating strategies to strengthen customer loyalty through AI chatbot engagements.

Extensive research on chatbots and their impact on customer behavior and attitudes is prevalent (Kim & Chang, 2020; Yun & Park, 2022). However, studies specifically addressing AI chatbots, with their distinct interaction and behavior patterns, are limited. Prior investigations have primarily concentrated on aspects like human-chatbot interaction and satisfaction (Eren, B.A., 2021; Chen et al., 2021), as well as attributes related to AI chatbot service quality, satisfaction, and loyalty (Chen et al., 2023). Notably, previous research (Jenneboer et al., 2022; Chen et al., 2023) has indicated an absence of a direct link between AI chatbot attributes and customer loyalty, highlighting a significant gap in the existing literature in this area. Akıl and Ungan (2022). confirmed that service quality significantly influences both user satisfaction and behavior. Acknowledging that consumer attitudes play a pivotal role in shaping behaviors within service-oriented contexts, it becomes imperative to consider whether chatbots can genuinely enhance the consumer experience in a fully digitalized environment. To understand this relationship, it is also crucial to look into other factors that may play a role such as the attitudes of user. This research endeavor seeks to explore the nuanced facets of AI-chatbot service quality dimensions and their substantial impact on favorable customer conduct such as their loyalty. The current research stands out by specifically evaluating both the direct and mediating impact of satisfaction and attitude on the correlation between AI chatbots' service quality and customer loyalty. This distinctive approach adds a valuable contribution to the existing body of literature.

Thus, the objectives of the research are:

1. How do AI-chatbots service quality dimensions influence satisfaction and attitude towards chatbot usage?
2. Does user satisfaction and attitude impact customer loyalty?
3. To explore the impact of service quality dimensions of AI-chatbots on customer loyalty via the mediating role of attitude and satisfaction.

LITERATURE REVIEW

Artificial intelligence (AI) has experienced a rapid resurgence and has exerted a widespread impact on the everyday lives of people (Rios-Campos et al., 2023). Media tools powered by AI, like chatbots, have brought new vitality to numerous industry sectors, achieving commercial success in recent decades (Cheng & Jiang, 2020). Chatbots facilitate real-time chats on multiple platforms, websites, social media platforms, or instant messaging applications from virtually any location (Hagberg et al., 2016). Furthermore, they offer personalized language that mimics human speech, enhancing user experience and fostering customer loyalty. A recent study by Patel and Trivedi (2020) studied a sample of 910 organisations and found that AI-based technology had a significant impact on customer loyalty. At the same time having AI-based technology does not necessitate loyalty. Service quality has an impact on consumers' feelings as well. Typically, it has been observed that high-quality service is favourably and significantly correlated with customers' positive feelings. Customers assess the quality of their experience based on the level of service they receive. User reviews are used to gauge service quality. The most popular tool for assessing service quality is the SERVQUAL scale, which was created by Parasuraman et al. (1985) and has been verified in a number of online and offline contexts. Researchers have developed several scales to measure the quality of online buying experiences, including 'Electronic Service Quality', 'Online Service Quality', and 'Online Retail Service Quality'. These scales are designed specifically for assessing the quality of services provided in online retail settings (Ashfaq et al., 2020). These metrics, nevertheless, have drawn criticism for being used to the evaluation of AI-powered financial chatbot services (Chen et al., 2022). Theoretically, the SERVQUAL dimensions might not be adequate to accurately represent the complexities of a chatbot service environment powered by artificial intelligence. The primary distinction between chatbots and human customer support is that the AI-based banking chatbot service is built on a state-of-the-art information system (Jenneboer et al., 2022). Nonetheless, SERVQUAL quality factors including "tangibles, reliability, responsiveness, assurance, and empathy" serve as the foundation for our investigation. DeLone and McLean (2003) highlighted that the selection of quality dimensions by researchers depends on the study setting and emphasis. Conversely, Parasuraman et al. (1985) proposed that the choice of service quality dimensions is influenced by the specific services under investigation. For the purpose of our examination, the distinctive nature of AI-chatbot services, which lacks tangible elements like physical facilities, staff appearances, and equipment, has directed scholars' attention towards emphasizing interactivity as a pivotal aspect of service quality. Furthermore, the significance of understandability is underscored in AI chatbot services, enabling them to simulate human speech and enhance the overall user experience, thereby serving as a surrogate for empathy. The present study advances conversation by substituting the two distinct dimensions of "understandability" and "interactivity" for the tangibility and empathy components of SERVQUAL.

Various theories and frameworks provide different perspectives on the same issue. By looking at a variety of sources, one might gain a better understanding of the possible interactions and mediating factors between the variables in issue that would not be apparent when looking at just one theory or framework. This study's conceptual model is well-founded in theory and takes into account all pertinent variables affecting the phenomena under investigation. By combining many academic models and theories this study takes an original approach, such as "The SERVQUAL Model" (Parasuraman et al., 1985) from where the dimensions of AI-chatbot service quality dimensions have been developed, "Social Presence Theory (Biocca et al., 2003)" and "DeLone and McLean Information Systems Success Model" (DeLone and McLean,2003) which have been studied to help understand how AI-chatbot service dimensions influence customer experiences (Ashfaq et al., 2020),"Theory of planned behaviour" (Ajzen, 1991), "The Unified Theory of Acceptance and Use of Technology (UTAUT)" (Venkatesh & Zhang, 2020), and "Technology Acceptance Model (TAM)" (Venkatesh & Davis, 2000) which are extensively employed frameworks for modeling the acceptance of new financial technologies and services. As per the theory of planned behaviour, attitudes are a key concept that describe how favorable or unfavorable a person's position is towards the behaviour of interest (Soares et al., 2022). Customers are likely to have a positive position if a chatbot can quickly handle their problems since it allows for quick replies and its service quality is up to their expectations. This attitude then has an impact on how they use and satisfaction of the available technology and how loyal they remain to the product or service. Based on the previously examined literature, a conceptual model is developed that takes into account how the quality of AI-chatbot service affects attitude and satisfaction, and how those two aspects affect customer loyalty.

Understandability

Understandability is a crucial component for the effective deployment of chatbot services. Customers want chatbots to be as natural-feeling as executive customer service representatives. The accuracy of comprehending human conversations is essential in meeting consumer expectations (Rapp et al., 2021). Abd-Alrazaq et al. (2021) and Skjuve et al. (2021) have highlighted the importance of ensuring that AI-enabled chatbots possess the ability to accurately comprehend human emotions and feelings. Numerous studies have explored the notion of comprehendibility within information systems and e-commerce, with a specific emphasis on enhancing the user experience. The concept of understandability in the context of information systems pertains to the ease with which users comprehend the data presented (Rapp et al., 2021). A platform's capacity to deliver information that is both understandable and clear determines the quality of its content (Go & Sundar, 2019). The level of understandability of a platform has a direct influence on user loyalty (Li et al., 2021). Users are inclined to attribute greater satisfaction to a chatbot when it delivers information that is easily understood (Skjuve et al., 2021). Understanding encompasses the user's assessment of the chatbot's ability to comprehend human queries, concerns, contexts, and the subtleties of human language (Abd-Alrazaq et al., 2021). According to Venkatesh and Davis (2000), the Technology Acceptance Model (TAM) suggests that consumers' attitudes towards technology are shaped by how easy they perceive it to be to us. Therefore, the following hypothesis has been proposed:

H2: Understandability is positively related to satisfaction while using AI-chatbots.

H7: Understandability is positively related to attitude while using AI-chatbots.

Responsiveness

Consumers now want AI apps to address their issues and complaints more quickly and efficiently (Abdulquadri et al., 2021). Chatbots that provide prompt and efficient replies have a good impact on user confirmation and intention to use. The chatbot's responsiveness influences the virtual flow experience (Chen et al., 2021). The impact of this element on communication quality and user satisfaction is shown by the previously stated research (Chen et al., 2021; Go & Sundar, 2019). It is important to swiftly address and resolve any various recommendations, comments, questions, or concerns that users may have (Nordheim et al.,2019). According to study by Eren (2021), there is a favourable correlation between chatbot response and perceived service quality. According to the existing body of literature, human agent-based service quality evaluation commonly incorporates dimensions such as assurance and responsiveness (Ashfaq et al., 2020). When the product feature is operational, AI-powered chatbots outperform human frontline staff in terms of responsiveness and performance (Li & Shang 2020). Responsive behaviour leads to increased customer satisfaction (Ruan & Mezei, 2022). Previous research studies have examined the specific metrics for assessing the quality of chatbot services (Przegalinska et al., 2019; Skjuve et al., 2021). Chatbots ought to deliver timely and accurate responses to user inquiries, mirroring the behaviour of human agents. This would enhance user confidence, trust, and intention. Therefore, to understand how responsiveness affects satisfaction and attitude, the following hypothesis has been proposed:

H1: Responsiveness is positively related to satisfaction while using AI-chatbots.

H6: Responsiveness is positively related to attitude while using AI-chatbots.

Reliability

The capacity of chatbots to comprehend requests, respond promptly, and efficiently handle consumer issues and effort within a short amount of time explains their reliability characteristic (Behera et al., 2021; Ashfaq et al., 2020). The assessment of service quality relies on the accurate and reliable performance of the application in delivering the desired service (Chung et al., 2020). Important variables include the impression of dependable performance and the suitability of user query resolution (Chung et al., 2020). Conversational assistants' dependability raises consumer confidence in e-commerce sites (Li et al., 2021; Behera et al., 2021). Customer trust in data security is crucial and can be established by ensuring system reliability (Lappeman et al., 2022). The acceptance rate of AI-enabled e-services can be enhanced by improving the reliability of chatbots. Improved performance and increased system efficiency of chatbots positively influence users' perception of meeting their initial performance expectations (Lee & Park, 2019). Relevant answers have a beneficial impact on users' confirmation and future desire to use these services. According to the UTAUT model, people who believe that a technological service is dependable and easy to use are likely to have greater effort expectancies, which represent their expectations that the service would be simple to use and take less work (Venkatesh & Zhang, 2020). Therefore, the subsequent hypothesis has been proposed:

H5: Reliability is positively related to satisfaction while using AI-chatbots.

H10: Reliability is positively related to attitude while using AI-chatbots.

Assurance

The capacity of personnel to build trustworthy connections with users, together with their expertise, knowledge, and politeness, may all be taken into account when evaluating the quality assurance of services (Parasuraman et al., 1985; Li et al., 2021). Research has shown that users' intention to utilise a chatbot service is positively impacted by the service's capacity to impart knowledge and instil confidence and trust (Nguyen et al., 2021). Assurance pertains to the perception of confidence, protection, and ease during one's exchanges with an automaton (Lee & Park, 2019). Customer satisfaction is favourably influenced by assurance, an independent variable. Positive word of mouth and repurchase intention are positively impacted by customer satisfaction (Ruan & Mezei, 2022). There is a guarantee for the security and privacy of user data that users provide to the chatbot (Park, 2020; Przegalinska et al., 2019; Skjuve et al., 2021). Increased assurance from chatbots leads to improved privacy, security, confidence, and trust among users (Lee & Park, 2019; Pereira & Díaz, 2018). Assurance pertains to the delivery of services without errors by chatbots. Assurance is a crucial aspect of service quality that leads to increased user satisfaction (Nguyen & Malik, 2022). The primary obstacle that impacts user confirmation and intention is a lack of confidence. Personifying the chatbot enhances user trust by creating a more natural conversational experience. According to Venkatesh and Zhang (2020), higher performance expectations are more common among users who see a technological service as dependable, responsive, and reassuring. This suggests that they believe the technology service will assist them in accomplishing their objectives. To explore this, the following hypothesis has been proposed:

H3: Assurance is positively related to satisfaction while using AI-chatbots.

H8: Assurance is positively related to attitude while using AI-chatbots.

Interactivity

Perceived interactivity in chatbot services pertains to the user's conviction that their engagements with the service resemble those with human agents (comprising numerous interactions). This perception empowers the user to exert authority over their individual requirements (Cho et al. 2019; Heeter 1989). Go and Sundar (2019) suggest that interactivity is an essential quality dimension for chatbot services. It is believed to be crucial in end user-facing systems as it enables personalized services and enhances user engagement. Furthermore, previous research has highlighted the significance of interactivity in enhancing the human-like qualities of chatbot-based system, the extent to which sensitive topics are discussed (Sannon et al., 2018). Additionally, the positive psychological impact of communicating with a chatbot might result in a positive opinion of the website or company (Go & Sundar, 2019). In online communication, when frontline staff are not in close proximity to the clients, chatbot interaction is crucial. According to the social presence theory (Kreijns et al., 2021), users' attitude might be influenced by how much social presence they feel they are experiencing in a technology-mediated connection. Close ties between consumers and the brand may be maintained and high customer satisfaction levels can result from interaction, which includes quick responses and problem-solving. The differentiation between understandability and interactivity pertains to the extent to which users perceive themselves as having control over interactive dialogues involving chatbots, as well as the chatbot's capacity to grasp the exchange. Thus, to understand the effect of Interactivity on Satisfaction and Attitude, we propose the following hypothesis:

H4: Interactivity is positively related to satisfaction while using AI-chatbots.

H9: Interactivity is positively related to attitude while using AI-chatbots.

Satisfaction and Consumer Loyalty

Loyalty is a crucial consequence of user satisfaction, in addition to intentions of ongoing use (Fornell, 2007). It is a frequently studied customer behavior in business communication research. It describes consumers' unwavering dedication to sticking with or repurchasing their favoured brands in the face of marketing initiatives from rival companies. (Godey et al., 2016). Prior research has emphasized the significance of user satisfaction in fostering loyalty among long-term users (Ruan & Mezei, 2022; Rizky & Hariasih, 2023). Customer satisfaction with a service encounter can increase their trust in recommendation agents, which in turn affects their intentions to purchase products or services from a brand (Kim & Ko, 2010, 2012). The enjoyment and satisfaction that customers experience when using social media or chatbots can have positive effects on brand perception, purchase intention, and brand awareness (Hess et al., 2009; Lu et al., 2016). Based on the literature review, we propose the following hypothesis in this study:

H11: Satisfaction positively influences customer loyalty using AI-chatbots.

Attitude and Costumer loyalty

The relationship between attitude and customer loyalty is a crucial aspect in the field of customer behaviour. Customer attitude, shaped by perceptions and experiences, significantly influences their loyalty to a brand or business (Soares et al., 2022). Positive attitudes often lead to increased customer satisfaction and loyalty, while negative attitudes may result in disengagement. Factors such as service quality, product satisfaction, and overall customer experience contribute to shaping attitudes

(Mehrolia et al., 2023). A positive attitude can foster a sense of trust and emotional connection, increasing the likelihood that customers will remain loyal to a brand over time (Tajeddini et al., 2021). Understanding and managing customer attitudes through effective communication, personalized experiences, and addressing concerns can play a pivotal role in building and sustaining customer loyalty. Researching and analyzing these dynamics can provide valuable insights for businesses aiming to enhance customer relationships and loyalty.

Therefore, we hypothesize that:

H12: Attitude positively influences customer loyalty using AI-chatbots.

Mediating Role of Satisfaction

Examining the subtleties within the literature reveals a clear pattern: when individuals engage with AI chatbots and perceive them as helpful and responsive, their satisfaction with the service increases (Hsu & Lin, 2023). This heightened satisfaction translates into positive emotions, trust, and a stronger affinity with the brand, ultimately fostering customer loyalty (Cheng & Jiang, 2020). An indispensable finding underscores that customers experiencing prompt and effective assistance from AI chatbots exhibit higher overall satisfaction (Dantsoho et al., 2021). The nexus between exemplary customer service and satisfaction plays a pivotal role in nurturing loyalty and cultivating a positive corporate reputation (Chen et al., 2021).

Moreover, the research underscores the crucial role of clarity in understandibilty. Businesses that communicate transparently, addressing the diverse informational needs of customers, contribute to a positive customer experience (Rapp et al., 2021). Therefore, companies should prioritize enhancing their communication methods to cater to the varied requirements of their customer base. Furthermore, the study highlights the necessity of assurance (Budur & Poturak, 2021).

Consistent demonstration of expertise and reliability by a company increases the likelihood of retaining satisfied customers and fostering loyalty. Additionally, interactive and engaging interactions with AI chatbots significantly contribute to customer satisfaction, creating a sense of connection and commitment(Ngo & Pavelková, 2017). Lastly, reliability is as a significant factor. Customers prefer services that are predictable and trustworthy, and maintaining a reliable track record is crucial for satisfying and retaining customers (Lappeman et al., 2023). Hence, satisfaction can serve as a mediating factor between the dimensions of AI chatbot quality (including responsiveness, understandability, assurance, interactivity, and reliability) and customer loyalty.

H13: Satisfaction acts as a mediator in between responsiveness and customer loyalty.

H14: Satisfaction acts as a mediator in between understandability and customer loyalty.

H15: Satisfaction acts as a mediator in between assurance and customer loyalty.

H16: Satisfaction acts as a mediator in between interactivity and customer loyalty.

H17: Satisfaction acts as a mediator in between reliability and customer loyalty.

Mediating Role of Attitude

The literature within the domains of information and marketing has delved into the antecedents of consumer satisfaction and behavior, emphasizing the role of service quality (Li et al., 2021; Akıl and Ungan, 2022). Notably, emerging research is shedding light on the significance of chatbot quality, investigating the interconnections among customer perceptions of utility, helpfulness, brand engagement, attitude, and trust (Cheng & Jiang, 2020; Hari et al., 2022). Upon examination of the research, certain scholars argue that both brand loyalty (Jenneboer et al., 2022) and the inclination to adopt intelligent technology are contingent upon fostering a favorable attitude toward its utilization (Li et al., 2020). In this context, businesses can capitalize on chatbots to integrate customers more deeply into their marketing strategies compared to traditional non-AI advertising platforms. A positive customer experience, facilitated by high-quality services, has the potential to enhance customers' trust and satisfaction, subsequently fostering loyalty and intentions to continue using the technology (Chen et al., 2022). Therefore, it would be reasonable to hypothesize that attitudes toward chatbots and individuals' perceptions of the quality of AI chatbot services exert an indirect influence on customer loyalty rather than a direct one. Empirical investigations have demonstrated that attitude serves as a mediating factor between behavioral intentions and various input factors. Chou and Hsu (2021), in their research, identified that user attitude plays a mediating role in the relationship between three interacting features of chatbots and user attitudes. A comprehensive study by Jenneboer et al. (2022) further supports this, revealing that positive attitudes directly result from favorable chatbot experiences, fostering customer loyalty.

In summary, the responsiveness, understandability, interactivity, dependability, and user confidence in the quality of AI chatbot services collectively influence customer behavior. Consequently, customers develop a positive perception of chatbots, leading to increased loyalty. Remarkably, to the authors' knowledge, there is a notable gap in the existing research regarding the mediating role of attitude between the five service quality dimensions—responsiveness, understandability, assurance, interaction, and reliability—and customer loyalty. Thus, we put up the following hypotheses:

H18: Attitude acts as a mediator in between responsiveness and customer loyalty.

H19: Attitude acts as a mediator in between understandability and customer loyalty.

Figure 1. Conceptual model

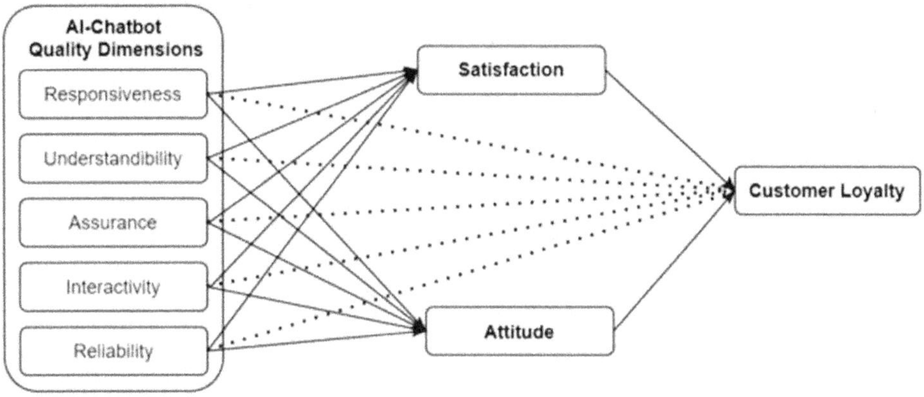

H20: Attitude acts as a mediator in between assurance and customer loyalty.
H21: Attitude acts as a mediator in between interactivity and customer loyalty.
H22: Attitude acts as a mediator in between reliability and customer loyalty.

METHODOLOGY

Measurements

Users of chatbots in India were surveyed for this study and were measured on a five-point Likert scales. Service quality consists of five dimensions with three items each, namely responsiveness, understandability, assurance, interactivity, and reliability (Mehrolia et al., 2023). Prior scales were utilised to operationalizc the researched constructs with five-point Likert scales. Adapted from Venkatesh et al. (2003), a four-item scale was used to examine attitudes about utilising chatbots. The authors adapted a four-item scale used in Fang et al. (2011) and Li et al. (2021) to measure satisfaction. Finally, Godey et al.'s (2016) four-item measure was used to evaluate customer loyalty. The questionnaire was pilot tested on 50 AI-chatbot users to adjust any difficult questions.

Procedure and Participants

The present research utilized data collected from people in Delhi-NCR region of India who have used AI-chatbots previously. The principal investigator's business links and social media sites like Facebook and LinkedIn have been employed for selecting respondents. An online platform for data gathering was used to gather information. They were asked to forward the link to the online survey to their colleagues. Participants were first asked if they had ever utilised chatbot services before moving on to the main questions. "Have you used the AI-chatbot services?" was the study's screening question. This was done in order to verify that the responses were actual users of the chatbot services. Due to the self-administered nature of this questionnaire, social desirability bias was less likely to occur. For data analysis, structural equation modelling (SEM) using SmartPLS4 was employed. 215 people made up that final sample in total. Male participants made up 57.21% of the total while female participants made up 42.79%. With 63.72% of the participants under 35, youth made up the majority. Only 11.16% of people were older than 46 years old, while 25.12% of people were in the 36 to 45 age range.

In accordance with the recommendations of Sarstedt et al. (2022), the study utilized Partial Least Squares Structural Equation Modeling (PLS-SEM) in Smart PLS 4 to validate the obtained results. As elucidated by Hair et al. (2020), PLS-SEM is recognized as a variance-based methodology that relies on least-squares functions, aiming to maximize the explained variance of dependent variables. Per Hair et al. (2019), a strong rationale for opting for Partial Least Squares Structural Equation Modeling (PLS-SEM) lies in its ability to estimate complex models without the need for a predetermined hypothesis regarding the data distribution. This flexibility is particularly beneficial when dealing with small sample sizes. Given its appropriateness for theory development and its ability to predict or enhance an existing structural theory, PLS-SEM was chosen as the analytical approach in this investigation. To thoroughly investigate the intricate aspects of AI-chatbot service quality dimensions and their significant influence on positive customer behaviors, including satisfaction, attitude and loyalty and to examine the mediating role of satisfaction and attitude, SEM came out to be the best approach of analysis.

RESULTS

Reliability and Validity Tests

Testing for validity and reliability was done on each concept before the study's hypotheses were tested. The outcomes are displayed in Tables 1 and 2. The constructs' outer loadings, which ranged from 0.723 to 0.946, were all higher than the advised 0.7 threshold. Each construct's Cronbach's Alpha score was higher than the acceptable 0.7, ranging from 0.711 to 0.909 which is acceptable, and the composite reliability score was from 0.724 to 0.941 (>0.7), which indicates strong internal consistency dependability. In terms of convergent validity, the constructs' AVE values varied from 0.579 to 0.827, above the threshold of 0.5 that is considered acceptable (Hair

Table 1. Reliability and validity

Items	Factor Loadings	Cronbach's Alpha	rho_a	rho_c	AVE
AS1	0.807	0.753	0.759	0.858	0.669
AS2	0.847				
AS3	0.798				
ATT1	0.855	0.909	0.941	0.936	0.785
ATT2	0.946				
ATT3	0.891				
ATT4	0.848				
CL1	0.776	0.890	0.905	0.925	0.756
CL2	0.910				
CL3	0.835				
CL4	0.946				
INT1	0.861	0.844	0.852	0.906	0.764
INT2	0.931				
INT3	0.826				
REL1	0.930	0.896	0.899	0.935	0.827
REL2	0.909				
REL3	0.890				
RES1	0.894	0.755	0.774	0.860	0.674
RES2	0.835				
RES3	0.723				
SAT1	0.767	0.757	0.762	0.846	0.579
SAT2	0.721				
SAT3	0.751				
SAT4	0.802				
UND1	0.792	0.711	0.724	0.834	0.627
UND2	0.769				
UND3	0.813				

et al., 2020). Furthermore, when it comes to identifying the absence of discriminant validity, the HTMT criteria performs better than conventional methods (Henseler et al., 2014). All scores fall below the established threshold values of 0.90, demonstrating the discriminant validity of our measures shown in Table 2.

Table 2. Discriminant validity: HTMT values

	AS	ATT	CL	INT	REL	RES	SAT
ATT	0.467						
CL	0.558	0.686					
INT	0.200	0.410	0.755				
REL	0.428	0.481	0.687	0.376			
RES	0.611	0.631	0.871	0.557	0.499		
SAT	0.556	0.519	0.754	0.543	0.619	0.792	
UND	0.612	0.636	0.889	0.607	0.642	0.831	0.854

Hypothesis Testing

Firstly, VIF values were checked to remove multicollinearity issues. No such issues were found since the values were ranging from 1.242 to 2.305, which is in the acceptable range. Predictive accuracy of the model i.e., R^2 were in the moderate range (Hair et al., 2020) as AI-chatbot quality dimensions account for 55% variation in satisfaction and 66% in attitude. R-square value of customer loyalty was 0.391. Next, the authors examined the path coefficient's (β) significance levels among both the dependent and independent variables. A bootstrapping estimate technique was used with 10,000 samples to test the assumptions, shown in Table 3. Path model analysis depicted that out of the five quality characteristics of chatbot quality only three had a positive and significant impact on attitude but all five had positive impact on user satisfaction. Findings show that among the dimensions of AI-chatbot quality responsiveness was associated with satisfaction ($\beta = 0.218, p<0.05$), understandability to satisfaction ($\beta = 0.259$, $p<0.05$), assurance was also positively associated with satisfaction ($\beta = 0.114$, $p<0.1$) fully supporting H1, H2 and marginally supporting H3. Interactivity was also positively associated to satisfaction ($\beta = 0.133$, $p<0.05$), and reliability to satisfaction ($\beta = 0.206$, $p<0.05$), thus supporting H4 and H5. The findings showed that attitude towards chatbots was affected by responsiveness ($\beta = 0.220$, $p<0.05$), Understandability ($\beta = 0.242$, $p<0.05$) and Reliability ($\beta = 0.162$, $p<0.05$), but was not associated to Assurance ($\beta = 0.117, p<0.05$) and Interactivity ($\beta = 0.081$, $p<0.05$). Thus, the hypotheses H6, H7 and H10 were supported, while H8 and H9 were not supported. In addition, outcome of analysis showed that customer loyalty was positively and significantly impacted by user satisfaction towards AI-chatbots ($\beta = 0.428$, $p<0.05$) and attitude ($\beta = 0.445$, $p<0.05$). Thus, H11 and H12 were supported.

The findings indicated that satisfaction significantly served as mediators in the relationships associated with service quality dimensions, achieving statistical

Table 3. Structural model results

Hypothesis	β	STDEV	t-Value	p Values	VIF	R^2
Direct Effects						
H1: RES -> SAT	0.218	0.079	2.774	0.006*	2.136	0.505
H2: UND-> SAT	0.259	0.081	3.188	0.001*	2.305	
H3: AS -> SAT	0.114	0.065	1.761	0.078**	1.379	
H4: INT -> SAT	0.133	0.065	2.059	0.040*	1.372	
H5: REL -> SAT	0.206	0.072	2.847	0.004*	1.425	
H6: RES -> ATT	0.220	0.087	2.516	0.012*	2.136	0.405
H7: UND-> ATT	0.242	0.098	2.467	0.014*	2.305	
H8: AS -> ATT	0.117	0.074	1.581	0.114 n.s.	1.379	
H9: INT -> ATT	0.081	0.081	0.991	0.321 n.s.	1.372	
H10: REL -> ATT	0.162	0.080	2.022	0.043*	1.425	
H11: SAT -> CL	0.428	0.065	6.575	0.000*	1.242	0.391
H12: ATT -> CL	0.445	0.079	5.640	0.000*	1.242	
Mediating Effects						
H13: RES -> SAT -> CL	0.093	0.038	2.483	0.013*		
H14: UND -> SAT -> CL	0.111	0.038	2.886	0.004*		
H15: AS -> SAT -> CL	0.049	0.028	1.749	0.080†		
H16: INT -> SAT -> CL	0.057	0.032	1.774	0.076†		
H17: REL -> SAT -> CL	0.088	0.035	2.530	0.011*		
H18: RES -> ATT -> CL	0.098	0.047	2.076	0.038*		
H19: UND -> ATT -> CL	0.108	0.041	2.626	0.009*		
H20: AS -> ATT -> CL	0.052	0.035	1.503	0.133 n.s.		
H21: INT -> ATT -> CL	0.036	0.041	0.878	0.380 n.s.		
H22: REL -> ATT -> CL	0.072	0.039	1.848	0.065†		

p<0.05*, †p<0.1, β= path coefficient, n.s. = non-significant

significance at either the 0.05 or 0.1 significance levels. Specifically, the path coefficient values were significant for responsiveness (β = 0.093, p<0.05), understandability (β = 0.111, p < 0.05), assurance (β = 0.049, p<0.1), interactivity (β = 0.057, p<0.1), and reliability (β = 0.088, p<0.05). Consequently, there is full support for hypotheses H13, H14, and H17, while partial support is evident for H15 and H16. Furthermore, the results indicated that attitude serves as a significant mediator in the relationship between responsiveness (β = 0.098, p<0.05), understandability (β = 0.108, p< 0.05), and partially mediated for reliability (β = 0.072, p<0.1) and customer loyalty. Thus, hypotheses H18 and H19 are fully supported, while H22

Figure 2. Bootstrapping results

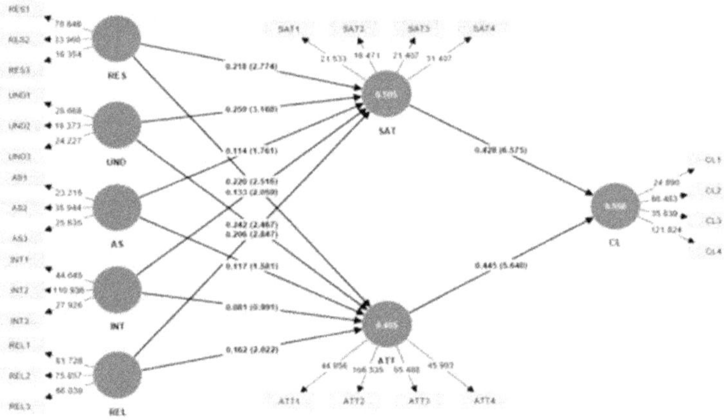

receives partial support. Conversely, no significant indirect mediation effect of attitude was observed for assurance and interactivity. As a result, hypotheses H20 and H21 were not supported.

DISCUSSIONS

The investigation aimed to discover the influence of AI-chatbot service quality dimensions through satisfaction and attitude on customer loyalty. Specifically, it sought to understand the effect of AI-chatbot service quality dimensions on user satisfaction and attitude towards chatbot usage. Additionally, the research investigated whether user satisfaction and attitude play a significant role in shaping customer loyalty. The result showed that among the five quality characteristics assessed for chatbots, only three demonstrated a positive and statistically significant impact on users' attitudes. However, it is noteworthy that all five dimensions of AI chatbot service quality had a positive influence on user satisfaction. First and foremost, responsiveness emerged as a critical factor impacting satisfaction. The statistically significant positive association between responsiveness and user satisfaction ($\beta = 0.218$, $p < 0.05$) underscores the pivotal role of prompt and efficient responses in enhancing overall user contentment. This outcome contrasts with the findings of Yun and Park (2022), who did not observe responsiveness to have an impact on satisfaction. This suggests that users who perceive a high level of responsiveness from AI chatbots are more likely to experience satisfaction, which is a crucial precursor to fostering loyalty. Research have noted that responsiveness is critical because it aligns with user expectations for timely interactions and solutions (Ruan & Mezei,

2022; Rizky & Hariasih, 2023). It directly affects user satisfaction by influencing the overall experience, whether in customer service, digital interactions, or product usage. As technology advances and communication channels evolve, maintaining and improving responsiveness will continue to be a key factor in enhancing user satisfaction (Comes et al., 2016). Furthermore, the study identified understandability as another key dimension positively influencing user satisfaction ($\beta = 0.259$, $p < 0.05$). The ability of AI chatbots to convey information in a clear and understandable manner contributes significantly to user satisfaction. This finding emphasizes the importance of designing chatbot interfaces and responses that align with user expectations and linguistic preferences. Enhancing user satisfaction is achieved when information is easily understood, interfaces are navigable, and tasks can be completed without confusion. A positive and enjoyable user experience is fostered by designing products and systems that prioritize clarity, intuitiveness, and user assistance (Ruan & Mezei, 2022). Moreover, assurance was found to be positively associated with satisfaction ($\beta = 0.114$, $p < 0.1$). Thus, the users who perceive a sense of reliability and competence in the AI chatbot's interactions are more likely to derive satisfaction from the service. Building user confidence through assurance in the chatbot's capabilities can contribute to a positive user experience, ultimately influencing satisfaction levels. assurance in AI services is closely tied to factors such as reliability, transparency, security, user education, and customer support. When users feel confident in the AI system's capabilities and trust its decision-making processes, it leads to increased satisfaction and a positive overall user experience as depicted by Yun & Park (2022). Interactivity was found to be poitively associated with user satisation ($\beta = 0.133$, $p<0.05$). This indicates that Interactivity enables AI services to gather and understand user preferences. By adapting responses and recommendations based on individual preferences, the AI can provide a more personalized and relevant experience, enhancing user satisfaction. As AI technology continues to advance, the effective incorporation of interactivity will likely remain a key factor in shaping positive user perceptions and ensuring the success of AI services (Ashfaq et al., 2020). The presence of reliability was discovered to have a positive correlation with satisfaction ($\beta = 0.206$, $p<0.05$), users are more satisfied when a chatbot consistently provides accurate and relevant information. Reliability in information retrieval ensures that users can trust the responses and rely on the chatbot as a valuable source of information. When users perceive a chatbot as consistently accurate, stable, and effective in understanding and addressing their needs, it fosters trust and contributes positively to the overall satisfaction of the user experience (Kim & Chang, 2020).

The results indicated that responsiveness had an impact on the attitude towards chatbots ($\beta=0.220$, $p<0.05$), which means that users appreciate chatbots that provide quick and timely responses to their queries. A responsive chatbot contributes to a sense of efficiency and attentiveness, positively influencing user attitudes (Lee & Yeo, 2022). In addition, understandability ($\beta = 0.242$, $p<0.05$), was also found to be positively related with attitude which depicts that users appreciate chatbots that provide clear and concise responses. When chatbots communicate information in an easily understandable manner, it enhances the user's overall perception and contributes to positive attitudes. Further, Reliability also had an impact on the attitude ($\beta = 0.162$, $p<0.05$), users are more likely to have positive perceptions when they can trust the chatbot's consistent performance, effective problem-solving capabilities, and transparent decision-making processes. Continuous efforts to enhance reliability through technology improvements, error mitigation, and user feedback integration are crucial for maintaining positive user attitudes over the long term (Li et al., 2020).

Interestingly, Assurance and interactivity are not significantly related to attitude. This depicts Assurance and interactivity might not be deemed crucial by users in shaping attitudes toward AI chatbots. If users prioritize other dimensions of service quality, like accuracy or responsiveness, the perceived importance of assurance and interactivity could be diminished. Moreover, the results indicated a positive and significant influence on customer loyalty from user satisfaction with AI-chatbots ($\beta = 0.428$, $p < 0.05$) and attitude ($\beta = 0.445$, $p < 0.05$). This indicates that when users are satisfied with their experiences interacting with AI-chatbots, it positively affects their loyalty. Satisfied users are more likely to continue using the AI-chatbot service, choose it over alternatives, and remain engaged with the product or brand (Hari et al., 2022). These results are also in line with Tajeddini et al. (2021) who also found that the attitude of customers have an impact on customer loyalty.

When discussing the role of satisfaction as a mediator between the quality of AI-chatbot services and customer loyalty, the findings indicate a significant mediation effect across all aspects of service quality. Nevertheless, satisfaction only offers limited support as a mediator for assurance and interactivity revealing a more intricate relationship that other factors may concurrently influence customer loyalty. This nuanced understanding is valuable for businesses, underscoring the importance of adopting a comprehensive approach to customer relationship management (Hsu & Lin, 2023). Managers should prioritize strengthening responsiveness, understandability, and reliability, while also considering contextual elements apart from satisfaction that influence the partial mediation of assurance and interactivity (Prentice et al., 2020). Our results align with the research conducted by Swaid and Wigand (2007) and Ismail and Yunan (2016), where they illustrated that the dimensions of service quality do affect satisfaction and subsequently impact loyalty.

Empirical evidence further supports the mediating role of attitude in shaping the customer experience and influencing subsequent customer loyalty, particularly between responsiveness, understandability, and reliability. The observed mediation effect suggests that these factors not only directly impact customer attitudes but also act as essential conduits, facilitating the translation of positive attitudes into heightened loyalty (Jenneboer et al. 2022). In contrast, assurance and interactivity did not demonstrate significant mediation effects, suggesting that their influence on loyalty may be more direct or contingent on other variables (de Cosmo et al., 2021). This nuanced understanding encourages a reevaluation of conventional assumptions about the mediating roles of assurance and interactivity in the context of customer loyalty. Consequently, businesses are advised to tailor their strategies, placing emphasis on improving responsiveness, understandability, and reliability to strengthen the link between positive attitudes and ensuing customer loyalty. This result is consistent with the findings of Bashir and Madhavaiah (2014), where the inclusion of attitude as a mediating variable proved to be a more accurate predictor of consumer behavior in technology adoption.

Implications

Numerous research efforts have established a correlation between customer experience and customer loyalty. However, there is a noticeable gap in the literature concerning the relationship between AI-chatbots and customer loyalty. This research offers significant theoretical and practical perspectives and ramifications. First off, to the best of our knowledge, this study is among the first in India to examine how the quality of AI chatbots' services affects a variety of consumer behavioural outcomes, including attitude and satisfaction, which in turn effects long-term behavioural intentions like loyalty. This research offers additional insights into the influence of AI chatbot service quality on customer loyalty by examining satisfaction and attitudes. The study is significant because it suggests and assumes that results may be measured in terms of several customer service quality variables that raise the likelihood that consumers would utilise chatbots in the future. This research makes a valuable addition to the body of knowledge on artificial intelligence, particularly in the context of AI chatbots. These chatbots are shown to bring about a revolutionary change in the field of marketing research. Introducing a novel and impactful strategy, this study enhances our understanding of chatbots and their potential to significantly alter the way online companies interact with and market to their customer base. Organizations may contemplate directing resources towards ongoing improvement and optimization of their AI chatbot services as a strategy to elevate customer satisfaction. Implementation of consistent updates and training for AI chatbots can be considered to ensure their alignment with the evolving needs and preferences of customers. Frequently collecting feedback and conducting surveys can aid companies in comprehending customer perceptions and pinpointing areas for enhancement in AI chatbot services.

LIMITATIONS AND FUTURE RESEARCH DIRECTIONS

The online feedback received was not derived from a randomly selected group. Those customers who chose to participate may not accurately reflect the broader customer population. Therefore, future research should strive to obtain responses from a more diverse range of services to assess the validity of the hypotheses. It's important to note that the current study is cross-sectional, and for more comprehensive insights, researchers could utilize longitudinal data in subsequent studies to evaluate the effectiveness of the research model over time. Subsequent research may explore diverse user populations, such as health chatbot users, tourism chatbot users, and e-commerce chatbot users, to gain a comprehensive understanding of chatbot service quality. While traditional service quality dimensions like tangibility and empathy are currently assessed as understandability and interactivity, these measurements have limitations. Future investigations should concentrate on identifying additional indicators within the dimensions of understandability and interactivity that effectively measure tangibility and empathy.

REFERENCES

Abd-Alrazaq, A. A., Alajlani, M., Ali, N., Denecke, K., Bewick, B. M., & Househ, M. (2021). Perceptions and opinions of patients about mental health chatbots: Scoping review. *Journal of Medical Internet Research*, *23*(1), e17828. doi:10.2196/17828 PMID:33439133

Abdulquadri, A., Mogaji, E., Kieu, T. A., & Nguyen, N. P. (2021). Digital transformation in financial services provision: A Nigerian perspective to the adoption of chatbot. *Journal of Enterprising Communities: People and Places in the Global Economy*, *15*(2), 258–281. doi:10.1108/JEC-06-2020-0126

Agarwal, R., & Wadhwa, M. (2020). Review of State-of-the-Art Design Techniques for Chatbots. *SN Computer Science*, *1*(5), 246. doi:10.1007/s42979-020-00255-3

Ajzen, I. (1991). The theory of planned behavior. *Organizational Behavior and Human Decision Processes*, *50*(2), 179–211. doi:10.1016/0749-5978(91)90020-T

Akbar, M. M., & Parvez, N. (2009). Impact of Service Quality, Trust, and Customer Satisfaction on Customers Loyalty. *ABAC Journal*, *29*(1), 1. http://www.assumptionjournal.au.edu/index.php/abacjournal/article/view/526

Akıl, S., & Ungan, M. C. (2021). E-Commerce logistics service quality. *Journal of Electronic Commerce in Organizations*, *20*(1), 1–19. doi:10.4018/JECO.292473

Ameen, N., Hosany, S., & Tarhini, A. (2021). Consumer interaction with cutting-edge technologies: Implications for future research. *Computers in Human Behavior*, *120*, 106761. doi:10.1016/j.chb.2021.106761

Ashfaq, M., Yun, J., Yu, S., & Loureiro, S. M. C. (2020). I, Chatbot: Modeling the determinants of users' satisfaction and continuance intention of AI-powered service agents. *Telematics and Informatics*, *54*, 101473. doi:10.1016/j.tele.2020.101473

Bashir, I., & Madhavaiah, C. (2014). Revisiting Technology Acceptance Model (TAM) at the Individual Internet Banking Adoption Level. *Metamorphosis*, *13*(1), 42–56. doi:10.1177/0972622520140107

Chen, J. S., Le, T. T. Y., & Florence, D. (2021). Usability and responsiveness of artificial intelligence chatbot on online customer experience in e-retailing. *International Journal of Retail & Distribution Management*, *49*(11), 1512–1531. doi:10.1108/IJRDM-08-2020-0312

Chen, Q., Gong, Y., Lu, Y., & Tang, J. (2022). Classifying and measuring the service quality of AI chatbot in frontline service. *Journal of Business Research*, *145*, 552–568. doi:10.1016/j.jbusres.2022.02.088

Cheng, Y., & Jiang, H. (2020). How Do AI-driven Chatbots Impact User Experience? Examining Gratifications, Perceived Privacy Risk, Satisfaction, Loyalty, and Continued Use. *Journal of Broadcasting & Electronic Media*, *64*(4), 592–614. do i:10.1080/08838151.2020.1834296

Cho, J., & Lee, G. (2019). A chatbot system for construction daily report information management. In *ISARC. Proceedings of the International Symposium on Automation and Robotics in Construction* (Vol. 36, pp. 429-437). IAARC Publications. 10.22260/ISARC2019/0058

Chou, E. Y., & Hsu, W. C. (2021). Conversational Service Experiences in Chatbots: A Perspective on Cognitive Load. *Management Review*, *40*, 111–130.

Comes, Y., Trindade, J. de S., Shimizu, H. E., Hamann, E. M., Bargioni, F., Ramirez, L., Sanchez, M. N., & Santos, L. M. P. (2016). Evaluation of user satisfaction and service responsiveness in municipalities enrolled in the Mais Médicos (More Doctors) Program. *Ciencia & Saude Coletiva*, *21*, 2749–2759. doi:10.1590/1413-81232015219.16202016 PMID:27653060

de Cosmo, L. M., Piper, L., & Di Vittorio, A. (2021). The role of attitude toward chatbots and privacy concern on the relationship between attitude toward mobile advertising and behavioral intent to use chatbots. *Italian Journal of Marketing*, *2021*(1-2), 83–102. doi:10.1007/s43039-021-00020-1

DeLone, W. H., & McLean, E. R. (2003). The DeLone and McLean model of information systems success: A ten-year update. *Journal of Management Information Systems*, *19*(4), 9–30. doi:10.1080/07421222.2003.11045748

Eren, B. A. (2021). Determinants of customer satisfaction in chatbot use: Evidence from a banking application in Turkey. *International Journal of Bank Marketing*, *39*(2), 294–311. doi:10.1108/IJBM-02-2020-0056

Fornell, C. (2007). *The satisfied customer: Winners and losers in the battle for buyer preference*. Macmillan.

Go, E., & Sundar, S. S. (2019). Humanizing chatbots: The effects of visual, identity and conversational cues on humanness perceptions. *Computers in Human Behavior*, *97*, 304–316. doi:10.1016/j.chb.2019.01.020

Hagberg, J., Sundstrom, M., & Egels-Zandén, N. (2016). The digitalization of retailing: An exploratory framework. *International Journal of Retail & Distribution Management*, *44*(7), 694–712. doi:10.1108/IJRDM-09-2015-0140

Hair, J. F. Jr, Howard, M. C., & Nitzl, C. (2020). Assessing measurement model quality in PLS-SEM using confirmatory composite analysis. *Journal of Business Research*, *109*, 101–110. doi:10.1016/j.jbusres.2019.11.069

Hair, J. F., Risher, J. J., Sarstedt, M., & Ringle, C. M. (2019). When to use and how to report the results of PLS-SEM. *European Business Review*, *31*(1), 2–24. doi:10.1108/EBR-11-2018-0203

Hari, H., Iyer, R., & Sampat, B. (2022). Customer Brand Engagement through Chatbots on Bank Websites– Examining the Antecedents and Consequences. *International Journal of Human-Computer Interaction*, *38*(13), 1212–1227. doi:10.1080/10447318.2021.1988487

Ismail, A., & Yunan, Y. M. (2016). Service quality as a predictor of customer satisfaction and customer loyalty. *LogForum*, *12*(4), 269–283. doi:10.17270/J.LOG.2016.4.7

Jenneboer, L., Herrando, C., & Constantinides, E. (2022). The impact of chatbots on customer loyalty: A systematic literature review. *Journal of Theoretical and Applied Electronic Commerce Research*, *17*(1), 212–229. doi:10.3390/jtaer17010011

Johnson, K., Li, Y., Phan, H., Singer, J., & Trinh, H. (2012). The Innovative Success that is Apple, Inc. Theses, Dissertations and Capstones. https://mds.marshall.edu/etd/418

Kim, M., & Chang, B. (2020). The Effect of Service Quality on the Reuse Intention of a Chatbot: Focusing on User Satisfaction, Reliability, and Immersion. *International JOURNAL OF CONTENTS*, *16*(4), 1–15.

Kreijns, K., Xu, K., & Weidlich, J. (2021). Social presence: Conceptualization and measurement. *Educational Psychology Review*, *34*(1), 139–170. doi:10.1007/s10648-021-09623-8 PMID:34177204

Lappeman, J., Marlie, S., Johnson, T., & Poggenpoel, S. (2023). Trust and digital privacy: Willingness to disclose personal information to banking chatbot services. *Journal of Financial Services Marketing*, *28*(2), 337–357. doi:10.1057/s41264-022-00154-z

Lee, D., & Yeo, S. (2022). Developing an AI-based chatbot for practicing responsive teaching in mathematics. *Computers & Education*, *191*, 104646. doi:10.1016/j.compedu.2022.104646

Lee, M. K., & Park, H. (2019). Exploring factors influencing usage intention of chatbot-chatbot in financial service. *Journal of Korean Society for Quality Management*, *47*(4), 755–765.

Li, C., Pan, R., Xin, H., & Deng, Z. (2020). Research on Artificial Intelligence Customer Service on Consumer Attitude and Its Impact during Online Shopping. *Journal of Physics: Conference Series*, *1575*(1), 012192. doi:10.1088/1742-6596/1575/1/012192

Li, F., Lu, H., Hou, M., Cui, K., & Darbandi, M. (2021). Customer satisfaction with bank services: The role of cloud services, security, e-learning and service quality. *Technology in Society*, *64*, 101487. doi:10.1016/j.techsoc.2020.101487

Li, L., Lee, K. Y., Emokpae, E., & Yang, S. B. (2021). What makes you continuously use chatbot services? Evidence from chinese online travel agencies. *Electronic Markets*, *31*(3), 1–25. doi:10.1007/s12525-020-00454-z PMID:35603227

McLean, G., & Wilson, A. (2016). Evolving the online customer experience … is there a role for online customer support? *Computers in Human Behavior*, *60*, 602–610. doi:10.1016/j.chb.2016.02.084

Nguyen, D. M., Chiu, Y. T. H., & Le, H. D. (2021). Determinants of continuance intention towards banks' chatbot services in Vietnam: A necessity for sustainable development. *Sustainability (Basel)*, *13*(14), 7625. doi:10.3390/su13147625

Nguyen, T. M., & Malik, A. (2022). Impact of knowledge sharing on employees' service quality: The moderating role of artificial intelligence. *International Marketing Review*, *39*(3), 482–508. doi:10.1108/IMR-02-2021-0078

Nordheim, C. B., Følstad, A., & Bjørkli, C. A. (2019). An initial model of trust in chatbots for customer service—Findings from a questionnaire study. *Interacting with Computers*, *31*(3), 317–335. doi:10.1093/iwc/iwz022

Parasuraman, A., Zeithaml, V. A., & Berry, L. L. (1985). A conceptual model of service quality and its implications for future research. *Journal of Marketing*, *49*(4), 41–50. doi:10.1177/002224298504900403

Patel, N., & Trivedi, S. (2020). Leveraging Predictive Modeling, Machine Learning Personalization, NLP Customer Support, and AI Chatbots to Increase Customer Loyalty. *Empirical Quests for Management Essences*, *3*(3), 1–24.

Pereira, J., & Díaz, Ó. (2018). Chatbot dimensions that matter: Lessons from the trenches. In Web Engineering: 18th International Conference, ICWE 2018, Cáceres, Spain, June 5-8, 2018 [Springer International Publishing.]. *Proceedings*, *18*, 129–135.

Przegalinska, A., Ciechanowski, L., Stroz, A., Gloor, P., & Mazurek, G. (2019). In bot we trust: A new methodology of chatbot performance measures. *Business Horizons*, *62*(6), 785–797. doi:10.1016/j.bushor.2019.08.005

Rahman, A. M., Mamun, A. A., & Islam, A. (2017). Programming challenges of chatbot: Current and future prospective. *2017 IEEE Region 10 Humanitarian Technology Conference (R10-HTC)*, 75–78. doi:10.1109/R10-HTC.2017.8288910

Rapp, A., Curti, L., & Boldi, A. (2021). The human side of human-chatbot interaction: A systematic literature review of ten years of research on text-based chatbots. *International Journal of Human-Computer Studies*, *151*, 102630. doi:10.1016/j.ijhcs.2021.102630

Rios-Campos, C., Viteri, J., Batalla, E., Castro, J., Núñez, J., Calderón, E., Nicacio, F., & Tello, M. (2023). Generative Artificial Intelligence. *South Florida Journal of Development*, *4*(6), 2305–2320. doi:10.46932/sfjdv4n6-008

Rios-Campos, C., Viteri, J. D. C. L., Batalla, E. A. P., Castro, J. F. C., Núñez, J. B., Calderón, E. V., Nicacio, F. J. G., & Tello, M. Y. P. (2023). Generative artificial intelligence. *South Florida Journal of Development*, *4*(6), 2305–2320. doi:10.46932/sfjdv4n6-008

Rizky, M., & Hariasih, M. (2023). Consumer Loyalty: Brand Perception, Trust, Product Quality, and the Mediating Role of Customer Satisfaction. *Academia Open*, *9*(2). Advance online publication. doi:10.21070/acopen.9.2024.5562

Ruan, Y., & Mezei, J. (2022). When do AI chatbots lead to higher customer satisfaction than human frontline employees in online shopping assistance? Considering product attribute type. *Journal of Retailing and Consumer Services*, *68*, 103059. doi:10.1016/j.jretconser.2022.103059

Rzepka, C., Berger, B., & Hess, T. (2022). Voice assistant vs. Chatbot–examining the fit between conversational agents' interaction modalities and information search tasks. *Information Systems Frontiers*, *24*(3), 839–856. doi:10.1007/s10796-021-10226-5

Sannon, S., Stoll, B., DiFranzo, D., Jung, M., & Bazarova, N. N. (2018, October). How personification and interactivity influence stress-related disclosures to conversational agents. In *Companion of the 2018 ACM conference on computer supported cooperative work and social computing* (pp. 285-288). ACM.

Sarstedt, M., Hair, J. F., Pick, M., Liengaard, B. D., Radomir, L., & Ringle, C. M. (2022). Progress in partial least squares structural equation modeling use in marketing research in the last decade. *Psychology &amp. Psychology and Marketing*, *39*(5), 1035–1064. doi:10.1002/mar.21640

Sivadas, E., & Baker-Prewitt, J. L. (2000). An examination of the relationship between service quality, customer satisfaction, and store loyalty. *International Journal of Retail & Distribution Management*, *28*(2), 73–82. doi:10.1108/09590550010315223

Skjuve, M., Følstad, A., Fostervold, K. I., & Brandtzaeg, P. B. (2021). My chatbot companion-a study of human-chatbot relationships. *International Journal of Human-Computer Studies*, *149*, 102601. doi:10.1016/j.ijhcs.2021.102601

Soares, A. M., Camacho, C., & Elmashhara, M. G. (2022, April). Understanding the impact of chatbots on purchase intention. In *World Conference on Information Systems and Technologies* (pp. 462-472). Cham: Springer International Publishing. 10.1007/978-3-031-04829-6_41

Swaid, S. I., & Wigand, R. T. (2007). Key dimensions of e-commerce service quality and its relationships to satisfaction and loyalty. *BLED 2007 Proceedings*, 29.

Tajeddini, K., Rasoolimanesh, S. M., Gamage, T. C., & Martin, E. (2021). Exploring the visitors' decision-making process for Airbnb and hotel accommodations using value-attitude-behavior and theory of planned behavior. *International Journal of Hospitality Management*, *96*, 102950. doi:10.1016/j.ijhm.2021.102950

Venkatesh, V., & Davis, F. D. (2000). A theoretical extension of the technology acceptance model: Four longitudinal field studies. *Management Science*, *46*(2), 186–204. doi:10.1287/mnsc.46.2.186.11926

Venkatesh, V., & Zhang, X. (2020). Unified theory of acceptance and use of technology. Encyclopedia of Education and Information Technologies, 13(1), 1750–1750. doi:10.1007/978-3-030-10576-1_300692

Yun, J., & Park, J. (2022). The Effects of Chatbot Service Recovery With Emotion Words on Customer Satisfaction, Repurchase Intention, and Positive Word-Of-Mouth. *Frontiers in Psychology*, *13*, 922503. doi:10.3389/fpsyg.2022.922503 PMID:35712132

Chapter 3 Revolutionizing the Financial Landscape: A Review on Human-Centric AI Thinking in Emerging Markets

Debora Dhanya Amarnath
Christ University, India

Stephen Jayamani Thimothy
Dhofar University, Oman

ABSTRACT

The emergence of Industry 4.0 has transformed the financial landscape by integrating unconventional technologies and artificial intelligence (AI) into consumer interactions. This chapter explores the evolving paradigm of human-centric AI-thinking in the context of emerging customer interactions in making financial decisions. The review analyses the opportunities and the challenges that arise from the integration of AI tools and human-centric approaches in addressing the diverse needs and behaviours of consumers within emerging financial markets. More specifically, the review critically examines the utilization of AI-driven technologies, such as predictive analytics, natural language processing (NLP), and machine learning algorithms, in customising the financial services to cater the emerging-market consumers. Moreover, the current study explicates how AI enables personalized customer interactions, risk assessments, and ethical decision making and financial inclusion strategies while considering the socioeconomic and cultural landscapes. The study has focussed on addressing the concerns related to data privacy, risk assessment, and transparency towards AI-powered financial solutions with ethical standards. Through an exhaustive analysis of current trends, and empirical evidence from the existing literature, this

DOI: 10.4018/979-8-3693-1503-3.ch003

review highlights the inevitability of human-centric AI-thinking approach towards financial services decision making. It emphasizes the importance of congruent AI-driven financial solutions in the context of banking where the determinants such as empathy, financial literacy, ethical considerations, and human values plays a significant role in finding the financial services in emerging markets. This research explores the challenges and prospects and has made commendations to all the major stakeholders such as industry stakeholders, policymakers, practitioners, customers, and service providers to create a dynamic financial landscape of Industry 4.0 in AI technologies that embrace a human-centric ethos to meet the evolving needs of consumers within emerging financial ecosystems.

INTRODUCTION

The emergence of artificial Intelligence (AI) in the financial landscape has brought significant improvements in the financial sector, predominantly in the interactions between consumers and AI-driven technologies. This review of the literature aims to provide an overview of the existing literature by identifying the knowledge gaps for future research towards the human-centric AI-thinking in banking and financial services. The phenomenon of AI applications has garnered greater interest towards digital financial accessibility for individuals in many developed and developing nations. Banking innovation started from the transition of a traditional banking system 1.0 to a self-service banking 2.0 through automated teller machines and the internet services. This banking 2.0 model was surpassed by the mobile banking 3.0 by the digital fintech systems for a convenient, manageable, and accessible banking services. Furthermore, AI has driven the banking into the next era of tech embedded, platform-based banking 4.0. This directs the attention towards customer centricity which helps on realizing and tailoring to the needs and preferences of the customer. This transition from existing mixed financing models across the world has obstacles while offering secured transactions, speed, transparency, and trust in the system. Financial inclusion is becoming an important aspect for the developing countries with a motive to improve the financial literacy and more informed decisions towards their investment decisions and credit availing decisions. These decisions encompass a range of services pertaining to the effective management of monetary resources, access to insurance coverage, facilitation of investments, and provision of loans with the aim of extending these services to all individuals (Chibba, 2009). The integration of AI in the digital financing services has brought a unprecedent change in the realm of banking services, presenting supreme levels of accessibility and convenience. Furthermore, these AI based services have also provided a promising potential for the developing countries in mitigating the pervasive issue of poverty. These AI based platforms now offer a wide range of financial services such as transmitting and receiving funds, accumulating financial resources tec., catering to the various demographic profile customers with diverse needs. Sethi and Acharya (2018), has stressed that as coin have both the sides it is imperative that the utilisation of this technology also presents potential susceptibilities such as security and privacy aspects. In light of these vulnerabilities, many Fintech companies are embracing latest technological algorithms with the aim of achieving operational efficiency and competitive advantage. With more than half of its people being deemed financially excluded or neglected, India has the second-biggest unbanked population in the entire globe (Yasir et al., 2022). Indian culture discourages taking risks; hence banks serve as essential financial institutions that guard the people from cash-related risks. With the aid of mobile banking technologies, banks were able to replace physical currency with flexible, economical, and less risky payment mechanisms (Pal & Herath, 2020; Chowdhury & Chowdhury, 2023). While AI can automate many tasks, human-centric AI thinking acknowledges the importance of human expertise in financial services. It promotes a collaborative approach where AI augments human capabilities rather than replacing them entirely Adel, 2022). Human-centric artificial intelligence (AI) when it comes to financial services and management, human-centric artificial intelligence (AI) refers to the application of AI technologies and systems that give human needs and experiences the top priority (Mhlanga, 2022). The approach strives to increase the efficacy, efficiency, and user-friendliness of financial operations while taking ethical issues, openness, and regulatory compliance into account. In the context of financial services, "human-centric artificial intelligence" (AI) refers to the use of AI technologies and systems with the main goal of improving customer experience and financial service delivery (Umamaheswari & Valarmathi, 2023).

However, many studies have explored the evolution and application of AI in financial services, particularly in the context of emerging-market. How (2020) and Riedel (2022) have emphasized that the potential of AI to advance financial inclusion, with political ideology. Sheth (2022) stressed the significance of human intervention in AI based banking services for a personalized experience. Hentzen's (2021) systematic literature review suggested the need for more conceptual and empirical studies on consumer financial behaviours. However, there are reservations about the complete replacement of human touch and customization in the financial industry (Mehrotra 2019). Addressing these issues, Zetzsche 2020 proposes a "regulatory roadmap" that emphasizes the importance of human involvement in AI based financial services. Pothumsetty 2020 further investigated the implementation of AI in various finance fields, highlighting its potential to augment companies' strategy for competitive advantage. The duality of AI's role in customer interactions is a growing area of interest.

LITERATURE REVIEW

Designing and implementing artificial intelligence systems with an eye on improving the human experience, building trust, and taking ethical issues into account is known as a human-centric AI strategy in the banking and financial services industry. Many earlier studies have investigated the determinants that influence consumers' adoption of AI technologies in the context of financial services. For example, Smith et al. (2018) have stated that perceived usefulness (PU)and perceived ease of use (PEOU) plays a significantly role in determining consumers' intention to adopt AI based financial services. Similarly, Chen et al. (2019) emphasized the significance of perceived risk and trust in determining the consumers' attitudes towards artificial intelligence-based applications in financial related decision making. This approach deals with various stakeholders such as customers and the various service providers that are put at the heart of AI-driven developments in the financial industry. Following are some aspects concerning the banking and financial sector human-centric AI thinking.

Table 1. Application of AI tools towards human-centric AI thinking in banking and financial services

Key Areas	Application of AI Tools	References
Customer Engagement	• Chatbots and Virtual Assistants uses natural language processing (NLP) • Personalized Recommendations • Predictive Analytics • Voice and Speech Recognition • Sentiment Analysis (AI analyses customer communication (emails, social media, etc.) to gauge sentiment. • Recommendation Engines • Behavioral Biometrics • Customer Segmentation metrics • AI-Powered Personal Financial Management (PFM) Tools • Automated Surveys and Feedback Analysis • Robotic Process Automation (RPA)	• Sørensen, 2012; • Suhel et al., 2020; • Kaur et al., 2020; • Subudhi, 2019; • Modwey & Elgabar, 2022; • Agarwal et al., 2021; • Elahi et al., 2021; • Tatineni, 2022; • Chhillar & Arora, 2022; • Choubey & Sharma, 2021;
Transparency and Explainability	• Explainable AI (XAI) Models • Decision Trees • Local Interpretable Model-agnostic Explanations (LIME) • Counterfactual Explanations • Model Documentation • Blockchain Technology • AI Governance Frameworks • Explanatory Interfaces that allow users to query the AI system for explanations. • Auditing and Model Monitoring • Simulations and Prototypes to showcase the decision-making process of AI models, making it more tangible and understandable for stakeholders.	• Burgt, 2020 • Hanif, 2021 • Hu & Wu, 2023; • Rane et al., 2023; • Nassar et al., 2020; • Hanif, 2021

continued on following page

Table 1. Continued

Key Areas	Application of AI Tools	References
Ethical Use of Data	• Data Governance Platforms • Privacy-Preserving AI Techniques such as federated learning, homomorphic encryption, and differential privacy • Data Masking and Anonymization Tools • Ethics and Bias Detection Tools • Algorithmic Impact Assessment Tools • Explainable AI (XAI) Models • AI Audit Tools • Consent Management Platforms • Ethics Training for AI Teams • Customer Data Portability Tools	• Ahmed, 2022; • Rabbani et al., 2022; • Rashmi & Nirmal, 2021; • Jain, 2023; Suresh & Rani, 2020; • Chambers-Jones, 2021
Financial Education	• Personalized Financial Advice Platforms • Chatbots for Financial Q&A • Mobile Apps with AI Financial Coaches • Gamification for Financial Literacy • Robo-Advisors with Educational Features • Personal Finance Management (PFM) Tools • Credit Score Simulators • AI-Enhanced Learning Platforms • Voice-Activated Financial Assistants • Behavioral Economics Applications	• Ashta & Herrmann, 2021; • Kuchciak & Wiktorowicz, 2021; • Noreen et al., 2023; • Andreou & Anyfantaki, 2021; • Samans, 2021; • Brenner & Meyll, 2020;
Empowering Human Decision-Making	• Predictive Analytics • Human-in-the-Loop (HITL) Systems • Augmented Analytics • Intelligent Process Automation (IPA • Robo-Advisors • Natural Language Processing (NLP) • Decision Support Systems • Cognitive Search Platforms • Feedback Loops and Continuous Learning • Dynamic Pricing Models • Fraud Detection Systems • Simulations and Scenario Analysis • Advanced Analytics for Credit Scoring	• Nagwani, 2023; • Gallego, et al., 2023; • Kulkarni and Ghosh, 2021; • Haddadian 2022; • Ferreira, 2021; • Chiu-Che Tseng, 2021 • Yu Lin 2005; • Macpherson, 2021;
Inclusive Access	• Voice-Activated Banking Service • Multilingual Chatbots and Interfaces • Accessible User Interfaces (UI) • AI-Enhanced Fraud Prevention for Vulnerable Populations • Financial Inclusion Analytics • Alternative access to credit for individuals with limited credit history. • Biometric Authentication • Digital Financial Literacy Tools • Remote Customer Support with AI • User-Friendly AI Interfaces	• Kandpal & Khalaf, 2020 • How et al., 2020 • Mhlanga, 2023; Tyagi, 2023 • Mhlanga, 2020; Chadha et a., 2024 • Marani et al., 2023 • Maseke, 2024
Fairness and Bias Mitigation	• Fairness Indicators • Bias Detection Algorithms • Ethical AI Frameworks • Explainable AI (XAI) • Adversarial Training • Equalized Odds Post-processing • Sensitive Attribute Removal • Regularization Techniques • Continuous Monitoring and Auditing	• Li et al., 2020; • Wang et al., 2019; • Zhang et al.,2020; • Liu et al.,2019; • Horvatic,2021; • Li,2021; • Steels,2020; • Harfouche,2023;

Human Centric AI Thinking and Its Influence in Customer Engagement

Human-centric AI enhances the customer experience by providing tailored financial services such as recommendations on various investments and advances, budgeting assistance, and debt management plans tailored to an individual's financial goals and circumstances which can significantly improve customer satisfaction. Where the 24/7 Support of AI-powered chatbots and virtual assistants offers round-the-clock customer support, addressing inquiries and requests at any time. In addition, Automation in AI can process transactions and approvals more quickly, reducing wait times for customers and helping the service providers complete the process on time (Sørensen, 2012).

AI tools play a crucial role in enriching customer engagement in the banking and financial sector, delivering custom-made and efficient services. Important AI tools utilised for customer engagement comprise Chatbots, Virtual Assistants and natural language processing (NLP) for real-time interaction, providing instant responses, assisting with inquiries, and guiding users (Suhel et al., 2020). AI Predictive Analytics, analyses historical and real-time data to anticipate customer needs, allowing banks to proactively address requirements and enhance customer satisfaction (Kaur et al., 2020). AI based Voice and Speech Recognition facilities ensures safe and appropriate customer verification through voice-enabled access (Subudhi, 2019). AI based sentiment analysis involves analysing communication to device sentiment, enabling financial institutions to respond prompt and preserve positive customer relationships (Modwey & Elgabar, 2022). In addition, AI driven recommendation engines analyse the transaction data to recommend relevant services, that improves cross-selling and up selling opportunities (Agarwal et al., 2021; Elahi et al., 2021). The AI application based behavioral biometrics focus on unique behavioral patterns with continuous authentication (Tatineni, 2022). AI-Powered Personal Financial Management (PFM) Tools offer visions into spending habits and offer customised financial advice (Chhillar & Arora, 2022). Automated Surveys and Feedback Analysis, enabled by AI, provides valuable perceptions into customer satisfaction and loyalty. Robotic Process Automation (RPA) mechanizes routine tasks, such as account updates and closures (Choubey & Sharma, 2021, May).

Human Centric AI Thinking and Its Influence in Transparency and Explainability

The employability of human-centric AI thinking significantly effects transparency and explainability. (Burgt, 2020; Hanif, 2021). The financial institutions and the developers prioritize "user-centric design" and ensure that AI systems are not only technically efficient but also comprehensible and understandable for human users with accessibility and accountability to the individuals they serve (Hu & Wu, 2023; Rane et al., 2023). The AI thinking approach includes features such as clear elucidations, innate and user-friendly interfaces, empowering individuals to understand and trust the decisions made by AI model approaches. Human-Centric AI tools are made-up with more transparency in their design, allowing users to access explanations for AI-driven outcomes, fostering a sense of control and understanding (Nassar et al., 2020). This human-centric approach improves overall transparency, aligning AI application systems with human values and preferences. Especially in the context of financial services, human-centric AI-thinking uses algorithms to evaluates the creditworthiness of the individuals in a fair manner. This clearly ensures that AI does not prejudice and provide recommendations to its consumers based on race, demographics, economic capacities, gender, or other personal characteristics, and instead emphases on pertinent financial indicators and metrics (Hanif, 2021). In addition, human-centric AI-thinking provides clear enlightenments on various factors considered by the financial institutions prior to the sanctioning loans and advances that helps individuals to self-evaluate their eligibility and the potential sanctioning amount and the interest rates. This can help to build the trust and the confidence in AI-powered lending systems (Rogha, 2023).

Human Centric AI Thinking in Ethical Use of Data

Human-Centric artificial intelligence (AI) systems emphasise ethical concerns in gathering data, processing, and application by establishing an emphasis on human principles, values, confidentiality, and user authorization (Ahmed, 2022). This system ensures transparency and knowledge of users regarding the use of their data. Human-centric AI solutions enable people to have control over their data as well as make sound choices regarding how they use it by embracing functions such as confidential information processing, security features, and graphical user interfaces (Rabbani et al., 2022). This approach promotes an ethical and accountable structure for handling information in a wide range of software, especially those in the financial services sector, and aims boost consumer trust in AI systems (Jain, 2023). The AI can analyse enormous volumes of data, forecast market trends, evaluate credit risk, and detect potential fraud, assisting businesses in proactively addressing problems and assisting financial professionals in making wise investment, lending, and risk management decisions. Further, Human-centric AI thought emphasizes ethical issues significantly (Rashmi & Nirmal, 2021). It seeks to get rid of prejudices in AI decision-making, take care of algorithm transparency, and uphold fairness and principles of equity (Chambers-Jones, 2021). Because humans are emotional beings, financial services can use artificial intelligence (AI) to assess consumer behaviour and emotions. Therefore, AI will help Fintech companies to better understand their potential customers' financial needs and help those who are facing financial stress. In addition to these the financial service providers should design human-centric AI-driven applications that are easily accessible to those with disabilities to deliver pertinent and valuable services, Artificial Intelligence thinking makes it possible for AI systems to adapt to dynamic customer preferences in line with financial market situations.

Human Centric AI Thinking Financial Education

The application of AI tools in financial education has radically altered the way individuals acquire financial literacy. Artificial Intelligence (AI) systems deploy advanced algorithms to analyse behaviour of users, choices, and financial data, enabling instructional materials to be customised (Ashta & Herrmann, 2021; Kuchciak & Wiktorowicz, 2021). Among the tools that are used to fulfil certain educational demands are "dynamic simulations, interactive learning modules, and personalised financial guidance". Furthermore, real-time input and insights are frequently offered by AI-driven financial education platforms, allowing users to easily understand complex financial concepts and make wise decisions (Noreen et al., 2023). Beyond traditional methods, artificial intelligence (AI) has an enormous effect on financial education through providing customised and engaging learning experiences that assist individuals acquire better information about money as well as more adept at making informed decisions (Andreou & Anyfantaki, 2021). AI can offer advice and educational materials to assist customers in becoming more financially literate, enabling them to make better financial decisions (Samans, 2021). AI can offer advice and instructional materials to assist people in making wise financial decisions. The AI-based chatbots, also known as virtual financial advisers, can help users reach their financial objectives by providing advice, resources for financial literacy, and answers to questions. Customers can deal with financial organizations more easily thanks to these interfaces' simplification of complex financial procedures and straightforward interactions. User-friendliness is taken into consideration while designing data-driven insights and user-friendly AI interfaces, including chatbots and virtual assistants. The most crucial factor is that AI improves financial literacy. To help financial professionals make intelligent investments, lending, and other decisions, improved AI analyses large amounts of data and choices in risk management. AI can forecast market trends, evaluate credit risk, and spot potential fraud for service providers, aiding firms in taking early measures to address problems. Emotional intelligence is encompassed in AI to assist users in managing the emotional side of finance, hence lowering stress and anxiety related to money (Brenner & Meyll, 2020).

Human Centric AI Thinking Empowering Human Decision-Making

There are so many financial Investment related decisions that AI helps in such as Asset Allocation Decisions, Security Selection Decisions, Tax Planning and Efficiency Decisions, Portfolio Management Decisions, Dividend policy decisions, Capital Budgeting Decisions, Risk Management Decisions, Investment Timing Decisions, Loan Evaluation Decision, AI Loan Bias.

Loan Evaluation Decision

Financial decision-making through the utilisation of artificial intelligence (AI) involves data derived from digital transactions, with the aim to develop tailored financial products and services that align precisely with individual customer unique needs and requirements. This phenomenon enables banks and financial organisations to track their customers online behaviour, thereby customised financial products according to the specialised needs. By leveraging artificial algorithms, these financial institutions can evaluate the creditworthiness of borrowers and later sanction loans. This technologies has significantly enhanced the accuracy of loan assessments through various credit rating agencies and based on the credit scores the financial institutions to make more informed lending decisions. Traditionally it is tedious to check the borrower's credibility involves the verify various documents and reports, including a comprehensive report on money management patterns, previously availed loans and loan settlement reports, as well as a statement of expenditures. These documents used to provide valuable insights regarding the consumers' financial behaviour and help assess their ability to manage and repay the debt. But thankfully the application of AI has more accurate data and collect this information from various domains, with process automation (Nagwani, 2023). Therefore, AI provides the process automation of loan approvals with high precision and speed through the Natural Language Processing (NLP) and Machine Learning techniques. This involves a thorough verification and extraction of the necessary information from the borrower's application (Nagwani, 2023). One of the distinguished advantages of digital financial services is to provide individuals to compare various financial services offerings and can make informed decision and reduces the time and the cost constraints and the effort of physically visit traditional brick-and-mortar banks or other financial institutions. The financial landscape has experienced significant transformations due to the pervasive adoption of smartphones and the internet connectivity. These advancements have had a profound impact on both the demand side, as well as the supply side, obvious by the emergence of novel products, services, and intermediaries (Gallego, et al., 2023). In a recent study conducted by Kulkarni and Ghosh (2021), aimed to study and analyse various aspects related to the topic under investigation.

Portfolio Optimization and Asset Allocation

Human-centric AI emphasizes the development of explainable AI models that provide transparent explanations for investment decisions. These models enable humans to understand how AI algorithms arrive at specific recommendations or conclusions, fostering trust and comprehension. Since the 1990s, when there was a rapid advancement in technology and widespread use of personal computers, the application of artificial intelligence (AI) to financial investing has garnered a great deal of attention from researchers. Choosing the best portfolio to meet investor goals or, to put it another way, optimizing returns on investments within investor constraints is the aim of investment decision-making. The ultimate objective is to create a humanist investment model in AI-intensive businesses that is intellectually sound, feasible for analysts, practical for portfolio managers, and trustworthy for investors, all while adhering to these metrics. Haddadian (2022) stated in his study that portfolio performance through the design of an intelligent and fully automated trading system that will enable investors to allocate resources optimally and find the best opportunities in the market. Specifically, this will involve fine-tuning technical indicator parameters, identifying the current market regime (trending or non-trending), issuing a clear signal (buy, sell, or hold) based on the indicators' signals, and finally rebalancing the portfolio support of this system will enable investors to do more than just identify the best opportunities in the market. In addition, Ferreira (2021) in his study have explained the application of AI in four categories such as financial sentiment analysis, portfolio optimization, stock market prediction and also mentioned that AI algorithms assist in optimizing portfolios by analysing historical data, market trends, and correlations between assets, recommending optimal asset allocation strategies based on risk tolerance, return objectives, and market conditions. Chiu-Che Tseng & Yu Lin (2005) have conducted an experimental comparison analysis using a variety of artificial intelligence systems, such as the Influence Diagram (a unique kind of Bayesian network), Decision Tree, and Neural Network, to assist users in making informed decisions when choosing the optimal portfolio. Finally, AI can help in this situation by offering analysis tools that sift through crucial data and act as a large-scale catalyst for sustainable investment. Pressure to measure the performance of portfolios is mounting for investment managers. (Macpherson, 2021).

Capital Budgeting Decisions

Human-centric AI systems assist in mitigating biases by considering human values, ethical principles, and long-term sustainability in investment decisions (Chen et al., 2021; Chiu, 1992; Griesser,1991). The AI tools can enhance traditional capital budgeting by providing transparent and understandable references while bring into line with organizational objectives and ethical aspects (Vuppalapaty, 2021). Chen et al. (2021) stressed that the integration machine learning algorithms and predictive analytics helps in efficient allocation of resources for long-term projects. Human-centric AI also assists in scenario planning, project evaluation and risk assessment (Tang, 2009; Valle-Cruz et al., 2022; Marotta & Au, 2022).

Risk Management Decisions

AI and machine learning are transforming the field of financial risk management (Kim et al., 2021). These technologies provide the potential consumers to make accurate risk prediction, optimize risk mitigation strategies and provides informed decision-making processes. Through analysing huge amounts of historical data and identifying patterns, artificial intelligence can aid in finding potential risks and creating more accurate risk models (Fritz-Morgenthal et al, 2021). These AI and ML technologies ensure more efficient risk assessment, more informed and quicker risk management decisions for both the financial institutions to gain a competitive advantage (Vučinić, M., & Luburić, 2022; Alzeaideen, 2019). Additionally, AI helps the financial service providers to forecast the price of securities effectively, estimate cash requirements and create more risk management models (Sujith et a., 2021).

Investment Timing Decisions

In recent years, there has been an increasing interest towards artificial intelligence and consumers are relying on these AI based applications in deciding the financial risk and the right time to invest. This approach involves machine learning techniques to track the historical data and identify trends and patterns that can help the consumers about the investment timing (Dirksen & Takahashi, 2020). The human centric AI models and its real-time data analysis, not only consumers even the fintech companies too can assess the risk associated with specific investment opportunities and make more informed decisions (Stone et al., 2020; Enholm et al., 2022). By considering the human centric element in artificial intelligence, Fintech companies can ensure that the technology not only provides accurate estimates but also considers distinct preferences, investment goals and risk tolerance. Additionally, human-centric artificial intelligence can also offer justifications for its decision-making process, enabling consumers to understand and trust the endorsements provided by the AI (Lui & Lamb, 2018).

Human Centric AI Thinking Inclusive Access

In the banking industry, promoting inclusive access is greatly aided by the implementation of human-centred AI thinking (Kandpal & Khalaf, 2020). Artificial intelligence (AI) solutions designed with a human-centric approach emphasise the specific requirements and varied characteristics of users, ensuring that digital financial services are accessible to a wide range of individuals (How et al., 2020). This inclusive strategy takes account of the requirements of those with various levels of expertise, linguistic backgrounds, and socioeconomic statuses (Mhlanga, 2023; Tyagi, 2023). Among the AI tools developed to enhance the accessibility and ease of use of financial services are controlled by voice assistants, chatbots that speak multiple languages, and readily available user interfaces. Through integrating Human Centric AI Thinking, institutions seek to establish a more diverse financial ecosystem that supports egalitarian access to banking services by meeting the various demands of all users (Mhlanga, 2020; Chadha et a., 2024). AI-thinking provides personalized financial advices and commendations that align with individuals' needs and wants. This includes AI-driven savings algorithms that track and analyse the trends and a spending pattern and suggest possible saving targets, or intelligent budgeting applications and help individuals to their expenses more effectively (Marani et al., 2023). Furthermore, human-centric AI-thinking also entails protecting individuals' privacy and security when it comes to their financial data. AI-powered financial platforms should prioritize robust data security measures and transparent data usage policies to ensure that users feel safe and confident in entrusting their financial information to AI systems (Maseke, 2024). Overall, human-centric AI-thinking in financial loans and savings aims to empower individuals to make informed financial decisions, while also promoting fairness, transparency, and ethical use of AI in the financial sector.

Human Centric AI Thinking Fairness and Bias Mitigation

Li et al. (2020) stated that AI-driven applications effectively personalize financial services based on consumers' needs and preferences. In the same line wang et al. (2019) also stressed that the customization enhances the consumers' satisfaction and loyalty towards AI based financial services. Zhang et al. (2020) revealed that the AI-driven algorithms help in deriving the transparent and ethical information for the consumers and in turn leads to informed decision making. Additionally, Liu et al. (2019) emphasized the ethical issues such as data privacy and security plays a significant role in building consumer trust and to ensure the successful adoption of AI technologies in financial services. The human-centric AI-thinking is an burgeoning interest in the field of financial services. Horvatic (2021) and Li (2021) both have emphasize the need for a harmonious and responsible relationship between humans and AI technology, with a emphasis on understanding cognitive, affective, and behavioural aspects. Steels (2020) ventures the technical hurdles and potential solutions in designing a human-centric AI. Harfouche (2023) extends this area of research by proposing a conceptual framework to mitigate AI biases through human-in-loop informed strategic process. Collectively the above stated studies highlight the pivotal role of human-cantered design and the ethical considerations in the development of AI systems.

Knowledge Gaps and Future Research Directions

While this research provides valuable insights into consumers' financial decisions with AI technologies in financial services such as investment decisions and loans decision, several knowledge gaps remain. Firstly, there is a need for further request for information into the specific challenges and opportunities faced by Fintech companies and the consumers in adopting human-centric AI-driven financial services. In future studies the researchers should focus in understanding the unique political, social, technological, cultural and economic determinants that impact consumers' perceptions and purchase behaviours and also in designing effective AI-driven financial solutions. Secondly, future research should focus on the long-term effects of personalized financial services enabled by AI technologies. In addition, the future studies can compare the human centric AI Financial solutions and Completely AI based personalized recommendations, tailored financial products, and its performance. Lastly, further research is needed to address the ethical implications such as ensuring data privacy and security, examining the fairness, developing frameworks and bias in algorithmic decision-making of Human centric responsible AI use in the financial sector. By addressing these research gaps, scholars can contribute to the development of human-centric AI-thinking models that prioritize consumer trust and informed decision making in the context of financial services.

CONCLUSION

In Conclusion, this review has navigated the labyrinth of human-centric AI-thinking in emerging-market consumer interactions, banking, and financial service AI. It has eloquently woven together threads on consumer adoption influencers by adopting automated services including autonomous account management and personalised transactions. In addition to the customer experience, the next optimum privilege is personalization's potential; banking involving tailored services to the customers need and preferences whereby gaining customer's trust and offering an end-to-end customer experience. The last concern is the ethical consideration where a bank's interference into the customers transaction transparency, algorithmic bias, and privacy infringement can be limited. AI has gradually been reinforcing a strong firewall to protect the customers identity, enhance banking cybersecurity, increase scalability, and satisfy customer relationship management. Yet, the quest remains unfinished, beckoning towards the enigmas surrounding emerging markets, personalized financial services' lasting impact, and the ethical conundrums inherent in AI. Venturing into these uncharted terrains via future research will shape the narrative of responsible and effective AI-driven financial services, centred on consumer welfare and trust.

REFERENCES

G20 Policy Recommendations for Advancing Financial Inclusion and Productivity Gains through Digital Public Infrastructure. (2023). *Global Partnership for Financial Inclusion.* Advance online publication. doi:10.1596/40421

Adel, A. (2022). Future of industry 5.0 in society: Human-centric solutions, challenges and prospective research areas. *Journal of Cloud Computing (Heidelberg, Germany), 11*(1), 1–15. doi:10.1186/s13677-022-00314-5 PMID:36101900

Agarwal, A., Singhal, C., & Thomas, R. (2021). *AI-powered decision making for the bank of the future*. McKinsey & Company. https://www. mckinsey. com/~/ media/mckinsey/industries/financial% 20services/our% 20insights/ai% 20powered% 20decision% 20making% 20for% 20the% 20bank% 20of% 20the% 20future/ai-powered-decision-making-forthe-bank-of-the-future. pdf

Ahmed, F. (2022). Ethical aspects of artificial intelligence in banking. *Journal of Research in Economics and Finance Management, 1*(2), 55–63. doi:10.56596/jrefm.v1i2.7

Al-Blooshi, L., & Nobanee, H. (2020). Applications of Artificial Intelligence in Financial Management Decisions: A Mini-Review. *Consumer Financial Fraud eJournal.*

Alzeaideen, K. (2019). Credit risk management and business intelligence approach of the banking sector in Jordan. *Cogent Business & Management, 6*(1), 1675455. doi:10.1080/23311975.2019.1675455

Andreou, P. C., & Anyfantaki, S. (2021). Financial literacy and its influence on internet banking behavior. *European Management Journal*, *39*(5), 658–674. doi:10.1016/j.emj.2020.12.001

Ashta, A., & Herrmann, H. (2021). Artificial intelligence and fintech: An overview of opportunities and risks for banking, investments, and microfinance. *Strategic Change*, *30*(3), 211–222. doi:10.1002/jsc.2404

Brenner, L., & Meyll, T. (2020). Robo-advisors: A substitute for human financial advice? *Journal of Behavioral and Experimental Finance*, *25*, 100275. doi:10.1016/j.jbef.2020.100275

Burgt, J. V. D. (2020). Explainable AI in banking. *Journal of Digital Banking*, *4*(4), 344–350.

Chadha, P., Gera, R., Khera, G. S., & Sharma, M. (2024). Challenges of Artificial Intelligence Adoption for Financial Inclusion. In Artificial Intelligence, Fintech, and Financial Inclusion (pp. 135-160). CRC Press.

Chambers-Jones, C. (2021). AI, big data, quantum computing, and financial exclusion: Tempering enthusiasm and offering a human-centric approach to policy. FinTech. *Artificial Intelligence and Law*, 193–210.

Chen, J., Lim, C. P., Tan, K. H., Govindan, K., & Kumar, A. (2021). Artificial intelligence-based human-centric decision support framework: An application to predictive maintenance in asset management under pandemic environments. *Annals of Operations Research*, 1–24. doi:10.1007/s10479-021-04373-w PMID:34785834

Chhillar, N., & Arora, S. (2022). Personal Financial Management Behavior Using Digital Platforms And Its Domains. *Journal of Financial Management. Markets and Institutions*, *10*(02), 2250009. doi:10.1142/S2282717X22500098

Chibba, M. (2009). Financial inclusion, poverty reduction and the Millennium Development Goals. *European Journal of Development Research*, *21*(2), 213–230. doi:10.1057/ejdr.2008.17

Chiu, C. Y. (1992). *Artificial intelligence and its applications to capital budgeting decisions under uncertainty*. Auburn University.

Choubey, A., & Sharma, M. (2021, May). Implementation of robotics and its impact on sustainable banking: A futuristic study. *Journal of Physics: Conference Series*, *1911*(1), 012013. doi:10.1088/1742-6596/1911/1/012013

Chowdhury, E. K., & Chowdhury, R. (2023). Role of financial inclusion in human development: Evidence from Bangladesh, India and Pakistan. *Journal of the Knowledge Economy*, 1–26. doi:10.1007/s13132-023-01366-x

Daud, S. N. M., & Ahmad, A. H. (2023). Financial inclusion, economic growth and the role of digital technology. *Finance Research Letters*, *53*, 103602. doi:10.1016/j.frl.2022.103602

Dirksen, N., & Takahashi, S. (2020). *Artificial intelligence in Japan 2020. Actors, Market, Opportunities and Digital Solutions in a Newly Transformed World.* Netherlands Enterprise Agency.

Elahi, M., Beheshti, A., & Goluguri, S. R. (2021). Recommender systems: Challenges and opportunities in the age of big data and artificial intelligence. *Data Science and Its Applications*, 15-39.

Enholm, I. M., Papagiannidis, E., Mikalef, P., & Krogstie, J. (2022). Artificial intelligence and business value: A literature review. *Information Systems Frontiers*, *24*(5), 1709–1734. doi:10.1007/s10796-021-10186-w

Fritz-Morgenthal, S. G., Hein, B., & Papenbrock, J. (2021). Financial Risk Management and Explainable, Trustworthy, Responsible AI. *Frontiers in Artificial Intelligence*, 5. PMID:35295866

Gallego-Losada, M., Montero-Navarro, A., García-Abajo, E., & Losada, R. G. (2023). Digital financial inclusion. Visualizing the academic literature. *Research in International Business and Finance*, *64*, 101862. doi:10.1016/j.ribaf.2022.101862

Giudici, P. (2018). Fintech risk management: A research challenge for artificial intelligence in finance. *Frontiers in Artificial Intelligence*, *1*, 1. doi:10.3389/frai.2018.00001 PMID:33733089

Griesser, J. W. (1991, January). Expert systems capital budgeting. In *1991 IEEE/ACM International Conference on Developing and Managing Expert System Programs* (pp. 249-250). IEEE Computer Society. 10.1109/DMESP.1991.171725

Hanif, A. (2021). Towards Explainable Artificial Intelligence in Banking and Financial Services. *arXiv preprint arXiv:2112.08441*.

How, M. L., Cheah, S. M., Khor, A. C., & Chan, Y. J. (2020). Artificial intelligence-enhanced predictive insights for advancing financial inclusion: A human-centric ai-thinking approach. *Big Data and Cognitive Computing*, *4*(2), 8. doi:10.3390/bdcc4020008

Hu, B., & Wu, Y. (2023). Unlocking Causal Relationships in Commercial Banking Risk Management: An Examination of Explainable AI Integration with Multi-Factor Risk Models. *Journal of Financial Risk Management, 12*(3), 262–274. doi:10.4236/jfrm.2023.123014

Jain, R. (2023). Role of artificial intelligence in banking and finance. *Journal of Management and Science, 13*(3), 1–4. doi:10.26524/jms.13.27

Kandpal, V., & Khalaf, O. I. (2020). Artificial intelligence and SHGs: enabling financial inclusion in India. In *Deep Learning Strategies for Security Enhancement in Wireless Sensor Networks* (pp. 291–303). IGI Global. doi:10.4018/978-1-7998-5068-7.ch015

Kaur, R., Sandhu, R. S., Gera, A., Kaur, T., & Gera, P. (2020). Intelligent voice bots for digital banking. In *Smart Systems and IoT: Innovations in Computing: Proceeding of SSIC 2019* (pp. 401-408). Springer Singapore.

Kim, D., Kang, H. G., Bae, K., & Jeon, S. (2021). An artificial intelligence-enabled industry classification and its interpretation. *Internet Research, 32*(2), 406–424. doi:10.1108/INTR-05-2020-0299

Krishnaraj Arul, O., & Megargel, A. (2023). Human-centred artificial intelligence in the banking sector. *Journal of Digital Banking, 7*(3), 266–279.

Kuchciak, I., & Wiktorowicz, J. (2021). Empowering financial education by banks—Social media as a modern channel. *Journal of Risk and Financial Management, 14*(3), 118. doi:10.3390/jrfm14030118

Kulkarni, L., & Ghosh, A. (2021). Gender disparity in the digitalization of financial services: Challenges and promises for women's financial inclusion in India. *Gender, Technology and Development, 25*(2), 233–250. doi:10.1080/09718524.2021.1911022

Lui, A., & Lamb, G. W. (2018). Artificial intelligence and augmented intelligence collaboration: Regaining trust and confidence in the financial sector. *Information & Communications Technology Law, 27*(3), 267–283. doi:10.1080/13600834.2018.1488659

Marani, M., Soltani, M., Bahadori, M., Soleimani, M., & Moshayedi, A. (2023). The role of biometric in banking: A review. *EAI Endorsed Transactions on AI and Robotics, 2*(1).

MarottaG.AuC. D. (2022). Budgeting in the Age of Artificial Intelligence–New Opportunities and Challenges. Available at SSRN 4168230. doi:10.2139/ssrn.4168230

Maseke, B. F. (2024). The Transformative Power of Artificial Intelligence in Banking Client Service. *South Asian Journal of Social Studies and Economics*, *21*(3), 93–105. doi:10.9734/sajsse/2024/v21i3787

Mhlanga, D. (2020). Industry 4.0 in finance: The impact of artificial intelligence (ai) on digital financial inclusion. *International Journal of Financial Studies*, *8*(3), 45. doi:10.3390/ijfs8030045

Mhlanga, D. (2022). Human-centered artificial intelligence: The superlative approach to achieve sustainable development goals in the fourth industrial revolution. *Sustainability (Basel)*, *14*(13), 7804. doi:10.3390/su14137804

Mhlanga, D. (2023). Artificial Intelligence (AI) Solutions for Financial Inclusion of the Excluded: What Are the Challenges? In *Economic Inclusion in Post-Independence Africa: An Inclusive Approach to Economic Development* (pp. 257–272). Springer Nature Switzerland. doi:10.1007/978-3-031-31431-5_14

Modwey, H. H. F., & Abd Elgabar, E. E. (2022). Using sentiment analysis technology to analyze bank customers' textual comments. *Humanities and Natural Sciences Journal.*

Nagwani, N. K., & Suri, J. S. (2023). An artificial intelligence framework on software bug triaging, technological evolution, and future challenges: A review. *International Journal of Information Management Data Insights*, *3*(1), 100153. Advance online publication. doi:10.1016/j.jjimei.2022.100153

Nassar, M., Salah, K., ur Rehman, M. H., & Svetinovic, D. (2020). Blockchain for explainable and trustworthy artificial intelligence. *Wiley Interdisciplinary Reviews. Data Mining and Knowledge Discovery*, *10*(1), e1340. doi:10.1002/widm.1340

Noreen, U., Shafique, A., Ahmed, Z., & Ashfaq, M. (2023). Banking 4.0: Artificial intelligence (AI) in banking industry & consumer's perspective. *Sustainability (Basel)*, *15*(4), 3682. doi:10.3390/su15043682

Pal, A., De', R., & Herath, T. (2020). The role of mobile payment technology in sustainable and human-centric development: Evidence from the post-demonetization period in India. *Information Systems Frontiers*, *22*(3), 607–631. doi:10.1007/s10796-020-09982-7

Rabbani, M. R., Sarea, A., Khan, S., & Abdullah, Y. (2022). Ethical concerns in artificial intelligence (AI): The role of RegTech and Islamic finance. In *Artificial Intelligence for Sustainable Finance and Sustainable Technology: Proceedings of ICGER 2021 1* (pp. 381-390). Springer International Publishing.

RaneN.ChoudharyS.RaneJ. (2023). Explainable Artificial Intelligence (XAI) approaches for transparency and accountability in financial decision-making. *Available at* SSRN 4640316. doi:10.2139/ssrn.4640316

Rashmi, R., & Nirmal, R. V. (2021). A study on the implementation and the impact of artificial intelligence in banking processes. *Asian Journal of Management, 12*(1), 47–54.

Rogha, M. (2023). Explain To Decide: A Human-Centric Review on the Role of Explainable Artificial Intelligence in AI-assisted Decision Making. *arXiv preprint arXiv:2312.11507.*

Samans, R. (2021). Financing human-centred COVID-19 recovery and decisive climate action worldwide: International cooperation's twenty-first century moment of truth (No. 40). ILO Working Paper.

Sethi, D., & Acharya, D. (2018). Financial inclusion and economic growth linkage: Some cross country evidence. *Journal of Financial Economic Policy, 10*(3), 369–385. doi:10.1108/JFEP-11-2016-0073

Shneiderman, B. (2020). Bridging the gap between ethics and practice: Guidelines for reliable, safe, and trustworthy human-centered AI systems. *ACM Transactions on Interactive Intelligent Systems, 10*(4), 1–31. doi:10.1145/3419764

Sobrino-García, I. (2021). Artificial intelligence risks and challenges in the Spanish public administration: An exploratory analysis through expert judgements. *Administrative Sciences, 11*(3), 102. doi:10.3390/admsci11030102

Sørensen, K. B. (2012). The Self-Leading Customer: A new human-centred financial service. *Proceedings of the 2nd Innovation for Financial Services Summit.*

Stone, M., Aravopoulou, E., Ekinci, Y., Evans, G., Hobbs, M., Labib, A., Laughlin, P., Machtynger, J., & Machtynger, L. (2020). Artificial intelligence (AI) in strategic marketing decision-making: A research agenda. *The Bottom Line (New York, N.Y.), 33*(2), 183–200. doi:10.1108/BL-03-2020-0022

Subudhi, S. R. I. H. A. R. I. (2019). Banking on artificial intelligence: Opportunities & challenges for banks in India. *International Journal of Research in Commerce, Economics and Management, 9*(7).

Suhel, S. F., Shukla, V. K., Vyas, S., & Mishra, V. P. (2020, June). Conversation to automation in banking through chatbot using artificial machine intelligence language. In *2020 8th international conference on reliability, infocom technologies and optimization (trends and future directions) (ICRITO)* (pp. 611-618). IEEE. 10.1109/ICRITO48877.2020.9197825

Sujith, A. V. L. N., Qureshi, N. I., Dornadula, V. H. R., Rath, A., Prakash, K. B., & Singh, S. K. (2022). A comparative analysis of business machine learning in making effective financial decisions using structural equation model (SEM). *Journal of Food Quality*, *2022*, 1–7. doi:10.1155/2022/6382839

Suresh, A., & Rani, N. J. (2020). Role of Artificial Intelligence (AI) in the Indian Banking Scenario. *Journal of Information Technology and Economic Development*, *11*(2).

Tang, Y. C. (2009). An approach to budget allocation for an aerospace company—Fuzzy analytic hierarchy process and artificial neural network. *Neurocomputing*, *72*(16-18), 3477–3489. doi:10.1016/j.neucom.2009.03.020

Tatineni, S. (2022). Customer Authentication in Mobile Banking-MLOps Practices and AI-Driven Biometric Authentication Systems. *Journal of Economics & Management Research.* doi. org/ (3). doi:10.47363/JESMR/2022

Tyagi, R. (2023). Empowering the unbanked: A revolution in financial inclusion through artificial intelligence. *International Journal of Research in Engineering. Science and Management*, *6*(10), 4–12.

Úbeda, F., Mendez, A., & Forcadell, F. J. (2023). The sustainable practices of multinational banks as drivers of financial inclusion in developing countries. *Finance Research Letters*, *51*, 103278. doi:10.1016/j.frl.2022.103278

Umamaheswari, S., & Valarmathi, A. (2023). Role of Artificial Intelligence in The Banking Sector. *Journal of Survey in Fisheries Sciences*, *10*(4S), 2841–2849.

Valle-Cruz, D., Fernandez-Cortez, V., & Gil-Garcia, J. R. (2022). From E-budgeting to smart budgeting: Exploring the potential of artificial intelligence in government decision-making for resource allocation. *Government Information Quarterly*, *39*(2), 101644. doi:10.1016/j.giq.2021.101644

Varsha, P. (2023). How can we manage biases in artificial intelligence systems – A systematic literature review. *International Journal of Information Management Data Insights, 3*(1), 100165. https://doi.org/. 2023.100165 doi:10.1016 /j.jjimei

VARTEQ Inc. (2023, July 11). *AI in Credit Scoring: Enhancing Loan Approvals and Financial Inclusion through Advanced Algorithms.* https://www.linkedin.com/pulse/ai-credit-scoring-enhancing-loan-approvals-financial-inclusion

Vučinić, M., & Luburić, R. (2022). Fintech, risk-based thinking and cyber risk. *Journal of Central Banking Theory and Practice*, *11*(2), 27–53. doi:10.2478/jcbtp-2022-0012

Vuppalapaty, P. (2021). *The Need for Agility in Capital Budgeting of Intelligent Automations for Knowledge and Service Work.* Temple University.

Yasir, A., Ahmad, A., Abbas, S., Inairat, M., Al-Kassem, A. H., & Rasool, A. (2022, February). How Artificial Intelligence Is Promoting Financial Inclusion? A Study On Barriers Of Financial Inclusion. In *2022 International Conference on Business Analytics for Technology and Security (ICBATS)* (pp. 1-6). IEEE. 10.1109/ICBATS54253.2022.9759038

Yeh, H. C., Yu, M. C., Liu, C. H., & Huang, C. I. (2023). Robo-advisor based on unified theory of acceptance and use of technology. *Asia Pacific Journal of Marketing and Logistics*, *35*(4), 962–979. doi:10.1108/APJML-07-2021-0493

Zeleznikow, J. (2021). Using artificial intelligence to provide intelligent dispute resolution support. *Group Decision and Negotiation*, *30*(4), 789–812. doi:10.1007/s10726-021-09734-1 PMID:33867681

Chapter 4
Understanding Evolution, Development, and Transitioning of Digital Financial Inclusion:
A Bibliometric Study

Santosh Satyanarayan Baheti
School of Business and Management, Christ University, India

Dippi Verma
https://orcid.org/0000-0001-7521-9267
School of Business and Management, Christ University, India

Debora Dhanya Amarnath
School of Business and Management, Christ University, India

ABSTRACT

Different countries across the globe are trying hard to address the challenges of poverty alleviation. Various studies conducted in the past have highlighted the essence of financial inclusion in poverty alleviation. Adoption of financial inclusion acts as a major trigger for developing countries to foster economic growth as it helps in fostering saving, investment, and helps society in attaining financial independence. Economies across the globe are striving hard to accomplish sustainable development goals. The speedy compliance with SDG goals can only be realized through the adoption of ICT. Some of the SDG goals like reduced inequalities (SDG10), quality education (SDG 4), and industry innovation and infrastructure (SDG 9) cannot be

DOI: 10.4018/979-8-3693-1503-3.ch004

attained without the adoption of technology. Effective blend of technology helps countries in achieving targets like digital financial inclusion, digital education, advanced healthcare services, green energy, and addressing other climate related issues. Financial inclusion consists of providing sufficient access to a diverse range of financial products and services. In an era of information technology, digital transformation has brought a major shift in demand and supply side of financial inclusion. In order to understand the progress of the past 23 years in digital financial inclusion, the study has conducted a systematic review and bibliometric analysis of digital financial inclusion domain. The study intends to explore the present status of digital financial inclusion, most prominent studies published in this domain, influential countries, influential authors, and collaborative tendencies between authors. Through Biblioshiny R and Vos-viewer software, the study intends to conduct temporal analysis of influential authors and countries as it helps to understand the emergence of new researchers, institutions, and countries over a time. The study also intends to explore thematic analysis of digital financial inclusion domain, influential theories derived from literature, and assessment of influential studies published for the past 23 years. In the final phase, the study intends to propose various antecedents of digital financial inclusion that have been identified through in-depth scrutiny of literature.

INTRODUCTION

Financial inclusion refers to the availability of practical and reasonably priced financial goods and services for the "individuals and businesses have access to useful and affordable financial products and services that meet their needs transactions, payments, savings, credit and insurance delivered in a responsible and sustainable way" (World Bank, 2021). More than 55 nations have committed to financial inclusion since 2010, while more than 60 countries have initiated or are developing national strategies (World bank, 2022). The phrase "financial inclusion (FI)" has gained relevance since the early 2000s (Ozili, 2021). FI has advanced significantly during the past twenty-three years: between 2000 and 2023, 515 million more people had access to financial services (Huang et al., 2023; Chisadza & Biyase, 2023). The creation of an inclusive financial system is an area of policy emphasis and priority because access to finance has traditionally been seen as one of the key indicators of economic growth (Ozturk & Ullah, 2022). As a result, FI is widely regarded as one of the most significant forces driving economic growth specially for the impoverished are enormous. Its contributions to the gross domestic product, to the welfare of individuals and society especially underprivileged, and to the establishment and growth of businesses, particularly small and medium-sized businesses, have been well-documented (Tay et al., 2022; Demirgüç-Kunt & Klapper, 2012). Additionally, the COVID-19 problem has emphasized the need for greater financial inclusion online. Digital financial inclusion entails the use of cost-effective digital means to provide populations that are currently underserved and financially excluded with a variety of formal financial services that are responsibly delivered at a cost that is affordable for customers and sustainable for providers (Dwivedi et al., 2022). Many stakeholders, including politicians, academics, and practitioners, have expressed concern about the need to establish an inclusive financial industry (Ullah et al., 2022). This has increased the necessity for developing various solutions to address noted constraints preventing the delivery of traditional financial services to remote areas and their adoption in most developing nations. Formal financing access can improve investments in human capital, decrease susceptibility to economic shocks, and promote the development of jobs. Financial inclusion is seen by seven of the Sustainable Development Goals (SDG) of the United Nations for 2030 as a critical facilitator for attaining global sustainable development. The creation of a National Strategy for Financial Inclusion (NSFI) is necessary to accomplish the goals in a coordinated and timely manner (RBI, 2020). More than 1.2 billion individuals have gained access to financial services since 2011, giving them a better chance to improve their lives (World Bank, 2022). In addition, more than fifty nations have implemented FI plans and strategies (United Nations, 2021). On the other hand, an estimated 1.7 billion individuals globally still lack access to fundamental financial services and banking. Therefore, the United Nations have proposed sustainable developmental goals and initiates for all the developing and underdeveloped nations. Financial inclusion has been identified as a key facilitator for seven of the 17 Sustainable Development Goals by United Nations, including SDG 1 (eliminate extreme poverty), SDG 2 (reduce hunger and promote food security), SDG 3 (achieve good health and well-being), SDG 4 (foster quality education), SDG 5 (enhanced women empowerment is the key to promoting gender equality), SDG 8 (promote shared economic growth), and SDG 9 (promote innovation and sustainable industrialization) (World Bank, 2021).

The major international regulators, the standard-setting bodies (SSBs), now regularly meet to discuss financial inclusion, and growing research demonstrates strong links between financial inclusion and important development goals (Demirgüç-Kunt et al., 2022; Khan et al., 2022). The recent global financial index has claimed that there has been significant progress in many areas over the past decade, according to a survey of 125,000 adults in 123 economies found that 76% of adults now have a bank or mobile account, up from just 51% in 2011 (World Bank, 2022 b). Employment was determined to be one of the biggest obstacles to financial inclusion and the main justification for not having a bank account (Geng & He, 2021). According to Findex, 77% of working-age persons have an account, compared to just 65% of those who are unemployed (Demirgüç-Kunt et al., 2022). Historically, women have been disproportionately left out of the financial system; globally, 55% of the unbanked population is female. The gender pay gap in finance, however, has been closing recently (Demirguc-Kunt et al., 2013). According to the research, the unbanked disparity in developing countries has decreased from 9 percentage points to 6 percentage points in 2021. In these areas, this translates to 74% of males and 68% of women. Another significant element was discovered to be education. According to the Findex survey, adults in developing nations with only a primary education had a 14-percentage point lower likelihood of having an account than those with a secondary degree. These adults are also more likely to become victims of fraud (World Bank, 2021, b). Despite increased financial inclusion, customers who have less banking knowledge find it difficult to take advantage of the benefits on their own. According to almost two-thirds of unbanked individuals, if they opened an account at a financial institution, they would require assistance utilizing it. The report issued a warning that these less knowledgeable customers would also be more susceptible to fraud and increased bank costs (World Bank, 2021, b)

According to Camara and Tuesta (2014), FI is a multifaceted notion that cannot be adequately represented by lone measures like bank account ratios and the quantity of ATMs. Additionally, most studies use a multidimensional approach and a variety of variables, including the number of household depositors and borrowers as well as per capita bank accounts, bank branches, ATMs, credit and debit cards, and bank branches etc., (Dabla-Norris et al., 2015; Mialou et al., 2017). According to several studies (e.g., Banerjee et al., 2015, Imai et al., 2012; Park & Mercado, 2015, 2018; Zhang & Posso, 2019), the empirical data on the influence of financial inclusion on development is still inconclusive.

Financial inclusion research has previously looked at a number of topics, including how to promote development via financial inclusion (Ghosh, 2013), the impact of financial inclusion on financial stability (Hannig and Jansen, 2010; Cull et al., 2012); the relationship between financial inclusion and economic growth (Mohan, 2006; Kim et al., 2018); country-specific financial inclusion practices (Fungáová and Weill, 2015; Mitton, 2008 However, the results of these research do not allow for cross-national or cross-regional comparison. A review of recent literature is required to find recent cross-country trends that may be compared to the experiences of other nations and areas. This current study review of the methodology is straightforward! The study intends to explore the present status of digital financial inclusion, most prominent studies published in this domain, influential countries, influential authors, and collaborative tendencies between authors. Through Biblioshiny R and Vos-viewer software the study intends to conduct temporal analysis of influential authors and countries as it helps to understand the emergence of new researchers, institutions, and countries over a time. The study also intends to explore thematic analysis of digital financial inclusion domain, influential theories derived from literature, and assessment of influential studies published for the past 23 years. In the final phase the study intends to propose various antecedents of digital financial inclusion that have been identified through in-depth scrutiny of literature. Following are some contributions that the analysis in this review article add to the literature on financial inclusion. One is that this review adds to the body of knowledge examining how financial inclusion promotes better development outcomes in underdeveloped nations. Second, this research adds to the ongoing discussion promoted by the World Bank in favour of financial inclusion as a successful means of reducing poverty in developing and impoverished nations. Thirdly, the debate in this review contributes to the growing body of literature on financial inclusion that aims to give strategies for lowering the existing level of financial exclusion in developing countries. In order to better understand the effects of financial exclusion on the excluded group and the general community, the ideas in this review article advocate for further joint study.

RESEARCH METHODOLOGY

Selection of Database

Among the various available database like Scopus, EBSCO, ProQuest, Inspec, and Web of Science. For the present study, we have considered Scopus as the best database as it is comprehensive and provides in-depth search results (Bartol et al., 2014). The Boolean operator AND was used to execute the search with key strings "Digital Finance" AND Financial Inclusion AND Digital Transformation AND Digital Economy. The search was expanded with the Boolean operator OR with the key string ("Digital Finance" OR "Digital Financial Inclusion") AND (Digital Transformation OR "Digital Revolution") AND Digital Finance AND Digital Economy. The language selected was English. In addition to specify the search the option was enabled by title and keyword resulted into total 1110 documents consisting from the period 1985-2023. The resulting database of 1110 documents downloaded as CSV file is used for bibliometric analysis through Biblioshiny and VOS Viewer software. In the filtration process in order to enhance quality of results several inclusion and exclusion criteria were adapted.

The generated pool of 1110 articles downloaded from the Scopus database was used for bibliometric analysis using VOS-Viewer and Biblioshiny R Software. The results are presented in four sections: 1) Characteristics and Performance, 2) Influential Author and Document, and 3) Thematic Analysis. The visualization software used for the study is VOS Viewer (van Eck & Waltman, 2010) and Biblioshiny, a bibliometrics R package.

Framing of Research Questions

The chapter intends to answer the following research questions:

RQ1: What is the pattern of growth in a publication related to the DFI since 2000?

RQ2: What characteristics of authors and their productivity in the domain of DFI research?

RQ3: Which studies are instrumental in shaping the knowledge base of DFI since 2000?

RQ4: Which are the relevant source of publication in domain of DFL research?

RQ5: Which are the important themes studied in DFL research?

RESULT AND DISCUSSION

RQ1: What are the characteristics and temporal publication dynamics of Digital Financial Inclusion Research?

To attain RQ1, the research examines the descriptive analysis of 1110 publications and scientific production of DFI research.

The given Table (1) offers a thorough descriptive analysis, dividing data into four distinct sections: Main Information, Document Content, Author Collaboration, and Document Type. The dataset contains 1110 publications related to green bonds, originating from 374 different sources spanning the years 1985 to 2023. It's worth noting that the yearly publication growth rate during this period averages at 15.36%, and the average document age is 2.82 years. This research related to DFI involved a totally of 2710 different authors, resulting in 808 unique keywords across the publications. Among the 1110 examined documents, 195 were written by a single author, involving 172 unique authors. Additionally, all documents within the sample were categorized as research articles.

The yearly publication trend reveals a noticeable surge in interest among researchers and academics regarding DFI. Starting from 2013, there has been a significant and consistent increase in the number of studies focused on DFI. Table (1) shows significant increase in studies from 2016 to 2017 and trend continued except the year 2018.The reason can be, In India, the concept of digital payments began gaining momentum in 2016 when the Digital India mission was launched. This initiative aimed to encourage the integration of digital technology into the lives of both Indian entrepreneurs and the general population, with the objective of strengthening the country's economy through transactions that are paperless, faceless, and cashless. Digital payment systems play a crucial role in socioeconomic development by promoting financial inclusion, reducing poverty, creating jobs,

Table 1. Key statistics of the study

Description	Results
MAIN INFORMATION ABOUT DATA	
Timespan	1985:2023
Sources (Journals, Books, etc)	374
Documents	1110
Annual Growth Rate %	15.36
Document Average Age	2.82
Average citations per doc	11.28
DOCUMENT CONTENTS	
Keywords Plus (ID)	808
Author's Keywords (DE)	2710
AUTHORS	
Authors	2476
Authors of single-authored docs	172
AUTHORS COLLABORATION	
Single-authored docs	195
Co-Authors per Doc	2.62
International co-authorships %	0
DOCUMENT TYPES	
Article	1110

enhancing economic efficiency, and providing opportunities for individuals and businesses to thrive in the modern economy.

RQ2: What characteristics of authors and their productivity in the domain of DFI research?

Table 3 shows a comprehensive assessment of the most influential authors DFL research.

To understand, RQ2: What characteristics of authors and their productivity in the domain of DFI research? The study conducts an analysis of authors, employing two criteria: 1) the quantity of publications per author, 2) the assessment of authors' influence determined by the average number of citations per author's articles. Table (3) shows information related to top ten authors such as Joseph Mapeera Ntayi, Makerere university of Business, Uganda . JM Ntayi has published 7 articles in the domain and received 126 citations. JM Ntayi along with Charles Akol Malinga JC Munene and George Okello Bongomin, Makerere university of Business, Uganda researched on focus of financial inclusion on the mediation of social capital in the

Table 2. Trend analysis of publications

Year	Studies	MeanTCperArt	MeanTCperYear	Citable Years
2000	1	7	0.18	39
2007	3	31.33	1.84	17
2009	1	4	0.27	15
2010	2	7.5	0.54	14
2011	5	9.8	0.75	13
2012	12	20.33	1.69	12
2013	11	33.91	3.08	11
2014	17	9.82	0.98	10
2015	22	11.45	1.27	9
2016	33	15.48	1.94	8
2017	69	27.8	3.97	7
2018	53	23.32	3.89	6
2019	116	16.41	3.28	5
2020	146	14.92	3.73	4
2021	168	11.76	3.92	3
2022	223	5.7	2.85	2
2023	228	1.43	1.43	1

Figure 1. Schematic representation of annual publication trend

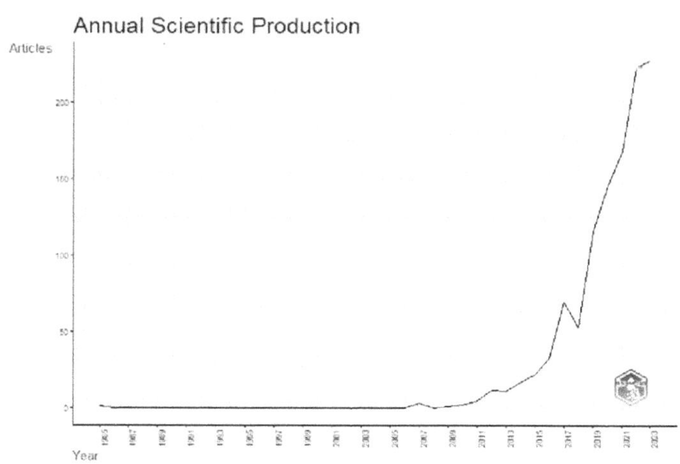

Table 3. List of influential authors and key matrices

Element	H_Index	G_Index	M_Index	TC	NC	Py_Start
Ntayi JM	6	7	0.75	126	7	2016
Karjaluoto H	5	5	0.625	267	5	2016
Malinga CA	5	5	0.714	74	5	2017
Munene JC	5	7	0.625	106	7	2016
Shaikh AA	5	5	0.625	267	5	2016
Bongomin GC	4	4	0.667	52	4	2018
Iheanachor N	4	5	0.8	83	5	2019
Okello Candiya Bongomin G	4	4	0.5	66	4	2016
Vismara S	4	4	1.333	96	4	2021
Wang Y	4	5	0.667	237	5	2018

Note-TC-Total Citations, NC-Normalized Citations

financial literacy-financial inclusion link in rural Uganda, with a focus on cognition and network moderation, revealing significant findings (Bongomin et al., 2018; Okello Candiya Bongomin, Ntayi, Munene, & Nabeta, 2016; Okello Candiya Bongomin, Ntayi, Munene, & Nkote Nabeta, 2016). Heikki Karjaluoto University of Jyvaskyla, Finland has received 267 citation and published five research papers in the domain of digital financial inclusion. The author researched on mobile money (MM) services as a robust catalyst for financial inclusion. It emphasizes the pivotal role of MM agents in the transition from conventional services to MM services, fostering customer engagement, advocacy, and empowerment, particularly benefiting those with limited financial resources (Shaikh et al., 2023). Salman Ahmed Sheikh, Department of Management Studies, SZABIST University, Pakistan, suggested a hybrid microfinance approach that leverages Fintech to seamlessly integrate Islamic commercial and social finance institutions, aiming for enhanced efficiency and substantial social impact. This model addresses financial and social intermediation needs, offering a range of financial services and non-financial assistance (Shaikh et al., 2023).

RQ3: Which studies are instrumental in shaping the knowledge base of DFI since 1985? to attain the research objective the study conducts citation analysis of influential documents. The focus of the research illuminates how digital technology accomplishes the financial inclusion of market segments that were previously marginalized (Leong et al., 2017). Few study in OIC countries examines the link between financial inclusion and economic growth using panel data and various analyses. Findings indicate a positive relationship between financial inclusion and economic growth (Kim et al., 2018), Over time, the financial industry has evolved

Table 4. List of influential studies and key matrices

Title	Authors	Journal	Year	TC	TCP	NTC
Digital Finance and FinTech: current research and future research directions	Peter Gombre, Jascha Alexender Koch, Michael Siering	Journal of Business Economics	2017	485	69.29	17.45
Measuring Financial Inclusion: Explaining Variation in Use of Financial Services across and within Countries	Asli Demirguc-Kunt,Leora Klapper	Brooking Institutional Press	2013	259	23.55	7.64
Financial inclusion and economic growth in OIC countries	Dai Won Kim, Jung Suk Yu, M Kabir Hassan	Research in International Business and finance	2018	258	43.00	11.06
Blockchain disruption and decentralized finance: The rise of decentralized business models	Yan Chen, Cristiano Bellovitis	Journal of Business Venturing Insight	2020	226	56.50	15.14
Digital finance, green technological innovation and energy-environmental performance: Evidence from China's regional economies	Shaopeng Cao,Liang Nie,Huaping Sun, Weifeng Sun,Farhad Tanghizadeh,Hesary.	Journal of Cleaner Production.	2021	200	66.67	17.01
Is financial inclusion good for bank stability? International evidence	M Mostak Ahmed	Sushanta K Mallick	2019	194	38.80	11.82
Nurturing a FinTech ecosystem: The case of a youth microloan startup in China	Carmen Leoang, Barney Tan,Xiao Xiao,Felix Ter Chian Ter,Yuan Sun	International Journal of Information Management.	2017	176	25.14	6.33
How perceived value drives the use of mobile financial services apps	Karjaluoto Heikki, Aijaz A Shaikh, Hannu Saarijarvi, Saila Saraneimi.	International Journal of Information Management.	2019	170	34.00	10.36
Mobile-banking adoption: empirical evidence from the banking sector in Pakistan	Maya F Farah, Muhammed Junaid Shahid Hasni, Abbas Khan Abbas	International Journal of Bank Marketing	2018	152	25.33	6.52
Sustainability, FinTech and Financial Inclusion	Douglas A Arner, Ross P Buckley, Dirk A Zetzsche, Robin Veidt	European Business Organization Law Review	2020	144	36.00	9.65

Note TC- Total Citations, NTC-Normalized Total Citations, TCP-Total Citations Per Year

Table 5. List of influential journals and key matrices

Element	H_ Index	Tc	Np	Publication
International Journal Of Bank Marketing	13	664	28	2011
International Journal Of Islamic And Middle Eastern Finance And Management	9	160	14	2015
Technological Forecasting And Social Change	9	288	21	2016
Financial Innovation	8	295	11	2017
International Journal Of Finance And Economics	8	149	20	2021
Research In International Business And Finance	8	492	15	2017
Banks And Bank Systems	7	117	21	2010
Emerging Markets Review	7	227	9	2012
African Journal Of Economic And Management Studies	6	174	13	2012
Journal Of Financial Services Marketing	6	172	17	2011

Source- Software Generated Results and Scopus Data

due to digitalization, shifting focus from improving traditional tasks to creating new opportunities through Digital Finance, including FinTech innovation (Gomber et al., 2017). Mobile information services, notably mobile banking and payment apps, have transformed consumer behavior. A study in Finland highlights self-congruence and novelty as key drivers of perceived value in mobile financial service apps. Positive perceptions of these apps enhance customer satisfaction and commitment to banks, suggesting valuable investments for financial institutions.(Karjaluoto et al., 2019). Study also reveals digital finance significantly improves environmental performance through green technology innovation, especially in less developed markets, supported by government regulations. The study advocates for accelerating financial digitization for environmental benefits (Cao et al., 2021).

Recent significant studies on digital financial inclusion highlight the versatile applicability of digital finance Table (4). These findings underscore that digital financial services, such as mobile banking, digital wallets, and online payment platforms, have the potential to bridge the gap in financial inclusion globally. The impact of these studies reveals the power of digital finance to provide essential financial services to underserved populations, stimulate economic growth, and enhance financial resilience. However, challenges like security and digital literacy must be addressed to fully realize these benefits.

To address" RQ4: Which is the relevant source of publication in domain of DFL research? The study conducts h index and total citation analysis for the 10-journal publishing highest number of studies Table (5).

Figure 2. Influential keyword analysis using Biblioshiny R

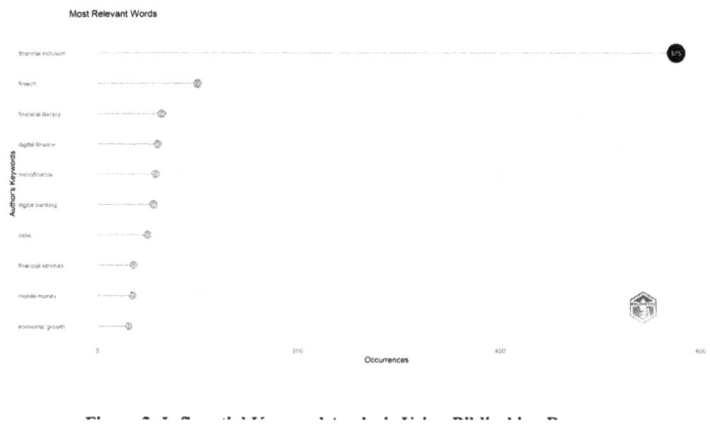

These journals exhibit diverse profiles when assessing their impact based on several key metrics. *"INTERNATIONAL JOURNAL OF BANK MARKETING"* stands out with a substantial h-index of 13 and a high total citation count of 664, underlining its influence in the field. It also boasts a significant number of publications at 28, signalling a consistent contribution to research since its inception in 2011. *"INTERNATIONAL JOURNAL OF ISLAMIC AND MIDDLE EASTERN FINANCE AND MANAGEMENT"* and *"TECHNOLOGICAL FORECASTING AND SOCIAL CHANGE"* have h-indices of 9, indicating their recognized scholarly value, although the former is a relatively newer journal compared to the latter. "FINANCIAL INNOVATION," with 8 in h-index and 295 total citations, highlights a notable impact given its brief existence since 2017. *"RESEARCH IN INTERNATIONAL BUSINESS AND FINANCE"* is marked by a high total citation count of 492, showcasing its substantial influence within its domain. *"BANKS AND BANK SYSTEMS"* and *"EMERGING MARKETS* REVIEW" both feature h-indices of 7, with the former having a commendable publication history since 2010, while the latter, starting in 2012, shows a significant total citation count of 227. The *"AFRICAN JOURNAL OF ECONOMIC AND MANAGEMENT STUDIES"* and the *"JOURNAL OF FINANCIAL SERVICES MARKETING*" have h-indices of 6, and the latter boasts a substantial 172 total citations, emphasizing their meaningful contributions to the academic community. Together, these journals encompass a spectrum of impact levels, demonstrating their distinctive roles in disseminating knowledge and shaping their respective research fields.

To attain RQ 5: Which are the important themes studied in DFL research? the study conducts keyword occurrence analysis and thematic map using Biblioshiny for R Studio.

Keyword Analysis

Keyword analysis is a fundamental research technique used to extract valuable insights from large volumes of textual data. Researchers employ this method to achieve various objectives, such as content summarization, topic identification, search engine optimization, and sentiment analysis. By identifying frequently occurring keywords or terms in a dataset, researchers can effectively categorize, cluster, and understand the subject matter of content, revealing trends and emerging topics.

The prevailing author-recommended terms in studies related to digital financial inclusion are "financial inclusion" and "fintech." In the chosen sample, "financial inclusion" was mentioned 100 times, closely followed by "fintech," while "digital finance" was explored 60 times. Additionally, "digital banking" and "mobile banking" were recurring subjects. The keyword analysis reveals a significant association between "financial inclusion" and "digital finance," with the shared aim of promoting economic growth. This stands as the primary objective of digital financial inclusion.

Thematic Analysis

The thematic map examines clusters of keywords, assessing their interconnections to identify underlying themes. These themes are distinguished by their density and centrality properties, with the Y-axis denoting density and the X-axis indicating centrality. These characteristics gauge the importance of themes, categorizing them as significant or insignificant. The more connections a node has within the thematic network, the greater its centrality and relevance. Likewise, cohesion among nodes signifies density, illustrating a theme's capacity to evolve and endure. The study constructs a thematic map using the first 250 keywords that appear at least five times, The results of the thematic map are presented in Figure (3).

An examination of digital financial inclusion through thematic analysis reveals that, despite three decades of research, the prominent themes remain in the foundational quadrant. There is potential for the advancement of themes like digital banking, mobile banking, and fintech within the context of digital financial inclusion. Additionally, there is a growing need to establish a knowledge base related to financial literacy and behavior, as this is essential for achieving comprehensive financial inclusion through technology integration.

The emerging and declining quadrant indicates digital for sustainable development is another theme which is moving towards basic quadrants. Digital financial inclusion, which extends banking services through digital channels, aligns closely with sustainable development's principles. The theme can be developed understanding dynamic partnership that can address diverse global challenges and opportunities,

Figure 3. Four quadrant analysis

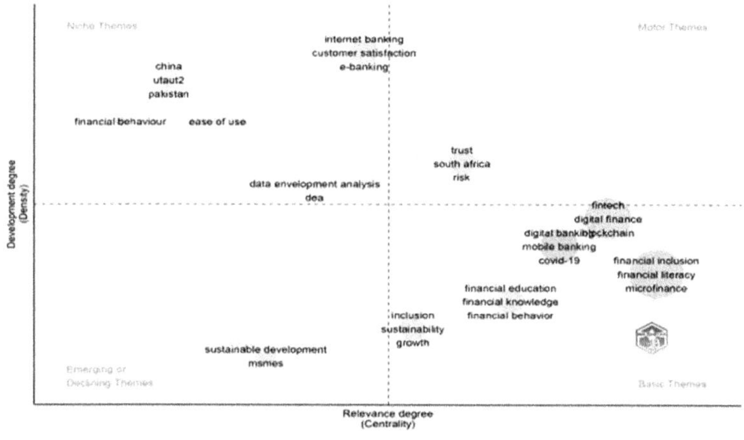

from economic well-being and environmental preservation to social equity and technological advancement (Chikalipah, 2020; Wadhwa et al., n.d.).

Thematic analysis of digital financial inclusion research uncovers recurring themes that shape our understanding of this evolving field. Key themes encompass access and accessibility, emphasizing inclusivity and overcoming barriers. Financial literacy and technology innovation play crucial roles in promoting digital financial inclusion (Chhatoi et al., 2023; Christiani & Kastowo, 2023; Mutamimah & Indriastuti, 2023). Additionally, policy (Ahmad & Satrovic, 2023), regulation, and data privacy are central concerns, as are the social and gender dimensions of inclusion. Economic empowerment, sustainability, and case studies from various regions further enrich the analysis. By identifying these themes and challenges, researchers and practitioners can better navigate the dynamic landscape of digital financial inclusion and work towards broader financial access, economic empowerment (Rohatgi et al., 2023; Sreenu, 2023), and social equity (Maity, 2023; Sharma et al., 1 C.E.) through digital channels.

In the thematic map's Quadrant 4, niche themes within the study are evident, with a focus on research conducted in China and Pakistan. Surprisingly, there is a limited emphasis on comprehensive interdisciplinary studies that encompass the entirety of digital financial inclusion. These studies should investigate its implications for customer satisfaction and the various factors that influence the adoption of digital finance, revealing a gap in the existing research landscape (Bankuoru Egala et al., 2021; Zouari & Abdelhedi, 2021).

Conclusive Remarks

Summarized findings of the studies are discussed as follows:

- These 1110 studies were drafted by 2476 authors.
- Documents selected for the study have received on average 11.28 citations.
- Average age of document is 3 years.
- 195 of the documents are contributed by the single author and 815 of the documents is the result of collaboration between the authors.
- Financial Inclusion, Fintech, digital finance, digital banking, and mobile banking are the most influential keywords in our assessment.
- Research productivity from developed countries is significant as the maximum contribution to the domain is from developed countries.
- International collaboration between the authors and associations is found to be is at the nascent stage and found to be negligible.
- Most influential studies are contributed by influential authors like Ntayi, J.M, Karjaluto, H, Malinga, C.A. and Munene, J.C.
- Most influential institutions that have contributed to the domain are Makere University of Business, Uganda, Heikki Karjaluto University, Finland, and Isfahan University.
- In terms of the nature of studies most of the studies are conceptual and empirical in nature. There are very few studies that have done systematic review of the domain.
- Co-authorship analysis shows that authors have formed collaboration within and between the institutions of their own country.
- Maximum percent of the research output is from the USA, UK and China.
- Digital Financial Inclusion theme has attracted research contributions from across the globe. In total, 54 countries contributed to the knowledge domain through their scientific contribution.
- Most of the authors, institutions, and countries have contributed once or twice to the knowledge domain.
- Academicians have contributed most of the research output on the interlinkage between digital finance and financial inclusion in comparison with practitioners.
- Practitioners have also contributed to the research domain, but their contribution is very few in number.
- Most of the authors, institutions, and countries have contributed once or twice to the knowledge domain.

- From 2011 onwards the theme of digital financial inclusion has attracted the attention of researchers and academicians and since then last one decade has appreciated considerable number of studies.

Limitations of Study

Our study has recognized a few limitations. They are discussed as follows:

- The study is review of literature in nature so we have not offered detailed propositions linking the elements, which would be a logical next step.
- Scopus assigns one-unit value to each author, study, institution, country, and publication. This implies that one study has an author; it will have the same value as if it had two or more authors.
- Database like Web of Science, EBSCO, PROQUEST are not considered while filtering out the necessary articles.
- The study has not discussed the conceptual model and proposed relationship between the identified factors.

Future Implications

- In future we wish to develop the conceptual model and define the relationship between identified factors of digital finance and its impact on financial inclusion through empirical relationship.
- The relationship between Digital Financial Inclusion and its applicability for the business organizations and individuals can be further explored.
- The role of digital finance in a global economy can be explored as there is a growing attention across the globe about digital economy.

REFERENCES

Banerjee, A., Karlan, D., & Zinman, J. (2015). Six randomized evaluations of microcredit: Introduction and further steps. *American Economic Journal. Applied Economics*, *7*(1), 1–21. doi:10.1257/app.20140287

Chisadza, C., & Biyase, M. (2023). Financial development and income inequality: Evidence from advanced, emerging and developing economies. *Annals of Financial Economics*, *18*(01), 2241002. doi:10.1142/S2010495222410020

Dabla-Norris, E., Ji, Y., Townsend, R., & Unsal, F. (2015). Identifying constraints to financial inclusion and their impact on GDP and inequality: A structural framework for policy (IMF Working Paper No. 15/22). doi:10.5089/9781498381598.001

Demirguc-Kunt, A., Klapper, L., & Randall, D. (2013). *The global Findex database* (No. 8). Note.

Demirgüç-Kunt, A., Klapper, L., Singer, D., & Ansar, S. (2022). *The Global Findex Database 2021: Financial inclusion, digital payments, and resilience in the age of COVID-19*. World Bank Publications. doi:10.1596/978-1-4648-1897-4

Dwivedi, R., Alrasheedi, M., Dwivedi, P., & Starešinić, B. (2022). Leveraging financial inclusion through technology-enabled services innovation: A case of economic development in India. *International Journal of E-Services and Mobile Applications*, *14*(1), 1–13. doi:10.4018/IJESMA.289633

Geng, Z., & He, G. (2021). Digital financial inclusion and sustainable employment: Evidence from countries along the belt and road. *Borsa Istanbul Review*, *21*(3), 307–316. doi:10.1016/j.bir.2021.04.004

Huang, W., Gu, X., Lin, L., Alharthi, M., & Usman, M. (2023). Do financial inclusion and income inequality matter for human capital? Evidence from sub-Saharan economies. *Borsa Istanbul Review*, *23*(1), 22–33. doi:10.1016/j.bir.2022.09.002

Imai, K. S., Gaiha, R., Thapa, G., & Annim, S. K. (2012). Microfinance and poverty—A macro perspective. *World Development*, *40*(8), 1675–1689. doi:10.1016/j.worlddev.2012.04.013

Khan, F., Siddiqui, M. A., & Imtiaz, S. (2022). Role of financial literacy in achieving financial inclusion: A review, synthesis and research agenda. *Cogent Business & Management*, *9*(1), 2034236. doi:10.1080/23311975.2022.2034236

Mialou, A., Amidzic, G., & Massara, A. (2017). Assessing countries' financial inclusion standing–a new composite index. *Journal of Banking and Financial Economics*, *2*(8), 105–126. doi:10.7172/2353-6845.jbfe.2017.2.5

Ozili, P. K. (2021, October). Financial inclusion research around the world: A review. *The Forum for Social Economics*, *50*(4), 457–479. doi:10.1080/07360932.2020.1715238

Ozturk, I., & Ullah, S. (2022). Does digital financial inclusion matter for economic growth and environmental sustainability in OBRI economies? An empirical analysis. *Resources, Conservation and Recycling*, *185*, 106489. doi:10.1016/j.resconrec.2022.106489

Park, C. Y., & Mercado, R. (2015). Financial inclusion, poverty, and income inequality in developing Asia. Asian Development Bank Economics Working Paper Series, (426).

Park, C. Y., & Mercado, R. Jr. (2018). Financial inclusion, poverty, and income inequality. *The Singapore Economic Review*, *63*(01), 185–206. doi:10.1142/S0217590818410059

RBI. (2020). National Strategy for Financial Inclusion (NSFI): 2019-2024. Retrieved 11/10/2023, 2023, from Reserve Bank of India - Press Releases (rbi.org.in)

Tay, L. Y., Tai, H. T., & Tan, G. S. (2022). Digital financial inclusion: A gateway to sustainable development. *Heliyon*, *8*(6), e09766. doi:10.1016/j.heliyon.2022.e09766 PMID:35785228

Ullah, S., Ali, K., Shah, S. A., & Ehsan, M. (2022). Environmental concerns of financial inclusion and economic policy uncertainty in the era of globalization: Evidence from low & high globalized OECD economies. *Environmental Science and Pollution Research International*, *29*(24), 36773–36787. doi:10.1007/s11356-022-18758-2 PMID:35064882

United Nations. (2021). The Imperative of Financial Inclusion. Retrieved on from 11/10/2023, Financial Inclusion | United Nations | UNSGSA Queen Máxima.

World Bank. (2021a). The Drive for Financial Inclusion: Lessons of World Bank Group Experience. Retrieved 11/10/2023, 2023, from ap_driveforfinancialinclusion.pdf (worldbankgroup.org).

World Bank (2021b). The Global Findex Database 2021 Financial Inclusion, Digital Payments, and Resilience in the Age of COVID-19. Retrieved 13/10/2023, from 9781464818974 (1).pdf

World bank. (2022a). Financial inclusion is a key enabler to reducing poverty and boosting prosperity.Retrieved 13/10/2023, from Financial Inclusion Overview (worldbank.org).

World Bank. (2022b). COVID-19 Drives Global Surge in use of Digital Payments. Retrieved 11/10/2023, 2023, from COVID-19 Drives Global Surge in use of Digital Payments (worldbank.org).

Zhang, Q., & Posso, A. (2019). Thinking inside the box: A closer look at financial inclusion and household income. *The Journal of Development Studies*, *55*(7), 1616–1631. doi:10.1080/00220388.2017.1380798

Chapter 5
Central Bank Digital Currency:
What It Can Achieve and Cannot Achieve in Africa

Peterson K. Ozili
https://orcid.org/0000-0001-6292-1161
Central Bank of Nigeria, Nigeria

ABSTRACT

This chapter presents a discussion on what a central bank digital currency (CBDC) can achieve in African countries and what a central bank digital currency may not achieve in African countries. The study shows that a central bank digital currency can achieve the following: CBDC can become a monetary policy tool; it can reduce the size of the informal economy; it can increase financial inclusion; it can increase digital financial literacy; it can reduce the circulation of counterfeit paper money; it can deepen existing payments system; it can improve social programmes and targeted welfare; it will increase transaction monitoring and surveillance; it can address tax evasion and increase tax revenue in African countries. The study also shows that a central bank digital currency may not completely replace cash in African countries; the issuance and use of CBDC won't make African countries earn a 'developed country' status; CBDC adoption may not stop institutional corruption; CBDC adoption will not stop illicit activities in African countries; and CBDC adoption may not reduce the level of poverty in African countries.

DOI: 10.4018/979-8-3693-1503-3.ch005

1. INTRODUCTION

The rapid rise of private digital currencies or cryptocurrencies, and the widespread adoption of private digital currencies by citizens in African countries, particularly in Nigeria and Kenya, have led African monetary authorities to assess the risks associated with using private digital currencies as a medium of exchange for economic activities. The monetary authorities in many African countries have raised concerns that private digital currencies or cryptocurrencies are too volatile which make them unfit to be used as money, and that cryptocurrencies are often used to hide illegal and criminal activities. The monetary authorities in North African countries have responded to the threat posed by cryptocurrencies by placing an outright ban on cryptocurrencies such as Egypt, Morocco, and Algeria. Meanwhile, the central bank in other African countries have either barred regulated financial institutions from facilitating cryptocurrency transactions such as Nigeria or have issued warnings about the risks of cryptocurrencies such as South Africa, Kenya, Uganda, Tanzania, Ghana, Tunisia and Rwanda. Although some African central banks resist cryptocurrency, they have been quite open-minded about the idea of issuing a central bank digital currency. A central bank digital currency is digital money issued by the central bank and is a liability of the issuing central bank (Ward and Rochemont, 2019; Ozili, 2023a).

Monetary authorities in some African countries have begun to research central bank digital currency, and plan to adopt a national central bank digital currency in the future as a counter-reaction to cryptocurrency while harnessing the potential benefits of a central bank digital currency for their economies. Analysts have offered mixed opinions on whether central bank digital currencies will become successful or a total failure (Ozili, 2024a). Some have argued that developed countries, such as Australia, Canada, and the United States, that have a fast, efficient, and reliable payment system infrastructure do not need a central bank digital currency as it will be a duplication of existing wholesale and retail payment products (Bjerg and Nielsen, 2018). Others have argued that adopting a central bank digital currency can allow central banks to bypass financial intermediaries to reach the people, but the consequence is that the future of financial intermediaries in the financial system may become uncertain (Wang and Gao, 2024). Others have also argued that adopting a central bank digital currency can save money for the government by reducing the cost of printing and managing cash or paper money (Babin et al, 2022). Despite these arguments, many central banks, such as the Reserve Bank of India, Bank of Ghana, the Central Bank of Tanzania, etc., have shown interest in issuing a central bank digital currency so as not to be left behind in the race to issue to a central bank digital currency.

In Africa, many central banks have shown interest in adopting a central bank digital currency (Ozili, 2023b), particularly, Nigeria, South Africa, Ghana, and Senegal. Most central banks in the region are studying central bank digital currency to understand it, to determine the best use case of CBDC, and to determine the design features that meet the payments need of their countries. Policy makers in African countries also want to understand what a CBDC can achieve and what a CBDC may not achieve in African countries. Such understanding is important as it can help to tame the over-optimism that is evident among CBDC enthusiasts in central bank policy circles in African countries. Consequently, the objective of this article is to discuss what a central bank digital currency (CBDC) can achieve in African countries and what a central bank digital currency may not achieve in African countries.

The discussion in this article contributes to the scant literature on central bank digital currency in African countries. Studies in this literature include Foster et al (2021), Edwards (2021) and Ozili (2022a). Focusing on African countries, this study presents a clear depiction of what a central bank digital currency can achieve in African countries and what a central bank digital currency may not achieve in African countries. Second, this study contributes to the monetary economics literature that examine non-traditional forms of money. Studies in this literature include Wang and Yip (1992), Rochon (1999) and Lucarelli (2011). This study shows that central bank digital currency is an alternative form of money which African countries can use as a medium of exchange and in settlement of debt.

The rest of the article is organized as follows. Section 2 presents the literature review. Section 3 presents the discussion on what a central bank digital currency can achieve in African countries. Section 4 presents the discussion on what a central bank digital currency may not achieve in African countries. Section 5 concludes.

2. LITERATURE REVIEW

There are very few studies on CBDC in developing countries. The reason for this is because CBDC is still a relatively new concept in developing countries. Náñez Alonso et al (2020) show that a reason for issuing a central bank digital currency in developing countries is to expand access to financial services to several geographical locations. Priyadarshini and Kar (2021) suggest that CBDC could offer developing countries a digital safety net and higher financial inclusion. Lee (2020) shows that financial inclusion is a primary motivation for issuing a central bank digital currency in emerging countries, and that for it to achieve success, there needs to be technical advancement in offline adaptability, identity management and traceability. Ozili (2022b) suggests that CBDC can increase financial inclusion by digitizing value chains, improving access to digital financial services, enlarging the digital economy, enhancing the efficiency of digital payments, and offering low transaction cost.

Foster et al (2021) identify the difficulty that may arise when the CBDC of a developing country is tied to foreign reserves. They argue that if a CBDC is pegged to a foreign currency, it could increase asymmetries in the international monetary system by reducing monetary policy autonomy in foreign economies. For instance, if a foreign government's CBDC is available in developing economies that have better control of monetary policy, but higher inflation, it is likely that the foreign government's CBDC could gradually substitute the local currency and have a negative impact on developing countries (Foster et al, 2021). In short, the developing economies' central banks would lose control of money supply because of gradual currency substitution, impacting sustainable development of that country (Foster et al, 2021).

Laboure (2021a) shows that, compared to CBDC, cryptocurrencies are gaining more attention in developing countries and are greatly benefiting from network effects. This means that the more people use it, the more valuable it becomes. Laboure et al (2021b) shows that the network effect is stronger in developing countries where payment systems are not efficient, and a significant part of the population do not have broad access to traditional financial services. Camara et al (2018) suggest that developing countries must consider some important factors when adopting a CBDC such as the level of informality, the costs associated with issuing and transporting cash, the penetration of mobile and data networks, the level of digital literacy, the degree of financial exclusion, among others.

Killingland and Dahl (2018) argue that developing countries should not issue a CBDC because they have weak institutions and low financial stability compared to developed countries. They further argue that members of the public may not accept a CBDC as an alternative to cash payments. Oh and Zhang (2020) emphasize that CBDC may not be accepted because households in developing countries value the anonymity in cash transactions and they do not want all their payments to be monitored by the government. In contrast, digital money such as a CBDC is likely to be traceable and subject to government monitoring, and for this reason, households in developing countries will prefer to use cash and are less likely to adopt and use CBDC widely. Oxford Analytica (2021) show that cash still dominates in many nations and CBDC adoption will be slower where people are reluctant to lose the anonymity of cash payments.

Duho et al (2022) explore the opportunities and risks of issuing a central bank digital currency in Ghana. They show that the Ghana e-Cedi can support monetary policy, ensure efficient payments, and increase financial inclusion. They also show that the e-Cedi could disrupt the financial system, reduce the use of physical cash and banking services among the uneducated, and the eCedi may be exposed to risks such as cyber-insecurity, and loss of privacy. Bludnik (2023) also argues that the use of a central bank digital currency in African countries, especially in Nigeria, will be difficult and that the risks associated with central bank digital currencies outweigh the benefits. Ahiabenu (2022) compares the central bank digital currency of Nigeria and Ghana and show that the two central bank digital currencies have more similarities than differences. However, the author notes the differences in central bank digital currency deployment, risk profiles, and plans. The author further notes that both Nigeria and Ghana have not developed legal and regulatory environments for central bank digital currency. Kumah (2024) compares the behaviour of Bitcoin and the fiat currencies of six African countries (i.e., Egyptian Pound, Cedi, ZAR, Naira, Rupee and Dinar) from 10th August 2015 to 31 December 2022. The author finds that, except for ZAR, Bitcoin is observed to be a viable alternative currency to the African currencies. Ozili (2023b), in a survey, showed that at least 14 African countries are interested in issuing a central bank digital currency, 13 African countries have announced that they are researching central bank digital currency, 4 African countries have reached the pilot test stage of issuing a central bank digital currency while only one African country has formally issued a central bank digital currency. Ozili (2023b) further argued that the reason for the low interest in central bank digital currency in African countries is due to the strong preference for cash payments, lack of a robust payment system, low use of digital payments, central banks' focus on other priorities, fear of failure, lack of government interest in digital currency and concerns about CBDC privacy risk and security threats.

3. WHAT CENTRAL BANK DIGITAL CURRENCY CAN ACHIEVE IN AFRICA

3.1. Interest-Bearing CBDC Can Become a Monetary Policy Tool

An interest-bearing CBDC is a central bank digital currency that pays interest on CBDC holdings. One important benefit of interest-bearing CBDC is that it can become a very effective monetary policy tool. When there is excess money supply in the economy, the central bank can reduce money supply by increasing the interest paid on CBDC holdings. This will mop-up the excess money in circulation in the commercial banking system as more people and businesses will increase their CBDC holdings and decrease their bank deposit balances (Ozili, 2024b). This will reduce the volume of bank lending, reduce money supply in the commercial banking system and decrease inflation. When there is too little money supply, the central bank can increase money supply by decreasing the interest paid on CBDC holdings. This will lead to CBDC-to-bank deposit migration as people will convert their CBDC holdings back to cash and keep them as deposit with banks. This will increase bank deposits and lead to increase in money supply in the commercial banking system and increase the volume of bank lending.

3.2. Reduce the Size of the Informal Economy

The informal economy or the black economy is where unregulated and unmonitored economic activities take place. Most financial transactions in the informal economy are cash-based transactions. Widespread CBDC adoption in African countries can reduce the size of the informal economy by reducing the supply of paper money or 'cash' in the hands of informal economic agents. The reduction in the supply of 'cash' would starve the informal economy of the cash it needs to survive. This will compel informal agents to use digital currency or digital payments for their transactions and will bring informal economic agents and their transactions into the formal sector, thereby, reducing the size of the informal economy.

3.3. CBDC Can Increase Financial Inclusion

Financial inclusion is one of the many benefits of issuing a central bank digital currency. Financial inclusion involves bringing unbanked adults into the formal financial sector so that they can have access to basic financial services which they can use to improve their welfare (Ozili, 2021; Ozili, 2018). The adoption of central bank digital currencies can increase financial inclusion in African countries by: (i) improving access to digital financial services, (ii) permitting people to hold CBDC even if they do not own a formal bank account, (iii) designing CBDC to have offline features so that people can perform CBDC transactions without internet connectivity, and (iv) low transactions cost. This suggests that the ability of CBDC to increase financial inclusion in African countries depends on CBDC design. In other words, the CBDC must be designed to have features that promote financial inclusion (Ozili, 2022b).

3.4. CBDC Adoption Will Increase Digital Financial Literacy

Central bank digital currency is one of many digital payment innovations. Just like every other innovation, people who want to use innovative products and services will have to learn how they work and how they can be used to meet their needs (Mallinson, 2021). Similarly, people who want to hold or use central bank digital currency in African countries will have to learn about central bank digital currency and how to hold a central bank digital currency in a wallet or token. They will also learn about how to download and install the CBDC app on their smart phones, and how to transfer CBDC from one party to another party. They will also learn about how to secure their CBDC account from unauthorized access. This means that the willingness to use central bank digital currency in African countries will drive people to learn more about central bank digital currency, thereby increasing their level of digital financial literacy. Some African citizens will gain basic knowledge about central bank digital currency. Other African citizens who are not contented with basic knowledge about central bank digital currency will seek to gain a deeper knowledge of central bank digital currency including digital money management skills and cybersecurity risk mitigation skills. Therefore, it is fair to say that central bank digital currency is a good thing because it can motivate people to become digital financial literate especially people who are willing to use CBDC. When this happens, it can increase the level of digital financial literacy in African countries and for the African continent.

3.5. CBDC Can Stop the Circulation of Counterfeit Paper Money

Much of the counterfeit paper money circulating in some African countries can be found in the informal sector where unregulated and illegal economic activities take place. Widespread usage of central bank digital currency in African countries can help to reduce the circulation of counterfeit paper money. Adopting central bank digital currency can make African central banks reduce the stock of printed paper money. The reduction in the stock of printed paper money will make paper money become limited in supply and it will reduce the opportunities to counterfeit paper money. This is because counterfeit paper money will become easy to detect when paper money becomes very limited in supply. On the other hand, central bank digital currency will be difficult to counterfeit because of its unique design features. Therefore, it is possible that the widespread adoption of central bank digital currency can reduce the circulation of counterfeit paper money.

3.6. CBDC Adoption Can Deepen Existing Payments System

The adoption of CBDC can improve and deepen the existing payments system by upgrading the entire digital payments infrastructure, introducing new payments technology, and the emergence of new Fintech players and payment system providers. The adoption of CBDC will, over time, facilitate the digitization of value chains in the economy. It will give businesses access to unlimited wholesale CBDC and encourage businesses to bring their activities into the digital financial system, thereby, enlarging the digital economy. CBDC can also lead to improved access to digital financial services and greater efficiency of digital payments.

3.7. CBDC Can Improve Social Programmes and Targeted Welfare

A CBDC in an African country can be used to fund social programmes to ensure that the basic needs of citizens are met. For example, CBDC can be used to fund local social programmes, state social programmes and federal social programmes such as health insurance, food assistance, housing subsidies, energy and utilities subsidies, and education and childcare assistance. This means that CBDC can play an important role in offering social security to African citizens. Also, CBDC can make it possible for the government to make targeted welfare payments to citizens directly, without needing any intermediary. This will reduce the cost of delivering welfare benefits to citizens in need of welfare support such as cash assistance. The absence of an intermediary means that citizens will receive their welfare disbursement into their CBDC wallet as quickly as possible.

3.8. CBDC Adoption Will Increase Transaction Monitoring and Surveillance

Central bank digital currency will enable African governments to effectively monitor all CBDC-based financial transaction in their countries. CBDC will increase government's monitoring and surveillance of all CBDC financial transactions and allow the government to make timely interventions to reduce frictions in existing payment systems, such as reducing the cost of CBDC transactions, and increasing the speed of CBDC transactions while ensuring finality of payments.

3.9. CBDC Can Address Tax Evasion and Increase Tax Revenue

When African countries fully adopt CBDC, 'tax evasion' will become more difficult to carry out since it would become impossible to use common methods, such as offshore banking, to hide financial activity from the central bank or the government. The absence of tax evasion means that the government will not lose tax revenue. Also, full adoption of CBDC in African countries will bring more economic activities into the formal economic system, and make such economic activities eligible to be taxed, thereby increasing the government's tax revenue.

3.10. CBDC Can Facilitate Remittance Inflows

A central bank digital currency can facilitate the inflow of remittances to African countries. Remittances into African countries are made through international money transfer operators who charge a fee ranging from 1 percent to 5 percent of the value of the remitted funds. Using CBDC to receive remittances can lower remittance transfer costs and make it easier for Africans working abroad to remit funds to their families back home. This can be done by obtaining central bank digital currency from international money transfer operators and transferring them to recipients in African countries at low-cost. Also, there will be a need to unify any disparity between the official and parallel exchange rates to enhance the incentives for using central bank digital currency to send remittances to African countries.

4. WHAT CENTRAL BANK DIGITAL CURRENCY MAY NOT ACHIEVE IN AFRICA

4.1. CBDC May Not Completely Replace Cash in African Countries

Presently, there is strong preference for cash over digital currency in many African countries particularly in East, West and Central African countries. This means that many people will continue to use cash even after a central bank digital currency is issued in African countries. What is more tenable in the region is that cash is likely to co-exist with central bank digital currency in African countries due to people's strong preference for cash in some African countries. However, a shift from cash to central bank digital currency in African countries will occur only if central bank digital currency offers more benefits to users than cash.

4.2. CBDC Adoption Won't Make African Countries Earn a 'Developed Country' Status

CBDC will revolutionize the payments system and expand digital financial services in African countries. However, it will not be enough to make African countries earn a "developed country" status. To earn a developed country status, African countries will need to address the poverty problem, increase GNP per capita, improve the standard of living of citizens, improve infrastructure, improve quality of life, develop their financial systems, and strengthen existing institutions.

4.3. CBDC Adoption Will Not Stop Institutional Corruption

Institutional corruption manifest when there is a systemic influence which may be legal, or even currently ethical, that undermines an institution's effectiveness by diverting it from its purpose or weakening its ability to achieve its purpose (Lessig, 2013). Adopting central bank digital currency may not stop institutional corruption in African countries because most institutionalized corruption often occur at the contract documentation stage, contract implementation stage and contract enforcement stage but not at the payment disbursement stage where contract payments can be made using central bank digital currency.

4.4. CBDC Adoption Will Not Stop Illicit Activities in African Countries

There are many illicit activities in African countries such as kidnapping for ransom, terrorism, smuggling or money laundering. These illicit activities are more pronounced in Sudan, Kenya, Mali, and Nigeria. Many of such illicit activities are carried out using cash. It has been argued that central bank digital currency can reduce cash-based illicit activities in African countries. The truth is that, while CBDC may reduce cash-based illicit activities, criminals will look for other sophisticated ways to engage in illicit activities when paper money is in limited supply due to widespread adoption of CBDCs. So, the argument that CBDC will reduce cash-based illicit activities in African countries is a weak argument.

4.5. CBDC May Not Reduce the Level of Poverty in African Countries

A central bank digital currency is just another medium of exchange or a means of payment. A central bank digital currency is not a welfare programme. It is not designed to be a welfare support system. Rather, it is designed to be an alternative payment solution. For this reason, a central bank digital currency does not have a 'direct' effect on the level of poverty in African countries. This is a very important distinction to make. A central bank digital currency may have an 'indirect' effect on the level of poverty because, arguably, a central bank digital currency can facilitate targeted welfare payment and increase financial inclusion for the poor, thereby empowering them to have access to finance which they can use to improve their well-being. But, these effects are 'indirect' effects of CBDC not a 'direct' effect of CBDC.

5. CONCLUSION

The purpose of this article was to discuss what a central bank digital currency can achieve in African countries and what a central bank digital currency may not achieve in African countries. This study showed that a central bank digital currency can achieve the following in African countries. A CBDC can become a monetary policy tool; it can reduce the size of the informal economy; it can increase financial inclusion; it can increase digital financial literacy; it can stop the circulation of counterfeit paper money; it can deepen existing payments system; it can improve social programmes and targeted welfare; it will increase transaction monitoring and surveillance; it can address tax evasion and increase tax revenue in African countries. On the other hand, the study showed that a CBDC may not achieve the following in African countries. A central bank digital currency may not completely replace cash in African countries; CBDC adoption won't make African countries earn a 'developed country' status; CBDC adoption may not stop institutional corruption; CBDC adoption will not stop illicit activities in African countries; and CBDC may not reduce the level of poverty in African countries.

Issuing a central bank digital currency in African countries is a big step towards payment system revolution for the African continent. It is recommended that the monetary authorities in African countries should understand the associated benefits, costs, and risks of issuing a CBDC. They should be ready to harness the full benefits of a central bank digital currency. While there is much expectation from a central bank digital currency, it is important for African bank central banks to understand what a central bank digital currency can achieve in African countries and what a central bank digital currency cannot achieve in African countries. Policy makers must understand the opportunities that central bank digital currency present, the foregone alternatives of issuing a central bank digital currency, and the limits of using a central bank digital currency. They should bear in mind that a central bank digital currency is, at best, an experiment. Therefore, it is yet to be seen whether central bank digital currency in African countries will become very successful and live up to its promise in African countries.

Future studies on CBDC in Africa can examine the socioeconomic effect of issuing a central bank digital currency in African countries. Such studies should assess the implications for poverty reduction and economic development. Such studies can offer insight into whether central bank digital currency can improve the general wellbeing of citizens in African countries.

REFERENCES

Ahiabenu, K. (2022). A comparative study of the design frameworks of the Ghanaian and Nigerian central banks' digital currencies (CBDC). *FinTech*, *1*(3), 235–249. doi:10.3390/fintech1030019

Babin, R., Smith, D., & Shah, H. (2022). Central bank digital currency: Advising the financial services industry. *Journal of Information Technology Teaching Cases*.

Bjerg, O., & Nielsen, R. H. (2018). *Who Should Make Kroner? A Review of Danmarks Nationalbank's Analysis of CBDC.* CBS Working Paper.

Bludnik, I. (2023). *Central bank digital currency and the cashless economy: The African experience.* Academic Press.

Camara, N., Dos Santos, E., Grippa, F., Sebastian, J., Soto, F., & Varela, C. (2018). *Central bank digital currencies: An assessment of their adoption in Latin America.* BBVA Researh Working Paper (No. 18/13).

Duho, K. C. T., Abankwah, S. A., Azu, G., Agbozo, D. A., Duho, V. S., & Atigodey, J. S. (2022). Central Bank Digital Currency in Ghana, the e-Cedi: Disruptions, Opportunities and Risks. Dataking Policy Brief, 6.

Edwards, S. (2021). *Central Bank Digital Currencies and The Emerging Markets: The Currency Substitution Challenge (No. w29489).* National Bureau of Economic Research. doi:10.3386/w29489

FosterK.BlakstadS.GaziS.BosM. (2021). Digital currencies and CBDC impacts on least developed countries (LDCs). The Dialogue on Global Digital Finance Governance Paper Series. doi:10.2139/ssrn.3871301

Killingland, M., & Dahl, L. B. (2018). Central bank digital currencies–fad or the future? a framework for country level assessment of central bank digital currencies (Master's thesis).

Kumah, S. P. (2024). Cryptocurrency and African fiat currencies: A peaceful coexistence? *Economic Notes*, *53*(1), e12229. doi:10.1111/ecno.12229

Laboure, M. (2021a). Corporate Bank Research: The Future of Payments: Series 2 – Part II. When Digital Currencies become Mainstream. Available from: https://research.db.com/Research/Article?rid=82185081-9b23-4f5a-8fd7-a454a9ee7b75-604&kid=RP0001&documentType=R&wt_cc1=IND-3015026-0000

Laboure, & Müller, Heinz, Singh, & Köhling. (2021b). Cryptocurrencies and CBDC: The Route Ahead. *Global Policy.* Advance online publication. doi:10.1111/1758-5899.13017

Lee, E. (2020). *Central bank digital currencies.* Economic Diplomacy Initiative, Harvard Kennedy School, Belter Centre.

Lessig, L. (2013). "Institutional corruption" defined. *The Journal of Law, Medicine & Ethics*, *41*(3), 553–555. doi:10.1111/jlme.12063 PMID:24088144

Lucarelli, B. (2011). *The economics of financial turbulence: alternative theories of money and finance*. Edward Elgar Publishing. doi:10.4337/9781849808798

Mallinson, D. J. (2021). Policy innovation adoption across the diffusion life course. *Policy Studies Journal: the Journal of the Policy Studies Organization*, *49*(2), 335–358. doi:10.1111/psj.12406

Náñez Alonso, S. L., Echarte Fernández, M. Á., Sanz Bas, D., & Kaczmarek, J. (2020). Reasons Fostering or Discouraging the Implementation of Central Bank-Backed Digital Currency. *A Review. Economies*, *8*(2), 41. doi:10.3390/economies8020041

Oh, E. Y., & Zhang, S. (2020). *Central bank digital currency and in-formal economy*. Working Papers in Economics & Finance, 2020-11.

Oxford Analytica. (2021). *Digital currencies mark a tectonic shift for banking*. Expert Briefings. doi:10.1108/OXAN-DB263446

Ozili, P. K. (2018). Impact of digital finance on financial inclusion and stability. *Borsa Istanbul Review*, *18*(4), 329–340. doi:10.1016/j.bir.2017.12.003

Ozili, P. K. (2021a). Financial inclusion research around the world: A review. *The Forum for Social Economics*, *50*(4), 457–479. doi:10.1080/07360932.2020.1715238

Ozili, P. K. (2022a). Central bank digital currency in Nigeria: opportunities and risks. In *The new digital era: digitalisation, emerging risks, and opportunities* (pp. 125–133). Emerald Publishing Limited. doi:10.1108/S1569-37592022000109A008

Ozili, P. K. (2022b). Can central bank digital currency increase financial inclusion? Arguments for and against. In *Big Data Analytics in the Insurance Market* (pp. 241–249). Emerald Publishing Limited. doi:10.1108/978-1-80262-637-720221013

Ozili, P. K. (2023a). Central bank digital currency research around the World: A review of literature. *Journal of Money Laundering Control*, *26*(2), 215–226. doi:10.1108/JMLC-11-2021-0126

Ozili, P. K. (2023b). A survey of central bank digital currency adoption in African countries. The Fourth Industrial Revolution in Africa: Exploring the Development Implications of Smart Technologies in Africa.

Ozili, P. K. (2024a). 100 Quotes about central bank digital currencies. Academic Press.

Ozili, P. K. (2024b). Central bank digital currency and the monetary policy and financial stability implications. In *Digital Currency Assets and Challenges to Financial System Stability* (pp. 52–62). IGI Global.

Priyadarshini, D., & Kar, S. (2021). Central Bank Digital Currency (CBDC): Critical Issues and the Indian Perspective. IEG Working Paper No. 44.

Rochon, L. P. (1999). *Credit, money, and production: an alternative post-Keynesian approach*. Edward Elgar Publishing. doi:10.4337/9781781959596

Wang, H., & Gao, S. (2024). The future of the international financial system: The emerging CBDC network and its impact on regulation. *Regulation & Governance*, *18*(1), 288–306. doi:10.1111/rego.12520

Wang, P., & Yip, C. K. (1992). Alternative approaches to money and growth. *Journal of Money, Credit and Banking*, *24*(4), 553–562. doi:10.2307/1992811

Ward, O., & Rochemont, S. (2019). *Understanding Central Bank Digital Currencies (CBDC)*. Institute and Faculty of Actuaries.

Chapter 6
Leveraging AI to Enhance the Global Mobility Experience:
Trends in Indian Higher Education

Shruti Bansal
M.M.H. College, Chaudhary Charan Singh University, India

Punjika Rathi
KIET Group of Institutions, India

Rachit Agarwal
https://orcid.org/0000-0003-0164-5292
Chandigarh University, India

Ramneek Ahluwalia
Chandigarh University, India

ABSTRACT

The study investigates how AI-driven solutions are revolutionizing student interactions, admissions processes, academic support, and cross-cultural adaptation. Through intelligent chatbots, personalized recommendations, and predictive analytics, universities are catering to individual needs and streamlining administrative procedures. Furthermore, AI-powered language translation tools are aiding international students in overcoming language barriers, fostering better communication, and enriching their learning experiences. In the Indian higher education landscape, this trend holds particular significance due to the nation's burgeoning student population and aspirations for global recognition. The chapter underscores the importance of continuous innovation, collaboration, and adaptability in integrating AI solutions effectively. By embracing these advancements, Indian universities can position themselves as attractive destinations for international

DOI: 10.4018/979-8-3693-1503-3.ch006

students, fostering diversity and cross-border learning. This study provides valuable insights into the symbiotic relationship between AI and global education mobility, accentuating the need for a dynamic approach to reshape the future of higher education on a global scale and helpful for policymakers to enhance the AI in higher education system.

INTRODUCTION

Global mobility in the context of higher education refers to the movement of students, researchers, and academic professionals across international borders to pursue educational and research opportunities. In recent years, advancements in artificial intelligence (AI) have significantly impacted various industries, and the field of education is no exception. ChatGPT, an AI-based conversational agent developed by OpenAI, is equipped with a sophisticated language model that empowers it to produce novel textual content in response to human instructions. The aforementioned technology, which was introduced in November of the previous year, may be used at no cost by those who own an OpenAI account (OpenAI, 2023). Nevertheless, the emergence of generative artificial intelligence (AI), exemplified as ChatGPT, has elicited apprehensions over its possible ramifications on many sectors and organisations. An area where ChatGPT might potentially be used is within the domain of higher education, wherein it offers a prospect to reassess the objective of evaluation and its ability to augment the process of learning. Instead of just relying on software for evaluation, educational institutions have the option to use ChatGPT as a tool to impart critical thinking skills, enhance writing abilities, and foster an understanding of the significance of artificial intelligence in contemporary society. ChatGPT is widely regarded as a useful instrument in fostering creative and inclusive pedagogical practises, facilitating both learning and evaluation processes, while also promoting a transformational approach to knowledge acquisition. In order to examine the prospective uses of ChatGPT in the context of higher education, it is essential to consider many domains. These domains include the generation of counterfeit citations, the creation of assignments, the facilitation of essay composition (Crawford et al., 2023), and the promotion of critical contemplation about the utilisation of artificial intelligence in society (van Dis et al., 2023). As academic institutions contemplate the consequences of AI chat systems, several educators have already included them into their assignments as a means to highlight their limits while examining the capabilities of this technology. The possible implications of ChatGPT on teaching and learning in higher education are being examined by universities, since its capabilities are extensive and have the potential to significantly alter the educational environment (Choi et al., 2023).

The goal of the branch of computer science known as artificial intelligence (AI) is to build machines with intellect similar to that of humans. Building machines that can think and learn like humans is at the heart of artificial intelligence. This calls for linguistic comprehension, pattern recognition, problem-solving, and judgement. Artificial intelligence is a broad field that encompasses many different technologies, including machine learning, natural language processing, robots, and more. AI has been incorporated more and more into the educational field, offering creative ways to improve teaching and learning. AI's potential in education is immense and is still expanding, ranging from personalised learning experiences to effective administrative procedures. Adaptive learning systems, intelligent tutoring systems, learning analytics, and educational data mining are a few applications of AI in education.

The application and scope of AI in education for international students must be explicitly defined by higher education institutions (Holmes & Tuomi, 2022). Universities may create theories and models that support the use of AI to maximise its benefits for all students and enhance the educational experience by carefully assessing the possible advantages and hazards of this technology. International students' educational experiences could be greatly improved by using artificial intelligence into higher education. To ensure that AI applications are applied to maximise their benefits and handle the particular demands and challenges of international students, careful analysis of the advantages and hazards is important. This study contributes to the continuing discussion on the use of AI in education and its trends in Indian Higher Education by examining present implementations of the technology, going through anticipated future advances, and addressing related issues.

Global Mobility in Higher Education

Global mobility is a critical component of modern higher education. It facilitates cross-cultural understanding, knowledge exchange, and the development of a global perspective. Indian students and scholars have increasingly participated in international mobility programs to gain exposure to diverse academic environments and enhance their career prospects. However, the traditional global mobility process faces challenges related to information dissemination, administrative procedures, and cultural adaptation.

Role of AI in Enhancing Global Mobility

AI technologies encompass a range of tools and applications, including natural language processing, machine learning, and data analytics. These technologies can be harnessed to improve the global mobility experience in several ways:

a. Information Access and Personalization

AI-powered chatbots and virtual assistants can provide real-time information to students regarding study abroad options, visa requirements, scholarship opportunities, and cultural insights. Personalized recommendations based on students' academic backgrounds, interests, and preferences can guide them toward suitable programs and destinations.

b. Application and Documentation Processes

AI-driven tools can streamline application processes by automating document verification, language proficiency assessments, and translation services. This reduces administrative burdens for both students and institutions, enabling quicker and more efficient application processing.

c. Predictive Analytics for Student Success

AI algorithms can predict students' likelihood of success in specific programs or countries based on historical data and academic profiles. This information assists students in making informed decisions about their mobility choices and institutions in offering appropriate support.

d. Cross-Cultural Adaptation and Support

AI-powered language learning applications, virtual cultural orientation programs, and communication platforms can help students adapt to new environments more effectively, enhancing their overall mobility experience.

e. Alumni and Network Engagement

AI can facilitate alumni engagement by suggesting relevant networking opportunities, career events, and mentorship connections, thereby enhancing the post-mobility outcomes for students.

Trends in Indian Higher Education and Global Mobility

a. Increased Outbound Mobility

The number of Indian students seeking international educational experiences has risen steadily. AI tools can address challenges such as information overload and provide tailored guidance for students considering mobility.

b. Collaboration Between Institutions

AI-driven platforms can facilitate collaborations between Indian and foreign universities, aiding in the development of joint programs, research initiatives, and faculty exchanges.

c. Skill Enhancement and Employability

AI-enabled education platforms can help students acquire skills aligned with the demands of the global job market, thereby enhancing their employability prospects.

d. Remote and Hybrid Mobility

The COVID-19 pandemic accelerated the adoption of remote and hybrid mobility models. AI technologies can enhance the quality of virtual mobility experiences by enabling personalized virtual exchanges and engagement.

Conceptual Framework

A comprehensive paper in this field is built on a conceptual framework for investigating the use of artificial intelligence (AI) in higher education, with a particular focus on Virtual Assistants, Automated Assessment, Intelligent Tutoring, and Personalised Learning. Understanding the function and effects of AI technology in higher education settings is made easier with the help of this framework. It is crucial to understand the linkages and potential synergies between different AI applications in higher education within this conceptual framework. For instance, virtual assistants can offer immediate assistance for individualised learning experiences, and automated assessment can give intelligent tutoring systems information to adjust their lesson plans and methods. To provide a thorough examination of the consequences of AI in higher education, ethical considerations, such as data protection, bias mitigation, and equity, should pervade every component of the framework. This conceptual framework ultimately acts as a research road map for AI applications in higher education. It promotes a

Figure 1. AI applications

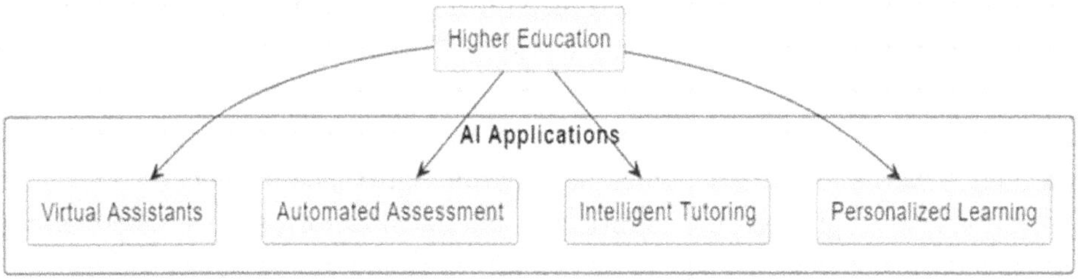

comprehensive viewpoint that takes into account the complex character of modern technologies, as well as its possible advantages, difficulties, and moral dilemmas. Researchers can contribute to a greater understanding of AI's revolutionary role in influencing the future of higher education by methodically researching Virtual Assistants, Automated Assessment, Intelligent Tutoring, and Personalised Learning within this framework.

AI in higher education is a comprehensive strategy that utilises artificial intelligence technology to improve teaching, learning, and administrative procedures in academic institutions. Essentially, this paradigm focuses on using AI tools and systems to customise educational experiences, optimise educational resources, and enable data-driven decision-making. AI-powered adaptive learning platforms have the ability to customise instructional content based on the unique requirements and learning styles of students. This promotes more student engagement and enhances academic performance. Intelligent tutoring systems offer individualised assistance and constructive criticism, enhancing conventional classroom teaching and fostering independent learning. In addition, AI-powered analytics empower instructors to get vital insights into student performance and development, permitting prompt intervention and focused interventions to successfully address learning gaps. From an administrative standpoint, AI technologies optimise and simplify repetitive duties like organising course schedules, evaluating student performance, and providing administrative assistance. This allows professors and staff to allocate more time and attention towards strategic projects and enhancing student support services.

LITERATURE REVIEW

In order to investigate the function of AI in the education of international students for this study, a thorough evaluation of the literature was carried out. Academic databases like JSTOR, ERIC, and Google Scholar were used to find scholarly articles, research papers, and reports. The study subject, the materials' freshness, and the publishing journal or institution's assessment of their trustworthiness all played a role in the selection process. The chosen texts were then subjected to a critical analysis to isolate significant themes and ideas. The study is categorised into four major variables of artificial intelligence contributing towards higher education such as virtual assistants, automated assessments, intelligent tutoring and personalized learning. Nevertheless, the theoretical structure of artificial intelligence (AI) in higher education also emphasises the significance of ethical factors, such as safeguarding privacy, ensuring transparency in algorithms, and addressing equity issues. This is done to guarantee that the integration of AI aligns with educational principles and fosters equal and inclusive access to learning opportunities. The conceptual framework of AI in higher education provides guidance for institutions aiming to use AI's transformational potential while maintaining ideals of justice, transparency, and student-centeredness in their educational processes.

Virtual Assistants

Virtual assistants are becoming more and more important in higher education and have the ability to improve the educational process. Here is a survey of the relevant literature on higher education and virtual assistants.

Dutsinma et al. (2022) does a thorough analysis of virtual assistant utilisation in higher education. The technology that powers them, as well as their usability and user experience, are the main topics. The paper suggests a taxonomy for categorising intelligent personal assistants. Gubareva et al. (2020) showed that the use of virtual assistants in education to streamline the learning process, better manage time, and boost motivation and engagement is explored in this research. The study offers perceptions into how virtual aides might improve the learning process. Hutson & Plate (2023) showed the impact of intelligent virtual assistants (IVAs) on education, particularly in the area of metacognition. The study emphasises how IVAs can assist students in acquiring metacognitive abilities. Curtis et al. (2021) literature on virtual health assistants for the prevention, management, or treatment of any physical or mental health condition is examined in this scoping overview of the field. The study sheds light on the virtual assistants' design traits and how they affect user experience. Cox (2021) in his study examined how literature-based design fictions can help us understand how AI and robotics will affect higher education. The study draws attention to the debates around the use of AI in education and how it might alter the learning process.

The research on AI applications in higher education is summarised in this systematic review. The study shows the potential for AI to improve learning and selects 146 papers for final synthesis (Zawacki Richter et al., 2019).

Automated Assessment

Higher education is becoming more and more relevant to automated evaluation, which has the ability to improve the assessment process. Here is a survey of the relevant literature on higher education and automated assessment.

Rawlusyk (2018) examined the question of whether assessment practises in higher education assist student learning, a topic of continuous academic concern. The study emphasised how crucial it is to match learning objectives with assessment, as well as the possibility for automated assessment to deliver prompt feedback. Crompton & Burke (2023) examined from 2016 to 2022, artificial intelligence (AI) in higher education. The paper emphasises how AI has the potential to improve evaluation through automated assessment, as well as the accessibility of massive student data and learning analytics.

This critical study does a systematic search of the best academic literature to determine how to advance research and analysis on AI. The study emphasised the value of coordinating assessment with learning objectives as well as the possibility of AI to improve the assessment process through automated assessment (Bearman et al., 2022). Crompton & Burke, (2023) in-depth analysis offers a novel look at AI in higher education from 2016 through 2022. The study emphasised the value of responsible implementation as well as the potential of AI to improve the evaluation process through automated assessment.

Intelligent Tutoring

Intelligent tutoring systems (ITS) have attracted a lot of interest in higher education because they have the ability to improve the educational process. Here is an overview of the literature on higher education and intelligent tutoring.

Nye (2015) emphasised how ITS has the ability to deliver personalised education and enhance learning results. The results of a thorough literature study on intelligent tutoring systems in developing countries were presented in this research. Wang et al. (2023) examined the applications of intelligent tutoring systems in actual educational environments. The study emphasised the difficulties in implementing and evaluating ITS as well as the promise of ITS to improve teaching and learning. The effect of intelligent tutoring systems on learning outcomes is investigated. The study emphasised how ITS has the ability to deliver personalised education and enhance learning results (Ma et al., 2014). Cox (2021) examined how literature-based design fictions can help us understand how artificial intelligence and robots will affect higher education. The study emphasises the debates around the use of AI in education and the potential for ITS to improve learning experiences.

Personalized Learning

Higher education has recognised the growing importance of personalised learning, which has the potential to improve the educational process. Here is a survey of the literature on higher education and personalised learning.

Walkington & Bernacki (2020) presented a special issue that contains research on initiatives to tailor learning across several academic disciplines. The study draws attention to the rise of personalised learning and the several definitions that outline its key characteristics. The contemporary research literature on personalised learning is reviewed. The study emphasised how crucial it is to address the need for a comprehensive definition of personalised learning that covers all of its various elements (Shemshack & Spector, 2020). The research on personalised learning is summarised. The study emphasised how crucial it is for teachers to modify their lessons in order to deliver diversified and individualised education based on learner needs (Bernacki et al., 2021).

AI is used in personalised learning experiences to develop learning materials that are specifically tailored to the learner's background and abilities, assuring relevance (Chaipidech et al., 2022); (Furini et al., 2022). This new approach has the ability to push students beyond their zones of proximal development while also giving international students useful examples that are relevant to their own cultures (Ballard & Butler, 2011) . Such a learning design would, however, have an impact on the educator's considerations for instructional design, as the AI would create learning experiences (lightening the load on the educator), but would also require more supervision for each student (increasing the need for individualised help) (Vandewaetere & Clarebout, 2014).

Ethical Consideration to AI

Within the domain of higher education, ethical questions regarding the use of artificial intelligence (AI) are of utmost importance. AI technologies have the potential to improve teaching, learning, and administrative operations. However, they also give rise to problems of privacy, equality, and prejudice. Institutions must prioritise maintaining openness in the utilisation of AI, guaranteeing that students and faculty comprehend the methods by which their data is gathered, used, and safeguarded. Furthermore, it is essential to establish protective measures to ensure that AI algorithms do not perpetuate prejudices or engage in discriminatory practices against certain populations. In order to effectively incorporate AI into education, institutions must actively participate in continuous dialogue and introspection to navigate the ethical challenges involved. This entails giving priority to principles such as fairness, accountability, and inclusivity, with the aim of creating an environment that maximizes the advantages of AI while minimizing potential risks.

Zeb et al. (2024) concluded that the use of AI technologies, namely ChatGPT, in higher education offers both advantageous prospects and complex obstacles. Universities may address these issues by adopting a proactive and ethical stance towards the usage of these technologies. This study proposes that colleges should create rules and protocols, and provide training and assistance, to identify and deter intents of academic dishonesty. AI has the capacity to profoundly revolutionise educational practices. However, in order to fully harness the advantages of AI in the educational sector, it is crucial to focus on integrating it effectively, resolving ethical issues, and adequately preparing students for future technological difficulties (Sarwar et al., 2024). The incorporation of ethical considerations is crucial in the process of developing and implementing artificial intelligence (AI) owing to the significant influence AI systems have on people, societies, and the wider global context. Artificial intelligence (AI) technologies have significant influence in moulding decision-making processes in numerous fields such as healthcare, finance, transportation, and education. In the absence of ethical constraints, AI systems pose a potential threat of propagating prejudices, violating privacy rights, or exacerbating pre-existing disparities. Furthermore, as artificial intelligence gains more autonomy, the likelihood of unforeseen repercussions or ethical quandaries grows. Hence, ethical deliberation guarantees the responsible development and utilisation of AI, prioritising ideals like as openness, impartiality, responsibility, and the welfare of humanity. By including ethical frameworks into the process of developing and implementing AI, we can cultivate trust, reduce potential dangers, and optimise the social advantages of this revolutionary technology.

AI in Education: Current Applications

According to (Seldon & Abidoye, 2018), integrating AI applications into education has the potential to completely transform the educational experience for overseas students. Since the applicability of this technology has rapidly advanced, there has been a noticeable surge in research on AI and education (Chichekian & Benteux, 2022). Additionally, AI-based learning may be adapted to help students from all backgrounds acquire the knowledge and skills that employers value (Santa Barletta et al., 2022). Through various computing technologies, including intelligent education, cutting-edge virtual learning, and data analysis and prediction, AI might potentially increase the value and effectiveness of learning (L. Chen et al., 2020). A significant area where AI is having an impact on education administration for international students is the creation of curricula and content as well as teaching and learning procedures (including examining assignments, grading, and providing feedback)

(X. Chen et al., 2020a). Platforms for interactive learning environments, including AI-assisted ACTIVE Math, MATHia, and Why2Atlas, have been implemented to track student progress, manage learning outcomes, enhance teaching resources, and support instructor-student communication and feedback (Chassignol, Khoroshavin, …, et al., 2018). Plagiarism detection, grading, and writing improvement are just a few of the administrative features provided by AI-powered programmes like Grammarly, Ecree, and PaperRater that might be useful to overseas students (Johnson et al., 2009).

The use of learner-centered AI applications, such as Deep Tutor and Auto Tutor, has been demonstrated to cultivate personalised and customised content based on the ability and requirements of the international learners, thereby improving the learning experience and potentially resulting in better learning outcomes for international students (Rus et al., 2013). The international students were pleased with their use of Google Translate for English writing to assess and enhance their level of ability. Additionally, gamification has improved the effectiveness and quality of learning for international students when combined with virtual reality and 3D technologies (Lee & Hammer, 2011).

Pokrivcakova (2019) further supported the idea that chatbots powered by machine learning algorithms AI could enhance students' learning experiences by tailoring course material to their needs and skills. Academic integrity is also promoted through the use of AI-based writing and revision tools like Turnitin and Pearson's Write-to-Learn (Sutton, 2019). (Crowe et al., 2017) stated that the tools would encourage students to use paper mill websites or platforms, endangering academic integrity and inciting dishonest behaviour. AI-powered translating and writing tools, voice recognition and dictation tools, and language learning tools can help international students whose home language is not English learn in English-speaking nations. For instance, Grammarly, a writing assistance programme, along with Google Translate, makes academic writing easier for international students, faculty members, and researchers (O'Neill & Russell, 2019); (Pratama, 2021). Similar programmes like ProWritingAid, Quillbot, and Ginger have a favorable effect on academic writing in English for students who are learning English (YÜCE, 2022); (Penelitian et al., 2023).

Teachers' Perception About AI

The perspectives of faculty members about the incorporation of AI in higher education differ significantly, encompassing a broad range of views that span from eagerness to doubt. Leoste et al. (2021) suggested that prior experience with supportive technology can help to build favorable attitudes and applications of such technologies in educational institutions. Faculty members held positive expectations regarding technologies and embraced them as means of enhancing their teaching practices. Conversely, discourse regarding the adverse consequences of AI's was minimal. In some other studies, teachers expect trainings on AI as well. They were interested to launch AI in the course curriculum but also want training to enhance their AI literacy (Wood et al., 2021). In Africa, in-service teachers also reported about training on existing AI and machine learning based tools for the uplift their skill standard (Sanusi et al., 2022). Furthermore, the involvement of teachers must be in designing of course curriculum based on AI, so that they can understand the real phenomenon about changing technologies. Teachers also emphasised the need of enhancing teachers' data literacy and fostering collegiality with AI. However, they also expressed the expectation for AI to possess Technological Pedagogical and Content Knowledge (TPACK) as well as dispute resolution abilities (Kim, 2023). Furthermore, educators have conveyed that the implementation of Internet of Things (IoT) in classrooms, the establishment of a structured curriculum for AI in education, ongoing professional development within schools, collaborations between research, practice, and policy, and the cultivation of a culture that promotes continuous learning and readiness for artificial intelligence are all of great importance.

Application Development for Academic Libraries

Academic libraries could undergo a considerable transformation as a result of current AI uses in education. According to (Cox et al., 2019), AI may have an impact on the search and recommendation systems, customization, text and data mining, and analytics used in libraries. Such innovations might improve library spaces' general usability and user experiences. Academic librarians are usually open to incorporating AI into their operations, according to research by (Lund et al., 2020) notwithstanding some hesitation in academia regarding AI adoption. They frequently use new information and communication technology before others do. According to (Yoon et al., 2022), AI is now a trustworthy replacement for some human services, helping with a variety of user services.

Amidst the COVID pandemic, the Department of School Education and Literacy, Ministry of Human Resources Development (MHRD) has introduced several initiatives to combat the crisis. These include Diksha, Swayam Prabha Channel, Shiksha Van, E- Pathshala, and National Repository of Open Educational Resources (NROER) (Singh et al., 2021). It is important to mention that in addition to the efforts made by the Indian central government, each state has implemented unique online education projects that are specifically designed to meet their individual needs.

Practical Implications for AI

The application of AI technology in higher education has brought about a new era of customized learning, streamlined administration, and inventive teaching approaches.

An important use case is seen in adaptive learning systems, where artificial intelligence algorithms examine students' learning patterns and customize course contents to match their particular demands, pace, and learning styles. This promotes a more interactive and efficient learning encounter, accommodating various student demographics. In addition, virtual assistants powered by artificial intelligence improve administrative work by handling questions, managing appointments, and offering direction for navigating the campus. This helps to save important staff time. Furthermore, the utilization of AI-powered analytics empowers institutions to effectively utilize large quantities of data to optimize the allocation of resources, forecast student results, and pinpoint areas that require improvement. Machine learning algorithms aid in detecting plagiarism, automating grading, and generating personalized feedback, so expediting assessment procedures while upholding academic integrity. In addition, the integration of artificial intelligence into virtual reality and augmented reality simulations provides students with immersive learning environments, enabling them to acquire hands-on experience in disciplines such as medicine, engineering, and architecture. These practical applications showcase the revolutionary capacity of AI in higher education, transforming conventional teaching and learning methods while empowering both teachers and students.

According to the OECD (2022), there is a growing trend of students seeking higher education and advancing through academic levels by studying in other countries. Remarkably, a little fraction of students may be classified as "internationally mobile," as stated by the OECD (Verbik & Lasanowski, 2007). On average, this group comprises just 5% of bachelor's degree students, 14% of master's degree students, and 24% of PhD students in OECD nations.The field of education administration for foreign students is significantly impacted by AI, which includes the automation of procedures and tasks, the development of curriculum and material, and the enhancement of teaching and learning processes (such as evaluating assignments, grading, and providing feedback (X. Chen et al., 2020b). In order to oversee academic accomplishments, monitor student progress, enhance instructional resources, facilitate communication and feedback among instructors and international students spanning various subject areas and level levels, interactive learning environment platforms have been integrated, including AI-assisted MATHia, Why2Atlas, and ACTIVE Math (Chassignol, Khoroshavin, Klimova, et al., 2018). AI-driven tools like Grammarly, Ecree, and PaperRater provide features like as plagiarism detection, grading, and writing enhancement, along with other administrative capabilities that might be advantageous for overseas students (Johnson et al., 2010). Foreign students whose primary language is not English and who are pursuing their studies in English-speaking nations may benefit from the use of language learning tools, voice recognition and dictation applications, and translators and writing tools propelled by artificial intelligence. One illustration of this is Grammarly, a writing support application that aids international students, faculty members, and researchers in their academic writing, in addition to Google Translate (ONeill & Russell, 2019). Imagine an overseas student who is trying to adapt to a new academic setting in a foreign country while also managing the challenges posed by cultural and linguistic disparities. Given the additional difficulties, it is essential for the student to have access to services that may facilitate their academic success. For instance, when a student has difficulty with a certain subject or task, a chatbot may serve as a valuable resource by offering prompt and precise answers to their inquiries. While the chatbot cannot substitute a professor's invaluable experience and counsel, it may function as an additional resource for students to use until they have the opportunity to meet with their professor during office hours. Utilising a chatbot enables overseas students to optimise their educational capabilities and remain aligned with their academic pursuits, while encountering language or cultural obstacles that restrict their direct interaction with their professor. Moreover, the chatbot offers a prompt and effective method of acquiring information. Furthermore, in some instances, the chatbot may have the capability to guide the learner towards pertinent resources or provide potential resolutions to intricate issues.

AI Applications' Limitations and Issues

The integration of AI in higher education has complex and extensive long-term consequences. AI has the ability to completely transform teaching and learning. It can personalise education experiences, increase student engagement, and improve academic achievements by using adaptive learning systems and intelligent tutoring (Rabbianty et al., 2023). Furthermore, administrative solutions powered by artificial intelligence may simplify processes, optimise the allocation of resources, and enhance the productivity of institutions. Nevertheless, these progressions also provide difficulties, such as worries about job displacement, ethical dilemmas regarding data privacy and algorithmic prejudice, and the necessity to enhance the skills of educators to proficiently use AI technology. In addition, the growing dependence on AI might potentially alter the responsibilities of educators, redirecting their attention towards mentoring, facilitating, and designing curriculum, rather than conventional teaching methods. In summary, the integration of AI in higher education has significant prospects for innovation and enhancement. However, it is essential to carefully evaluate its long-term consequences to ensure that it is in line with educational principles and objectives, and that it benefits all parties involved.

As using data to design learning experiences may necessitate gathering personal information that may be subject to legislation in their home countries, personalised learning experiences may pose privacy and security concerns for these students (Butcher et al., 2004). For international students, adaptive testing might potentially pose dangers, particularly with regard to language proficiency. For instance, employing algorithms to gauge question difficulty may not effectively represent a student's linguistic proficiency or capacity for understanding subtle wording. This could produce skewed test results that don't accurately reflect the student's skills or knowledge (T. Wang & Kolen, 2001). For international students, predictive analytics in education may potentially have ethical ramifications. For instance, identifying students who are at risk of failing or struggling can call for the use of information that is not appropriate to or relevant for international students, which could result in forecasts that are unreliable or deceptive. Additionally, there is a chance that the information used to create predictions may be governed by various privacy laws or rules in the users' native countries (Slade & Prinsloo, 2013). Last but not least, employing chatbots in education and research might spark questions about how language and cultural limitations may affect the reliability and accuracy of the information delivered (Lund et al., 2023).

DISCUSSION

Generative AI, Chatbots, Analytics, and International Student Success" provide insight into how AI can enhance international students' learning effectiveness in higher education. The function of AI in education and its possible effects on the educational experiences of foreign students are both examined in this essay. Among the main findings are:

AI Intelligence Chatbot: Using AI chatbots on platforms for higher education can enhance the educational experiences of students.

Generative AI: It has the potential to improve learning effectiveness because it includes AI systems producing new information.

Analytics: AI analytics can assist pinpoint areas for improvement and offer insightful information about students' learning habits.

Success of International Students: AI has the ability to help international students succeed in higher education.

These results help us comprehend how AI may improve the global mobility experience for Indian higher education students. Educational institutions may offer personalised learning experiences and assist the success of international students by utilising AI technologies like generative AI, chatbots, and analytics. India is positioned as a global source for AI expertise due to its growing adoption of AI and its rich talent pool in data and AI capabilities. The use of AI in higher education can promote personalised learning, increase learning effectiveness, and offer insightful data that is essential for student success. Universities may make the most of AI by actively specifying its application and scope (Pagano & Marengo, 2021). Higher education institutions can then assess the benefits and drawbacks of AI and decide how to best use it to meet the needs of their students (X. Chen et al., 2022). Although AI has the potential to revolutionise education for overseas students, it is critical to recognise the dangers and constraints involved (Alam, 2021). For instance, AI-powered tools may have trouble understanding accents, dialects, and constrained views of language and culture, which could make it harder for pupils to comprehend other viewpoints. Therefore, it's essential to strike a balance between using AI to improve the educational experience and maintaining the key function of human instructors. It is crucial to understand that artificial intelligence cannot take the role of human instructors' knowledge and leadership (X. Chen et al., 2022); (Zawacki Richter et al., 2019). Despite the potential advantages of AI in education for students from outside, it is not a cure-all. Although AI can offer helpful support and direction, it cannot entirely take the position of human educators in fostering students' academic and personal development. In order to improve the educational experience while maintaining the crucial function of human educators, higher education institutions must manage the usage of AI.

It is clear from comparing the study's findings to earlier research that the topic of integrating AI in education is one that is rapidly developing. The current uses of AI that are covered in this paper reflect important developments with the potential to improve learning effectiveness and offer personalised educational help. Recognising the drawbacks and dangers of AI technologies, such as privacy issues, cultural nuances, linguistic proficiency, and ethical ramifications, is crucial. The results of this study highlight the necessity for higher education institutions to actively define the use and reach of AI in education for Indian students. Institutions may guarantee that AI technologies are adopted to maximise their benefits and address the unique requirements and problems of Indian students by carefully weighing the advantages and hazards. Overall, the study shows how AI has the power to revolutionise the learning environment for international students in higher education and emphasises the significance of utilising AI technology to improve global mobility in Indian higher education.

CONCLUSION

Finally, the introduction of artificial intelligence in India's higher education sector has an important promise to revolutionize learning. It is impossible to overestimate the revolutionary power of AI-driven solutions, from personalized learning to effective administrative procedures. However, caution is required to address the social repercussions of this. India's higher education can use the power of artificial intelligence to significantly improve global mobility experience by focusing on data protection, promoting diversity and investing in skills development to reduce the possibility of job displacement. The entire promise of artificial intelligence in this environment can only be realized through the delicate balance of innovation, ethics and flexibility, so that students, educators and administrators benefit from a more integrated and enriching educational journey.

In conclusion, incorporating artificial intelligence (AI) into Indian higher education has the potential to completely change how students perceive international travel. A number of noteworthy factors are influencing how AI is affecting higher education in India and, as a result, how students who are interested in studying abroad will experience mobility. First and foremost, AI-driven personalization and recommendation algorithms aid students in selecting the best study abroad programme for them. The decision-making process can be streamlined and a better fit between students and schools is ensured by AI, which can adjust recommendations to specific student preferences, academic ambitions, and financial limits by analysing large amounts of data. Additionally, personalised content distribution, adaptive learning platforms, and intelligent tutoring systems are all ways that AI is improving the learning experience. This not only raises the standard of education in India but also gives students the information and abilities they need to succeed in worldwide academic settings.

Furthermore, the value of AI in removing bureaucratic obstacles and streamlining administrative procedures cannot be overstated. The shift to studying abroad is becoming easier and more effective thanks to AI-powered chatbots and virtual assistants that streamline visa applications, enrollment procedures, and even offer vital advice on accommodations and cultural adaption. Another encouraging development is how AI could improve international networking chances for Indian students and research collaborations. AI can locate new collaborators, sources of financing, and conferences, allowing students to broaden their academic horizons and participate in global research projects.The problems and ethical issues that come with the growing use of AI in higher education must be acknowledged, though. To guarantee equal access to AI-driven advantages, concerns like data privacy, algorithmic bias, and the digital gap must all be resolved.

In conclusion, trends in AI use within Indian higher education are poised to greatly improve students' experiences with global mobility. AI is changing how students interact with chances for international higher education by providing personalised assistance, enhancing learning results, streamlining administrative procedures, and encouraging international partnerships. As these trends develop, it is essential for educators, policymakers, and institutions to collaborate in order to fully utilise AI while protecting students' interests and rights. This will ultimately result in a brighter future for Indian students looking to study abroad.

Limitations of the Study

The study largely focuses on the higher education landscape in India, and while it provides insightful information for this particular location, there may be major differences in how well these trends apply to other nations or regions. The impact and uptake of AI in higher education can be influenced by the different educational systems, cultural norms, and legal frameworks that exist in various nations. The ethical and social ramifications of AI deployment in Indian higher education may not be fully covered by the study. These intricate problems, like privacy issues, fairness concerns, and cultural consequences, might call for deeper investigation outside the purview of this study. Even though the study pinpoints existing tendencies, it may not be able to precisely forecast future advancements in AI and education. The subject of artificial intelligence is developing quickly, and unanticipated technology advances or modifications to educational laws and practises may have a big impact on where AI goes in higher education.

It is important to understand the research study's limitations in terms of generalizability, data accessibility, ethical considerations, and the dynamic nature of AI and education, even though it offers insightful information about trends and the potential of leveraging AI to improve the global mobility experience in Indian higher education. When translating the findings to real-world decision-making and future research endeavours, researchers and policymakers should be mindful of these limitations.

Implications

Indian higher education institutions are increasingly integrating artificial intelligence to improve the experience of global mobility, which has exciting potential and important social impacts. Moreover, AI-powered solutions can tailor learning experiences, accelerate administrative procedures, and promote intercultural links, improving the educational experience of international students. These developments also raise questions about data privacy, equity and the possibility of automation replacing the work of administrative personnel. To ensure that global mobility experiences are inclusive, ethical and transformative for all stakeholders, a balance must be found between using AI's benefits and managing its social implications.

The effects on the educational field are significant. AI-driven improvements to the experience of international travel may also apply to domestic education. Indian higher education institutions can include personalised learning, adaptable curricula, and intelligent tutoring technologies to enhance learning results for students all around the nation. Investments in AI technologies and educator training should be given top priority by educators and politicians in order to promote a more flexible and dynamic educational system. There will be several prospects for innovation and growth in the technology sector. Higher education is a growing sector for AI applications. By creating goods and services specifically for Indian institutions, tech companies that specialise in AI solutions for education can prosper. This might result in efforts for research and development, the creation of new jobs, and an overall improvement of the ecosystem for technology.

The study's ramifications in terms of economics are extensive. More Indian students may pursue prospects for international education if the global mobility experience is made simpler for them. Increased foreign exchange inflow will result from this, spurring economic expansion. Additionally, the creation and export of AI-based educational technologies has the potential to evolve into a successful sector, strengthening India's position in the global technology market. Equally important are the societal effects. Improved global mobility opportunities promote cross-cultural exchange and international engagement, broadening Indian students' viewpoints. This may lead to a society that is more connected and aware of the world around it. To make sure that the advantages of AI in education are available to all facets of society, it is essential to address ethical issues surrounding AI, such as data privacy and algorithmic prejudice. To fully realise the promise of AI in higher education, government agencies and educational authorities should be central in developing the laws and policies. They should take into account problems like data security, student privacy, and fair access to AI-driven learning tools. It is crucial to have a legal system that supports innovation while defending students' rights and interests.

Therefore, utilising AI to improve the global mobility experience in Indian higher education has far-reaching and revolutionary ramifications. Adopting AI technologies can improve educational standards, spur economic expansion, and create a society that is more aware of the world around it. To guarantee that every student has access to the opportunities provided by AI-driven education, these advantages must be matched with ethical governance and a focus on equity.

Future Scope of Study

Future studies should examine how improvements generated by AI may affect Indian students' experiences travelling abroad in the long run. Studying students who have benefited from AI-supported decision-making and learning includes looking at their academic and career outcomes as well as their cultural and personal growth. Gaining insight into how AI affects a student's complete educational experience can be quite beneficial. Research might look into the creation of AI-driven career advising systems as an extension of the usage of AI for educational decision-making. These tools can assist students in matching their academic preferences with potential future employment possibilities both domestically and abroad. It will be crucial to evaluate how well these technologies promote successful job changes.

Research should concentrate on the changing ethical and data privacy problems as AI continues to play a significant role in higher education. Studies can look at how organisations and decision-makers might find a balance between using AI's promise and defending students' rights and privacy. This entails looking at recommended practises, rules, and compliance requirements. Future studies can look into how AI can help students who are studying abroad adapt to unfamiliar social and cultural settings. The efficiency of AI-driven solutions for language acquisition, cultural sensitivity instruction, and mental health support in fostering student achievement in international contexts can be researched.

Another intriguing direction is to investigate how AI can promote worldwide faculty cooperation and research alliances. Research can look at the ways in which AI can find research synergies, recommend suitable collaborators, and simplify the administrative parts of cross-border research projects. It can be beneficial to comprehend how AI affects innovation and research productivity. Beyond conventional higher education, there is a bright future for education. Research can look into how AI can promote ongoing education and lifetime learning, as well as professional growth and upskilling for working professionals. Investigations may focus on credential recognition in various global contexts and AI-driven personalised learning routes.

REFERENCES

Alam, A. (2021). Possibilities and Apprehensions in the Landscape of Artificial Intelligence in Education. *2021 International Conference on Computational Intelligence and Computing Applications, ICCICA 2021*. 10.1109/ICCICA52458.2021.9697272

Ballard, J., & Butler, P. (2011). Personalised learning: Developing a Vygotskian framework for e-learning. *International Journal of Technology, Knowledge and Society*, *7*(2), 21–36. doi:10.18848/1832-3669/CGP/v07i02/56198

Bearman, M., Ryan, J., & Ajjawi, R. (2022). Discourses of artificial intelligence in higher education: A critical literature review. *Higher Education*, *86*(2), 369–385. doi:10.1007/s10734-022-00937-2

Bernacki, M. L., Greene, M. J., & Lobczowski, N. G. (2021). A Systematic Review of Research on Personalized Learning: Personalized by Whom, to What, How, and for What Purpose(s)? *Educational Psychology Review*, *33*(4), 1675–1715. doi:10.1007/s10648-021-09615-8

Butcher, A. (2004). International students in New Zealand: Needs and responses. *International Education Journal, 5*(4).

Chaipidech, P., Srisawasdi, N., Kajornmanee, T., & Chaipah, K. (2022). A personalized learning system-supported professional training model for teachers' TPACK development. *Computers and Education: Artificial Intelligence*, *3*, 100064. Advance online publication. doi:10.1016/j.caeai.2022.100064

Chassignol, M., Khoroshavin, A., Klimova, A., & Bilyatdinova, A. (2018). U. (2018). Artificial Intelligence trends in education: A narrative overview. *Procedia Computer Science*, *136*, 16–24. doi:10.1016/j.procs.2018.08.233

Chassignol, M., Khoroshavin, A., Klimova, A., & Bilyatdinova, A. (2018). Artificial Intelligence trends in education: A narrative overview. *Procedia Computer Science*, *136*, 16–24. doi:10.1016/j.procs.2018.08.233

Chen, L., Chen, P., & Lin, Z. (2020). Artificial Intelligence in Education: A Review. *IEEE Access : Practical Innovations, Open Solutions*, *8*, 75264–75278. doi:10.1109/ACCESS.2020.2988510

Chen, X., Xie, H., Zou, D., & Hwang, G. J. (2020). Application and theory gaps during the rise of Artificial Intelligence in Education. *Computers and Education: Artificial Intelligence*, *1*, 100002. Advance online publication. doi:10.1016/j.caeai.2020.100002

Chen, X., Zou, D., Xie, H., & Cheng, G. (2022). Two decades of artificial intelligence in education. *Journal of Educational Technology & Society*, *25*(1).

Chichekian, T., & Benteux, B. (2022). The potential of learning with (and not from) artificial intelligence in education. *Frontiers in Artificial Intelligence*, *5*, 903051. Advance online publication. doi:10.3389/frai.2022.903051 PMID:36177366

Choi, E. P. H., Lee, J. J., Ho, M.-H., Kwok, J. Y. Y., & Lok, K. Y. W. (2023). Chatting or cheating? The impacts of ChatGPT and other artificial intelligence language models on nurse education. *Nurse Education Today*, *125*, 105796. doi:10.1016/j.nedt.2023.105796 PMID:36934624

Cox, A. M. (2021). Exploring the impact of Artificial Intelligence and robots on higher education through literature-based design fictions. *International Journal of Educational Technology in Higher Education*, *18*(1), 1–19. doi:10.1186/s41239-020-00237-8

Cox, A. M., Pinfield, S., & Rutter, S. (2019). The intelligent library: Thought leaders' views on the likely impact of artificial intelligence on academic libraries. *Library Hi Tech, 37*(3), 418–435. doi:10.1108/LHT-08-2018-0105

Crawford, J., Cowling, M., & Allen, K.-A. (2023). Leadership is needed for ethical ChatGPT: Character, assessment, and learning using artificial intelligence (AI). *Journal of University Teaching & Learning Practice, 20*(3). Advance online publication. doi:10.53761/1.20.3.02

Crompton, H., & Burke, D. (2023). Artificial intelligence in higher education: The state of the field. *International Journal of Educational Technology in Higher Education, 20*(1), 1–22. doi:10.1186/s41239-023-00392-8

Crowe, D., LaPierre, M., & Kebritchi, M. (2017). Knowledge Based Artificial Augmentation Intelligence Technology: Next Step in Academic Instructional Tools for Distance Learning. *TechTrends, 61*(5), 494–506. doi:10.1007/s11528-017-0210-4

Curtis, R. G., Bartel, B., Ferguson, T., Blake, H. T., Northcott, C., Virgara, R., & Maher, C. A. (2021). Improving User Experience of Virtual Health Assistants: Scoping Review. *J Med Internet Res, 23*(12), e31737. doi:10.2196/31737

Dutsinma, F. L. I., Pal, D., Funilkul, S., & Chan, J. H. (2022). A Systematic Review of Voice Assistant Usability: An ISO 9241–11 Approach. *SN Computer Science, 3*(4), 1–23. doi:10.1007/s42979-022-01172-3 PMID:35531568

Furini, M., Gaggi, O., Mirri, S., Montangero, M., Pelle, E., Poggi, F., & Prandi, C. (2022). U. (2022). Digital twins and artificial intelligence: As pillars of personalized learning models. *Communications of the ACM, 65*(4), 98–104. doi:10.1145/3478281

Gubareva, R. (2020). Virtual Assistants for Learning: A Systematic Literature Review. *Proceedings of the 12th International Conference on Computer Supported Education (CSEDU 2020).* 10.5220/0009417600970103

Holmes, W., & Tuomi, I. (2022). State of the art and practice in AI in education. *European Journal of Education, 57*(4), 542–570. doi:10.1111/ejed.12533

Hutson, J., & Plate, D. (2023). *Human-AI Collaboration for Smart Education: Reframing Applied Learning to Support Metacognition.* IntechOpen.

Johnson, M., & Nádas, R. (2009). Marking essays on screen: An investigation into the reliability of marking extended subjective texts. *Wiley Online Library.* doi:10.1111/j.1467-8535.2009.00979.x

Johnson, M., Nádas, R., & Bell, J. F. (2010). Marking essays on screen: An investigation into the reliability of marking extended subjective texts. *British Journal of Educational Technology*, *41*(5), 814–826. doi:10.1111/j.1467-8535.2009.00979.x

Kim, J. (2023). Leading teachers' perspective on teacher-AI collaboration in education. *Education and Information Technologies*. Advance online publication. doi:10.1007/s10639-023-12109-5

Lee, J. J., & Hammer, J. (2011). Gamification in Education: What, How, Why Bother? *Academic Exchange Quarterly, 15*(2), 146.

Leoste, J., Jõgi, L., Õun, T., Pastor, L., San Martín López, J., & Grauberg, I. (2021). Perceptions about the Future of Integrating Emerging Technologies into Higher Education—The Case of Robotics with Artificial Intelligence. *Computers*, *10*(9), 110. doi:10.3390/computers10090110

Lund, B. D., Omame, I., Tijani, S., & Agbaji, D. (2020). Perceptions toward Artificial Intelligence among Academic Library Employees and Alignment with the Diffusion of Innovations' Adopter Categories. *College & Research Libraries*, *81*(5), 865. doi:10.5860/crl.81.5.865

Lund, B. D., Wang, T., Mannuru, N. R., Nie, B., Shimray, S., & Wang, Z. (2023). ChatGPT and a new academic reality: Artificial Intelligence-written research papers and the ethics of the large language models in scholarly publishing. *Journal of the Association for Information Science and Technology*, *74*(5), 570–581. doi:10.1002/asi.24750

Ma, W., Adesope, O. O., Nesbit, J. C., & Liu, Q. (2014). *Intelligent Tutoring Systems and Learning Outcomes: A Meta-Analysis*. doi:10.1037/a0037123.supp

Nye, B. D. (2015). Intelligent tutoring systems by and for the developing world: A review of trends and approaches for educational technology in a global context. *International Journal of Artificial Intelligence in Education*, *25*(2), 177–203. doi:10.1007/s40593-014-0028-6

O'Neill, R., & Russell, A. M. T. (2019). Stop! Grammar time: University students' perceptions of the automated feedback program Grammarly. *Australasian Journal of Educational Technology*, *35*(1), 42–56. doi:10.14742/ajet.3795

ONeill, R., & Russell, A.ONeill. (2019). Stop! Grammar time: University students' perceptions of the automated feedback program Grammarly. *Australasian Journal of Educational Technology*, *35*(1). Advance online publication. doi:10.14742/ajet.3795

OpenAI. (2023). https://openai.com/chatgpt

Pagano, A., & Marengo, A. (2021). Training Time Optimization through Adaptive Learning Strategy. *2021 International Conference on Innovation and Intelligence for Informatics, Computing, and Technologies, 3ICT 2021*, 563–567. 10.1109/3ICT53449.2021.9582096

Penelitian, J., Pembelajaran, P., Nurmayanti, N., Stkip, S., & Banten, S. (2023). The Effectiveness Of Using Quillbot In Improving Writing For Students Of English Education Study Program. *Jurnal Teknologi Pendidikan : Jurnal Penelitian Dan Pengembangan Pembelajaran*, *8*(1), 32–40. doi:10.33394/jtp.v8i1.6392

Pokrivcakova, S. (2019). Preparing teachers for the application of AI-powered technologies in foreign language education. *Journal of Language and Cultural Education*, *7*(3), 135–153. doi:10.2478/jolace-2019-0025

Pratama, Y. D. (2021). The investigation of using grammarly as online grammar checker in the process of writing. *English Ideas. Journal of English Language Education*, *1*(2).

Rabbianty, E. N., Azizah, S., & Virdyna, N. K. (2023). AI in academic writing: Assessing current usage and future implications. *INSANIA : Jurnal Pemikiran Alternatif Kependidikan*, *28*(1a), 14–35. doi:10.24090/insania.v28i1a.9278

Rawlusyk, P. E. (2018). Assessment in Higher Education and Student Learning. *Journal of Instructional Pedagogies*, *21*, 1.

Rus, V., D'Mello, S., Hu, X., & Graesser, A. C. (2013). Recent advances in conversational intelligent tutoring systems. *AI Magazine*, *34*(3), 42–54. doi:10.1609/aimag.v34i3.2485

Santa Barletta, V., Cassano, F., Marengo, A., Pagano, A., Pange, J., & Piccinno, A. (2022). Switching learning methods during the pandemic: A quasi-experimental study on a master course. *Mdpi.ComVS Barletta, F Cassano, A Marengo, A Pagano, J Pange, A PiccinnoApplied Sciences, 2022•mdpi. Applied Sciences (Basel, Switzerland)*, *12*(17), 8438. Advance online publication. doi:10.3390/app12178438

Sanusi, I. T., Oyelere, S. S., & Omidiora, J. O. (2022). Exploring teachers' preconceptions of teaching machine learning in high school: A preliminary insight from Africa. *Computers and Education Open*, *3*, 100072. doi:10.1016/j.caeo.2021.100072

Sarwar, M. A., Saima, M., & Gul, A. (2024). The Role of Artificial Intelligence in Shaping the Future of Education at Higher Secondary Level. *Journal of Education and Social Studies*, *5*(1), 34–45. doi:10.52223/jess.2024.5104

Seldon, A., & Abidoye, O. (2018). *The fourth education revolution*. Academic Press.

Shemshack, A., & Spector, J. M. (2020). A systematic literature review of personalized learning terms. *Smart Learning Environments*, *7*(1), 33. Advance online publication. doi:10.1186/s40561-020-00140-9

Singh, M., Adebayo, S. O., Saini, M., & Singh, J. (2021). Indian government E-learning initiatives in response to COVID-19 crisis: A case study on online learning in Indian higher education system. *Education and Information Technologies*, *26*(6), 7569–7607. doi:10.1007/s10639-021-10585-1 PMID:34177350

Slade, S., & Prinsloo, P. (2013). Learning Analytics: Ethical Issues and Dilemmas. doi:10.1177/0002764213479366

Sutton, H. (2019). Minimize online cheating through proctoring, consequences. *Recruiting & Retaining Adult Learners*, *21*(5), 1–5. doi:10.1002/nsr.30434

van Dis, E. A. M., Bollen, J., Zuidema, W., van Rooij, R., & Bockting, C. L. (2023). ChatGPT: Five priorities for research. *Nature*, *614*(7947), 224–226. doi:10.1038/d41586-023-00288-7 PMID:36737653

Vandewaetere, M., & Clarebout, G. (2014). Advanced technologies for personalized learning, instruction, and performance. Handbook of Research on Educational Communications and Technology: Fourth Edition, 425–437. https://doi.org/doi:10.1007/978-1-4614-3185-5_34/COVER

Verbik, L., & Lasanowski, V. (2007). International Student Mobility: Patterns and Trends. *World Education News and Reviews*, *20*(10), 1–16.

Walkington, C., & Bernacki, M. L. (2020). Appraising research on personalized learning: Definitions, theoretical alignment, advancements, and future directions. doi:10.1080/15391523.2020.1747757

Wang, H., Tlili, A., Huang, R., Cai, Z., Li, M., Cheng, Z., Yang, D., Li, M., Zhu, X., & Fei, C. (2023). Examining the applications of intelligent tutoring systems in real educational contexts: A systematic literature review from the social experiment perspective. *Education and Information Technologies*, *28*(7), 9113–9148. Advance online publication. doi:10.1007/s10639-022-11555-x PMID:36643383

Wang, T., & Kolen, M. J. (2001). Evaluating comparability in computerized adaptive testing: Issues, criteria and an example. *Journal of Educational Measurement*, *38*(1), 19–49. doi:10.1111/j.1745-3984.2001.tb01115.x

Wood, E. A., Ange, B. L., & Miller, D. D. (2021). Are We Ready to Integrate Artificial Intelligence Literacy into Medical School Curriculum: Students and Faculty Survey. *Journal of Medical Education and Curricular Development, 8*. doi:10.1177/23821205211024078 PMID:34250242

Yoon, J. W., Andrews, J. E., & Ward, H. L. (2022). Perceptions on adopting artificial intelligence and related technologies in libraries: Public and academic librarians in North America. *Library Hi Tech, 40*(6), 1893–1915. doi:10.1108/LHT-07-2021-0229

Yüce, E. (2022). The Immediate Reactions of EFL Learners towards Total Digitalization at Higher Education during the Covid-19 Pandemic. *Journal of Theoretical Educational Science, 15*(1), 1–15. doi:10.30831/akukeg.939836

Zawacki Richter, O., Marín Juarros, V. I., Bond, M., & Gouverneur, F. (2019). Systematic review of research on artificial intelligence applications in higher education: where are the educators? *International Journal of Educational Technology in Higher Education, 16*, 6. doi:10.1186/s41239-019-0171-0

Zeb, A., Ullah, R., & Karim, R. (2024). Exploring the role of ChatGPT in higher education: Opportunities, challenges and ethical considerations. *The International Journal of Information and Learning Technology, 41*(1), 99–111. doi:10.1108/IJILT-04-2023-0046

Chapter 7
Fraud in Insurance and the Application of Artificial Intelligence (AI) in Preventing Fraud:
Definitions, Types, Consequences, Techniques, and Real Examples

Dharmendra Singh
Modern College of Business and Science, Muscat, Oman

Amal Khalil Al-Zadjali
Modern College of Business and Science, Muscat, Oman

Rasha Ahmed Al Mamari
Modern College of Business and Science, Muscat, Oman

Omar AbdulAziz Al Ansari
Modern College of Business and Science, Muscat, Oman

ABSTRACT

This research investigates insurance fraud, with a specific focus on the role of artificial intelligence (AI) in detection and prevention. It begins by defining key terms and providing an overview of insurance fraud. The study recognizes the global significance of insurance fraud in various insurance lines and the limitations of traditional fraud prevention methods. The research underscores the importance of clear legal frameworks and consistent enforcement in deterring insurance fraud. While previous research has acknowledged the potential of technology in fraud prevention, this study delves deeper into the application of AI. In summary, this research underscores the critical importance of addressing insurance fraud comprehensively and highlights the potential of AI as a powerful tool in safeguarding the integrity of the insurance industry, protecting policyholders, and mitigating the broader economic impact of fraud.

DOI: 10.4018/979-8-3693-1503-3.ch007

INTRODUCTION

Insurance is an integral part of modern economic systems because it provides individuals and businesses with the means to hedge risks by transferring them to insurance companies. However, the insurance field faces the problem of fraud committed through many different means, whether through false claims, staged accidents, identity theft, etc. These frauds can damage the financial stability of insurance companies, increase premiums for policyholders and undermine public confidence in the insurance system. In response to these challenges, the application of artificial intelligence has become a magic tool for fraud prevention and detection in the insurance industry.

This research endeavors to examine the critical definitions associated with insurance, fraud, and insurance fraud. Furthermore, it aims to explain the various categories of fraudulent activities within the insurance domain. Additionally, this study will explore the consequences of fraud on insurance companies, policyholders, and society.

Moreover, this research will offer concrete, real-world examples of insurance fraud to illustrate the gravity of the issue. Finally, it will explore the roles played by legal frameworks, insurance entities, and artificial intelligence in effectively combating this problem. It will comprehensively investigate the core technologies and practical applications of artificial intelligence within the insurance sector by emphasizing their paramount impact in the mitigation of fraudulent activities.

The study will conclude by presenting the significant findings that have been obtained, accompanied by recommendations to enhance the insurance system and encourage application of AI in detecting and preventing fraud.

1. DEFINITIONS

1.1 Insurance

It is a contract between an individual, business, or corporation (policyholder) and an insurance company called an "insurance company." A policyholder, also known as an insured, pays a premium to an insurance company in exchange for protection by providing solvency or coverage against a particular risk. These risks include property damage, accidents, illness, and death.

By this contract "the company pools clients' risks to make payments more affordable for the insured. Most people have some insurance: for their car, their house, their healthcare, or their life" (*Insurance*, n.d.).

1.2 Fraud

It is a deceptive act aimed at obtaining a benefit in a fraudulent manner. These methods include intentionally misrepresenting or concealing facts and deceiving others through manipulating information. Fraud can occur in multiple areas and ways, including financial transactions, most notably insurance transactions.

It can be said that the term fraud does not have a unified definition, as it varies depending on the context. Meanwhile "the definition of fraud given in the (*UK HM Treasury Fraud Report 1994-1995 - Google Search*, n.d.,p.10) is more favorable in describing fraud in the economy sector as: 'The use of deception with the intention of obtaining advantage, avoiding an obligation or causing loss to a third party" (Mohamed, 2013)

1.3 Insurance Fraud

It refers to an act in which an attempt is made to defraud an insurance company or even the insurer regarding a claim for compensation. Its purpose is to obtain benefits, as we previously explained in the general statute of frauds, but it differs in this context that benefits are claims for insurance benefits or unearned monetary benefits. Thus, two forms of insurance fraud can be distinguished:

-Soft fraud: This type of fraud is carried out by exaggerating the value of the insured object in the hope of higher compensation.

-Hard Fraud: A person intentionally makes an entirely fictitious or fictitious claim. For example, faking injuries, arson or creating false documents to support a false claim.

2. TYPES OF INSURANCE FRAUD

A common way to categorize fraud is to categorize it by intent. Whether it's against an organization or someone committing fraud on behalf of an organization.

The types of fraud can be listed as follows: Benefit fraud, Embezzlement, Management fraud, Investment Scams, Vendor or Supplier Fraud, Customer Fraud, Miscellaneous/Specific Fraud.

However, a distinction can be made between ordinary types of fraud and insurance fraud. In insurance fraud, there are three types of insurance fraud that can be discussed which are Claims fraud, Application fraud, and Premium fraud.

Firstly: Insurance Claims Fraud: it occurs when a policyholder or claimant makes a false or exaggerated claim to an insurance company. This can be divided into four sections:

a) Exaggeration of loss: The policyholder values the loss or damage to the insured property in the hope of obtaining more compensation than should be paid. If you exaggerate.
b) Staged Incident: Occurs when an individual or group initiates an orchestrated incident for the purpose of fabricating a claim for injury or property damage. Note that in these accidents, multiple parties may collude to defraud the insurance company, including: some types of car accidents.
c) Double Dipping: Some people defraud insurance companies by filing claims for the same loss or injury with multiple insurance companies. This is essentially "double dipping" where you get multiple payouts for one accident.
d) Fictitious or Phantom Claims: This includes hypothetical scenarios or losses by some beneficiaries with the purpose of making fraudulent claims to obtain compensation.

To summarize, claims fraud is where an individual or organization makes a fictitious or intentionally inflated insurance claim. For example, someone claiming for non-existent jewelry or for a slip or trip which never took place. (*Insurance Fraud Taskforce Final Report. (2016, January 21). GOV.UK. Https://Www.Gov.Uk/Government/Publications/Insurance-Fraud-Taskforce-Final-Report - Google Search*, n.d.)

Secondly: Application Fraud: Insurance companies are known to have two departments which are underwriting and actuarial. Application fraud or "insurance application fraud" occurs when a person or entity deceives the underwriting department by providing false or misleading information to the policyholder on an insurance application to receive more insurance coverage than necessary. For example, someone falsely stating that they have never made an insurance claim before). This can be done by the following way:

a) Concealing Information: An applicant hides important information, such as pre-existing conditions or previous insurance claims, from applications seeking coverage or lower premiums.
b) Misrepresentation of Information: Policyholders may provide false information about their background or lifestyle in order to obtain more favorable insurance terms.
c) Identity fraud: Individuals use false identities when applying for insurance, making it difficult for insurance companies to assess the true risk they pose.

Thirdly: Premium fraud: it occurs when an insurance policy holder or broker manipulates premium payments to reduce the cost of insurance. The Premium fraud relates to data misrepresentation committed by an insurance customer with the intent to benefit from unjustifiably low premiums when underwriting an insurance policy. (Vandervorst et al., 2022) This comes in many forms:

a) Underreporting of wages or income: This can be seen with workers' compensation or business insurance.
b) Employee Misclassification: Employers might mistype employees as independent contractors to deny them coverage, resulting in lower insurance costs.
c) Stand-off: Stand-off or Fronting occurs when a company uses some other more suitable insurance to cover its activities instead of the real hazards. This usually means that the parent company ensures a less risky subsidiary in order to get lower premiums.

3. CONSEQUENCES OF INSURANCE FRAUD

The effects of insurance fraud which involve dishonest conduct intended to extract unjustified financial advantage from insurance companies, go well beyond the immediate financial loss suffered by insurers. Deliberately misleading insurance companies for financial gain which has serious repercussions that affect insurers as well as society at large (Viaene & Dedene, 2004).

a) Financial Impact on Insurers

The significant financial burden that insurance fraud causes on insurers is one of the most direct effects. For insurance firms, fraudulent claims result in immediate financial losses, which have an effect on their profitability and undermine their primary goal of sharing risks. The capacity of an insurer to invest in expansion and innovation as well as its financial stability may be negatively impacted by these losses over time. Insurance companies incur the cost of processing and paying out bogus claims. The profitability of insurance firms is directly impacted by these losses, which may be considerable. Insurance fraud immediately undercuts the primary purpose of insurers, which is to aggregate risks and provide policyholders with financial protection. The capital accessible to paying out legitimate demands and ensuring financial stability is decreased as a result of money being diverted to settle false claims.

b) Costs of Fraud Detection

For the purpose of detecting and preventing fraud, insurance firms must make significant investments in cutting-edge technology. These detection techniques include forensic study of claims, machine learning algorithms, and data analysis. These tools are crucial for preventing fraud, but they have their own expenses, which further affect insurers' bottom lines (Niemi, 1995).

c) Regulation and Legal Consequences

Both insurers and society may be impacted by the legal and regulatory repercussions of insurance fraud. Insurance companies are frequently required by regulatory organizations to disclose fraud cases, and legal actions can be drawn-out and expensive. In criminal investigations, which may be time-consuming, insurers may need to work with law enforcement.

d) Impacts on Accessibility for Insurance

Some people and companies may decide not to get insurance entirely as a result of rising rates brought on by the costs associated with fraud. This choice puts them at greater risk financially and burdens society by increasing the number of uninsured people who will need help from the government or social services in the case of an accident or disaster. Infrastructure and public resources may be further strained as a result (Picard, 2000).

e) Fraud as an Insurance Innovation Driver

It's interesting to note that innovation in the insurance sector has been sparked by the necessity to combat insurance fraud. The development of more sophisticated fraud detection technologies and methods by insurers can eventually help honest policyholders by lowering premium rises brought on by fraud.

f) Education and Prevention Initiatives

The socioeconomic effects of insurance fraud must be addressed, and educational and preventative measures are crucial. Insurance companies frequently launch public awareness efforts to inform people and companies about the effects of insurance fraud. Furthermore, community-based programs can aid in the detection and reporting of fraud, making it harder for criminals to act freely.

g) Sector-Specific and Global Implications

Insurance fraud is not limited to a certain area or industry. It has worldwide repercussions and may have an impact on a number of insurance categories, including those for property, vehicle, health, and workers' compensation (Viaene & Dedene, 2004). Depending on the level of fraud in each sector of insurance, the outcomes vary and can have economic and societal effects.

h) Strain on Resources

Insurance fraud places a significant financial pressure on insurance firms, with far-reaching effects on both the sector and its clients (Picard, 2000).

1. **Increased Premiums:** Insurance firms need to make up for their losses when there are more false claims filed against them. They do this, among other things, by raising rates for all policyholders. Because of the deeds of a dishonest minority, honest people who follow the rules wind up paying more for their policies.
2. **Reduced Coverage and Benefits:** To mitigate the financial burden caused by fraudulent claims, insurance companies may limit coverage options and reduce the benefits offered to policyholders. This means that innocent customers may face reduced protection, higher deductibles, or increased out-of-pocket costs due to the need to compensate for losses caused by insurance fraud (Feinman, 2017).
3. **Insufficient Resources for Genuine Claims:** The substantial resources spent investigating and dealing with fraudulent claims divert attention and funds away from providing efficient services for legitimate policyholders. Insufficient resources may result in slower claims processing, delays in resolving disputes or providing coverage, and reduced overall customer satisfaction.

i) Investigation Costs

Insurance fraud investigations are sometimes complicated and need a lot of time, knowledge, and money to get clear results.

1. **Hiring and Educating Professionals:** To spot and investigate fraudulent activity, insurance firms frequently work with specialist professionals like fraud investigators and auditors. For these specialists to identify and support false claims, substantial training and experience are necessary. The entire charges

faced by insurance firms are considerably impacted by the hiring and training expenses related to maintaining an investigation team.

2. **Technology Advancements:** Insurance firms must invest in technological developments to stay up with new risks as fraudsters adapt their techniques to take advantage of systemic flaws. The expense of using sophisticated fraud detection software, data analytics tools, and other technical solutions increases the financial burden of looking into fictitious claims (Viaene & Dedene, 2004).
3. **Legal Action:** Insurance fraud investigations can result in legal action. It can be expensive to take legal action against fraudsters, including paying attorneys and traveling to court. These expenses add to the overall cost of the inquiry and further burden insurance companies due to the drawn-out legal process (Niemi, 1995).

j) Premium Increases for Honest Policyholders

For sincere policyholders, insurance fraud can have serious repercussions, raising premiums. Insurance firms base the premiums they charge on a number of variables, including the risk involved with a certain policyholder and the possibility that a claim would need to be paid. However, when insurance fraud happens, it may upset this delicate balance and raise expenses for all parties. Insurance fraud costs insurance companies money, which is one of its effects. Insurance companies are required to look into false claims, which takes time, resources, and labor.

Ultimately, these expenses are transferred to policyholders in the form of increased premiums. Additionally, paying out erroneous claims might force insurance firms to incur financial losses (Feinman, 2017).They increase premiums across the board to make up for these losses. Insurance fraud also damages the relationship of trust between policyholders and insurers. Mutual trust is a key component of insurance, with insurers assuming that information provided by policyholders is reliable and genuine. This trust is violated through fraud, which weakens the entire system. The implementation of tougher verification processes by insurers to reduce the risk of fraud can be time-consuming and inconvenient for loyal customers. Higher premiums may also result from these extra precautions. Honest policyholders may suffer from diminished benefits and coverage in addition to financial repercussions from higher premiums. When fraud forces insurers to make larger payouts, they may make up the difference by limiting coverage options or raising deductibles. Honest policyholders may have fewer alternatives accessible to them as a result, and filing valid claims may cost them more out of pocket. Insurance fraud also affects society. Resources are taken away from individuals who legitimately need financial help and valid claims. These fraudulent actions drain money from insurers, making it more difficult for them to rapidly pay out legitimate claims. Honest policyholders may experience delays in the claims procedure as a result, which may have an effect on their financial situation (Niemi, 1995).

k) Other Consequences of Insurance Fraud on Honest Policyholders

1. **Rate Disparities:** Insurance fraud can result in rates for policyholders that are not competitive. Insurance firms may raise rates for particular policyholders or geographical areas when they suffer financial losses as a result of fraud. As a result, even those that weren't involved in fraudulent activity may see increased rates.
2. **Limited Coverage Options:** In regions with high incidences of fraud, insurance firms could be less likely to provide coverage options or policies. Honest policyholders may have fewer options, which will make it more challenging for them to get enough insurance coverage at a reasonable price (*Group, I. N. (2018, October 5). What Are the Consequences of Insurance Fraud? Cataño Insurance Brokers - Google Search*, n.d.).
3. **Less Accessibility:** For certain people, getting insurance may become more difficult and expensive due to higher rates brought on by insurance fraud. Low-income policyholders may be particularly impacted since they may find it difficult to pay higher rates. As a result, these people could be compelled to forgo insurance protection, making them susceptible in the event of unforeseen circumstances or mishaps.
4. **Exposure to Uninsured Drivers:** When it comes to vehicle insurance, insurance fraud may be a factor in the rise of uninsured drivers. Some drivers may choose to drive without the required insurance because they cannot afford the higher costs brought on by fraud. In the case of a collision involving an uninsured driver, this may put defenseless policyholders in danger.
5. **Time and Effort:** Insurance fraud investigations may be drawn-out and time-consuming, necessitating extra information from honest policyholders and their cooperation with insurers throughout the course of the inquiry. This might be a hassle and add time to the process of getting benefits or resolving valid claims. Through awareness programs, strict regulation, and efficient investigation procedures, insurance fraud must be stopped.

Insurance fraud has serious repercussions that put a burden on insurance companies' resources and raise the cost of investigations. Honest policyholders are put under pressure since they have to pay higher rates, have less coverage, and wait longer to get services. Collaboration between insurance firms, law enforcement, and legislators is crucial for effectively combating insurance fraud. The negative effects of insurance fraud may be reduced, which is advantageous for both the insurance sector and customers, by introducing stronger measures to dissuade and identify fraudulent actions, such as public awareness programs, thorough investigation processes, and strict legal punishments.

4. TECHNIQUES AND REAL EXAMPLES OF FRAUD

4.1 Techniques of Insurance Fraud

a) Inflating or exaggerating claims: Fraudsters may exaggerate the value of a valid claim to obtain larger compensation, for as by asserting that stolen goods were worth more than they actually were.
b) Staged Accidents: This tactic, which involves both genuine and phony individuals, involves purposefully provoking collisions or accidents and then submitting claims for injuries or damages.
c) Fictitious Claims: Some people submit totally false claims for incidents that never happened, such as claiming an erroneous automobile theft.
d) Identity theft: People who commit healthcare insurance fraud may use the identity of another person to receive medical care or prescription medications.
e) Arson and Property Damage: Deliberate vandalism or acts of arson to destroy property with the intent to file insurance claims are well-known strategies.
f) Application fraud: People applying for insurance coverage may give misleading information or omit crucial facts. Although it might result in cheaper rates, this deception is insurance fraud.
g) Fake documents: To support their false claims, fraudsters will occasionally provide counterfeit documents, such as invoices, repair estimates, or medical bills.
h) Collusion: In certain instances, policyholders may work with experts, such insurance adjusters or doctors, to inflate claims or fabricate claims that pass muster as real.
i) Hit and Run: A driver may create an accident before scurrying away, making it challenging for law enforcement to locate them. They then submit a claim for damages in an effort to avoid being prosecuted (*Cydni. (2016, April 18). Insurance Fraud - Definition, Examples, Cases, Processes. Legal Dictionary.* Https://Legaldictionary.Net/Insurance-Fraud/ - *Google Search*, n.d.).

4.2 Real Examples of Insurance Fraud

a) The "Phantom" Accident Rings: Organized criminal groups have staged fictitious car accidents involving many vehicles, making false injury claims on behalf of passengers who weren't in the cars when the incidents occurred.

b) Healthcare Billing Fraud: Some healthcare practitioners have overcharged insurance companies for treatments that were never performed, billed for needless procedures, or falsified diagnoses.

c) Property arson: It has been shown that some property owners have set their houses or businesses on fire with the intent of recouping insurance costs.

d) Life Insurance Fraud: Some people have tried to collect life insurance benefits by pretending to die and using false identification and paperwork.

e) Workers' Compensation Fraud: In order to get workers' compensation benefits inadvertently, employees may misrepresent their injuries or assert that accidents happened when they were not working.

f) Scams using mortgage insurance: People tried to conduct mortgage insurance fraud during the housing crisis by purposefully going into default on their mortgages and faking being eligible for insurance benefits.

g) Hurricane Katrina fraud, number seven: Numerous instances of insurance fraud surfaced following Hurricane Katrina in 2005. Some policyholders misrepresented their properties as primary residences when they were actually second homes. They were able to receive greater insurance benefits as a result.

h) Healthcare Pill Mills: A few medical centers, sometimes referred to as "pill mills," have taken advantage of loose laws to prescribe and disseminate excessive amounts of banned medications. After that, they charge insurance companies for these pointless prescriptions.

i) Fraudulent Mortgage Insurance Practices: People tried to conduct mortgage insurance fraud during the housing crisis of the late 2000s by purposefully defaulting on their mortgages and fraudulently asserting they were entitled to mortgage insurance benefits.

j) Forgery and Art Theft - Through the manufacture of phony artworks, high-value art thefts have resulted in insurance fraud. A priceless painting may be stolen by a criminal, who would then fake a copy and submit a claim for the loss of the real piece.

k) The "Whiplash" Epidemic: Following vehicle accidents, whiplash injuries have frequently been used as a cover for insurance fraud. Fraudsters make difficult-to-disprove claims of neck and back ailments, which result in exorbitant medical care and compensation claims.

l) Dental professionals have been linked to insurance fraud schemes by invoicing for treatments that were never rendered or by advising needless procedures to boost claims.

5. THE FRAUD IN OMANI LAWS

The issue of fraud in insurance does not only impact the financial stability of insurance companies but also corrodes trust in the overall insurance system. Therefore, Oman as many other countries considered insurance fraud as illegal practice and is subject to legal penalties. It has established institutions & provisions in place to detect, prevent, and penalize those engaged in fraudulent activities within the insurance domain.

In sultanate of Oman, the Capital Market Authority undertakes the pivotal role of overseeing insurance companies and brokers. Moreover, it bears the responsibility of advancing the capital market and insurance domains, accomplished by conducting comprehensive studies and formulating legislation and regulations in accordance with globally recognized best practices (*About CMA, Capital Market Authority Website, Capital Market Authority, Sultanate of Oman - About CMA, Accessed on 27/08/2023. - Google Search*, n.d.).

Moreover, Oman has enacted a series of laws aimed at combating fraud, both in a general context and with a specific emphasis on the insurance sector. The subsequent explanation would examine these legislative measures:

a) Omani Supreme Court

It defined the crime of fraud in one of its principles as using fraudulent methods to mislead the victim in order to deceive him or seize his money, while supporting the lie with external appearances in which the offender obtains an illegal benefit for himself or others (*The Supreme Court of Oman, a Set of Judgments Issued by the Criminal Chamber of the Supreme Court and the Principles Derived from It, Principal No. (76/2008), Supreme Criminal, the Eighth Judicial Year, Pg. 520. - Google Search*, n.d.).

b) Penal Law No. (2018/7)

It has discussed the crime of fraud and attempted fraud in articles (349-353). It outlines the cases in which a person is considered to have committed the crime of fraud including obtaining unjustified benefits for oneself or others through fraudulent methods, or by using a false name or inaccurate qualification (*Article 349 of Omani Penal Law No. (2018/7). - Google Search*, n.d.).

Hence, Omani Penal Code discussed the specific events that define when someone is considered to have committed the crime of fraud. One of the events is gaining advantages or benefits that a person does not rightfully deserve. In the context of fraud, it refers to situations where a person obtains these benefits through dishonest or deceiving means and there are many strategies used to mislead others and achieve personal gain. However, committing fraud should involve intentionally using such methods to deceive others.

Another event of fraud is situations where someone assumes a false identity or provides misleading information about their qualifications, skills, or background. This false information could be used to gain trust, secure a position, or obtain benefits.

The punishment in such cases involves imprisonment for a period not less than three months and not exceeding two years, and a fine of no less than (100) Omani Rials, and not exceeding (300) Omani Rials. Alternatively, one of these two punishments may be applied. The punishment will be increased to not exceed double if the fraudulent act is committed against a person under the age of 18 or against an adult who does not possess their full distinguishing capacities.

Furthermore, the Omani Penal Code penalizes attempted fraud with a punishment that does not exceed half of the maximum penalty set for the crime (*Article 353 of Omani Penal Law No. (2018/7). - Google Search*, n.d., p. 353). This means that even if someone doesn't fully carry out a fraudulent act, they could still face legal consequences for the attempt.

c) Motor Vehicles Insurance Law No.) 34/94)

Article (15) stated that: *"The insurer has the right to refer to the insured and/or his equivalents in implementation of this obligation, and to refrain from compensating any bodily injury or death that may be caused to them or their family members (if the vehicle insurance policy covers such injuries) or what affects the body of the insured vehicle (if its insurance is comprehensive) in the following cases:*

(a) If it is proved that the insurance was concluded based on the insured's false material statements or concealment of material facts, which affects the company's acceptance of the risk coverage or the price or conditions of the insurance.

(d) If it is proved that the accident, death or bodily injury arose from an act committed by the insured with the intention of harming."

We understand from the above article that, the Motor Vehicles Insurance Law outlines the circumstances under which the insurance company has the right to deny compensation for bodily injury, death, or damage. These circumstances include providing false information or concealing important facts during the insurance application process and intentionally causing harm that leads to accidents or damage. The purpose of this clause is to ensure that the insured acts honestly and responsibly, and to prevent fraudulent claims.

d) Insurance Companies Law No. (79/12)

This law discusses two types of fraud:

1. Fraud from Third Party Side

Article (49) addressed and explained the actions and consequences related to making false or misleading statements when attempting to persuade someone to enter into a contract or apply for an insurance agreement with an insurance company. It states that if an individual knowingly provides a statement that contains false information, a promise that they know is deceptive, or deliberately hides important facts to create a misleading impression, they will be considered in violation of this clause. This applies whether the misleading statement is made in good faith (with genuine intent) or bad faith (with intent to deceive).

This law doesn't explicitly specify whether it refers to an agent or broker of an insurance company. However, the actions described in the clause could apply to both agents and brokers, as they both have roles in facilitating insurance contracts.

2. Fraud From Insurance Company Side

Article (54) outlines the consequences or penalties that an insurance company may face if they engage in certain activities:

i. **Providing False Information for a License:** If any person provides information that they know is incorrect with the intention of obtaining an insurance license, they may be subject to punishment.
ii. **Negligence in Submitting Information:** any person will be subject to punishment if negligently inserts or uses incorrect information in their application for an insurance license, or in a report or statement submitted to the relevant authorities (the Minister, Ministry, or Office). Also, if they negligently omit any material fact or document from such applications, data, or reports. This means that even if the incorrect information was inserted or omitted due to negligence (carelessness) rather than intentional deception, they can still be fined.

In these cases the penalties consist of fines ranging from 1,000 Omani Rials to 5,000 Omani Rials depending on the circumstances (*Article (54- a,f) of Insurance Companies Law No. (79/12). - Google Search*, n.d.). These penalties are likely in place to ensure the integrity and accuracy of information provided in the insurance industry in Oman.

6. ANTI-FRAUD IN INSURANCE

It's important to consider that insurance fraud prevention is an ongoing effort that requires the combined efforts of insurers, regulators, law enforcement, and other stakeholders. Laws and regulations provide a legal framework to address fraud. However, effective prevention also involves proactive measures and constant adaptation to new fraud schemes and techniques.

6.1 The Role of Laws and Regulations in Preventing Fraud

Laws and regulations are considered the foundation of insurance fraud prevention. Governments establish regulations that define what constitutes insurance fraud, how it should be investigated, and the penalties for those found guilty. These legal frameworks vary by jurisdiction but generally encompass acts such as false claims, misrepresentation and deceptive practices (*Naif Arab University for Security Sciences (NAUSS)*, n.d.).

6.2 The Role of Insurance Companies in Preventing Fraud

Insurance companies play a crucial role in preventing fraud within the insurance industry. Fraudulent activities can lead to financial losses for both the insurance company and its policyholders, and it can also drive-up insurance premiums for everyone. We will discuss some ways that insurance companies should work on to prevent fraud:

- It has become necessary for insurance companies to establish indicators and policies to combat fraud by organizing their administrative structure. They should also prepare an approved and effective plan to address fraud in all its forms and degrees. This can be achieved by establishing a fraud prevention department consisting of administrative and technical members specialized in addressing the phenomenon of fraud, if the insurance company deems it necessary to implement these precautions to combat fraud (*Malcolm Clarke,*

Policies and Perceptions of Insurance Law, Oxford University Press, 2012, P48 - Google Search, n.d.).

- Insurance companies, through their underwriting departments, should carefully assess the risk associated with each policyholder before issuing a policy. Thus, they need to verify the information provided by policyholders during the application process. This includes reviewing all relevant details to ensure that the information provided in the insurance application is accurate and complete. During this stage, they should use various tools and data sources to evaluate an applicant's background and history. Insurance companies can use the central databases that are used between insurance companies and government departments to confront any illegal practices during the verification stage. This will help them to identify any potential fraud risks.
- Insurance companies should have claims departments that investigate suspicious or unusual claims. They shall use experienced investigators who may interview claimants, gather evidence, and review medical records, police reports, and other documents to determine the validity of a claim. Likewise, insurance companies should collaborate with law enforcement agencies to investigate and prosecute any insurance fraud practices. They should share all required information and evidences to assist in criminal cases against fraudsters.
- Insurance companies should provide training and resources to their employees to help them recognize and prevent fraud. This includes training claims adjusters, underwriters, and other personnel on fraud detection techniques.
- Insurance policies should include clear language regarding the consequences of fraudulent claims. This can act as a deterrent and make policyholders aware of the legal and financial risks associated with insurance fraud (*Malcolm Clarke, Policies and Perceptions of Insurance Law, Oxford University Press, 2012, P48 - Google Search*, n.d.).

6.3 The Role of Artificial Intelligence in Detecting and Preventing Fraud

With the advent of modern technologies in the insurance industry, the expenditure on cognitive and artificial intelligence systems in the insurance sector increased to $77.6 billion in 2022 according to reports from the International Data Foundation.

Due to the increase of practices and behaviors carried out by some individuals for illegal purposes which suspected of being fraudulent, many specialized technology companies in predictive analytics have developed advanced systems based on artificial intelligence techniques to analyze insurance claims submitted to insurance companies.

This is aimed at facilitating automatic approvals without human intervention. This positively impacts the speed of processing insurance claims and reduces operational costs for insurance companies.

These technologies examine insurance claims and compare them with the data of the policyholder and their insurance history. When there is a suspicious claim that differs from the normal context, by using predictive analytics, the system then notifies the person responsible for claims at the insurance company of suspected fraud in that claim which requiring human intervention and manual inspection (Mall et al., 2023).

In the following, we will mention some of these specialized technology companies and their roles:

- One of the most well-known companies that develops artificial intelligence systems for insurance companies is "Lemonade" which sells insurance to renters and homeowners. In fact, it is a licensed insurance company itself and has developed a "Chatbot" program to collect customer information and process claims. It has been revealed that 30% of these claims do not require human intervention to be resolved. "Lemonade" now has over half a million customers where the majority of whom are first-time insurance buyers.
- The company "Shift Technology" is one of the emerging French companies operating in Paris, Tokyo, Boston, and Singapore. It uses artificial intelligence to help insurance companies to detect fraud and process claims. In this context, it has designed a program called "Force" to identify fraudulent insurance claims with a success rate of 75%. One of the largest insurance companies in Asia named "Tokio Marine Indonesia" has announced the use of this program to combat fraud.
- The company "Work Fusion" created the "Intelligent Automation Cloud" platform. It helps insurance companies to improve claims processing and settlement disputes using artificial intelligence techniques. It also verifies documents more quickly by extracting identification data from documents such as passports and driver's licenses and comparing them with customer data and identifying any discrepancies. Accordingly, the system has been able to reduce costs by 50% (*How Does the Insurance Sector Benefit from Artificial Intelligence Applications?, Samar Al-Mashata,* Https://Www.Alarabiya.Net - *Google Search*, n.d.).

These smart systems will significantly contribute to improving the efficiency and effectiveness of processing insurance claims and will prevent any fraudulent activities to mitigate their negative impact on the insurance sector. They will play a crucial role in reducing the accompanying risks of insurance operations and implementing new actuarial standards, which will be a fundamental and influential element in re-pricing insurance services. This ultimately will lead to a reduction in insurance premium rates.

6.3.1 How AI be used in Insurance Companies

Artificial intelligence is the capacity of computers to do jobs and solve problems that would otherwise need human intelligence more quickly and efficiently. AI is used in the insurance sector to speed up operations and make use of an ever-expanding universe of data to provide tailored, proactive coverage.

In recent years, the AI revolution in insurance has gained traction. Consumer acceptance of digital channels for purchasing and administering insurance has led property and casualty insurers to rapidly digitize more of their operations, a trend that has only exacerbated in the aftermath of the COVID-19 outbreak. The criterion for success for digitally aware insurance clients is no longer only other insurers. It consists of Amazon, Google, and Netflix.

New data sources, and the capacity to use it through AI, will become an increasingly important differentiating source of insight and value for property insurers. This capacity to introduce new products and services makes the globe more insurable, accelerates claims in ways that assist insured during what may be a stressful time, and improves fraud control in ways that reduce the financial burden on families.

In some respects, the AI revolution in property insurance makes acquiring talent and the capacity to utilize external, cloud-connected solutions more important than depending only on internal development resources more urgent (*Ways AI Is Transforming Property Insurance - CAPE Analytics. (2023, February 1). CAPE Analytics - Google Search*, n.d.).

6.3.1.1 How Artificial Intelligence Is Used in Different Departments

1. AI in the Health Insurance Industry:

Artificial intelligence is set to become a game changer in healthcare. Traditional analytics and clinical decision-making techniques are not as effective as AI health insurance.

AI in health insurance improves healthcare providers' capacity to better understand the day-to-day patterns and requirements of the individuals they care for, allowing them to give greater feedback, advice, and support for keeping healthy.

It provides a cloud-based software platform for home healthcare practitioners. The platform includes clinical documentation, back-office functions, remote patient monitoring, and telehealth. It also aids in the analysis of wearable devices to get patient data for processing using machine learning technology by providing real-time insights to care providers.

2. AI for Automobile Industry:

The automobile sector is on the verge of a massive revolution. To keep one step ahead of competitors in the market, automakers throughout the world have begun implementing new technology into their products and operations.

AI for auto insurance firms has been seen working its magic in an autonomous automobile utilizing machine learning, as well as automating auto insurance underwriting with AI.

3. AI in Underwriting Department:

Using AI in underwriting may broaden and increase access to multiple data sources, optimizing risk assessments. Insurance companies have already experienced benefits from bringing big data, machine learning, and predictive analytics models and algorithms into their departments (*Top 7 Reasons to Transform Insurance Underwriting with AI. Saxon - Google Search*, n.d.).

Errors are unavoidable no matter how bright, rational, or keen individuals are. However, AI and machine learning do not make mistakes, regardless of how simple and repetitive the task is or how many figures are involved. As a result, adopting AI for underwriting is crucial. AI in insurance underwriting can synthesis enormous datasets in many forms, reducing the likelihood of mistakes.

6.3.1.2 How Artificial Intelligence Is Used in Customer Communications

Customers' shifting demands and expectations are taken into account by insurers, especially since they no longer accept lengthy insurance applications or complicated claims procedure. Integrating AI and automation into insurance businesses' customer communication models is crucial.

Insurers can handle the demand for dynamic products and gain a new client base comprised of younger generations by leveraging conversational AI. AI in client communications in the insurance sector has improved customer experiences and operational efficiency significantly.

How AI in customer communications could change the customer experience?

1. Increased Claim Process Efficiency: AI aids in reshaping the claims process for both new and current policyholders. Voice AI can assist in handling large call volumes by relieving the burden on human agents.

2. Policy Management: Using an AI-enabled Chabot to automate typical client requests such as document assistance will improve the customer experience.
3. Creating Quotes: After obtaining a quotation, most customers have questions. Voice AI can assist consumers with simple queries, saving insurers' time until a complicated inquiry occurs.

6.3.1.3 Benefits of AI in Insurance Industry

- Efficiency: Process automation, natural language processing (NLP), and chatbots may all be used to speed up insurance operations, saving both the consumer and the insurer time and money.
- Product development: The introduction of new technologies enables for the development of new items. Usage-based insurance plans, such as 'pay how you drive' models, for example, are becoming increasingly popular. These insurance options offer a more tailored insurance experience.
- Saving money: Fewer human mistakes and less manual intervention result from automation and greater accuracy. This results in substantial cost reductions for insurance companies.
- Customer satisfaction has increased: Customers enjoy a seamless and customized experience with rapid replies and unique policy ideas (*How Does the Insurance Sector Benefit from Artificial Intelligence Applications?, Samar Al-Mashata,* Https://Www.Alarabiya.Net - *Google Search*, n.d.).

6.3.2 How Can AI Be Used Effectively in Insurance Detection and Prevention?

Fraudulent insurance claims are causing a significant financial burden with an estimated annual cost of €13 billion in Europe. This means that dishonest individuals and parties are making false insurance claims which can lead to higher premiums for honest policyholders and financial losses for insurance companies.

Therefore, Insurance companies are increasingly recognizing the importance of adopting digital innovations to combat fraud and enhance their overall operations. Insurtech refers to technology-driven solutions and innovations specifically designed for the insurance industry. These innovations can include advanced analytics, artificial intelligence (AI), machine learning, and data analytics.

Insurance fraud is prevalent in various sectors including property, automotive and healthcare. In these sectors, individuals or organizations may submit false claims to receive insurance payouts to which they are not entitled.

According to a report (*Global Investments in Insurtech, Forrester Helps Organizations Grow Through Customer Obsession, 2022 - Google Search*, n.d.), global investments in Insurtech exceeded $15 billion in 2021. This indicates that insurance companies and investors are putting significant resources into developing and implementing technology solutions to improve the efficiency, accuracy, and security of insurance processes.

6.3.2.1 Using of Machine Learning Models

6.3.2.1.1 Concept:

Detecting fraudulent insurance claims is a complex and resource-intensive task. Insurance companies receive a large volume of claims daily, making it physically impossible to thoroughly investigate each one. Early computerized systems used rudimentary analysis and red flag indicators which were limited in their ability to detect fraud.

Machine learning, as a subset of AI, is a powerful tool for insurance companies to improve fraud detection accuracy, speed up processes and save money. By analyzing historical data, machine learning models can identify patterns and anomalies that might indicate fraudulent claims.

Technology, specifically Robotic Process Automation (RPA), has been a game-changer for insurance companies. RPA assists in verifying information from various sources to detect fraudulent data. This has led to significant efficiency improvements such as reducing claims cycle time.

In the context of machine learning and data analysis, "ground truth" refers to the correct or known outcomes or labels for each data point in the dataset. For insurance fraud detection, these labels indicate whether a particular insurance claim is legitimate ("valid") or fraudulent based on historical information and investigations. Accordingly, machine learning models as they are computer algorithms that can learn patterns and make predictions based on data, they will learn to recognize common characteristics, behaviors, or patterns that are indicative of insurance fraud. These patterns might include unusual claim amounts, frequent claim submissions by the same individual, or inconsistencies in the information provided.

After the machine learning model has been trained on the historical dataset, it can be applied to new, incoming insurance claims. When a new claim is submitted, the model uses its learned knowledge to assess the claim and predict whether it is likely to be fraudulent or valid. This prediction can assist human investigators in prioritizing their efforts and resources (*Detecting Insurance Claims Fraud Using Machine Learning Techniques,* Https://Managementevents.Com/, *2022 - Google Search*, n.d.).

6.3.2.1.2 Techniques of Machine Learning Model:

Firstly: Supervised Learning Techniques for Fraud Detection:

Supervised learning is a common approach in machine learning for fraud detection. In supervised learning, a dataset is used where each example has a labeled or known output which is typically whether a transaction or claim is fraudulent or not.

This labeled dataset is used to train a machine learning model by allowing it to learn the relationships between the input features (attributes) and the corresponding labels (fraudulent or not). Once trained, the model can make predictions on new, unlabeled data. Supervised Learning approach has two common methods:

a) Decision Trees:

It makes predictions based on a sequence of binary splits. Each internal node in the tree represents a decision based on the value of a specific attribute (feature), and the leaf nodes provide the final predictions.

Decision trees can handle both numerical and categorical data, and they are relatively easy to understand and interpret. However, one drawback is that they can be prone to overfitting especially when the tree becomes too deep and captures noise in the data.

b) Logistic Regression:

It is a linear model designed for binary classification problems such as determining whether a claim is false (0) or true (1). It assesses the likelihood of an event occurring and categorizes it as either 0 or 1 based on a predetermined threshold.

Compared to decision trees, logistic regression is less prone to overfitting, and it is generally easier to implement and interpret. However, it may not perform well if the relationships between input features and labels are highly nonlinear.

Secondly: Unsupervised Learning Techniques for Fraud Detection:

It is a machine learning technique used in fraud detection where the model doesn't rely on labeled examples. Instead, it discovers patterns, relationships, or anomalies in the data independently. It has two common methods:

a) K-Means Clustering:

The primary objective of K-Means is to divide the dataset into a predefined number of clusters based on the similarity of data points. In the context of fraud detection, the assumption is that fraudulent cases will form their own distinct cluster within the data. Once identified, these clusters can be flagged as potential fraud.

K-Means is relatively easy to implement and can handle large datasets. However, it is sensitive to initial conditions and its effectiveness may vary depending on the quality of the initial cluster centroids. It may not always find the most optimal solution.

b) Anomaly Detection:

This method identifies cases in the data that are significantly different from the majority of data points and flags them as potential fraud. Anomaly detection is particularly useful for detecting rare and unusual cases of fraud that might not be identified by more traditional methods.

However, it can produce a relatively high number of false positives as it might flag legitimate but uncommon transactions or behaviors as anomalies. Additionally, it may not be as effective at detecting more common types of fraud.

Thirdly: Semi-Supervised Learning for Fraud Detection:

It is a machine learning approach that combines elements of both supervised and unsupervised learning. In this approach, the model is trained on a dataset that is partially labeled. Thus, some of the data points have known labels (supervised data), while others do not (unlabeled data). The goal of semi-supervised learning is to leverage the labeled data to improve the model's performance on both the labeled and unlabeled cases.

Support Vector Machines (SVMs) are a popular technique used in semi-supervised learning. SVMs operate by finding a hyperplane in a high-dimensional space that best separates different classes or categories of data points. They are known for their effectiveness in a wide range of applications and their ability to handle high-dimensional data effectively (*Machine Learning Techniques for Detecting Insurance Claims Fraud, Aarathi Jaikrishnan - Google Search*, n.d.).

6.3.2.1.3 Advantages of Machine Learning Model:

Machine learning models offer several advantages, which have made them increasingly popular and impactful in insurance field:

- Machine learning models can automate tasks that would be time-consuming or even impossible to accomplish manually. This includes tasks such as data analysis, pattern recognition, and decision-making.
- It can handle large and complex datasets, making them scalable to a wide range of applications, from small-scale data analysis to big data processing.
- It can provide high levels of accuracy and precision in tasks such as image recognition, natural language processing, and predictive analytics. With

proper training and optimization, they can outperform human experts in some domains.

- It has the ability to generalize from the data they are trained on, which means they can make predictions or decisions on new, unseen data. This generalization capability is a key strength of ML models.
- It can adapt to changing data patterns and can be retrained to improve their performance over time. This adaptability is crucial in dynamic environments where data distributions may change.
- Once trained, machine learning models can make predictions or decisions in real-time or near-real-time, which is valuable in applications like fraud detection, recommendation systems, and autonomous vehicles.
- Automating tasks with machine learning models can lead to cost savings by reducing the need for human labor in tasks such as data entry, data analysis, and customer support. To prove that, a Turkish insurer saving $5.7 million and achieving a 210% increase in Return on Investment (ROI), after investing in a fraud prevention system which demonstrates the potential financial benefits.
- It makes decisions based on predefined algorithms and patterns, ensuring consistent and unbiased decision-making, which can be challenging for human operators.
- ML models can handle complex, multidimensional data and extract meaningful insights from it, even when the relationships within the data are not obvious to humans.
- With access to new data and improved algorithms, machine learning models can be continually improved to enhance their performance and accuracy.
- Machine learning models enable the creation of personalized experiences for users in applications like recommendation systems, marketing, and content delivery.
- By automating tasks, machine learning models can reduce the risk of human errors, particularly in tasks that require repetitive or monotonous actions.
- It can help discover hidden patterns, correlations, and insights within data, which can inform decision-making and strategy development.
- ML models can optimize resource allocation in various processes, such as supply chain management, energy consumption, and resource utilization.
- ML models can predict when equipment or machinery is likely to fail, enabling proactive maintenance and reducing downtime.

It's important to note that while machine learning models offer numerous advantages, they also come with challenges including the need for high-quality data, potential biases in the data, model interpretability and ethical considerations (Kose et al., 2015).

6.3.2.2 The Application of AI-in Fraud Detection by Major Players in the Insurance Industry

Insurance companies have recognized the importance of protecting themselves from fraudulent claims, where people may try to deceive the insurance company for financial gain. To combat this, many AI companies have developed and offering solutions that use AI technology to detect and prevent fraudulent insurance claims. In the following, we will explain how the top global insurers are using AI to detect fraud:

a) Anadolu Sigorta:

It is a prominent insurance company in Turkey known as the first and one of the largest insurers in the country. In the past, they employed a team of 50 individuals who manually assessed each insurance claim for potential fraud. These assessments were based on somewhat flexible rules and the team members' personal experience in detecting fraudulent claims.

However, in an effort to streamline and enhance their fraud detection process, Anadolu Sigorta decided to adopt an artificial intelligence (AI) software solution. They acquired predictive analytics software from a company called "Friss" which specializes in fraud detection and prevention. The results of this transition were quite impressive:

- According to the customer success story, Anadolu Sigorta saw a remarkable 210% return on investment within just one year of implementing the "Friss" software. This suggests that the investment in the AI software yielded significant financial benefits for the company.
- Anadolu Sigorta faced a substantial volume of claims, with 25,000 to 30,000 claims to evaluate for potential fraud indicators each month. Prior to implementing the AI solution, this was a time-consuming process that took almost two weeks to complete for each claim.
- The "Friss" software allowed Anadolu Sigorta to assess the risk of fraud associated with a claim in real-time. This means that they could quickly and efficiently identify suspicious claims and potentially prevent fraudulent payouts.
- The customer success story also highlights that Anadolu Sigorta saved a significant amount of money, specifically \$5.7 million, in fraud detection and prevention costs by using the "Friss" software. This indicates that the AI solution not only improved efficiency but also reduced the financial impact of fraudulent claims.

Overall, the case of Anadolu Sigorta demonstrates how adopting AI technology, specifically predictive analytics software from "Friss" helped them to enhance their fraud detection process, reduce costs and significantly improve their return on investment within a relatively short period of time.

b) AXA:

It is a prominent French life insurance company. It is collaborating with the UK-based startup Darktrace to implement an AI-driven fraud detection solution.

AXA's primary concern was to monitor their entire network and detect emerging threats from advanced cybercriminals. They wanted to identify and address potential security breaches before they escalated into larger problems.

AXA has a complex infrastructure due to its acquisition of various companies with different levels of integration. This complexity required a solution capable of adapting to different circumstances depending on the specific branch or subsidiary being analyzed.

Darktrace's solution, called the "Enterprise Immune System" is designed to detect anomalies in the behavior of computer and network users within AXA. It accomplishes this by learning the typical patterns of each user's activity throughout the workday. After learning these patterns, the Enterprise Immune System uses AI to correlate the data and identify relationships between the responsibilities and activities of different users within the organization. This can help identify suspicious or unusual behavior that may indicate a security threat.

Darktrace's solution includes "Antigena," an autonomous response software. When Antigena detects behavior consistent with data security threats, fraud, or preparations for fraud based on its training, it can take action within AXA's network. This action may include shutting down users or taking other protective measures to mitigate the threat.

c) CNA Financial:

It is a large insurance company that has decided to use AI software for detecting fraud in insurance claims. CNA Financial's primary goal was to automate their claims fraud detection process. They wanted to make the process more efficient and effective.

They chose Shift Technology as their preferred vendor to help them to achieve this goal. Shift Technology provided them with a software solution called "FORCE" for automating fraud detection.

In addition to automating fraud detection, CNA Financial also aimed to understand the context surrounding the detected fraud. This means they wanted to not only identify fraudulent claims but also gain insights into why and how fraud was occurring. They intended to optimize their special investigations by focusing on the most suspicious claims. They used predetermined analytical paths to guide their investigative efforts and ensuring that all known fraud methods are thoroughly examined.

The mention of "predetermined paths for fraud analysis" and the software's ability to provide "contextual information regarding the best next step" suggests that Shift Technology's FORCE software is a predictive analytics application. It not only identifies potential fraud but also recommends actions or investigative steps based on the detected fraud patterns.

In summary, CNA Financial partnered with Shift Technology to automate fraud detection in insurance claims while also gaining a deeper understanding of the fraud context. The software they adopted "FORCE" appears to be a predictive analytics tool that not only detects fraud but also assists in deciding the best course of action when fraud is suspected. This approach can help them improve their fraud investigation efforts and enhance their overall fraud prevention strategy (*Artificial Intelligence-Based Fraud Detection in Insurance, Niccolo,* Https://Emerj.Com/, *2019 - Google Search*, n.d.).

7. STATISTICS

Innovation is crucial in determining how insurers assess risks while offering coverage in the always changing insurance sector. The use of artificial intelligence (AI) in underwriting is one of the most revolutionary advances in recent years. This development has transformed risk assessment and stimulated market expansion, providing insurers and policyholders with a more specialized and effective insurance experience.

Underwriting has historically involved a systematic process that relied on historical data and fundamental demographics. However, a new era of accuracy and customisation has arrived due to AI-powered underwriting models

According to Statista, the worldwide insurtech industry is predicted to reach $16.4 billion by 2025. This increase will be driven by the use of AI in underwriting.

While the insurance tech market will be worth $166.4 billion by 2030 with an average yearly increase of 39.1%,(*Wilson, F. (2023) INSURTECH Market Size to Reach USD 166.4 Billion by 2030. Retrieved from* Https://Www.Acumenresearchandconsulting.Com/Press-Releases/Insurtech-Market - *Google Search*, n.d.)

The size of the worldwide insurance fraud detection market was estimated at US$2.5 billion in 2019, US$3.3 billion in 2021, and is anticipated to reach US$28.1 billion by 2031, expanding at a CAGR. of 24.2 from 2022 to 2031%. (Https://

Figure 1. Insurance fraud detection market

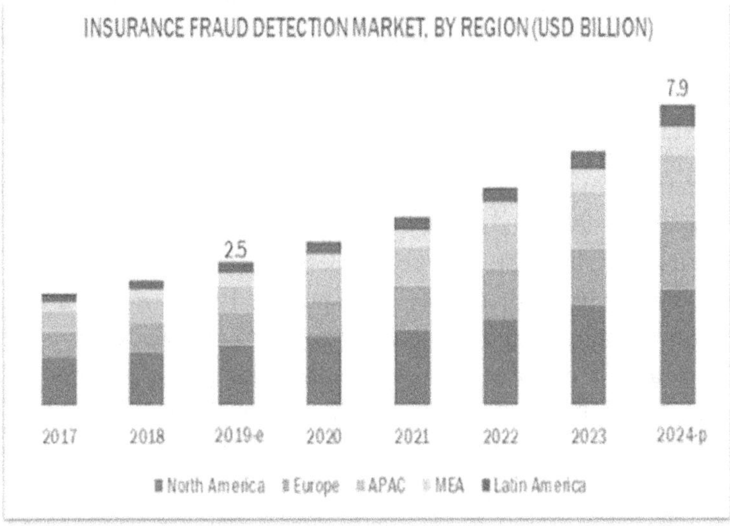

Www.Marketsandmarkets.Com/Market-Reports/Insurance-Fraud-Detection-Market-139715396.Html. - *Google Search*, n.d.).

By 2024, the market is anticipated to grow at a CAGR of 25.8% and reach US$7.9 billion. The adoption of sophisticated analytics, regulatory compliance, improved operational efficiency, improved customer experience, and effective identity management are some key growth drivers According to the attached figure 1 (Https:// Www.Alliedmarketresearch.Com/Insurance-Fraud-Detection-Market-A06948. - *Google Search*, n.d.).

CONCLUSION

In conclusion, insurance fraud poses significant challenges to the insurance industry, policyholders, and society as a whole. Hence, insurance fraud lead to substantial financial losses to insurance companies and increased premiums for policyholders. It encompasses various deceptive practices aimed at obtaining illegitimate payouts from insurance companies. However, with the application of AI and a collaboration between all stakeholders, it is possible to mitigate the impact of fraud, reduce financial losses, and ensure that insurance remains a reliable and cost-effective risk management tool for individuals and businesses.

Results

- This research defines key concepts related to insurance, fraud, and insurance fraud. Also, it effectively explores various types of insurance fraud and explains its significant consequences for both insurers and policyholders.
- This paper provided real examples of fraudulent activities which enhances the understanding and demonstrates the real-world impact of insurance fraud.
- This paper has discussed the status of insurance fraud in accordance of Omani laws and highlighted the legal consequences and implications.
- The research provided insights into anti-fraud measures by explaining the role of laws and regulations in preventing fraud and maintaining the integrity of the insurance industry. Also, by emphasizing the importance of proactive measures taken by insurance companies to prevent fraud.
- This paper provides a clear understanding of how AI is used in the insurance sector for fraud detection and prevention.

Recommendations

- Encourage legislators and policymakers to collaborate with the insurance industry to continually update and strengthen legal frameworks that address emerging fraud tactics.
- Promote collaboration between insurance sector and other relevant sectors by Sharing information and best practices through advanced electronic linking program that can lead to a more universal approach to fraud prevention.
- Ensure that insurance industry professionals receive ongoing training in fraud detection and prevention techniques. This education should include the latest fraud schemes and should evolve technologies to stay ahead of fraudsters.
- Collaborate with government agencies and industry associations to launch public awareness campaigns about insurance fraud. This aims to educate the general public about the costs and consequences of fraud and encourage reporting of suspicious activities.
- Establishing specialized units in insurance companies entrusted with the task of investigating and detecting fraudulent acts.
- Implement AI systems that can analyze multiple data sources and modalities including structured data (e.g., claims data) and unstructured data (e.g., text, images, and voice). This comprehensive approach improves fraud detection capabilities.

REFERENCES

About CMA. (n.d.). Capital Market Authority, Sultanate of Oman.

An Interactive Machine-Learning-Based Electronic Fraud and Abuse Detection System in Healthcare Insurance. (2015). Faculty of Engineering and Natural Sciences, Sabanci University.

Artificial Intelligence-Based Fraud Detection in Insurance. (2019). Niccolo. https://emerj.com/

Clarke, M. (1990). the control of insurance fraud, a comparative view. *British Journal of Criminology*, *30*(1).

Clarke, M. (2012). Policies and perceptions of insurance law. Oxford University Press.

Cydni. (2016, April 18). *Insurance fraud - definition, examples, cases, processes*. Legal Dictionary. https://legaldictionary.net/insurance-fraud/

Data misrepresentation detection for insurance underwriting fraud prevention. (2022, May 5). ScienceDirect. https://doi.org/ doi:10.1016/j.dss.2022.113798

Detecting insurance claims fraud using machine learning techniques. (2022). https://managementevents.com/

Feinman, J. M. (2017). Insurance Fraud, Agency, and Opportunism: False Swearing in Insurance Claims. *Agency, and Opportunism: False Swearing in Insurance Claims*.

Group, U. M. (2018, October 5). *What are the consequences of insurance fraud?* Cataño Insurance Brokers. https://catanoinsures.com/insurance-fraud-consequences/

How does the insurance sector benefit from artificial intelligence applications? (n.d.). Samar Al-Mashata. https://www.alarabiya.net

Insurance fraud report 2022: Real Time Data, a crucial asset in fraud fighting. (2022, March 17)._Business Wire. https://www.businesswire.com/news/home/20220317005223/en/Insurance-Fraud-Report-2022-Real-Time-Data-A-Crucial-Asset-In-Fraud-Fighting

Insurance Fraud Taskforce final report. (2016, January 21). GOV.UK. https://www.gov.uk/government/publications/insurance-fraud-taskforce-final-report

Jolly, J. (2023, August 29). *Top 7 Reasons to Transform Insurance Underwriting with AI*. Saxon. https://saxon.ai/blogs/top-7-reasons-to-transform-insurance-underwriting-with-ai/#:~:text=In%20this%20case%2C%20using%20AI,predictive%20analytics%20models%20and%20algorithms

Kagan, J. (n.d.). *Insurance.* Investopedia._https://www.investopedia.com/terms/i/insurance.asp

Machine Learning Techniques for Detecting Insurance Claims Fraud. (2023). Aarathi Jaikrishnan. https://experionglobal.com/

Mohamed, M. (2013). *Countering fraud in the insurance industry: A case study of Malaysia.* Academic Press.

Muhammad Bitar, M. (2016). *The Role of Criminal Legislation in Fraud Prevention.* Naif University for Security Sciences.

Niemi, H. (1995). Insurance fraud. *Eur. J. on Crim. Pol'y & Rsch., 3*, 48.

Patel, S. (2023, May 23). *Top Benefits & Use Cases of AI in Insurance Industry.* REVE Chat. https://www.revechat.com/blog/insuranceai/#:~:text=Insurers%20can%20rely%20on%20AI,them%20based%20on%20customer%20needs

Picard, P. (2000). *Insurance fraud: theory. Handbook of Insurance*. Kluwer.

Rotaru, I. (n.d.). *How do insurance companies use AI in 2023? Benefits and examples.* Chatfuel. https://chatfuel.com/blog/ai-insurance

Viaene, S., & Dedene, G. (2004). Insurance fraud: Issues and challenges. *The Geneva Papers on Risk and Insurance-Issues and Practice, 29*, 313-333.

Wilson, F. (2023). *INSURTECH market size to reach USD 166.4 billion by 2030.* Retrieved from https://www.acumenresearchandconsulting.com/press-releases/insurtech-market

Chapter 8
Frauds and Cyber Security Issues in the Finance Sector

Rajeev Tripathi
School of Management Science, India

Smita Tripathi
School of Management Science, India

ABSTRACT

In today's digital age, the importance of cybersecurity cannot be overstated, as it directly affects an individual's or organization's ability to protect themselves from various types of fraud. Organizations and individuals must stay vigilant, continuously update their security practices, and invest in cybersecurity technologies to minimize the risk of falling victim to fraudsters. Cybersecurity is the proactive defense against digital threats, while fraud prevention involves safeguarding against deceptive and dishonest activities. To effectively combat fraud, individuals and organizations must implement robust cybersecurity measures, stay informed about emerging threats, and educate themselves and their employees about the tactics used by fraudsters. Fraud and cyber security are two closely related topics that revolve around protecting sensitive information, assets, and systems from unauthorized access, manipulation, or theft.

In today's digital age, the importance of cybersecurity cannot be overstated, as it directly affects an individual's or organization's ability to protect themselves from various types of fraud. Organizations and individuals must stay vigilant, continuously update their security practices, and invest in cybersecurity technologies to minimize the risk of falling victim to fraudsters. cybersecurity is the proactive defense against

DOI: 10.4018/979-8-3693-1503-3.ch008

digital threats, while fraud prevention involves safeguarding against deceptive and dishonest activities. To effectively combat fraud, individuals and organizations must implement robust cybersecurity measures, stay informed about emerging threats, and educate themselves and their employees about the tactics used by fraudsters.

Frauds and cyber security are two closely related topics that revolve around protecting sensitive information, assets, and systems from unauthorized access, manipulation, or theft. Frauds often leverage weaknesses in cybersecurity to carry out their activities. This is why it's crucial for individuals and organizations to implement robust cybersecurity measures to protect against fraud and other cyber threats. Both frauds and cybersecurity are evolving fields. As technology advances, new fraud tactics emerge, and cybersecurity measures must adapt to counter these threats (Ng & Kwok, 2017). Staying informed about the latest trends and practices in both areas is essential for individuals, businesses, and organizations to protect themselves in the digital landscape.

Fraud refers to any deceptive activity or act designed to gain an unfair or unlawful advantage, typically involving deceit, trickery, or misrepresentation. It can occur in various forms, such as financial fraud, identity theft, and online scams. Frauds can occur in various domains, including finance, commerce, healthcare, and more. Some common types of fraud include:

- **Financial Fraud:** This involves activities such as credit card fraud, investment scams, Ponzi schemes, and identity theft. Attackers may use stolen information to make unauthorized transactions or gain access to victims' financial accounts.
- **Phishing:** Phishing is a cyber-attack in which attackers impersonate legitimate entities (often via emails, websites, or messages) to trick individuals into revealing sensitive information like passwords, credit card numbers, or personal data.
- **Social Engineering:** This involves manipulating individuals into divulging confidential information or performing actions that compromise security. Techniques include pretexting (creating fabricated scenarios), baiting (luring victims into traps), and tailgating (gaining unauthorized physical access).
- **Online Shopping Scams:** With the rise of e-commerce, scammers create fake online stores or listings to sell nonexistent products, resulting in financial loss for unsuspecting buyers.
- **Tech Support Scams:** Attackers pose as technical support personnel and convince victims to grant remote access to their computers or pay for unnecessary services to fix nonexistent issues.

- **Identity Theft**: Obtaining someone's personal data, such as their social security number or credit card information, in order to pass yourself off as them and profit financially.
- **Credit Card Fraud**: Unauthorized use of someone's credit card information to make purchases.
- **Investment and Ponzi Schemes**: Deceptive investment opportunities that promise high returns but actually use funds from new investors to pay returns to earlier investors.
- **Insurance Fraud**: Faking accidents, injuries, or other events to file false insurance claims.
- **Employee Fraud**: Fraudulent activities conducted by employees within an organization, such as embezzlement or manipulating financial records.
- **Tax Evasion**: Illegally reducing tax liability through misrepresentation of income or expenses.

Investment and Ponzi Schemes: Investment schemes and Ponzi schemes are two distinct financial structures with significantly different purposes and outcomes. Understanding the differences is crucial to protect yourself from fraudulent activities.

Investment Schemes

- Legitimate Investment: An investment scheme, in its legal and legitimate form, involves individuals or organizations investing their money in various financial instruments or assets with the expectation of earning a return on their investment. These investments can include stocks, bonds, mutual funds, real estate, or other assets.
- Transparency and Regulation: Legitimate investments are typically transparent, and investors have legal protections. The financial industry is often regulated to ensure that investors' rights are safeguarded.
- Risk and Returns: Investments carry varying degrees of risk, and returns are generally commensurate with the level of risk. Legitimate investors understand and accept the potential for both gains and losses.
- Investment Advisors: Many investors work with licensed investment advisors or professionals who help them make informed investment decisions.

Ponzi Schemes

- Illegal Scheme: A Ponzi scheme is an illegal investment scheme designed to defraud investors. It promises high, consistent returns but doesn't actually invest the money as claimed.

- High Returns: Ponzi schemes attract investors by offering abnormally high returns, often significantly higher than what legitimate investments can offer. These returns are usually paid to early investors using funds from newer investors.
- Lack of Real Investments: In a Ponzi scheme, there are no real investments generating returns. The returns paid to early investors come from the capital of newer investors, creating a facade of profitability.
- Unsustainable: Ponzi schemes are unsustainable by nature. As long as there is a continuous influx of new investors, the scheme can appear to work. However, when the flow of new investments slows down or stops, the scheme collapses, and most investors lose their money.
- Criminal Consequences: Operating or participating in a Ponzi scheme is illegal in most jurisdictions and can result in criminal charges and imprisonment for those involved.
- Red Flags: Red flags for Ponzi schemes include promises of consistently high returns with little to no risk, a lack of transparency about how the investments work, and pressure to recruit new investors.

Phishing: Phishing is a type of cyberattack in which malicious actors attempt to deceive individuals or organizations into revealing sensitive or confidential information, such as login credentials, credit card numbers, or personal identification details. This is typically done by posing as a trustworthy entity, such as a legitimate company, financial institution, or government agency. Phishing attacks are often carried out through various communication channels, including email, text messages, social media, and even phone calls (Bajracharya et al., 2023). To protect yourself or your organization from phishing attacks, it's essential to remain cautious when receiving unsolicited messages or communications, especially if they request sensitive information. Look for signs of phishing, like generic greetings, typos, and suspicious email addresses. Always verify the legitimacy of requests for sensitive information, whether through a different communication channel or by contacting the supposed sender directly. Employing cybersecurity measures like email filtering, two-factor authentication, and educating users about phishing risks can also help mitigate these threats. Here are some common types of phishing attacks:

- **Email Phishing:** In email phishing, attackers send fraudulent emails that appear to be from a reputable source. These emails often contain links to fake websites or malicious attachments, aiming to trick recipients into providing personal information.
- **Spear Phishing:** Spear phishing is a targeted form of phishing. Attackers customize their messages to specific individuals or organizations, often using

personal information gathered from social media or other sources to make their emails seem more convincing.

- **Phishing Websites:** Attackers create fake websites that closely resemble legitimate ones, tricking users into entering their login credentials or other sensitive information. This is often done through email links or by manipulating search engine results.
- **Smishing:** This type of phishing occurs through text messages (SMS). Users receive fraudulent texts that ask them to click on links or respond with personal information.
- **Vishing:** Vishing, or voice phishing, involves attackers making phone calls to individuals and pretending to be from trusted organizations, such as banks or government agencies, to extract sensitive information.
- **Clone Phishing**: In clone phishing, attackers take a legitimate email, make a copy of it with malicious alterations, and then send the altered version to the recipient, often containing malicious links or attachments.
- **Whaling:** Whaling attacks specifically target high-profile individuals within an organization, such as executives or senior management, to gain access to sensitive data or financial information.

Financial Fraud: Financial fraud refers to a broad category of illegal activities that involve deceptive practices to gain financial benefits or advantages at the expense of others. These fraudulent activities can occur in various contexts, such as personal finance, business, investments, and more. Preventing and combatting financial fraud involves awareness, vigilance, and taking steps to protect your personal and financial information (Saha & Shaw, 2019). This includes safeguarding personal data, regularly monitoring financial statements, and reporting any suspicious or fraudulent activity to the relevant authorities. Additionally, it's essential to be cautious of offers that seem too good to be true and to conduct due diligence before making financial decisions or investments. The common types of financial frauds are as follows:

Check Fraud: Check fraud includes activities like forging or altering checks, creating counterfeit checks, or using stolen checks to make unauthorized payments or withdrawals from bank accounts.

Mortgage and Real Estate Fraud: This type of fraud may involve misrepresenting information on mortgage applications, engaging in predatory lending practices, or other forms of deceit related to real estate transactions.

Investment Scams: Investment fraud includes schemes where individuals or entities promise high returns on investments but misuse the invested funds. Examples include Ponzi schemes, pyramid schemes, and pump-and-dump schemes.

Insurance Fraud: Insurance fraud can be committed by policyholders, claimants, or even insurance professionals. It involves filing false or exaggerated insurance claims to receive undeserved payouts.

Tax Fraud: Tax fraud encompasses activities such as underreporting income, inflating deductions, or using illegal tax shelters to evade taxes owed to the government.

Bank Fraud: Bank fraud can involve fraudulent activities related to banking institutions, such as making false statements on loan applications, embezzlement by bank employees, or using stolen or counterfeit checks to withdraw funds.

Wire Fraud: Wire fraud is a federal crime involving the use of electronic communication systems, such as emails or phone calls, to commit fraudulent schemes. This can include scams related to phishing, advance fee fraud, or business email compromise (BEC).

Pyramid Schemes: Pyramid schemes are illegal investment schemes where participants are promised high returns for recruiting new members. Money from new recruits is used to pay earlier participants, and the scheme eventually collapses, leaving many participants with losses.

Embezzlement: Embezzlement is the misappropriation of funds or property entrusted to someone's care, often occurring within an organization, business, or nonprofit.Embezzlement is a white-collar crime that involves the misappropriation or theft of funds or assets entrusted to an individual's care or control, typically by an employee or a person in a position of trust within an organization (Goutam, 2015). It occurs when someone who is responsible for managing or safeguarding the assets of another person or entity diverts those assets for their personal gain or unauthorized use.

- Trust and Responsibility: Embezzlement typically occurs in situations where a person is given access or control over funds or assets due to their role or position within an organization, such as an employee, financial manager, treasurer, or accountant. They are entrusted with these assets because they are expected to handle them responsibly.
- Misappropriation: Embezzlement involves the wrongful appropriation of the assets or funds. The person committing embezzlement does not have legal ownership of the assets but has access to them as part of their job responsibilities.
- Concealment: Embezzlers often try to cover up their activities by manipulating financial records, creating fraudulent documentation, or using other deceptive means to hide the theft.
- Types of Assets: Embezzlement can involve a wide range of assets, including money, stocks, bonds, property, intellectual property, or any item of value that belongs to the victim, which is taken without authorization.

- Motivation: People engage in embezzlement for personal gain, such as enriching themselves, paying off debts, funding a lavish lifestyle, or covering up other financial improprieties. In some cases, embezzlement may be driven by desperation or addiction.
- Legal Consequences: Embezzlement is considered a criminal offense and is subject to legal penalties. The severity of the penalties depends on the amount embezzled and the jurisdiction's laws. Penalties may include fines, restitution to the victim, probation, or imprisonment.
- Detection and Prevention: Organizations often implement internal controls and audit procedures to detect and prevent embezzlement. This may involve segregation of duties, regular financial audits, and strong oversight of financial transactions.
- Reporting: If embezzlement is suspected or detected, it should be reported to law enforcement and appropriate legal action taken to address the issue.

Tax evasion: Tax evasion is the illegal act of not paying the full amount of taxes owed to the government by underreporting income, inflating deductions, hiding money or assets, or using other fraudulent means to reduce one's tax liability. It's important to note that tax evasion is a serious crime and can result in significant legal and financial consequences. It is in everyone's interest to pay their fair share of taxes and comply with tax laws to support government services and programs.

Key Points About Tax Evasion Include

- Illegal Activity: Tax evasion is illegal, and those found guilty of it can face serious legal consequences, including fines and imprisonment.
- Deception: Tax evasion involves intentionally deceiving tax authorities by providing false or misleading information on tax returns. This can include underreporting income, inflating expenses, hiding assets in offshore accounts, or using fake invoices.
- Difference from Tax Avoidance: Tax evasion is distinct from tax avoidance, which involves using legal methods to minimize tax liability. Tax avoidance may involve using tax deductions, credits, or other legitimate strategies to reduce taxes owed.
- Consequences: The penalties for tax evasion can vary by jurisdiction but typically include fines, imprisonment, or both. In some cases, assets may be seized to satisfy tax debts.
- International Implications: Tax evasion involving offshore accounts or international financial transactions can have global implications. Many countries have signed international agreements, such as the Common

Reporting Standard (CRS) and the Foreign Account Tax Compliance Act (FATCA), to share financial information and combat tax evasion.

- Whistleblower Programs: Some countries offer whistleblower programs that reward individuals for reporting tax evasion. These programs can incentivize individuals with knowledge of tax evasion to come forward and provide information to tax authorities.
- Prevention and Compliance: To avoid legal trouble, individuals and businesses should ensure they accurately report their income and comply with tax laws. Working with tax professionals and accountants can help ensure compliance.

Credit Card Fraud: Credit card fraud is a type of financial fraud in which someone uses another person's credit card information without their permission to make unauthorized purchases or transactions. This can happen in various ways, and it is a serious criminal offense.

Types of Credit Card Fraud

1 -Card Not Present (CNP) Fraud: This occurs when a fraudster uses stolen credit card information to make online or phone purchases where the physical card is not required.

- ◦ Card Present Fraud: In this type of fraud, the criminal uses a physical card to make unauthorized transactions, often through methods like skimming or card cloning.
- ◦ Application Fraud: This involves applying for a credit card using someone else's identity or false information.
- ◦ Lost or Stolen Card Fraud: When a credit card is lost or stolen, it can be used by someone other than the cardholder to make unauthorized transactions.

2- Methods of Committing Credit Card Fraud:

- ◦ Skimming: Criminals install devices on card readers, such as ATMs or gas station pumps, to capture card information when the card is swiped.
- ◦ Phishing: Fraudsters may use phishing emails or websites to trick individuals into providing their credit card details.
- ◦ Data Breaches: Large-scale data breaches of businesses or financial institutions can lead to the theft of credit card information.
- ◦ Carding: Criminals test stolen credit card information by making small, inconspicuous transactions before attempting larger purchases.

3- Consequences of Credit Card Fraud:

- ◦ Victims of credit card fraud may face financial losses if unauthorized charges are not promptly reported and resolved.

- Credit card companies and banks often have fraud protection measures in place, and most cardholders are not liable for fraudulent charges if they report them promptly.
- Perpetrators of credit card fraud can face legal consequences, including fines and imprisonment.

4-Prevention and Protection:

- Protect your physical cards and card information. Be cautious when sharing card details online.
- Regularly monitor your credit card statements for unauthorized transactions.
- Use strong and unique passwords for online accounts and consider two-factor authentication.
- If your card is lost or stolen, report it to your card issuer immediately to limit potential damage.

5-Reporting Credit Card Fraud:

- If you suspect credit card fraud, contact your card issuer or bank immediately to report the unauthorized charges and request a card replacement.
- In many cases, you will need to file a police report to document the fraud.

Advance Fee Frauds: In advance fee frauds, scammers convince victims to pay an upfront fee for a promised benefit, such as a lottery win, job opportunity, or business deal. Once the fee is paid, the promised benefit never materializes.

Cyber Scam: It is an online scam, is a fraudulent activity conducted over the internet with the intention of deceiving individuals or organizations for financial gain or other malicious purposes. Cyber scams come in various forms and can target a wide range of victims, from individuals to businesses. There are several types of cyber scam:

Phishing Scams: Phishing involves sending deceptive emails or messages that appear to be from a legitimate source, such as a bank or a well-known company. These messages often contain links or attachments that, when clicked, can lead to the theft of personal information, including usernames, passwords, and financial data.

Online Shopping Scams: In these scams, fraudsters create fake online stores or auction sites to trick people into buying products or services that don't exist. Victims make payments but never receive the promised goods or services.

Advance Fee Fraud: This type of scam involves convincing victims to pay an upfront fee with the promise of a larger benefit in the future. Common examples include lottery scams, inheritance scams, and job offer scams. Once the initial fee is paid, the promised benefit never materializes.

Tech Support Scams: Scammers often pretend to be tech support agents from well-known companies and claim that the victim's computer has a problem. They request remote access to the victim's computer, install malware, and demand payment to fix non-existent issues.

Romance Scams: In romance scams, criminals create fake online dating profiles and build romantic relationships with victims. Eventually, they request money for various reasons, such as medical emergencies or travel expenses, and disappear once they receive payments.

Social Engineering Scams: These scams involve manipulating people through psychological tactics to reveal sensitive information or perform actions that they wouldn't normally do. This can include impersonating a trusted colleague or family member to gain access to sensitive data.

Ransomware Attacks: Ransomware is a type of malware that encrypts a victim's data and demands a ransom to provide the decryption key. Paying the ransom is discouraged, as it doesn't guarantee the return of your data.

Job Scams: Fraudulent job postings are used to extract personal information, such as Social Security numbers or bank account details, from job seekers. These scams can also involve fake job offers that require upfront fees.

Cybersecurity: Protecting computer systems, networks, and data against theft, damage, or unauthorised access is the practise of cybersecurity. It encompasses various measures and best practices to ensure the confidentiality, integrity, and availability of digital assets. It involves a range of technologies, processes, and practices to safeguard digital assets. Key aspects of cybersecurity include:

- **Network Security**: Protecting networks from unauthorized access and cyberattacks using firewalls, intrusion detection systems, and encryption.
- **Endpoint Security**: Ensuring the security of individual devices like computers, smartphones, and tablets through antivirus software, device encryption, and patch management.
- **Information Security**: Safeguarding sensitive data through encryption, access controls, and data loss prevention measures.
- **Application Security**: Securing software applications from vulnerabilities and exploitation, typically through secure coding practices and regular updates.
- **Incident Response**: Developing plans and procedures to respond effectively to security incidents and data breaches.
- **Security Awareness Training**: Educating employees and users about cybersecurity best practices to reduce human error and social engineering attacks.

- **Cloud Security**: Protecting data and applications hosted in cloud environments through access controls, encryption, and continuous monitoring.
- **IoT (Internet of Things) Security**: Ensuring the security of interconnected devices and sensors, which can be vulnerable to attacks. Internet of Things (IoT) security refers to the measures and practices designed to protect the connected devices, networks, and data associated with the IoT ecosystem. IoT involves a wide range of devices, from smart thermostats and wearable technology to industrial sensors and autonomous vehicles, and securing these devices is essential to prevent potential vulnerabilities and breaches.

Device Authentication and Authorization

Ensuring that IoT devices are only accessible and controllable by authorized individuals or systems is crucial. This involves strong authentication methods, such as device certificates and user credentials, to verify the identity of devices and users.

Data Encryption

Data transmitted between IoT devices and servers or other devices should be encrypted to protect it from interception or tampering. Strong encryption protocols, like TLS (Transport Layer Security), are essential.

Firmware and Software Updates

Regularly updating the firmware and software on IoT devices is vital to patch security vulnerabilities. Manufacturers should provide a mechanism for easy and secure updates.

Network Security

Securing the network infrastructure through which IoT devices communicate is crucial. This includes using firewalls, intrusion detection systems, and network segmentation to prevent unauthorized access.

Access Control

Implementing strict access control policies is essential to limit who can interact with IoT devices and their data. Role-based access control can help manage permissions effectively.

Secure Boot and Hardware Security

Ensuring the integrity of the device's boot process and using secure hardware components can protect against physical and software-based attacks.

Device Management

Centralized device management solutions can help monitor, update, and enforce security policies for large IoT deployments.

Privacy Protection

IoT devices often collect sensitive data. Privacy measures should be in place to protect the data and ensure that users have control over what information is shared.

Security by Design

Security should be a fundamental consideration in the design and development of IoT devices and systems. This includes threat modeling and risk assessments during the design phase.

IoT Ecosystem Security

Securing the entire IoT ecosystem, including cloud services and applications, is critical. All components need to be protected to prevent vulnerabilities at any point.

Regulatory Compliance

Ensure compliance with relevant data protection and privacy regulations, which can vary by region (e.g., GDPR in Europe, CCPA in California).

Education and Training

Users and administrators should be educated about IoT security best practices to minimize the risk of human error.

Vulnerability Assessment and Penetration Testing

Regularly test IoT devices and systems for vulnerabilities and weaknesses through security assessments.

- **Threat Intelligence**: Staying informed about current cybersecurity threats and vulnerabilities to proactively defend against them.
- **Authentication and Access Control:** Ensuring that only authorized users can access systems and data through strong authentication methods (like multi-factor authentication) and proper access control policies.
- **Data Encryption:** Encrypting sensitive data both in transit and at rest to prevent unauthorized parties from reading or modifying the information.
- **Firewalls and Intrusion Detection/Prevention Systems:** Firewalls act as barriers between trusted internal networks and potentially malicious external networks. Intrusion detection/prevention systems monitor network traffic for suspicious activities and respond to them.
- **Regular Software Updates:** Keeping software, operating systems, and applications up to date with the latest security patches helps protect against known vulnerabilities.
- **Employee Training:** Educating employees about cybersecurity best practices, such as recognizing phishing attempts, using strong passwords, and being cautious about sharing sensitive information, is crucial.

Relationship Between Frauds and Cybersecurity: Frauds often leverage weaknesses in cybersecurity to carry out their activities. This is why it's crucial for individuals and organizations to implement robust cybersecurity measures to protect against fraud and other cyber threats. Both frauds and cybersecurity are evolving fields (Baur-Yazbeck et al., 2019). As technology advances, new fraud tactics emerge, and cybersecurity measures must adapt to counter these threats. Staying informed about the latest trends and practices in both areas is essential for individuals, businesses, and organizations to protect themselves in the digital landscape. Cybersecurity plays a fundamental role in preventing, detecting, and mitigating fraud in the digital age. The increasing reliance on digital platforms and the internet for financial transactions and communication makes it imperative for individuals, businesses, and organizations to invest in robust cybersecurity measures to protect against various forms of fraud.

1. **Prevention**: Effective cybersecurity measures can help prevent many forms of fraud. For example, strong authentication mechanisms can reduce the risk of identity theft, and robust network security can thwart phishing attempts.
2. **Detection**: Cybersecurity tools and practices often play a crucial role in detecting fraudulent activities. Intrusion detection systems (IDS) and security information and event management (SIEM) systems can identify suspicious behavior.

3. **Investigation**: In the event of a fraud, cybersecurity experts may be called upon to investigate the breach, identify the culprits, and determine how the fraud occurred.
4. **Mitigation**: Cybersecurity experts also help in mitigating the impact of fraud by isolating compromised systems, restoring data, and implementing additional security measures to prevent future incidents.
5. **Phishing Attacks:** Cybercriminals use phishing emails to trick individuals into revealing sensitive information. Effective email security measures are essential to mitigate this threat.
6. **Data Breaches:** Large-scale data breaches can lead to identity theft and other forms of fraud. Robust data security practices are crucial to prevent breaches.
7. **Malware:** Malicious software can steal financial information or provide unauthorized access to systems. Good endpoint security is necessary to combat malware.
8. **Social Engineering:** Fraudsters manipulate individuals into divulging sensitive information or performing actions that benefit the attacker. Security awareness training helps prevent such attacks.
9. **Online Payment Frauds:** Strong encryption and secure payment gateways are essential to protect against credit card fraud and unauthorized transactions.
10. **Business Email Compromise (BEC):** BEC is a type of fraud that often involves cybercriminals compromising business email accounts to impersonate company executives and manipulate employees into transferring funds. Enhanced email security and authentication methods are essential in preventing BEC attacks.
11. **Regulatory Compliance:** Many industries are subject to cybersecurity regulations and standards, which help protect against fraud. Compliance with these regulations, such as GDPR or HIPAA, often includes measures to safeguard sensitive data and prevent fraud.
12. **Secure Communication:** Secure communication channels are critical in preventing fraud. Cybersecurity measures, including end-to-end encryption, ensure that sensitive information shared between parties remains confidential and is not intercepted by malicious actors.
13. **Ransomware and Extortion**: Cybersecurity efforts are crucial in protecting organizations from ransomware attacks. Ransomware can be a form of digital extortion, where criminals encrypt critical data and demand a ransom to restore access. Effective cybersecurity measures can prevent and mitigate such attacks.
14. **Protection of Online Accounts:** Cybersecurity is essential in protecting online accounts, including email, social media, and financial accounts. Unauthorized access to these accounts can lead to various forms of fraud, such as unauthorized purchases or identity theft.

Effect of Frauds and cybersecurity in daily life: The effects of frauds and cybersecurity in daily life are significant and influence individuals, businesses, and society as a whole. In daily life, individuals and organizations must remain vigilant and proactive in addressing cybersecurity challenges and preventing fraud. This involves using secure practices, keeping software and systems up to date, educating oneself about fraud prevention, and staying informed about the latest cybersecurity threats. Additionally, reporting fraud and suspicious activities to the appropriate authorities helps protect others and hold perpetrators accountable.

1. Financial Loss:

Individuals: Fraud can result in significant financial losses for individuals. Identity theft, credit card fraud, and online scams can deplete savings and damage credit scores.

Businesses: For businesses, fraud can lead to monetary losses due to unauthorized transactions, embezzlement, and payment fraud. It can also damage their reputation.

2. Personal Privacy and Security:

Individuals: Cybersecurity is essential for protecting personal data and privacy. Frequent data breaches can lead to the exposure of sensitive information, potentially causing emotional distress and identity theft.

Businesses: Organizations hold a vast amount of personal and sensitive data. Failing to secure this data can have legal and financial consequences.

3. Psychological Impact:

Individuals: Falling victim to fraud can be emotionally distressing. It erodes trust, leading to increased anxiety, stress, and a sense of violation.

Businesses: For companies, fraud incidents can harm the morale of employees who may feel vulnerable to scams or internal dishonesty.

4. Trust and Reputation:

Individuals: Experiencing fraud can make individuals more cautious and less trusting in their daily interactions, both online and offline.

Businesses: Maintaining a trustworthy reputation is critical for businesses. A breach in cybersecurity leading to fraud can damage customer trust, leading to lost sales and customers.

5. Time and Resources:

Individuals: Dealing with the aftermath of fraud, such as canceling compromised accounts and resolving fraudulent charges, can consume a significant amount of time and effort.

Businesses: Businesses must allocate resources to investigate fraud, invest in cybersecurity measures, and manage the fallout from any incidents.

6. Regulatory Compliance:

Businesses: Many businesses must adhere to cybersecurity regulations to protect customer data. Failure to do so can lead to legal consequences and financial penalties.

7. Impact on Online Activities:

Individuals: Due to concerns about cybersecurity and fraud, individuals may limit their online activities, hesitate to share information, or avoid certain online transactions.

Businesses: E-commerce businesses must work hard to establish trust and security to encourage customers to make online purchases.

8. Adaptation to Technological Advances:

Individuals: Staying informed about cybersecurity practices and evolving fraud tactics is necessary for individuals to protect themselves effectively.

Businesses: Organizations must continually invest in cybersecurity technology and training to adapt to the changing threat landscape.

Frauds and Cybersecurity in the Finance Sector

The finance sector is particularly vulnerable to fraud due to the large volumes of sensitive financial data it handles. Effective cybersecurity is crucial in this sector to protect assets, customer information, and maintain trust. Here's how fraud and cybersecurity intersect in the finance sector:

1. Types of Financial Fraud:
   a. **Payment Card Fraud**: Criminals steal credit card information and use it for unauthorized transactions.
   b. **Account Takeover (ATO)**: Fraudsters gain access to customer accounts through various means, such as phishing or password cracking.

c. **Identity Theft**: Thieves steal personal information to impersonate individuals and open fraudulent accounts or obtain loans.
d. **Phishing**: Emails or websites imitating legitimate financial institutions are used to trick individuals into revealing sensitive information.
e. **Insider Fraud**: Employees or insiders with access to financial systems may engage in fraudulent activities.
f. **Investment Scams**: Fraudulent investment schemes promising high returns can result in significant financial losses for investors.

2. Cybersecurity Measures in Finance:
    a. **Encryption**: Encrypting sensitive data to protect it from unauthorized access in transit and storage.
    b. **Two-Factor Authentication (2FA) and Multi-Factor Authentication (MFA):** Adding an extra layer of security by requiring multiple forms of authentication.
    c. **Firewalls**: Implementing robust firewalls to block unauthorized access to networks and data.
    d. **Security Information and Event Management (SIEM):** Using SIEM tools to monitor network traffic and detect unusual activity.
    e. **Data Loss Prevention (DLP)**: Implementing policies and tools to prevent the unauthorized transfer of sensitive data.
    f. **Regular Software Patching**: Updating software and systems to patch known vulnerabilities.
    g. **Anti-Phishing Solutions**: Employing technologies to detect and block phishing attempts.
    h. **Employee Training**: Educating employees about cybersecurity best practices and how to recognize potential threats.
3. Regulatory Compliance:

The finance sector is subject to numerous regulations, such as the Payment Card Industry Data Security Standard (PCI DSS) and the Gramm-Leach-Bliley Act (GLBA) in the United States. These regulations impose specific cybersecurity requirements on financial institutions to protect customer data.

4. Incident Response:

Having a robust incident response plan is critical in the finance sector. When a breach or fraud occurs, a well-prepared response can help minimize damage and restore trust.

5. Third-Party Risk Management:

Financial institutions often rely on third-party vendors for various services. Managing and accessing the cybersecurity of these vendors is crucial to prevent vulnerabilities from entering the financial ecosystem.

6. Machine Learning and AI:

Many financial institutions are turning to machine learning and artificial intelligence to detect patterns of fraudulent behavior in real-time. These technologies can analyze large volumes of data to identify suspicious activities.

In the finance sector, the battle against fraud is ongoing, and cybersecurity is an integral part of this effort. As financial technologies continue to evolve, so do the tactics used by fraudsters. Financial institutions must continually adapt and enhance their cybersecurity measures to stay ahead of emerging threats and protect both their assets and their customers' financial well-being. Robust cybersecurity measures are essential to protect both the institutions and their customers from the various types of fraud that can occur (Sharif & Mohammed, 2022). Regular monitoring, updating of security protocols, and collaboration with law enforcement agencies are crucial components of maintaining cybersecurity in the finance sector.

Prevention From Fraud and Cybersecurity in the Finance Sector

Preventing fraud and enhancing cybersecurity in the finance sector requires a multi-faceted approach that combines technology, processes, and employee training. Here are key prevention strategies:

1. **Implement Strong Authentication**:

Enforce multi-factor authentication (MFA) for both customers and employees. This adds an extra layer of security by requiring multiple forms of verification before granting access.

2. **Regularly Update and Patch Systems**:

Keep all software, including operating systems and applications, up to date with the latest security patches. Vulnerabilities in outdated software are often exploited by cybercriminals.

3. **Encrypt Sensitive Data**:

Encrypt sensitive financial data at rest and in transit to protect it from unauthorized access. This includes customer information, transaction data, and other critical financial records.

4. **Monitor Network Traffic**:

Employ intrusion detection and prevention systems (IDS/IPS) to monitor network traffic for suspicious activities or unauthorized access attempts. Implement firewalls to filter incoming and outgoing traffic.

5. **Data Loss Prevention (DLP):**

Use DLP solutions to monitor and control the movement of sensitive data within and outside your organization. This helps prevent data leaks and theft.

6. **Regular Security Audits and Penetration Testing**:

Conduct regular security audits and penetration tests to identify vulnerabilities and weaknesses in your systems and processes. Address any issues promptly.

7. **Access Controls**:

Implement strong access controls to restrict who can access sensitive financial data and systems. Ensure that employees only have access to the information necessary for their roles.

8. **Security Awareness Training**:

Educate staff members on good cybersecurity practises, such as how to spot phishing scams and social engineering tricks. Update training often to handle new dangers.

9. **Incident Response Plan**:

Develop a comprehensive incident response plan that outlines the steps to take in the event of a security breach. Ensure that employees are familiar with the plan and conduct drills.

10. **Vendor Risk Management**:

Assess the cybersecurity practices of third-party vendors and partners who have access to your financial systems or data. Ensure they meet your security standards.

11. **Regulatory Compliance:**

Stay current with financial industry regulations and compliance requirements, such as GDPR, PCI DSS, and AML/KYC regulations. Ensure your organization meets these standards.

12. **Employee Background Checks:**

Conduct thorough background checks on employees, particularly those who have access to sensitive financial information.

13. **Secure Mobile and Remote Access**:

Securely manage mobile devices and remote access to your systems, ensuring that they meet security standards and policies.

14. **Machine Learning and AI**:

Implement machine learning and artificial intelligence solutions to detect unusual patterns and potential fraudulent activities in real-time.

15. **Customer Education**:

Educate your customers about common fraud risks and how to protect themselves. Encourage them to use strong passwords, regularly monitor their accounts, and report any suspicious activity.

16. **Whistleblower Program**:

Establish a whistleblower program where employees and stakeholders can report suspicions of fraud or cybersecurity issues anonymously and without fear of retaliation.

Forthcoming technologies for prevention from Frauds and cybersecurity:The future of fraud prevention and cybersecurity will likely be shaped by advancements in technology as well as the evolving threat landscape. Here are some emerging technologies and trends that are expected to play a crucial role in preventing fraud and enhancing cybersecurity:

Artificial Intelligence (AI) and Machine Learning

AI and machine learning algorithms can be used to analyze vast amounts of data to detect patterns indicative of fraudulent activity. They can adapt and improve over time, making them increasingly effective at identifying new and sophisticated fraud schemes.

Behavioral Analytics

Behavioral analytics examines how users interact with systems and devices. By establishing a baseline of normal behavior, it can detect anomalies and suspicious activities, helping prevent fraud and unauthorized access.

Blockchain Technology

Blockchain's inherent security features, like immutability and decentralized consensus, make it a promising technology for enhancing the security and transparency of financial transactions and supply chains. It has the potential to reduce fraud in areas like payments and identity verification.

Zero Trust Architecture

Zero Trust is a security model that assumes that no one, whether inside or outside an organization, should be trusted by default. Access is strictly controlled and authenticated, making it more difficult for attackers to move laterally within a network.

Quantum-Safe Cryptography

With the advent of quantum computing, traditional cryptographic methods may become vulnerable. Quantum-safe or post-quantum cryptography is being developed to ensure the security of data in a post-quantum world.

Biometrics and Multi-Factor Authentication (MFA)

Biometric authentication, such as fingerprint and facial recognition, along with MFA, are becoming more widespread for securing access to devices and systems. They enhance security by requiring multiple forms of authentication.

Cybersecurity Automation and Orchestration

Automation and orchestration tools are increasingly used to respond to security incidents more quickly and effectively. They can identify and mitigate threats in real time.

Threat Intelligence Sharing

Collaborative platforms and information sharing between organizations, industries, and governments can help in the early detection and mitigation of emerging threats and vulnerabilities.

Cloud Security

As more businesses move to the cloud, advanced cloud security solutions, including cloud-based firewalls and security services, are essential for protecting sensitive data and applications.

Homomorphic Encryption

Homomorphic encryption allows computations to be performed on encrypted data without decrypting it. This technology has the potential to enhance data privacy and security in various applications.

Deception Technologies

Deception technologies involve setting traps or decoys to detect and deceive attackers. They can identify malicious activity early in the attack cycle.

5G Security

As 5G networks become more widespread, the need for robust 5G security measures is paramount to protect against new threats that high-speed, low-latency networks may introduce.

Social responsibility of prevention from Frauds and cybersecurity: The social responsibility of preventing frauds and enhancing cybersecurity is a crucial aspect of creating a safer and more secure digital environment for individuals, organizations, and society as a whole. Preventing frauds and enhancing cybersecurity is not just the responsibility of security experts or law enforcement agencies; it's a collective effort that involves individuals, businesses, governments, and the wider community

(Dzomira, 2014). Social responsibility in this context means working together to create a safer and more secure digital world for everyone.

Education and Awareness

Promoting awareness about the risks of fraud and the importance of cybersecurity is essential. This includes educating individuals and businesses about common fraud schemes, safe online practices, and how to recognize and respond to threats.

Data Privacy Advocacy

Encouraging individuals and organizations to respect and protect the privacy of personal data is a key social responsibility (Tripathi & Tripathi, 2023). This includes advocating for strong data protection laws and compliance with these regulations.

Promoting Ethical Conduct

Encouraging ethical behavior and responsible online conduct is vital. This involves discouraging any form of digital wrongdoing, including hacking, cyberbullying, and online harassment.

Supporting Vulnerable Populations

Recognizing that certain individuals may be more vulnerable to fraud and cyberattacks, such as the elderly or children, and taking steps to protect and support them.

Collaboration and Reporting

Encouraging individuals and organizations to collaborate and share information about threats and incidents. Reporting cybercrimes and fraud helps law enforcement and cybersecurity professionals take appropriate action.

Supporting Nonprofit Organizations

Many nonprofits and NGOs work to raise awareness about cybersecurity and provide assistance to victims of cybercrimes. Supporting these organizations helps further the social responsibility of fraud prevention.

Advocating for Stronger Cybersecurity Policies

Encouraging policymakers and legislators to create and enforce cybersecurity policies and regulations that protect the public interest. This includes advocating for measures to hold organizations accountable for data breaches and other security failures.

Mentoring and Education Programs

Providing mentorship and educational opportunities, especially in underprivileged communities, to foster cybersecurity skills and awareness. This can help individuals pursue careers in cybersecurity and protect themselves online.

Promoting Secure Software Development

Encouraging software developers to prioritize security in their products and services. This can be achieved by emphasizing secure coding practices and promoting the use of encryption and other security features.

Responsible Product Design

Advocating for the responsible design of products and services to prioritize security and user privacy. This includes considerations like privacy by design and security assessments of new technologies.

Supporting Cybersecurity Research

Backing research initiatives that focus on improving cybersecurity technologies and strategies. Advancements in cybersecurity research benefit everyone by enhancing online safety.

Corporate Social Responsibility

Holding companies accountable for cybersecurity and data protection. Encouraging businesses to take steps to protect customer data and to support fraud prevention initiatives.

Community Engagement

Engaging with local communities to raise awareness about cybersecurity and fraud prevention. Community-level efforts can have a significant impact on reducing risks.

Preventing fraud and enhancing cybersecurity in the finance sector is an ongoing effort that requires continuous monitoring, adaptation to new threats, and a culture of security awareness throughout the organization. Collaboration with industry peers and sharing threat intelligence can also be beneficial in staying ahead of evolving threats.

REFERENCES

Bajracharya, A., Harvey, B., & Rawat, D. B. (2023, March). Recent Advances in Cybersecurity and Fraud Detection in Financial Services: A Survey. In *2023 IEEE 13th Annual Computing and Communication Workshop and Conference (CCWC)* (pp. 368-374). IEEE. 10.1109/CCWC57344.2023.10099355

Baur-Yazbeck, S., Frickenstein, J., & Medine, D. (2019). Cyber Security in Financial Sector Development. *CGAP Background Documents, 5*(2).

Dzomira, S. (2014). Electronic fraud (cyber fraud) risk in the banking industry, Zimbabwe. *Risk Governance and Control: Financial Markets and Institutions, 4*(2), 16–26. doi:10.22495/rgcv4i2art2

Goutam, R. K. (2015). Importance of cyber security. *International Journal of Computer Applications, 111*(7). https://en.unesco.org/unesco_science_report/sdg9

Ng, A. W., & Kwok, B. K. (2017). Emergence of Fintech and cybersecurity in a global financial centre: Strategic approach by a regulator. *Journal of Financial Regulation and Compliance, 25*(4), 422–434. doi:10.1108/JFRC-01-2017-0013

Saha, S., & Shaw, P. (2019). Revisiting industrialisation and innovation in India: roadmap for SDG 9. *2030 Agenda and India: Moving from Quantity to Quality: Exploring Convergence and Transcendence*, 41-64.

Sharif, M. H. U., & Mohammed, M. A. (2022). A literature review of financial losses statistics for cyber security and future trend. *World Journal of Advanced Research and Reviews, 15*(1), 138–156. doi:10.30574/wjarr.2022.15.1.0573

Tripathi, R., & Tripathi, S. (2023). Identifying Fraud Detection Techniques Using Text Analytics Processing. *Adhyayan: A Journal of Management Sciences, 13*(1), 5-8.

Chapter 9
Deep Learning Models for Detecting Software Defects

Kalpana Singh
https://orcid.org/0000-0003-0131-9905
Chandigarh University, India

Alankrita Aggarwal
https://orcid.org/0000-0002-0931-1118
Chandigarh University, India

ABSTRACT

Software defect classification must be automated in order to ensure software dependability, as the use of automatic software-based applications grows. This chapter suggests an automatic software defect classification approach that is expert-based. The technique of grouping defects into predetermined categories is known as defect report categorization. Recently, numerous machine learning (ML) techniques have been introduced to classify defects into different categories. This study suggests a classification model that creates new word embeddings from defect reports using deep learning (DL) models, specifically the long short-term memory (LSTM) network, recurrent neural network (RNN), convolution neural network (CNN), and multilayer perceptron (MLP). The outcomes are compared to pre-trained word embedding using Google's word2vec in terms of recall, accuracy, and precision. The experimental results show that LSTM outperforms the other models used in the investigation. The maximum accuracy that LSTM can attain on the redmine dataset is 70%.

DOI: 10.4018/979-8-3693-1503-3.ch009

1. INTRODUCTION

Software dependability and defect classification are vital due to the growing dependence on software-based systems. Scholars started focusing their attention on how software processes affect software defects. To examine the reasons behind software faults and improve the development process, software defects need to be categorised. Additionally, this keeps software flaws from improving the organization's software maturity and software quality (Abdu, A. et al., 2022, Druzhkov, P. N. & Kustikova, V. D., 2016, Gao, J. et al,2019). According to definitions, a software bug is "a deficiency in a work product that does not meet its specifications and must be replaced or repaired. (Shi, M., Wang, K., & Li, C., 2019, Wang, H., & Yuan, L., 2022, Xiao, Y. et al., 2019, Zhou, P. et al., 2019). A report on software defects is a document that documents various anomalies seen and reported by users of software products. There are various attributes associated with a fault, such as Id, Status, Description, Severity, Resolution, and Priority. Bug reports are monitored via bug tracking systems. Redmine Bug Tracker is an online project management tool that assists software developers, businesses, and professionals by storing defect data (Lopes, F. et al., 2020). The flaw follows a cycle that begins with faults being categorised in order to be validated. After that, the expert is tasked with analysing the flaw report in order to remedy it. Additionally, the specialists categorise the defect. Thus, it is imperative to classify software issues; yet, as the volume of defect reports increases, the process of manually classifying issues gets more challenging and intricate.

Methods for automating the process of classifying flaws have been provided by researchers (Aizawa, A., 2000). The proposed techniques represented the fault reports' textual descriptions as supervised and semi-supervised text classification tasks. Before text is input into machine learning (ML) algorithms, it is preprocessed and transformed into vectors of actual value vectors in a text classification problem. It undergoes testing and training for reported hidden flaws. The suggested methods either used the BoW (Bag of Words) model or the TF-IDF (Term Frequency-Inverse Document Frequency) model to represent words as vectors of real valued values (Aizawa, A. 2000). The meaning of the text or words is not understood by either model. We used deep learning (DL) models, such as CNN (Convolution Neural Network) and LSTM (Long Short Term Memory network), to automatically classify defects in a report. LSTM networks are capable of remembering a long sequence or pattern for a longer period and hence solve the gradient descent problem. The information is updated across time steps using input and output gates. CNN is a feed forward neural network having two or more hidden layers known as convolution and pooling layers (Deng, J. et al,2014).

It learns dependencies and works effectively for image processing (Yan, L., Zheng, Y., & Cao, J., 2018). CNN is also used in text classification problems (Khan, T., & Mollah, A. F., 2019, Rehman, A. U., Malik, A. K., Raza, B., & Ali, W., 2019, Basiri, M. E et al., 2021, Liu, P. et al., 2016 Mikolov, T et al., 2010). RNN is type of artificial neural network with loop and hence well suited for sequential data (Miao, Y., Gowayyed, M., & Metze, F., 2015, Graves, A. et al., 2013). The loop in RNN makes it remember the previous information. MLP is a feed forward neural network consisting of various layers like I/P, hidden layer and an O/P layer. A MLP can have multiple hidden layers (Hornik, K., Stinchcombe, M., & White, H.,1989). Each layer consists of multiple neurons interconnected to each other between the layers. Applications for these DL models can be found in computer vision (Gao, J., Zhang, L., Zhao, F., & Zhai, Y., 2019) speech recognition (Graves, A. et al., 2013).and picture classification (Jappelli, R., & Marconi, N.,1997, Jorayeva, M. et al., 2022). Word embedding is used by DL techniques to acquire a vector representation for text classification issues (Jorayeva, M. et al,2022, Krizhevsky, A. et al,2017, Lopes, F. et al,2020, Xiao, Y et al., 2019). One method for creating a vector representation of a word is word embedding.

The highlights of the study are as follows:

- Based on textual descriptions of the defects, a classification model that automatically classifies defect reports into specified categories has been constructed using DL models CNN, RNN, MLP and LSTM.
- We put our model to the test using newly produced word embeddings from the defect report corpus. To produce word vectors, Google's word2vec, the frequently used pre-trained embedding, was employed.
- Using freshly generated word embeddings from the defect report corpus, we evaluate our model. Google's word2vec, a popular pre-trained embedding, was used to generate word vectors.

Sections make up the remaining paper. Current methods that attempt to automatically categorize the flaws using the written description or synopsis of the flaws in section 2. In Section 3, the suggested classification model based on DL techniques is covered. Section 5 provides a summary of the work, while Section 4 discusses the results that are examined and contrasted with previous methods.

2. METHODOLOGY

A brief overview of the methodology, including details on the training process, hyperparameter tuning, and data preprocessing steps typically employed in deep learning studies:

Data Collection and Preprocessing

Identify relevant datasets suitable for the task at hand.

Preprocess the data, which may include steps like data cleaning, normalization, handling missing values, and feature extraction.

Model Architecture Selection

Choose a suitable deep learning architecture based on the nature of the problem. This could be Convolutional Neural Networks (CNNs) for image data, Recurrent Neural Networks (RNNs) for sequential data, or Transformer models for natural language processing tasks.

Training Process

Split the dataset into training, validation, and test sets to evaluate the model's performance.

Train the deep learning model using the training set.

Hyperparameter Tuning

Tune hyperparameters such as learning rate, batch size, dropout rate, number of hidden units or layers, etc., to optimize the model's performance.

Figure 1 shows the suggested approach. We started by compiling defect reports from Redmine databases.

2.1. Text Preprocessing

Numerous fields are included in a defect report, including description, bug ID, status, operating system, severity, keywords, priority, and quantity of comments. The defect's textual explanation is found in the description. Preprocessing is needed in order to extract the relevant words from this textual description.

Figure 1. Proposed methodology

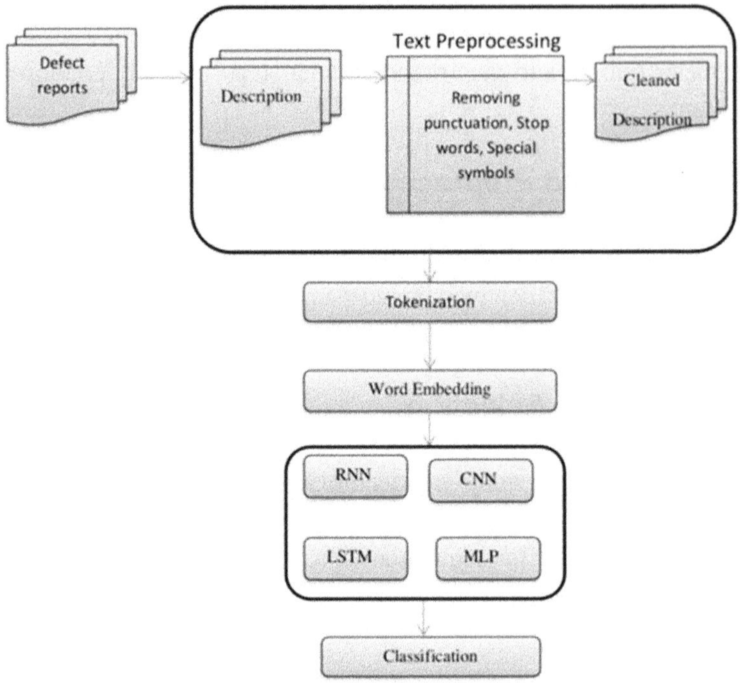

2.2. Word Embedding

An A method for turning words into low-dimensional vectors with actual value is called word embedding. In this study, we employed pre-trained word embedding from Google's word2vec.

2.2.1 Long Short-Term Memory

LSTM networks are capable of remembering a long sequence or pattern for a longer period and hence solve the gradient descent problem. The information is updated across time steps using input and output gates. The input gate (i) determines what to be entering to the memory cell using equation 2. The forget gate (f) forgets the past information and modifies the cell state using equation 1. Finally output gate (y) determines the information passed to the next state.

Figure 2. LSTM network

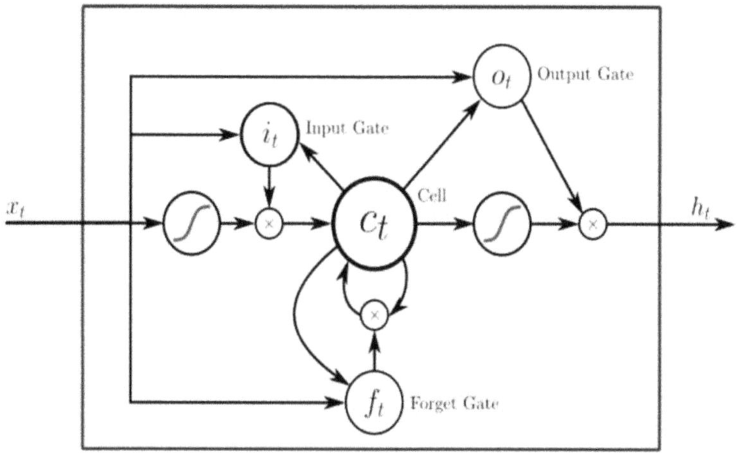

2.2.2 Convolution Neural Network (CNN)

CNN is a feed forward neural network having two or more hidden layers known as convolution and pooling layers (Deng, J. et al, 2014). It learns dependencies and works effectively for image processing. CNN is also used in text classification problems.The convolution neural network is outlined in figure 5. In this study, we have used two convolution layers with average pooling.

Figure 3. Convolution neural network

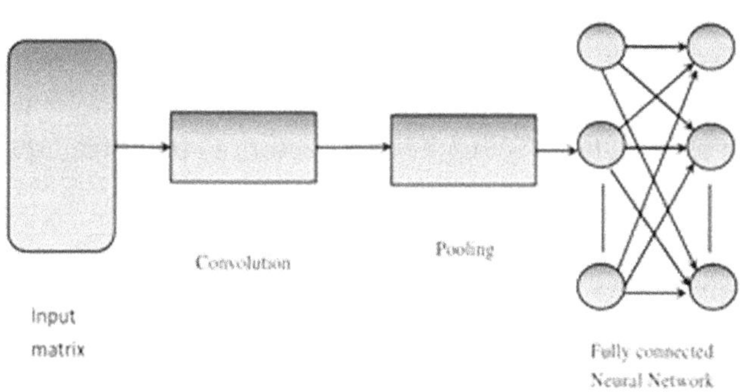

Figure 4. Recurrent neural network

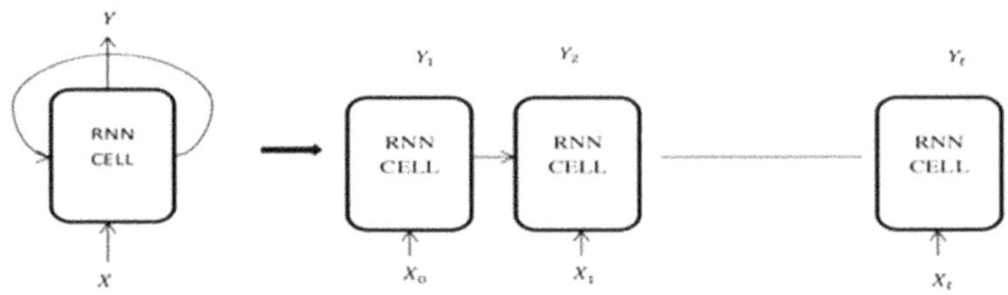

2.2.3 Recurrent Neural Network (RNN)

RNN is type of artificial neural network with loop and hence well suited for sequential data [28-30]. The loop in RNN makes it remember the previous information. A RNN is outlined in figure 6, X represents the input feed to the RNN cell and outputs a value Y. A number of RNN cell is connected to each other where $x_0,x_1,\ldots\ldots,x_t$ are the input sequences and $y_0,y_1,\ldots\ldots,y_t$ are the outputs. RNN are widely used in solving natural language processing (NLP) tasks like speech recognition, predicting the context (Kumar, S. et al., 2024) and many more.

2.2.4 Multilayer Perceptron (MLP)

[1] MLP is a feed forward neural network consisting of various layers like I/P, hidden layer and an O/P layer as shown in figure 5. A MLP can have multiple hidden layers (Hornik, K et al., 1989). Each layer consists of multiple neurons interconnected to each other between the layers. MLP is widely used in text classification problems i.e. medical text (Srivastava, S. K., et al., 2020). SMS text classification (Rusli, A et al., 2020).and other text classification tasks (Varghese, A. et al., 2020, LeCun, Y et al., 1998, Deng, J. etal., 2014).

The neurons are connected by weights. The output of a neuron is calculated with the help of connecting weight. It is further fed forward to the neurons of the next layer that acts as an input to the next neuron. So another name for MLP is a feed forward neural network. A simple structure of a neuron is depicted in figure 6.Neurons take features X=x_1, $x_2,\ldots,x_n$ as input and weights W= w_1, $w_2,\ldots$, w_n is associated with each feature. We took word vectors as Input features.

Figure 5. Multilayer Perceptron with One Hidden Layer

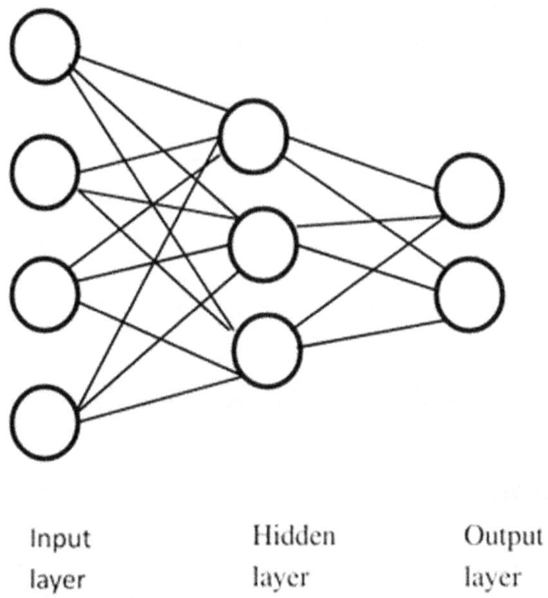

Figure 6. Structure of a neuron

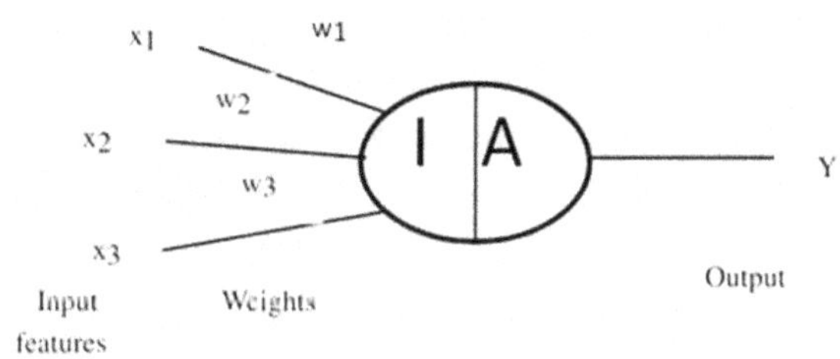

3. DATA SETS DESCRIPTION

3.1. Data Sets

Using datasets, the suggested classification model is assessed and put into practise. Defect reports gathered from Redmine comprise the dataset. A total of 3,020 reports from 2007 to June 2022 make up the gathered dataset.

There are fifty categories in the defect report collection. As Table 1 illustrates, we only looked into 9 categories in this work because there weren't enough defect reports for the other categories.

Table 1. Redmine dataset details

Categories	Counts
Issue	580
UI	266
REST API	172
SCM	318
Custom fields	218
Email notification	316
Administration	99
Time tracking	123
Projects	140

3.2 Hyper Parameter Tuning

To get the best results, the hyper parameters need to be tuned. So in this section, we present the best value that leads to the best results for MLP, RNN, LSTM and CNN deep neural network models. For MLP, the three hidden layers use 800 neurons i.e. nodes. For RNN, the appropriate number of hidden units, dropout and learning rate are tuned as 32, 0.2 and 0.001. The number of convolutional layers, size of filters and pooling size are the hyper parameters tuned to get the best result for CNN. First and second convolution layers use six and eight filters respectively. The size of filter is taken to be 6×6. The size of pooling is 2×2. LSTM, a special type of Recurrent Neural Network having a memory cell, we had tuned the following parameters to achieve the best value: hidden unit counts, drop out and rate of learning. The number of hidden units is confined to 64 while drop out and learning rates are set to the values 0.5 and 0.001.

3.3 Evaluation Metrics

In assessing the performance of different deep learning techniques, such as CNN, RNN and LSTM, three metrics were taken into account: recall, precision, and accuracy. The following equations can be used to calculate recall, precision, and accuracy:

$$Accuracy = \frac{tp_i + tn_i}{tp_i + fp_i + tn_i + fn_i} \tag{1}$$

$$Precision = \frac{tp_i}{tp_i + fp_i} \tag{2}$$

$$Recall = \frac{tp_i}{tp_i + fn_i} \tag{3}$$

where tp_i represents the true positive, which is the number of cases accurately categorized and classed by the class *i*; and tn_i represents the true negative, which is the number of instances classified as *i* but belong to other classes. The false positive is represented by fp_i, which is the number of cases correctly not identified as *i*. tp_i denotes the true negative, which is the number of instances assigned to other classes while they are members of class *i*.

Automated software defect classification, while offering numerous benefits, also comes with several limitations. Here are some of the key limitations:

1. **Limited Training Data**: Automated defect classification systems heavily rely on labeled training data to learn patterns and make accurate predictions. However, obtaining sufficiently large and diverse datasets with accurately labeled defects can be challenging.
2. **Feature Engineering**: Extracting meaningful features from raw data is crucial for the performance of machine learning models.
3. **Class Imbalance**: In many real-world scenarios, the number of defective instances is significantly lower than the number of non-defective instances, leading to class imbalance.

The practical implications of the results obtained from using Long Short-Term Memory (LSTM) models in software defect classifications.

1. **Improved Software Quality Assurance**: By accurately identifying defects in software code, LSTM models can contribute to enhancing software quality assurance processes.
2. **Efficient Bug Triage and Prioritization**: LSTM models can aid in automating the bug triage process by automatically categorizing incoming bug reports or issues based on their severity and impact.
3. **Reduced Maintenance Costs**: Identifying and fixing software defects can be time-consuming and costly. LSTM models that accurately classify defects can help reduce maintenance costs by streamlining the defect identification and resolution process.

Table 2. Classification results without using pre-trained (i.e. new generated) word embedding

Dataset	Metric	LSTM	CNN	RNN	MLP
Redmine	Accuracy	**63.84**	61.28	60.09	58.12
	Precision	**62.96**	54.31	58.73	57.30
	Recall	**57.10**	49.64	53.82	55.42
No SQL database (Cassandra, Hbase, MongoDB)	Accuracy	60.76	60.41	48.09	52.06
	Precision	56.69	53.09	44.41	50.48
	Recall	46.62	38.40	33.20	45.26

4. RESULTS

We looked at the different test results that ML techniques produced. The suggested models perform better than the ML-based models listed in Table 2 demonstrates when DL techniques' performance is contrasted with ML algorithms'.

We discover that DL models exhibit superior performance in terms of accuracy, precision, and recall. Accuracy, precision, and recall are achieved by the suggested work in the following ranges: 20.3% to 31.6%, 20.3 to 31.6%, and 21.4% to 34.4%, respectively. However, using the suggested DL-based framework, we train and test on word embedding and obtain an average accuracy, precision, and recall of 60%, 55%, and 50%.

We build a DL based classification model by using pre-trained word embedding word2vec.

Table 2 shows the results without utilizing pre-trained word embedding. The word vectors are produced using the Keras API. In terms of recall, precision, and accuracy, LSTM surpasses the other DL models i.e. CNN and RNN. Table 3 presents the results when the studied deep learning models are trained and tested using the pre-trained embedding generated using Google's word2vec model. Figure 7 shows visual representation of the results without utilizing pre-trained word embedding. Figure 8 shows visual representation of the Recall comparison with pre trained embedding Google's word2vec.

5. CONCLUSION

Research on a flaw detection and classification system for software engineers is presented in this paper. The suggested classification models for defect report categorization, CNN (Convolution Neural Network), MLP (Multilayer Perceptron),

Figure 7. Visual representation of the results without utilizing pre-trained word embedding

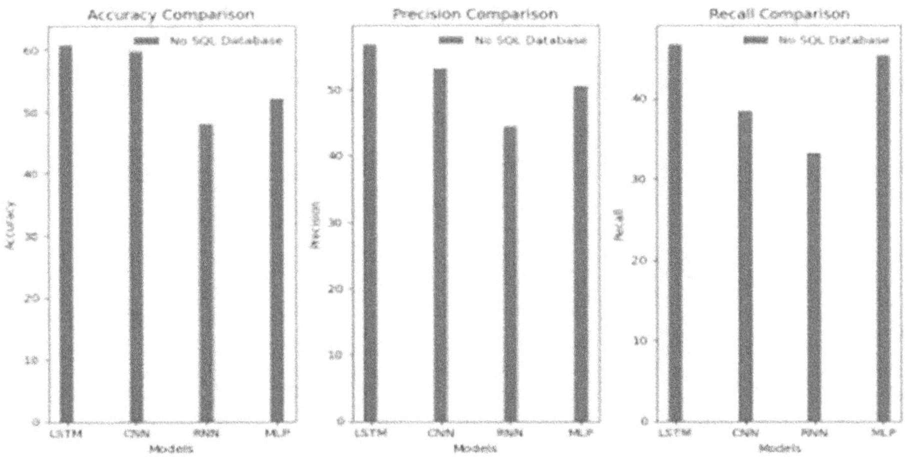

RNN (Recurrent Neural Network) and LSTM (Long Short Term Memory), are based on DL models and use word embedding. We compared the accuracy, precision, and recall of DL models with and without pre-trained word embedding (Google word2vec). On the redmine dataset, DL models achieve up to 70% accuracy using pre-trained word embedding. Previous ML-based models performed worse than our recommended models. We found that deep learning models achieve maximum accuracy 70% with pre-trained word embedding for the redmine dataset. Experimental results show that LSTM performs better among the other deep learning models used in the study. Our proposed models improved the existing machine learning based models. Using pre-trained Google word2vec, proposed models improve by 29.16%, 25.09% and 12.22% in terms of accuracy, precision and recall for LSTM. Proposed

Table 3. Classification results with pre-trained embedding Google's Word2vec

Dataset	Metric	LSTM	CNN	RNN	MLP
Redmine	Accuracy	**70.02**	59.27	65.71	56.34
	Precision	**66.83**	53.18	59.08	52.46
	Recall	**64.11**	50.30	53.94	46.43
No SQL database (Cassandra, Hbase, MongoDB)	Accuracy	67.13	62.60	59.10	64.42
	Precision	63.49	52.75	55.37	60.75
	Recall	60.91	38.29	48.15	54.31

Figure 8. Visual representation of the recall comparison with pre-trained embedding Google's Word2vec

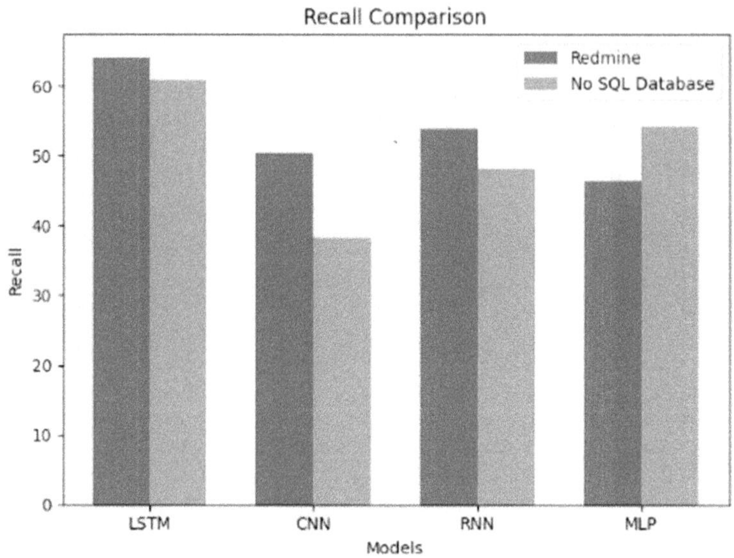

models improve by 35.53%, 31.89% and 26.51% in terms of accuracy, precision and recall using new word embedding for LSTM. Further for future research, project specific word embedding for sentences or documents can be generated.

REFERENCES

Abdu, A., Zhai, Z., Algabri, R., Abdo, H. A., Hamad, K., & Al-antari, M. A. (2022). Deep learning-based software defect prediction via semantic key features of source code—Systematic survey. *Mathematics*, *10*(17), 3120. doi:10.3390/math10173120

Aizawa, A. (2000, July). The feature quantity: an information theoretic perspective of tfidf-like measures. In *Proceedings of the 23rd annual international ACM SIGIR conference on Research and development in information retrieval* (pp. 104-111). 10.1145/345508.345556

Basiri, M. E., Nemati, S., Abdar, M., Cambria, E., & Acharya, U. R. (2021). ABCDM: An attention-based bidirectional CNN-RNN deep model for sentiment analysis. *Future Generation Computer Systems*, *115*, 279–294. doi:10.1016/j.future.2020.08.005

Deng, J., Russakovsky, O., Krause, J., Bernstein, M. S., Berg, A., & Fei-Fei, L. (2014, April). Scalable multi-label annotation. In *Proceedings of the SIGCHI Conference on Human Factors in Computing Systems* (pp. 3099-3102). 10.1145/2556288.2557011

Druzhkov, P. N., & Kustikova, V. D. (2016). A survey of deep learning methods and software tools for image classification and object detection. *Pattern Recognition and Image Analysis*, *26*(1), 9–15. doi:10.1134/S1054661816010065

Gao, J., Zhang, L., Zhao, F., & Zhai, Y. (2019, March). Research on software defect classification. In *2019 IEEE 3rd Information Technology, Networking, Electronic and Automation Control Conference (ITNEC)* (pp. 748-754). IEEE.

Graves, A., Mohamed, A. R., & Hinton, G. (2013, May). *Speech recognition with deep recurrent neural networks. In 2013 IEEE international conference on acoustics, speech and signal processing*. Ieee.

Hornik, K., Stinchcombe, M., & White, H. (1989). Multilayer feedforward networks are universal approximators. *Neural Networks*, *2*(5), 359–366. doi:10.1016/0893-6080(89)90020-8

Jappelli, R., & Marconi, N. (1997). Recommendations and prejudices in the realm of foundation engineering in Italy: A historical review. In Geotechnical engineering for the preservation of monuments and historic sites (pp. 191-214).

Jorayeva, M., Akbulut, A., Catal, C., & Mishra, A. (2022). Deep learning-based defect prediction for mobile applications. *Sensors (Basel)*, *22*(13), 4734. doi:10.3390/s22134734 PMID:35808230

Khan, T., & Mollah, A. F. (2019). AUTNT-A component level dataset for text non-text classification and benchmarking with novel script invariant feature descriptors and D-CNN. *Multimedia Tools and Applications*, *78*(22), 32159–32186. doi:10.1007/s11042-019-08028-8

Krizhevsky, A., Sutskever, I., & Hinton, G. E. (2017). ImageNet classification with deep convolutional neural networks. *Communications of the ACM*, *60*(6), 84–90. doi:10.1145/3065386

Kumar, S., Mahadev, R. G., Kamal, P., & Aggarwal, A. (2024). Original Research Article An optimized deep learning-based fault-tolerant mechanism for energy efficient data transmission in IoT. *Journal of Autonomous Intelligence*, *7*(4). Advance online publication. doi:10.32629/jai.v7i4.1380

LeCun, Y., Bottou, L., Bengio, Y., & Haffner, P. (1998). Gradient-based learning applied to document recognition. *Proceedings of the IEEE*, *86*(11), 2278–2324. doi:10.1109/5.726791

Liu, P., Qiu, X., & Huang, X. (2016). Recurrent neural network for text classification with multi-task learning. *arXiv preprint arXiv:1605.05101*.

Lopes, F., Agnelo, J., Teixeira, C. A., Laranjeiro, N., & Bernardino, J. (2020). Automating orthogonal defect classification using machine learning algorithms. *Future Generation Computer Systems*, *102*, 932–947. doi:10.1016/j.future.2019.09.009

Miao, Y., Gowayyed, M., & Metze, F. (2015, December). EESEN: End-to-end speech recognition using deep RNN models and WFST-based decoding. In 2015 IEEE workshop on automatic speech recognition and understanding (ASRU) (pp. 167-174). IEEE.

Mikolov, T., Karafiát, M., Burget, L., Cernocký, J., & Khudanpur, S. (2010, September). Recurrent neural network based language model. *Interspeech*, *2*(3), 1045–1048. doi:10.21437/Interspeech.2010-343

Rao, K., Sak, H., & Prabhavalkar, R. (2017, December). Exploring architectures, data and units for streaming end-to-end speech recognition with rnn-transducer. In 2017 IEEE Automatic Speech Recognition and Understanding Workshop (ASRU) (pp. 193-199). IEEE. doi:10.1109/ASRU.2017.8268935

Rehman, A. U., Malik, A. K., Raza, B., & Ali, W. (2019). A hybrid CNN-LSTM model for improving accuracy of movie reviews sentiment analysis. *Multimedia Tools and Applications*, *78*(18), 26597–26613. doi:10.1007/s11042-019-07788-7

Rimavicius, T., & Gelzinis, A. 2017. A comparison of the deep learning methods for solving seafloor image classification task. In *Information and Software Technologies: 23rd International Conference, ICIST 2017, Druskininkai, Lithuania, October 12–14, 2017, Proceedings* (pp. 442-453). Springer International Publishing. 10.1007/978-3-319-67642-5_37

Rusli, A., Young, J. C., & Iswari, N. M. S. (2020, July). Identifying fake news in Indonesian via supervised binary text classification. In *2020 IEEE International Conference on Industry 4.0, Artificial Intelligence, and Communications Technology (IAICT)* (pp. 86-90). IEEE. 10.1109/IAICT50021.2020.9172020

Shi, M., Wang, K., & Li, C. (2019, June). A C-LSTM with word embedding model for news text classification. In *2019 IEEE/ACIS 18th International Conference on Computer and Information Science (ICIS)* (pp. 253-257). IEEE. 10.1109/ICIS46139.2019.8940289

Srivastava, S. K., Singh, S. K., & Suri, J. S. (2020). A healthcare text classification system and its performance evaluation: A source of better intelligence by characterizing healthcare text. In *Cognitive informatics, computer modelling, and cognitive science* (pp. 319–369). Academic Press. doi:10.1016/B978-0-12-819445-4.00016-3

Varghese, A., Agyeman-Badu, G., & Cawley, M. (2020). Deep learning in automated text classification: A case study using toxicological abstracts. *Environment Systems & Decisions*, *40*(4), 465–479. doi:10.1007/s10669-020-09763-2

Wang, H., & Yuan, L. (2022). Software engineering defect detection and classification system based on artificial intelligence. *Nonlinear Engineering*, *11*(1), 380–386. doi:10.1515/nleng-2022-0042

Xiao, Y., Keung, J., Bennin, K. E., & Mi, Q. (2019). Improving bug localization with word embedding and enhanced convolutional neural networks. *Information and Software Technology*, *105*, 17–29. doi:10.1016/j.infsof.2018.08.002

Yan, L., Zheng, Y., & Cao, J. (2018). Few-shot learning for short text classification. *Multimedia Tools and Applications*, *77*(22), 29799–29810. doi:10.1007/s11042-018-5772-4

Zhou, P., Liu, J., Liu, X., Yang, Z., & Grundy, J. (2019). Is deep learning better than traditional approaches in tag recommendation for software information sites? *Information and Software Technology*, *109*, 1–13. doi:10.1016/j.infsof.2019.01.002

Chapter 10
Investigating the Moderating Impact of Institutional Quality on the Digitalization and Financial Development Nexus:
The Case of Small Island Development

Sheereen Fauzel
https://orcid.org/0000-0002-5297-1808
University of Mauritius, Mauritius

Jeevita Matadeen
University of Mauritius, Mauritius

ABSTRACT

It is crucial to assess the impact of digital transformations on the financial sector given the rapid emergence of digitalisation. As such, the study aims at identifying the extent to which digitalization has impacted on financial sector development in a sample of small island developing states, over the period 2000 to 2020. Additionally, given the crucial importance of institutional quality in reducing banking sector risk, and therefore enhancing the level of development in the financial sector, the study investigates the nexus between digitisation and financial development through the moderating impact of institutional quality. The study adopts the PVECM framework to investigate the link. The results demonstrate digitalization is important to boost financial development and digitalization coupled with good quality institutions will further promote financial development. More so, FDI and trade openness are also determinants of financial development for the case of the small island economies considered in the present study.

DOI: 10.4018/979-8-3693-1503-3.ch010

1. INTRODUCTION

Over the years, information and communication technologies have not only witnessed a rapid evolution, but have also become more accessible to a growing number of individuals. Indeed, according to the data on The World Bank, only 7% of the world population in 2000, a value that has skyrocketed to 40% in 2015, before continuously exponentially rising to 63% in 2021. Similarly, data show that the number of mobile cellular subscriptions rose from 738,157,897 in 2000 to 8.49 billion in 2021 (The World Bank). These changes in the information and communication technology realm have brought forward a tremendous digital revolution in all aspects of human life, including the way people live, work, learn and communicate. This restructuring of social life around digital communication and media infrastructures is referred to as digitalization according to Brennen and Kreiss (2016).

The advances in technology have also impacted all the industry sectors of the global economy. However, each industry sector seems to adopt the new technologies at different paces as not all the technologies can be equally implemented (Kutnjak et al., 2019). As for the financial sector, it has also undergone significant transformations and improvements with the ever-evolving technologies. Similarly, different financial services providers will be affected to a different extent, based on their "current market positions and ability to leverage technology." Gomber et al. (2018) argue that there are three key aspects for the current FinTech revolution: technological innovation, process disruption and services transformation. Subsequently, the adoption of the new technologies has forced the financial sector to shift from the traditional systems to systems that offer digitalized services. The banking sector is no exception and is also experiencing disruptive changes with the extremely rapid ongoing digital transformation. Indeed, online banking, mobile banking, and digital payments, although being relatively new financial innovations, have rapidly become a thing of the past with the disruptive changes being speedily brought forward by technological advancements such as artificial intelligence, machine learning, big data, block chain, robo-advisors, chatbots and digital money. These recent innovative technologies have rapidly transformed the banking sector as we know it. Indeed, while increased mobile access and internet connection only enhance connectivity between customers and firms, newer technologies such as big data, artificial intelligence, distributed ledger technology, and cryptography help design new customized financial products, synchronize and record transactions among a network of individual computers, and ensure robust security for electronic transactions (He et al., 2017). These new technologies have altered the business models of the banks (Cappiello, 2020), reduced the number and size of the banks, as well as the number of employees (Sibanda et al. (2020), slashed down the prices of digital transactions ((Liu et al., 2017), enhanced a hybrid client-bank interaction (Sibanda et al., 2020; Hodson, 2021), provided an algorithm-driven services through robo advisors and chat bots (Cappiello, 2020), improved the risk profiling of the clients (Sibanda et al., 2020) and even built credit scores to provide loans (Gomber et al., 2018). Given the numerous impacts of these digital transformations and disruptions, it becomes primordial to investigate the nexus between digitalization and financial development.

The main goal of the study is to explore the nature and the direction of the relationship, if any, between digitalisation and banking sector development, in a sample of small island developing states (SIDS) for the period 2000 to 2020. Additionally, the study endeavors assess the moderating impact of institutional quality on the potential link between digitalization and economic growth. This study is believed to depart and add on to previous literature for several reasons. Firstly, while the link between digitalization and economic growth is well anchored in the literature (Stiglitz and Greenwald, 2015; Jepsen and Drahokoupil, 2017; Habibi and Zabardast, 2020; Myovella et al., 2020), there are fewer studies investigating the causal relationship between digitalisation and financial development. As such, this nexus must be further investigated and discussed. Additionally, given the rapid pace at which the technologies are evolving, the literature needs to be updated to assess the effect of the more recent and, undeniable more disruptive technological revolution. Indeed, while there are numerous studies that consider digitalization through technological innovations like internet banking and online banking, only a relatively scant number of studies has explored this particular link during periods of disruptions from the new technological revolution, which is largely driven by artificial intelligence and blockchain. Secondly, the paper innovatively adds a moderating factor, institutional quality within the link under investigation. While it has been empirically acknowledged that digitalisation and institutional quality each affect the banking sector development (Tresierra et al., 2018; Kaur et al., 2020; Bousrih, 2023), to the best of our knowledge, no study has tried to assess whether, both digitalisation and institutional quality have a combined influence on the financial sector development. Thirdly, the study focuses on SIDS. While digitalization impacts different industry sectors at different extents, it also gets transmitted to different countries at different speeds. Developed countries were seen to adopt the new technologies more rapidly, and as early as the beginning of the century, while emerging economies, have only been catching up in recent years. Besides, SIDS, have their own unique specificities and distinct characteristics, which differentiate them from other developing economies. These peculiarities might not only slow down the adoption process of new technologies, but also tamper the adaptation ability of the SIDS. Therefore, the potential impact of digitalization on the banking sector of these islands, is believed to be contingent on their distinct attributes. Fourthly, this paper opts for a PVAR/PVECM model catering for dynamism as well as the possibility of reverse causation and other indirect links between the variables.

The rest of the study is structured as follows: Section 2 provides a review of the links between digitalization and financial development. Section 3 gives a brief overview of the technological and financial landscape in SIDS. This is followed by section 4, which outlines the methodology used and section 5, which analyses the findings of the research. Finally, section 6 provides a brief summary of the study, including some key policy recommendations.

2. LITERATURE REVIEW

While there is a general consensus that digitalization triggers economic growth (Stiglitz and Greenwald, 2015; Habibi and Zabardast, 2020; Myovella et al., 2020), and, financial development boosts economic growth (example, McKinnon (1973), monitoring (Diamond 1984; Rousseau and Wachtel, 2000; Beck, 2003; Matadeen and Seetanah, 2015), the link between digitalization and financial development has been less widely explored. Nevertheless, this link is crucial: if there is indeed a positive relationship digitalization and economic growth, it would imply that economic development would indirectly be enhanced. There are several channels through which digitalization can potentially help expand financial development. For instance, theoretically, digitalization is believed to enhance financial development by increasing access to information, enhancing accessibility to credit, inducing competitiveness, and lowering multiple costs, thereby promoting bank efficiency, and minimizing information asymmetries. Additionally, Feyen et al. (2021) mention that apart from reduced economic frictions and creating opportunities for new entries, the technological revolution is also shifting economies of scale. Nevertheless, it is also important to consider the other side of the coin. The impact of digitalization on financial development can also be curbed by the multiple cyberthreats involved, which instill a lack of trust in the customers (Forcadell et al., 2020).

i. Theoretical Linkages

Both Asongu and Nwachukwu (2019) and Forcadell et al. (2020) argue that technological innovations ensure that banks can enhance information sharing, which eventually reduces information asymmetries. Likewise, Feyen et al. (2021) also maintain that technology has facilitated information exchange. Forcadell et al. (2020) further states that by building up proprietary information systems, the banks' lending processes and performances will be improved. Along the same vein, Asongu and Nwachukwu (2019) also concur that the use of new technologies will better equipping financial institutions to evaluate the risk profiles of borrowers, prompting an increase the availability of credit. Additionally, big data, which is part of the new technologies reshaping the financial sector, enhance the bank's predictive power with regards to lending customer behavior (Davenport and Dyché, 2013; George et al., 2014). Such technologies will further enhance the bank's screening efficiency.

Furthermore, Allen and Santomero (1997) argue that reducing the cost of information will also minimize the information asymmetries, which are traditionally inherent in the banking system (Andonova, 2006; Kuzmina et al., 2020; Horobet et al., 2022). In fact, digitalisation can help lower several costs incurred by the banks. While Davenport and Dyché (2013) and George et al. (2014) agree that big data can also lower the cost of information, Feyen et al. (2021) argue that financial innovation has also minimized several costs such as customer acquisition costs, funding costs, assembly costs, switching costs and transaction costs. Similarly, Goel and Hsieh (2022) also maintain that the internet has the potential to reduce the costs. The latter also believe that digitalization can increase the geographical reach of the banks, leading to a drastic decrease the investment costs of the banks. This is in line with Niemand et al. (2017), who also argue that when the financial services turn branchless with the evolving digital technologies, they will be able to lower several other costs, including investment costs, and subsequently, the efficiency of the banks will increase (Perez-Saiz, H. and Sharma, 2019; Forcadell et al., 2020).

Additionally, digitalization is also seen to be a driver of competition in the financial sector. Indeed, Perez-Saiz and Sharma (2019) describe technology in the financial sector as a "disruptive competitive force". Along the same vein, Goel and Hsieh (2022) postulate that the internet can make markets more competitive by being more contestable due to the low sunk costs. Ultimately, this competitive force will drive financial development forward. Moreover, Feyen et al. (2021) argue that financial innovation, through digitalization, has not only minimized transaction costs, but also prompted the creation of new business models and new entrants. Indeed, they believe that financial services will disaggregated by key players, thereby allowing customers to customize their products. Furthermore, Feyen et al. (2021) argue believe that a more intense competition will promote economies of scale. This will in turn further reduce information asymmetries between the banks and the customers. Similarly, Perez-Saiz and Sharma (2019) believe that the new technologies will cause the market structure to change in four different ways: First, the cost of financial services will be curbed; second, more opportunities will be available for new entrants; third, accessibility to new market segments and different customer base will be increased; and fourth, competitiveness will be enhanced. This eventually result in both financial inclusion and deepening.

ii. Brief Empirical Review

Empirically, only there is a relatively small number of studies that focus on investigating the effect of digitalization on financial development. Indeed, most studies focus on the impact of digitalisation on economic growth (Arsić, 2020; Solomon and Klyton, 2020). Nevertheless, the recent studies have been innovative and insightful. For instance, Alshubiri et al. (2019) investigate the role of information and communication technology on the financial development in six oil-dependent economies from the Gulf Cooperation Council countries, during the time span 2000 to 2016. They make use of two measures for information and communication technology, namely, fixed broadband and internet users. As for the financial development index, it is captured through domestic credit to private sector (% of GDP) and broad money supply (% of GDP). By applying fixed effects estimation as well as a generalized method of moments estimator to their data generate results that confirm the positive and significant impact of fixed broadband on both proxies of financial development. Interestingly, the broadband proxy of information and communication technology has a higher impact than internet users on both financial development proxies. Similarly, Owusu-Agyei et al. (2020) empirically investigate the effect of internet use in a sample of 48 Sub-Saharan African countries for the period 2000-2016. They confirm, through the use of three models (a pooled OLS, a Feasible Generalised Least Squares (FGLS) and an Instrumental Variable (IV) approach), a consistent positive link between internet use and various measures of financial development. Interestingly, apart from bank assets (% of GDP), they have used five different proxies to capture different aspects of financial development in terms of banking development and stock market development, bank assets (% of Central Bank assets), domestic credit, credit from financial institutions, stock market capitalization and total value traded.

On the other hand, some studies have considered an interaction among different digitalisation proxies. For instance, Asongu and Nwachukwu (2019) examine the link between the interaction of both internet and mobile phone penetration and financial development on financial access. The study is conducted on a sample of 53 African countries for the period 2004-2011. They make use of the Generalised Method of Moments methods, and estimate 8 different models for each dependent variable (internet and mobile phone penetration) in order to capture different aspects of financial access (two proxies of financial activity, two proxies of financial allocation efficiency) and two aspects of financial development (financial formalization and informalization). They provide evidence that the interaction between the digitalization proxy and financial formalization decreases financial activity. On the contrary, when financial informalization is considered, it is seen to bring about an increase in financial activity. Along the same vein, Ejemeyovwi et al. (2021) analyses the impact of digital interaction (between information and communication technology adoption and innovation) on financial development in 54 Africa for a period of 16 years. They innovatively make use of a Bayesian Vector Auto-Regressive (BVAR) model in order to examine transmission effects between variables. To capture financial development, the authors have resorted to the computation of a financial development index, consisting of financial depth, financial activity, financial size, financial stability, and financial efficiency, by using the principal component analysis method. The results demonstrate that that digital interaction shock positively and significantly impacts financial development, both in Africa and in 6 sub-samples considered.

Innovatively, the possibility of a nonlinear relationship has also been considered. Indeed, Chien et al. (2020) adds on to the literature by assessing both the linear and non-linear effects of information and communication technology on financial development in a sample of 81 countries during 1990–2015. As such, they employ two methodologies to capture linearity and non-linearity: the generalized-momentum method and panel smooth transition regression. Three different indicators are used for both the financial development variable (deposit money among bank assets (% GDP), liquid liabilities (% GDP), and private credit by deposit money bank (% GDP)), and the information and communication technology variable (Internet users, fixed telephone subscriptions, and mobile cellular subscriptions). As far as the linear model is concerned, all proxies of information and communication technology are seen to drive financial development. However, when two sub samples are considered (high-income group and the middle- & low-income group), both Internet users and fixed telephone subscriptions boost financial development. However, when the mobile cellular subscriptions proxy is used, it is seen to have a favorable impact on the financial development of middle- & low-income countries, but an unfavorable effect on that of high-income countries. On the other hand, for the nonlinear model, the information and communication technology variable generally drive financial development in the lower regime, while in the higher regime, the link becomes a negative one.

While various approaches and proxies have been used to analyse the relationship, it is still hard to pin down whether the link is a positive one or a negative one. Indeed, a look at the most recent articles reveals that the results seem to be vary based on the proxies used and the countries being examined. Given the varying impacts that digitalisation has on financial development, it becomes crucial to investigate the nature of this relationship in SIDS. Indeed, their unique specificities will entail that the relationship might not be comparable to the results obtained for the past studies.

3. OVERVIEW

Generally, SIDS face several challenges with respect to internet connectivity due to their distinct characteristics, such as their remoteness, small population, enhanced susceptibility to natural disasters, and higher vulnerability to global economic disruptions. Additionally, the small population coupled with long open sea distance along with small economies of scale, often entail high connectivity costs. However, SIDS have progressed remarkably over the past. Indeed, according the United Nations Development Programme (2024)1, SIDS are not only leaders in internet gender parity, but their performance in the Global Cybersecurity Index is also exceptional. They are gradually paving their way towards becoming "Small Island Digital States" (United Nations Development Programme, 2024).

The figures below illustrate the difference in terms of technology in a sample of SIDS. Zooming in on Figure 1 which illustrates the Telecommunications Infrastructure Index, it can be seen that Singapore and Bahrain lead the way, with an index value above 0.8. However, Federated States of Micronesia, Papua New Guinea and Tonga are lagging behind.

Similarly, from Figure 2, which displays the online service index, it can be clearly seen that Singapore is still ranked first among the other SIDS (with an index value of 0.96). It is followed Bahrain, Dominican Republic and Mauritius with index values of 0.79, 0.76 and 0.7 respectively. Unfortunately, Federated States of Micronesia is still ranked last, with an index of 0.11.

Figure 3 below illustrates the readiness for frontier technologies in a sample of SIDS. As expected, Singapore's performance is by far better than the others, with an index value of 0.95. Barbados is ranked 2nd, with an index of 0.58, while Bahrain comes 3rd, with an index of 0.54. Haiti is the least ready among them all, with an index of 0.04.

Moving on to Figure 4, the same pattern is detected, with Singapore ranking 1st with an index of 0.91. It is closely followed by Bahrain (index value 0.82) and Mauritius (index value 0.71) and Bahamas (0.70). Guinea-Bissau, Comoros and Haiti are among the ones ranked last for this index.

As for Figure 5, it depicts the cybersecurity index. The differences among the countries are highly noticeable, with Singapore and Mauritius clearly winning the race, with a value of 98 and 97 respectively. However, Bahrain is not too far behind, with a value of 78. However, most of the other SIDS have values below 20.

As shown above, each SIDS has a different level of digitalization. Overall, their readiness for frontier technologies appears weak. Moreover, despite the emergence in new technologies in the SIDS, the cyberthreats are expected to weigh down their evolution as most of the islands record poor scores for the cybersecurity index. However, E-government seems to be developing rapidly, and they seem to be fairing

Figure 1. Telecommunications infrastructure index, 2020

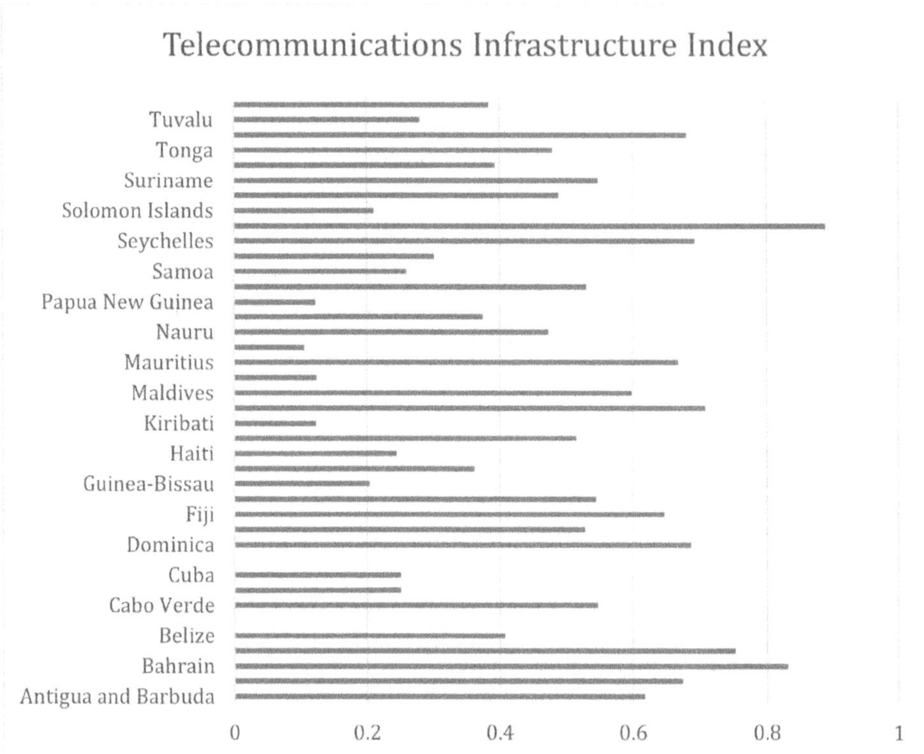

satisfactorily with respect to their telecommunications infrastructure. These are expected to have a significant impact on the financial development of the SIDS.

4. METHODOLOGY

The objective of this study is to investigate the relationship between digitalization and financial development for the case of small island developing states. Another important aspect of the study is to analyse the extent to which government institutions coupled with digitalization boosts financial development in these small island economies. For this purpose, an interactive term between digitalization and government institution is used in the model and annual data have been used. Following studies like Horobet et al, 2022, Fauzel (2016) and Iddrisu et al, (2022) the following model has been used under the present study;

$$FD = f(DIG, DIG*INST, GDPPC, FDI, TO) \quad (1)$$

Figure 2. Online service index, 2020

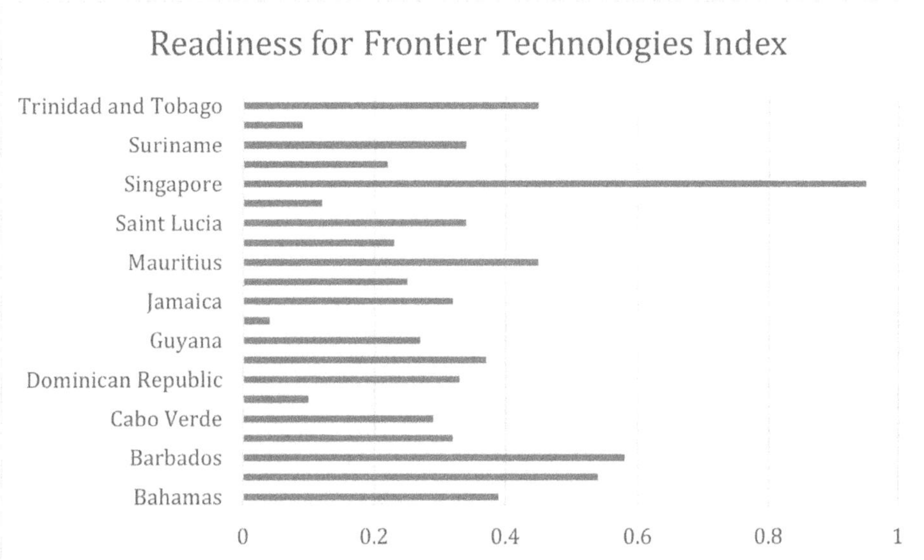

Because of the variance stabilizing properties of log transformation, the log values of the variables are used. In fact, logged variables yield a more clear-cut interpretation of the coefficients in terms of percentage change.

Converting all the variables in logarithmic terms yields:

$$lnFD_{it} = \alpha_0 + \beta_1 lnDIG_{it} + \beta_2 lnlnDIG * INST_{it.} + \beta_3 lnGDPPC_{it} + \beta_4 lnTO_{it} + \beta_5 lnFDI_{it} + \varepsilon_{it} \quad (2)$$

$\beta_1 \ldots \beta_5$ represent the parameter estimates and ε_{it} is the random disturbance term. All data has been downloaded from the World Development Indicators.

Panel Unit Root Tests

It is crucial to make an investigation of the time series properties before estimating the model. As identified by Granger et al., (1974) and Phillips, (1986), one may get biased results from regressing time series data mainly because of the likelihood that the data might be non-stationary. Hence, because of this situation, the panel unit root tests are performed to analyse the order of integration of the different variables used in the study. The Im, Pesaran, and Shin (2003) panel unit root tests have been utilised under the present study. The findings show that stationarity is

Figure 3. Readiness for frontier technologies index, 2021

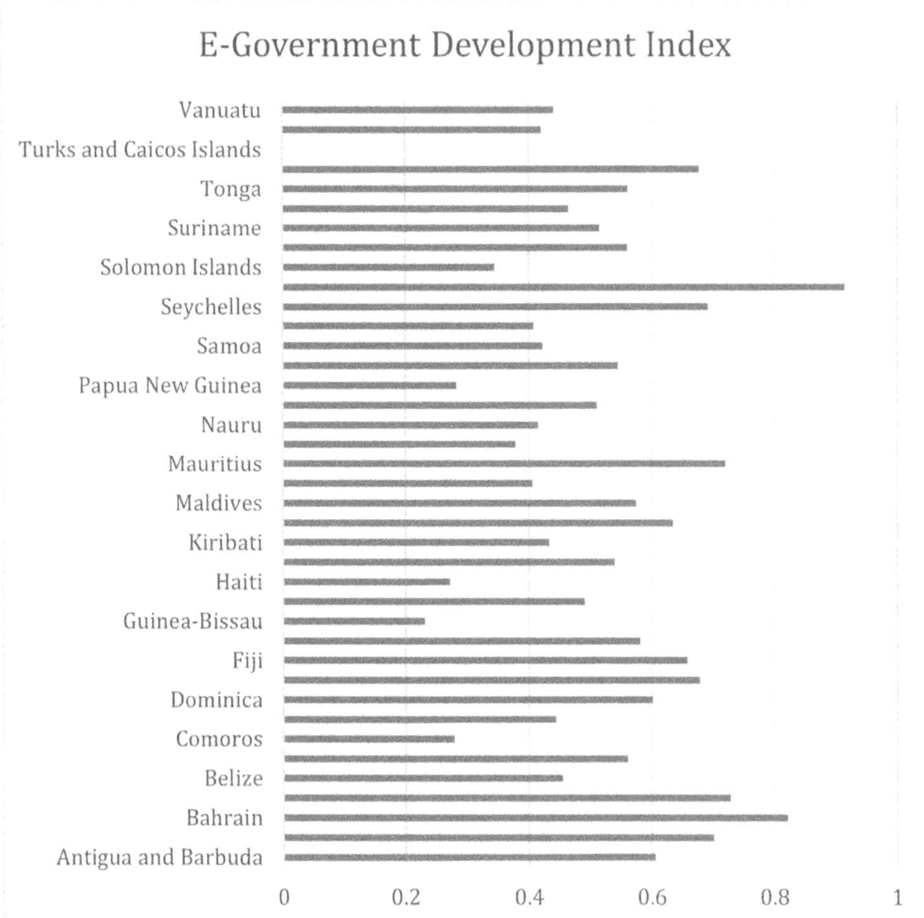

achieved after differencing each variable once. This implies that the variables are integrated of order one.

Panel Cointegration Test

After checking for stationarity of the variables, we proceeded to investigate whether co-integration exists between the variables or whether there is a long run link between the variables. The Kao Residual Cointegration Test has been used which shows the existence of co-integrating association amid the variables. Hence, the study proceeded with the use of a panel vector error correction model.

Figure 4. E-government development index

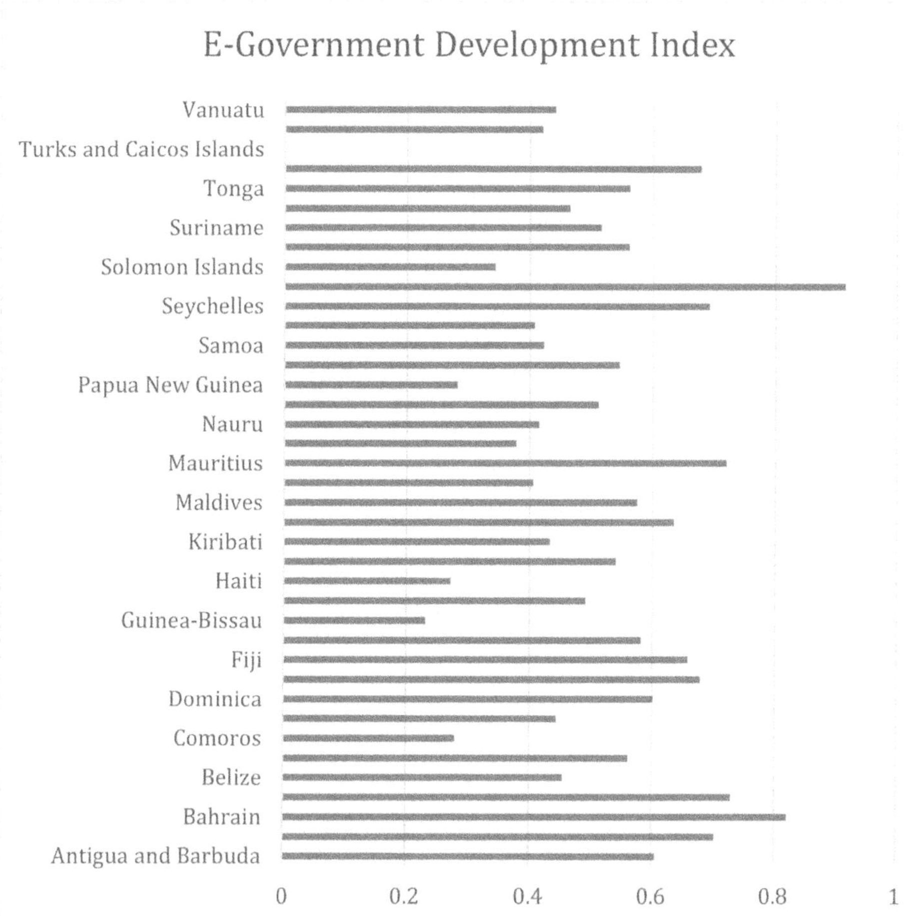

5. ANALYSIS OF RESULTS

In the presence of cointegration, we used a PVECM model which also caters for dynamism in the model. More so, by adopting a PVECM, we not only appropriately analyse the potential effect of digitalization on financial development in Small Island Economies but also any reverse causality which might exist between them. An investigation of other feedback and indirect effects in the hypothesized link becomes also possible. In fact, this framework resembles a series of equations where each determinant comes as the explained variable in a system which is then solved simultaneously. We estimated a VAR in an error correction model (VECM) for the purpose of our analysis. The pth order PVECM is specified as follows:

Figure 5. Cyber security index, 2020

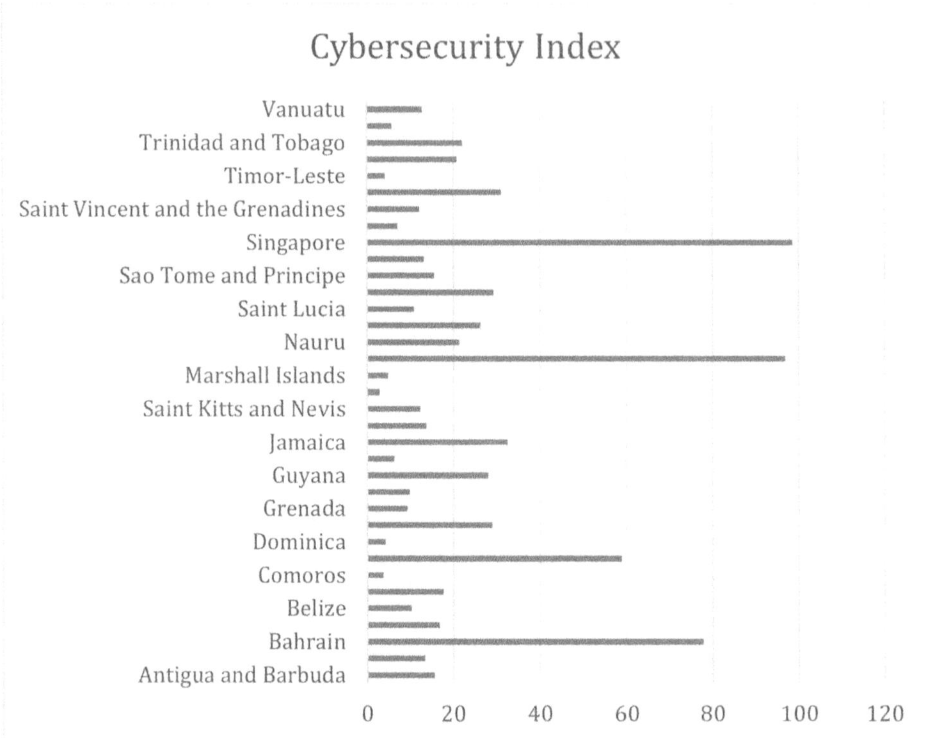

$$\Delta Z_{it} = \prod_i Z_{i't-1} + \Gamma_{i1} \Delta Z_{i't-1} + \ldots\ldots + \Gamma_{i,p-1} \Delta Z_{i,t-p+1} + \mu_{it} \quad (3)$$

Zit = [*FDit, (DIG*INST)it, DIGit, GDPPCit, FDIit, TOit*]

i denote the different countries in the sample and t denotes the time dimension. μ is a standard white noise process. The PVECM is estimated by using an optimal lag length of 1, and the results of the model are reported in Table 1.

Analysing the results from table 1, it is observed from column 2 that the coefficient measuring the impact of digitalization on financial development is positive and significant. It implies that a 1% increase in digitalization, increases financial development by 0.21% in the long run. Similar results have been obtained by Alshubiri et al. (2019) and Owusu-Agyei et al. (2020). Indeed, digitalization enhances financial development as digital platforms help financial institutions to disseminate financial information (Haenssgen, 2018, Hommel and Bican, 2020), reduce the risk of fraud (Siano et al., 2020) and provide services at affordable rates (Feyen et al., 2021). Moreover, digitalization in the financial sector reduces

Table 1. Variable definition

Proxy Used	Variable Used	Variable Definition	Related Literature
FD	Financial Development	Domestic credit to the private sector as a percentage of GDP	Horobet et al, 2022, Fauzel, (2016), Baltagi et al. (2009),
DIG	Digitalisation	Telephone subscription	Owusu-Agyei et al. (2020), Iddrisu et al, 2022
GDPPC	Gross domestic product per capita	Gross domestic product per capita	Horobet et al, 2022, Iddrisu et al, 2022
FDI	Foreign direct investment	FDI inflow as a % of GDP	Alfaro et al. (2004), Dutta and Roy (2011), Hermes and Lensink (2003), and Kholdy and Sohrabian (2005, 2008)). Adam and Tweneboah (2009
TO	Trade openness	The sum of imports and exports to GDP.	Horobet et al, 2022, Baltagi et al. (2009) and Hanh (2010)
DIG*INST	Digitalisation*Government institution	Digitalisation* Quality of Institutions (quality of institutions and governance)	Labhard et al, 2022

Source: Authors' Compilation

information asymmetries as well as transaction costs, hence resulting in greater economic stability (Feyen et al. 2021; Hommel and Bican, 2020). Services provided by the financial sector have also improved with digital platforms used by financial institutions and have helped to improve financial inclusions. (Ongo Nkoa and Song, 2020). Ozili, (2018) further posits that households and firms can benefit from digitalization of the financial system as it enables a higher access to a wide range of financial products and services. Better access to finance and investment is realized with digital financial platforms, thus boosting economic activities. As argued by

Table 2. Long-run results

Variables	*Coefficient*	*T-Statistics*
LDIGIT	0.208653**	1.72957
LDIGIT*LINST	0.068256***	5.75198
LGDPPC	-0.072588	0.65280
LFDI	0.064343**	1.75774
LTO	0.226559***	2.41423
Constant	1.938210	

** represents significance at 5% and *** represents significance at 1%.

Narayan, (2020), financial technology improves the financial sector performance as well as economic stability.

Zooming on the impact of the interaction variable, that is digitalisation and institutions on the financial development of the small island economies, it is found that the combined effect of these two variables increases financial development, which implies that the joint effect of digitalization and institution has a positive and significant influence on financial development. Hence, while digitalization boosts financial development, the presence of good and high-quality institutions coupled with technology contribute further to financial development. It implies that good quality institution is a moderating factor in the financial development model. While a 1% in digitalization boost financial development by 0.21, a 1% increase in digitalization coupled with good quality institutions boost financial development by 0.28%.

Further analysing the results shows that foreign investment in small island developing states has positively contributed to the development of the financial market. This result is in line with Hanh (2010) whose results shows that financial development as measured by domestic credit to private sector enters the equation with a positive and significant coefficient. It is observed that FDI have been flowing more significantly in the Caribbean SIDS mainly due to their proximity to large American markets. Nevertheless, SIDS located in Africa, Asia and Oceania has also been performing well and has registered relatively higher FDI growth during the 2000s. In fact, SIDS have a limited domestic resource base, and a high degree of structural openness to trade. These economies have been able to attract foreign investment mainly because of several advantages. For instance, they have trade preferences regimes that give them principally preferential access to markets of developed countries. Also, oceans, sizeable exclusive economic zones, coastal environments and biodiversity have attracted FDI to tourism and fishing activities. Large nonrenewable natural resources have stimulated large foreign investments in mining and related downstream activities in some of these countries. These economies also have limited institutional and financial capacities to manage and use natural resources on a sustainable basis. It is also observed that some of them are endowed with natural resources as well as human resources. For example, SIDS like Papua New Guinea, Trinidad and Tobago, and Timor-Leste are resource rich. Foreign investors from developing economies have invested mainly on Papua New Guinea, Maldives, Mauritius and Jamaica.

In addition to that, SIDS provides various powerful incentives for foreign firms to create headquarters, financial and trading operations. All these incentives have encouraged FDI in the business and offshore financial services (UNCTAD, 2013). Hence, one can argue that FDI can help the small island developing states to develop their financial market.

Moreover, an increase in trade openness can lead to more financial development as it may lead to an increase in the supply of new financial instruments (Svaleryd and Vlachos, 2002). The present study supports this idea. Analysing the results, it is observed that there is a positive and significant relationship between trade openness and financial development for the sample of small island developing states included in the study. Moreover, the results are also in line with Abida et al (2014). Their study was on an examination of whether financial development helps a country to benefit more from trade openness. Their results show that trade openness when interacted with the financial development indicators; the interaction term is positive and significant, shedding light on the role of financial development in benefiting from trade openness. Hence, the more open an economy is, the better will be the financial development of the country.

CONCLUSION

By using a PVECM approach, this empirical study investigates the potential relationship between digitalization and financial market development in selected small island developing states over the period 2000-2020. The main findings show that indeed digitalisation has helped the development of the financial market of small island economies. Moreover, the results show the effect of digitalisation on financial development is magnified with the existence of good quality institutions in the economies. The research further examines other relationships like the extent to which foreign capital flow in the host countries and trade openness affect financial development. Indeed, a positive relationship between foreign direct investment and financial development is found. Similar results were obtained for trade openness and financial development.

Hence both digitalisation and good quality institutions are important ingredients for boosting financial development. Yet for sustainable financial development, policy makers should devise policies which further encourage the usage of digital finance and at the same time devise risk management tools to instill security in the use of financial technology. There is also a need to improve digital and financial literacy in the countries. Furthermore, policies to further stimulate investment in digital infrastructure will help the financial sector to develop further and also result in financial innovation.

REFERENCES

Allen, F., & Santomero, A. M. (1997). The theory of financial intermediation. *Journal of Banking & Finance*, *21*(11-12), 1461–1485. doi:10.1016/S0378-4266(97)00032-0

Alshubiri, F., Jamil, S.A. & Elheddad, M. (2019). The impact of ICT on financial development: Empirical evidence from the Gulf Cooperation Council countries. *International Journal of Engineering Business Management, 11.*

Andonova, V. (2006). Mobile phones, the Internet and the institutional environment. *Telecommunications Policy*, *30*(1), 29–45. doi:10.1016/j.telpol.2005.06.015

Arsić, M. (2020). Impact of digitalisation on economic growth, productivity and employment. *Economic Themes*, *58*(4), 431–457. doi:10.2478/ethemes-2020-0025

Asongu, S. A., & Nwachukwu, J. C. (2019). ICT, financial sector development and financial access. *Journal of the Knowledge Economy*, *10*(2), 465–490. doi:10.1007/s13132-017-0477-x

Bayar, Y., Gavriletea, M. D., & Păun, D. (2021). Impact of mobile phones and internet use on financial inclusion: Empirical evidence from the EU post-communist countries. *Technological and Economic Development of Economy*, *27*(3), 722–741. doi:10.3846/tede.2021.14508

Beck, T. (2003). Stock markets, banks, and economic development: theory and evidence. *EIB papers, 8*(1), 37-54.

Bousrih, J. (2023). The impact of digitalization on the banking sector: Evidence from fintech countries. *Asian Economic and Financial Review*, *13*(4), 269–278. doi:10.55493/5002.v13i4.4769

Brennen, J. S., & Kreiss, D. (2016). Digitalization. The international encyclopedia of communication theory and philosophy, 1-11.

Cappiello, A. (2020). The technological disruption of the insurance industry: A review. *International Journal of Business and Social Science*, *11*(1), 1–11. doi:10.30845/ijbss.v11n1a1

Chien, M. S., Cheng, C. Y., & Kurniawati, M. A. (2020). The non-linear relationship between ICT diffusion and financial development. *Telecommunications Policy*, *44*(9), 102023. doi:10.1016/j.telpol.2020.102023

Davenport, T. H., & Dyché, J. (2013). Big data in big companies. *International Institute for Analytics*, *3*, 1–31.

Ejemeyovwi, J. O., Osabuohien, E. S., & Bowale, E. I. (2021). ICT adoption, innovation and financial development in a digital world: Empirical analysis from Africa. *Transnational Corporations Review*, *13*(1), 16–31. doi:10.1080/19186444.2020.1851124

Feyen, E., Frost, J., Gambacorta, L., Natarajan, H., & Saal, M. (2021). *Fintech and the digital transformation of financial services: implications for market structure and public policy*. BIS Papers.

Forcadell, F. J., Aracil, E., & Úbeda, F. (2020). The impact of corporate sustainability and digitalization on international banks' performance. *Global Policy*, *11*(S1), 18–27. doi:10.1111/1758-5899.12761

George, G., Haas, M. R., & Pentland, A. (2014). Big data and management. *Academy of Management Journal*, *57*(2), 321–326. doi:10.5465/amj.2014.4002

Goel, R. K., & Hsieh, E. W. (2002). Internet growth and economic theory. *NETNOMICS: Economic Research and Electronic Networking*, *4*(2), 221–225. doi:10.1023/A:1021225514442

Gomber, P., Kauffman, R. J., Parker, C., & Weber, B. W. (2018). On the fintech revolution: Interpreting the forces of innovation, disruption, and transformation in financial services. *Journal of Management Information Systems*, *35*(1), 220–265. doi:10.1080/07421222.2018.1440766

Habibi, F., & Zabardast, M. A. (2020). Digitalization, education and economic growth: A comparative analysis of Middle East and OECD countries. *Technology in Society*, *63*, 101370. doi:10.1016/j.techsoc.2020.101370

He, M. D., Leckow, M. R. B., Haksar, M. V., Griffoli, M. T. M., Jenkinson, N., Kashima, M. M., Khiaonarong, T., Rochon, M. C., & Tourpe, H. (2017). *Fintech and financial services: Initial considerations*. International Monetary Fund.

Hodson, D. (2021). The politics of FinTech: Technology, regulation, and disruption in UK and German retail banking. *Public Administration*, *99*(4), 859–872. doi:10.1111/padm.12731

Horobet, A., Mnohoghitnei, I., Zlatea, E. M. L., & Belascu, L. (2022). The interplay between digitalization, education, and financial development: A european case study. *Journal of Risk and Financial Management*, *15*(3), 135. doi:10.3390/jrfm15030135

Jepsen, M., & Drahokoupil, J. (2017). The digital economy and its implications for labour. 2. The consequences of digitalisation for the labour market. *Transfer: European Review of Labour and Research*, *23*(3), 249–252. doi:10.1177/1024258917714659

Kaur, S., Kaur, H., & Singh, N. (2020). A study on digitalization and technology environment and its impact on banks. *Globus-An International Journal of Management and IT, 11*(2), 17–20. doi:10.46360/globus.mgt.120201004

Kutnjak, A., Pihiri, I., & Furjan, M. T. (2019, May). Digital transformation case studies across industries–literature review. In *2019 42nd International Convention on Information and Communication Technology, Electronics and Microelectronics (MIPRO)* (pp. 1293-1298). IEEE. 10.23919/MIPRO.2019.8756911

Kuzmina, O. Y., Konovalova, M. E., & Chulova, E. S. (2020). Transformation of the banking system as a way to minimize information asymmetry. In Digital Age: Chances, Challenges and Future 7 (pp. 12-18). Springer International Publishing. doi:10.1007/978-3-030-27015-5_2

Liu, J., Abhishek, V., & Li, B. (2017). *The impact of mobile channel adoption on customeromni-channel banking behaviour.* Available at SSRN 2912691.

Matadeen, J., & Seetanah, B. (2015). Stock market development and economic growth: Evidence from Mauritius. *Journal of Developing Areas, 49*(6), 25–36. doi:10.1353/jda.2015.0120

Myovella, G., Karacuka, M., & Haucap, J. (2020). Digitalization and economic growth: A comparative analysis of Sub-Saharan Africa and OECD economies. *Telecommunications Policy, 44*(2), 101856. doi:10.1016/j.telpol.2019.101856

Niemand, T., Rigtering, J. P. C., Kallmünzer, A., Kraus, S., & Matijas, S. (2017). Entrepreneurial orientation and digitalization in the financial service industry: A contingency approach. In *Proceedings of the 25th European Conference on Information Systems (ECIS), Guimarães, Portugal, 2017* (pp. 1081-1096). Academic Press.

Owusu-Agyei, S., Okafor, G., Chijoke-Mgbame, A. M., Ohalehi, P., & Hasan, F. (2020). Internet adoption and financial development in sub-Saharan Africa. *Technological Forecasting and Social Change, 161*, 120293. doi:10.1016/j.techfore.2020.120293

Perez-Saiz, H., & Sharma, P. (2019). *FinTech in Sub-Saharan African Countries: A Game Changer*. International Monetary Fund.

Rousseau, P. L., & Wachtel, P. (2000). Equity markets and growth: Cross-country evidence on timing and outcomes, 1980–1995. *Journal of Banking & Finance, 24*(12), 1933–1957. doi:10.1016/S0378-4266(99)00123-5

Sibanda, W., Ndiweni, E., Boulkeroua, M., Echchabi, A., & Ndlovu, T. (2020). Digital technology disruption on bank business models. *International Journal of Business Performance Management, 21*(1-2), 184–213. doi:10.1504/IJBPM.2020.106121

Stiglitz, J. E., & Greenwald, B. C. (2015). *Creating a learning society: A new approach to growth, development, and social progress.* Columbia University Press. doi:10.7312/stig17549

Solomon, E. M., & van Klyton, A. (2020). The impact of digital technology usage on economic growth in Africa. *Utilities Policy, 67*, 101104. doi:10.1016/j.jup.2020.101104 PMID:32904493

Tresierra, A. E., & Reyes, S. D. (2018). Effects of institutional quality and the development of the banking system on corporate debt. *Journal of Economics, Finance and Administrative Science, 23*(44), 113–124. doi:10.1108/JEFAS-03-2017-0053

Horobet, A., Mnohoghitnei, I., Zlatea, E. M. L., & Belascu, L. (2022). The interplay between digitalization, education, and financial development: A european case study. *Journal of Risk and Financial Management, 15*(3), 135. doi:10.3390/jrfm15030135

Iddrisu, A.G. & Chen, B. (2022). Economic growth through digitalization in Africa: does financial sector development play a mediating role? *International Journal of Emerging Markets.*

Labhard, V. & Lehtimäki, J. (2022). *Digitalisation, institutions and governance, and growth: Mechanisms and evidence.* Academic Press.

ENDNOTES

1 https://www.undp.org/blog/developing-digital-charting-course-sids-transformation

2 Based on the availability of data; Data was obtained from UNDP.

Chapter 11
E-Payments in Microfinance:
Evolution and Benefits

Kavita Joshi
Amity University, Noida, India

Ritesh Dwivedi
https://orcid.org/0000-0003-3921-5458
Symbiosis Institute of Business Management, Noida, India

ABSTRACT

The integration of e-payment systems in digital microfinance marks a pivotal intersection between financial inclusion and fintech innovation. This chapter traces the evolutionary trajectory of e-payment methods, from their origins to contemporary tools like mobile wallets. It underscores the profound benefits of these platforms, emphasizing unparalleled accessibility, efficiency, and benefits for underserved regions. However, merging technology with finance presents challenges, including limited adoption, technological barriers, and regulatory complexities. The chapter highlights the RBI's regulatory role, showcasing how e-payment platforms are reshaping the microfinance sector through real-world examples. Ultimately, it advocates for these platforms as essential drivers for achieving comprehensive financial inclusion.

1. INTRODUCTION

The world is really growing fast and rapidly going digital, in this era the handling of money is also changing. Financial sector has been under great influence by advancement of technologies and adapted changes to provide its financial services

DOI: 10.4018/979-8-3693-1503-3.ch011

through it e.g. mobile applications and online platforms (Bruton et al., 2015). Microfinance services are all about providing services to those under privileged people with lack of collateral and excluded from regular banks services. The e-payments platforms are design to make the transactions of money value between the parties through electronic commerce transactions(Raja et al., 2008). The combination of microfinance with electronic payments (E-payments) is a huge portion of this change, Also (Kauffman & Riggins, 2010) has discussed that electronic payment (e-payment) platform in microfinance sector has an extreme impact on both the clients and their institutions.

The contribution to understanding the e-payment system in the microfinance sector is very important. The evolution of e-payment system is described, looking back on its retrospective journey and tracing the growing arc of E-payments system. Readers gain a Comprehensive view of how these sophisticated platforms which are prevalent today, e.g. mobile wallets, mobile banking, and other digital services.

E-payments make services easier and quicker for many in this new era by identifying the unparalleled accessibility, streamlined efficiency and rapidity. The tangible benefits bought by the E-payment systems in the field of finance and in the lives of people are discussed. But, it is also important to discuss the challenges faced by these platforms as there is need to maintain human touch element in the growing digitalization of microfinance services (Ray et al., 2018). The list of challenges like issues of adoption, technological barriers, low digital financial literacy, Legal intricacies and Infrastructure limitation(Abid, 2016) other obstacles that comes in between growth of digital microfinance is uncovered.(Singh & Singh, 2024) also made discussion which includes implementing digital literacy programs, collaboratively evolving customized products, trust-building and incorporating e-payment mechanisms into social welfare programs.

A comprehensive exploration of digital payment systems delves into their transformative influence on the financial world through real world-examples covering different dimensions (Gillon, 2017; Musa Abdullahi Sakanko, 2019; Mwafise & Stapleton, 2012). Based on historic trends and informed predictions, the e-payment system is poised to shape the future of the microfinance sector in the upcoming period. This chapter offers valuable resource for formulating regulatory guidelines and policy implications.

2. HISTORICAL BACKGROUND OF MICROFINANCE

Microfinance has made progress over the time and it has recent history compare to others in finance sector. The concept of involving poor people in financial services is very ancient but now these services are tagged with the name “Microfinance”. In

19th century microfinance can be traced as financial initiative in North America and Europe(Copestake et al., 2016). At earlier time in Asia, micro financing was done by moneylenders from their own funds imposing high interest rates(Zainuddin & Yasin, 2020). The thought of microfinance gained traction when professor Muhammad Yunus and his formation, the Grameen Bank came up with collateral-free model of micro financing to impoverished, especial focus on women, collective lending system was used. This strategy utilized trust, social capital and peer oversight to mitigate information discrepancies. The successful models by Grameen Bank, along with other similar organizations, paved the way for global proliferation of microfinance(Yunus, 1999).

2.1. Early Adaptation of Technology in Microfinance

Capacity-building programs in beginning of 2000s prioritize the integration of technologies advancement and microfinance sector to support sustainability and outreach. Pilot projects like e-Grama, Computer Munshi and branch automation were launched for betterment of book-keeping, refining backend processes and productivity in field workers(Ray et al., 2018). For efficiency gains many tools were introduced and gained widespread acceptance such as Automatic teller Machines (ATMs), Management Information System (MIS), and Interactive Voice Response (IVR). This era also witnessed the specialized software especially designs for accounting, loan management, monitoring and human resource management. Numbers of software solutions were adopted by microfinance institutions such as Bijli, Efimo, Delfix Nano, and Ganaseva. The importance of technology driven solutions to minimize transaction costs and enhancement of financial inclusion was mentioned by Rangarajan Committee (*Report of the Committee on Financial Inclusion*, 2008). These early signs underlined the rising appreciation of technology's participation in amplifying the breath and effectiveness of microfinance offerings.

What Is E-Payment?

Electronic payment systems enclose all transactions done through digital communication technologies applying numerous payment tools, including credit and debit cards, direct account debits, online transfers, and transactions via set-top boxes or mobile phones. This system also covers pre-paid cards, stored-value solutions, one click transactions and e-money. Ensuring the credibility of these digital payments is important for the seamless operation of the electronic transaction market and, therefore to the growth of e-commerce.

Figure 1. E-payment
Source: (Abid, 2016)

> *What is E-Payment?*
>
> Electronic payment systems enclose all transactions done through digital communication technologies applying numerous payment tools, including credit and debit cards, direct account debits, online transfers, and transactions via set-top boxes or mobile phones. This system also covers pre-paid cards, stored-value solutions, one click transactions and e-money. Ensuring the credibility of these digital payments is important for the seamless operation of the electronic transaction market and, therefore to the growth of e-commerce.

WHAT IS E-PAYMENT?

The transfer of Funds through digital or electronic platform via the internet is termed as e-payment.

2.2. Need of E-Payment

The platform must ensure customer privacy and safety, preventing companies from tracing user information. The switch towards e-payment system was in pursuit of efficiency and convenience (Yu et al., 2002). After demonetization phase in India, people started adopting digital payment methods instead of using paper currency because of shortfall and it also saved time. (Hurdawaty & Tukiran, 2024) also mention that how e-payments systems can enhance access to government support and financial resources for future growth. The government also supported people to become more reliant on e-payments. (jain, 2022) COVID-19 pandemic forced the government to take urgent step in spreading the awareness regarding digital platforms among the nation. For example, most of the online stores, groceries and many other essential items were only accepting e-payments (Benni, 2021). (Esperance, 2024; Refat, 2023) in his study highlighted e-payment mechanisms can encourage financial inclusion and economic growth.

3. EVOLUTION OF E-PAYMENT SYSTEM

An early example of E-payment system was first seen when the Federal Reserve Bank in U.S transferred its currency using telegraph in 1918. New system was introduced by the U.S in 1972 named as Automated Clearing House (ACH) where the central treasury and commercial banks can transfer currency without doing cheque payments. Some regions in Europe were also started using cards to make

Figure 2. Evolution of e-payments
Source: (Aldaas, 2021)

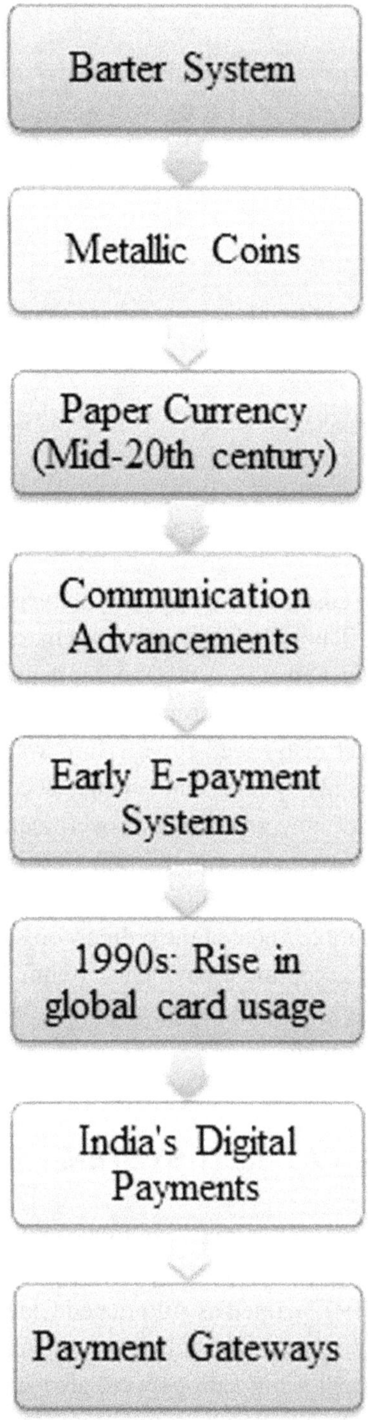

payments in 1914. But, card payments become more frequent and popular in 1990s after Internet and computers added more value in digital technologies. Across the globe, the usage of credit and debit card is growing for all the transaction payments (Al-Laham et al., 2009). India's journey in the digital landscape began quite early. In 1996, the Industrial Credit and Investment Corporation of India (ICICI), was among the groundbreaker, which first provide digital platform to its retail branches to performing banking services. In 2008, another milestone was achieved with the formation of the National Payments Corporation of India (NPCI) For Nation's payment and arrangement infrastructure. Different innovative services and product was developed by the NPCI including India's exclusive digital identity system Aadhar in 2010. Banking system came up with modern day innovative tool known as unified payment interface (UPI) where one can manage numerous bank accounts in from single mobile application (of any engaging intermediary) and merging various banking features (Rastogi et al., 2021). In the list of innovative financial tool one more item is added that is an electronic wallet (E-wallet). It is a digital form of the regular wallet with additional features describe by The National Payment Corporation of India (NPCI). For future transactions, E-wallet can use as a prepaid account where we can store money in advance (Syifa & Tohang, 2020). Here are some E-wallets examples like Gpay, Paytm, BHIM, ICICI Pockets, Amazon Pay, Freecharge, PhonePe etc. A payment Gateway is an intermediary organization in market where seller and buyer authorizes and approves digital transaction using e-wallets, cards, bank details and other data (Aldaas, 2021). Razorpay is most popular payment gateway in 2023. Also, companies like Visa and MasterCard connects with banking institutions across the globe to provide credit/debit cards to support digital transaction through payment gateways.

4. TYPES OF E-PAYMENTS IN MICROFINANCE

The Microfinance landscape is experiencing great changes, especially in the domain of technology. These platforms while participating in operational performance also play a significant role in developing financial inclusion, notably in regions where formal banking systems might not be included. Here's a brief explanation of types of e-payment in microfinance.

- **Mobile Banking/ Mobile Money**: Many microfinance customers are adapting mobile banking because of growing mobile penetration in India. Peer-to-peer digital fund transfers are done with services like BHIM (Bharat Interface for Money). The adoption and usage of digital platform in microfinance sector can serve as a link to connect traditional banking and unorganized populations,

Figure 3. Types of e-payments in microfinance
Source:(Raja et al., 2008; Rastogi et al., 2021; Shaikh et al., 2017; Syifa & Tohang, 2020)

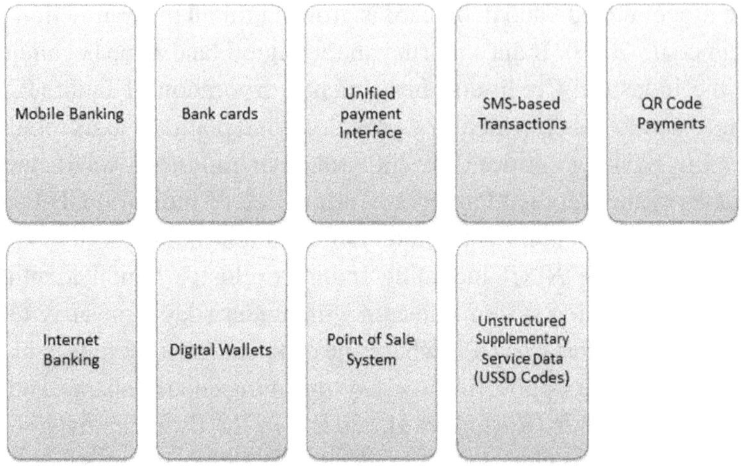

by giving access to financial products and services and contributing to financial inclusion(Shaikh et al., 2017). Blending of m-banking services into microfinance sector will open innovative opportunity and new investments for clients but, there is still research is needed on the combination of m-banking and microfinance (Shaikh & Karjaluoto, 2015).

- **Internet Banking**: As Internet coverage increases globally, MFIs started offering internet banking to its clients for easy operation of their accounts and secure digital transaction. One can apply for loan online using internet banking without visiting bank in physical mode. Microfinance providers can directly approach to their potential users by using internet banking and can promote integrity and usefulness of their services (Bryson et al., 2015). These advancements brings competitive environment in microfinance sector which results in innovation of new financial services and products (Safari et al., 2020).
- **Bank Cards**: Bank cards are financial instrument which consist of credit cards, debit cards, stored-value cards (prepaid debit cards) and prepaid credit cards. MFISs are now issuing cards to their clients for easy and digital access to their funds. By using these cards one can do many activities such as withdrawing cash from ATMs, transferring funds and making purchases. There are many advantages of this instrument in microfinance sector like convenience in operation, cost saving, Financial inclusion and financial empowerment (Dang & Vu, 2020)

- **Digital Wallets/E-Wallets**: Digital wallets facilitate payment and fund transfer capabilities, making it easier and highly convenient for both individuals and small-medium businesses (SMEs) to perform microfinance solutions (Wewege et al., 2020). E-wallets like GooglePay, Amazon Pay, Paytm and many more have gained immense popularity.
- **UPI (Unified Payments Interface)**: The UPI is gaining suction in the microfinance field. Microfinance client use this platforms largely for repayment of loan. UPI provides many benefits like enhanced security, innovative features, convenience, simplified complaint resolution and seamless merchant transactions (Rastogi et al., 2021).
- **POS (Point of Sale) Systems**: For payments of services and goods, cardholder uses these platforms. Some MFIs provided POS machines in outlying regions to help their customers transact more easily. Additionally, POS system expanding its outreach by offering services available 24/7, it boosts customer allegiance and contentment (Hishigsuren, 2006). Overall, the POS system is an important tool for microfinance operations, efficiency, offering convenience, security and better access to financial products and services for both MFIs and customers.
- **SMS-based Transactions**: The system allows traders, villagers and microfinance bank officials to perform banking functions using 2G mobile equipped with SMS feature. It is built on mobile Bank servers operating on mobile stations and mobile devices capable of receiving and sending SMS. The system give access to its users to perform basic banking activities like opening accounts, balance checking, lending and transferring money through SMS. The system utilizes one time passcodes to authenticate both senders and buyers for additional security. During a pilot study, participants executed 804 transactions and sent 2412 SMS messages over a three hour period. The results indicates that the system has the capacity to serve over 15,000 micro business owners, making it suitable for microfinance institutions and micro-banking (Song et al., 2014).
- **Unstructured Supplementary Service Data (USSD) Codes**: USSD codes play a crucial role in microfinance by promoting both affordable transactions and digital access. These codes provide loan application services and customer feedback, collect loan repayment, disburse loans, and oversee account withdrawals. This approach not only improves access to financial services for less privileged but also boosts the development of the microfinance sector (Sinha et al., 2018).
- **QR Code payments**: QR codes have become essential in microfinance sector by offering a simple and consistent payment solution and more. Their quick readability and large storage capability make them preferred choice. QR

codes can simply be read by smartphone camera, point-of-sale terminals and many other devices. OR codes covers broad audience. Using this platform, microfinance banks and lenders can streamline their processes, improve security, and provide customers prompt updates related to their loan status (Otuonye et al., 2022). In essence, QR codes offer a beneficial technique to enhance both operational efficiency and security within the microfinance sector.

Various digital payment types exist both in our country and the globe, here mentioned just a more are covered under this framework. The integration of digital payment systems also comes under this supervision.

5. ROLE OF THE RESERVE BANK OF INDIA (RBI)-THE REGULATORY BODY

Regulatory changes in electronic payments plays crucial role in how digital payments expand and stay safe. Its Goal is to maintain balance among ensuring competition, fostering innovation, maintain the stability and integrity of the financial system, and protecting consumers. Reserve Bank of India (RBI) primarily oversees the microfinance sector and e-payment system in it. The role of RBI in e-payments in microfinance can be summarized as follows:

- **Supervision and Regulations**: Under the regulatory framework, Non-Banking Financial Company-Micro Finance Institutions (NBFC-MFIs) are regulated by RBI (*Reserve Bank of India*, 2022), ensuring that MFIs works under specific guidelines. The guidelines on lending practices, interest rates, and
- Grievance redressal mechanism should be maintained by MFIs.
- **KYC Norms**: Know Your Customers (KYC) norms are imposed by RBI and it is mandatory for all financial institutions, it acknowledges the problems faced by the MFIs in providing services to low-income clients. Therefore, RBI introduce simplified version of KYC procedures for microfinance clients, simplifying the onboarding process while accessing e-payment systems.
- **Capital Adequacy and Liquidity**: Even though MFIs concentrate on micro loans, the penetration of potential digital saving services and e-payment system makes it paramount for them to maintain adequate capital and liquidity.
- **Data Security**: In the era of digital transactions, data safety becomes essential. According to RBI's guidelines, like other financial institutions it is mandatory for MFIs to adopt robust security practices for keeping customer

data safe during e-transactions. The Payment and Settlement System Act of 2007 was introduced to regulate the payment and settlement system in India. (Payment and Settlement Systems Act, 2007) According to Section 4 of this Act, no person other than the Reserve Bank of India (RBI) has the authority to operate payment system in India, unless other party receives approval from the RBI.

- **Supporting Innovation**: For the benefits of microfinance sector, RBI collaborates with other institutions like the National Payments Corporation of India (NPCI) to encourage innovations in the payment space.
- **Financial Literacy and Training**: Knowing that many microfinance clients might be fresh to digital transactions, the RBI highlights the role of MFIs in organizing necessary training and creating awareness about financial literacy, especially regarding e-payment tools.
- **Reporting and Monitoring**: RBI keeps periodic records of MFIs. With adoption of digital payment systems, these periodic reports would keep data on electronic transactions, ensuring rules are met and evaluating the impact of digital initiatives.
- **Interoperability**: For greater adoption and comfort, the RBI is very much interested in promoting interoperability. This means that a client of one MFI accessing a particular digital payment system can easily transact with another.
- **Financial Inclusion**: RBI encourages the use of digital payment systems to promote further financial inclusion. (*MFIN INDIA*, 2023) MFIs can cover remote areas where the physical infrastructure of banking is not available with the help of digital platforms.
- **Consumer Protection**: RBI pays more attention towards fairness and transparency as microfinance clients are vulnerable. It makes sure that there should be clear communication regarding Interest rates, transaction fees, and any other charges. Few familiar ones. It is important to understand that the adoption of these e-payment systems can differ depending on the location, technological infrastructure, legal environment, and the specific preference and need of the targeted population. As technology grows, it's probable that fresh and innovative e-payment methods will emerge in the microfinance field.

Overall, while the initial aim of the RBI's regulatory mediation in microfinance is to look upon the safety of underserved and weaker sections of society, it also observes the transformative power of digital payment system (Dayal, 2019). Through its initiatives and guidelines, the RBI ensures that the advantages of digital financial services penetrate the grassroots level of the Indian economy (Sikdar & Kumar, 2016).

6. CASES HIGHLIGHTING E-PAYMENT SUCCESS

Case 1: User Adoption of Mobile Payment Systems in Microfinance: Case Study Cameroon

1.1 Introduction

The case study investigates the determinants of user adoption of mobile electronic payment systems in microfinance institutions, focusing on Cameroon (Mwafise & Stapleton, 2012). It explores the drivers behind individuals' use of these systems in developing nations and their significance in enhancing financial transactions and operational efficiency for MFIs. By highlighting the role of institutional and socio-technical factors, the study aims to contribute to the development of effective adoption strategies. Cameroon's microfinance sector serves as a pertinent context, offering insights into the challenges and opportunities of e-payment adoption in a developing country. Through a detailed analysis, the study aims to illuminate the broader implications of digital transformation in microfinance and provide valuable insights for practitioners and policymakers.

1.2 Challenges/Problems

- Narrow Studies: Existing studies often fail to comprehensively cover institutional and societal factors, necessitating a broader examination of e-payment system usage.
- Safety Concerns: Security-related issues, such as limited access to personal data, privacy protection, and transaction secrecy, are significant barriers to the adoption of mobile digital payment systems in microfinance.
- Usability: The usability of e-payment systems, encompassing both social and technical aspects, plays a crucial role in adoption. Ensuring ease of use and user-friendliness is essential for widespread adoption.
- Trust Issues: Establishing trust, including the credibility of MFIs and the accuracy of payment systems, is essential for customer adoption. Building trust among clients is a significant challenge that needs to be addressed.

1.3 Intervention/Solution

- Inception of Mobile Applications: MFIs in developing nations are introducing mobile applications to improve and expand their operations using mobile e-payment systems.

- Enhancing Security: Addressing safety concerns related to mobile digital payments, such as privacy protection and transaction secrecy, can increase adoption rates.
- Improving Usability: Enhancing the usability of digital payment systems from both social and technical perspectives can facilitate adoption.
- Regulatory Support: Government actions, such as promoting the importance of technology for government services and implementing pro-tech regulatory laws, can boost e-payment adoption in microfinance.
- Building Trust: Ensuring the credibility of MFIs and the electronic payment system can positively influence clients' adoption intentions.

1.4 Outcome

The research on mobile e-payment adoption in Cameroon revealed that while 56% of the population is aware of the system and 87% recognize its advantages, a majority still prefer cash over digital platforms, with only 37.5% using e-payments. The study investigated social-technical factors like privacy, system familiarity, on-time payment confirmation, and credibility, as well as institutional influences like regulatory support and competition pressures. Key findings highlight the importance of trust, security, market pressures, and usability in shaping mobile e-payment adoption in Cameroon.

1.5 Reflection

The study demonstrates that e-payment adoption in Cameroon is influenced by both social and technical factors, including trust, ease of use, and external pressures from trading and competition. It underscores the importance of considering regional contexts and balancing technological features with institutional factors when adopting e-payment systems in developing countries.

1.6 Summary

The study emphasizes that institutional and socio-technical factors significantly impact e-payment adoption in Cameroon's microfinance institutions. (Roy & Sinha, 2014) highlights the need for a holistic approach that considers both institutional and technological aspects to enhance adoption and promote financial inclusion.

CASE 2: TRANSFORMING INDIAN MICROFINANCE THROUGH DIGITAL INNOVATION

2.1 Introduction

The microfinance sector in India, historically focused on empowering women and alleviating poverty, is currently undergoing a significant transformation with the rise of digital technologies. This shift brings both challenges and opportunities, as the sector evolves and integrates digital payment solutions. This case study by (Gillon, 2017) explores how digital innovation is reshaping the Indian microfinance landscape, highlighting its progress and obstacles. It emphasizes the advantages of digital platforms in enhancing financial transactions, improving operational efficiency, and addressing regulatory constraints. Additionally, it showcases the positive impact of partnerships and innovative strategies in driving adoption and fostering financial inclusion, presenting a compelling narrative of e-payments' revolution in India's microfinance sector.

2.2 Challenges

- **Regulatory Hurdles**: The Reserve Bank of India (RBI) imposes strict regulations on loan structures and interest rates to maintain stability. However, these regulations sometimes limit the flexibility of microfinance institutions (MFIs) in adopting new digital solutions.
- **Cash Dependency**: India's economy is largely cash-based, with 90% of transactions being conducted in cash. This heavy reliance on cash was particularly evident during the demonetization period, highlighting the vulnerability of the system to disruptions.
- **Reluctance to Digital Innovation**: Traditional approaches of MFIs have been slow to embrace digital platforms. This reluctance has led to inefficiencies and missed opportunities for leveraging digital technologies to improve services and operations.

2.3 Proposed Solutions

- **Partnerships**: Collaborating with digital payment platforms like Vodafone's M-Pesa can facilitate the transition from cash to digital transactions. These partnerships can help MFIs offer more convenient and secure payment options to their clients.

- **Digital Payment Platforms**: Implementing successful digital payment platforms, such as Kenya's M-Pesa, can encourage the adoption of e-payment solutions in India. These platforms can provide a reliable and efficient way for MFIs to manage transactions and serve their clients.
- **Adaptation and Training**: Initiatives focused on training MFIs and their clients can ease the transition to digital systems. By providing education and support, MFIs can help their clients feel more comfortable and confident in using digital payment solutions.

2.4 Outcome

While the adoption of digital payment platforms like M-Pesa is still in its early stages in India, early collaborations between microloan companies and Vodafone show promise. Both urban and rural areas are gradually adopting digital solutions, offering potential resolutions to the challenges posed by cash dependency and regulatory hurdles.

2.5 Reflection

The demonetization period was a turning point for the microfinance sector, highlighting the need for a shift towards digital solutions. While the sector has shown positive responses to platforms like M-Pesa, scaling up and increasing adoption rates remain key challenges. Educating and training both MFIs and their clients will be crucial in ensuring the success of digital initiatives.

2.6 Summary

By integrating digital technologies with traditional approaches, the microfinance sector in India can overcome current challenges and continue its mission of socio-economic development. (Gillon, 2017) stated that the growing prevalence of mobile phones in developing areas presents an opportunity for the sector to embrace digital transformation, emphasizing education, flexibility, and collaboration as key drivers of success.

CASE 3: USER ADOPTION OF MOBILE E-PAYMENTS IN NIGER STATE MICROFINANCE BANK

3.1 Introduction

The case study focuses on the transformative impact of implementing an e-payment platform at COE-Minna Microfinance Bank in Niger State, specifically analysing its effects on the institution's financial performance(Musa Abdullahi Sakanko, 2019). With a targeted examination of 23 bank staff members, the study illuminates the challenges and outcomes associated with integrating digital payment systems in microfinance institutions. This adoption signifies a significant shift towards modernization and operational efficiency, highlighting the bank's commitment to embracing technological advancements. Despite the benefits, challenges such as lack of awareness, security concerns, and usability issues have emerged. Nevertheless, the potential advantages of digital payment adoption, including increased efficiency and enhanced customer experience, position this case study as a pivotal example of digital transformation in the microfinance sector in Nigeria.

3.2 Challenges Faced

- Lack of Awareness: A significant challenge was the 15% of staff members who were unaware of the bank's financial performance pre and post e-payment adoption. This lack of awareness could hinder the effective utilization of the new system.
- Variability in Opinion: Another challenge arose from the 25-30% of staff members who provided differing views on the acceptance timeline of the digital payment platform. This variability was influenced by their varying years of affiliation with the bank, highlighting potential communication gaps within the institution.
- Security Concerns: Ensuring the reliability of the digital payment platform for 100% of its users was a major concern. Security is paramount in e-payment systems, and any breach could lead to a loss of trust among staff and clients.
- Access & Usability: While 85% of staff members confirmed the bank's offering of services such as loans, withdrawals, and deposits using the digital payment system, there may still be issues regarding the ease of access and usability of the platform for all users.

3.3 Proposed Solutions

- Better Security: Enhancing the security of the digital payment system was proposed to gain trust among all staff members. This could involve implementing additional security measures and providing regular security training.
- Sensitization: Educating staff and clients about the benefits of the e-payment platform was seen as crucial. Approximately 65% of the staff mentioned that clients had already been sensitized to these benefits, indicating progress in this area.
- Variety in E-Payment Systems: The use of multiple platforms, including credit/debit cards, ATMs, internet payments, and mobile banking, was proposed to cater to the diverse needs and preferences of users, thereby enhancing adoption rates.

3.4 Outcome

Following the adoption of the e-payment system, 75% of respondents indicated a significant improvement in the bank's financial performance. The Ordinary Least Squares (OLS) regression method showed that the digital payment system, ATM facilities, mobile banking, and e-payment cards had a positive impact ranging from 14% to 29% on the bank's financial performance.

3.5 Reflection

The case study highlights the importance of addressing challenges such as lack of awareness, variability in opinion, security concerns, and issues related to access and usability in the adoption of e-payment systems. It also underscores the positive impact of solutions such as enhancing security, sensitization efforts, and offering a variety of e-payment systems on the bank's financial performance.

3.6 Summary

The adoption of the e-payment system at COE-Minna Microfinance Bank has proven beneficial, with a significant improvement in their financial performance. This case study emphasizes the importance of awareness and user trust in the successful implementation of e-payment systems in microfinance institutions(Musa Abdullahi Sakanko, 2019).

Table 1. Key insights

Cases	Key Insights
Case	• While the importance of e-payment platforms is understood, the adoption rate remains comparatively low in Cameroon. • Security, trust and usability plays vital role in deciding on adoption intention among users. • Competition and outer market pressure can highly influence decisions linked to adopting mobile payments.
Case 2	• The demonetization in India made to re-think on financial practices. • Kenya's M-Pesa achievements arranges a model for India, it commands significant changes in trust-building and education. • Infrastructure challenges and demographic areas need to be well planned for huge digital adoption rate in India.
Case 3	• Boost in financial outcomes has been seen in Niger state due to digital platforms. • Even with hesitation about e-payment systems for the economically deprived, actual results demonstrate their worth. • User trust and awareness still remains the paramount part in this digital age.

(Source: Authors)

7. DISCUSSION

All three case studies illuminate the challenges, potential, and transformative power of digital payment system in various contexts.

As discussed in table 1, through different dimensions from Cameroon, India and Niger state, a fascinating narrative unfolds- one of innovation, challenge, and transformation.

In the bustling streets of Cameroon's urban Centers, a digital revolution brews. Individuals are started using their mobile phones for financial transactions other than calls and texts. But why are few accepting this change while others are unenthusiastic? The answer lies in matrix of institutional dynamics and socio-technical factors. Yet shadows of trust issues and security concerns deter many, directing towards disparity between actual usage and digital finance awareness. In India, where an unplanned push for demonetization shove the microfinance sector into unexplored waters. The traditional cash-reliable landscape faces disruption, it's within these challenges that new solutions emerges. Lastly in Niger state, a deep dive discloses the tangible advantage of digital adoption. These MFIs are serving economically disadvantaged and semi-educated, are not just accepting digital platforms, but are booming because of them. Also, there is significant symbiosis between finance and technology.

According to global narration, ultimatum of commonality emerges. The unique challenges each area faces, demanding solutions should be customized according to their socio-economic factors.

Figure 4. Benefits of e-payments
(Source: Authors)

8. BENEFITS OF E-PAYMENTS

Features like straightforward and quick access are paramount for a digital payment system. Payment system gain from technological advancement, malfunctions and defaults can happen. Organizations should not fully depend on digital system, providing they have backup plans in place. These platforms can be aim for hackers and digital threats. A financial implication in a digital payment system is serious issue. The cost of establishing such an electronic system can be huge, with cost including agreement fees, technology infrastructure, legal costs, and revenue sharing, training and marketing costs. Despite of various advantages of e-payment system, there are few drawbacks like hidden charges, restrictions on usage of certain currency, uneasiness about ownership and maintenance, and inefficient complaints handling. (Henry et al., 1999) highlights the superiority of digital payment systems over traditional methods. . E-payment systems have many advantages like integrity, privacy, acceptability, effective transaction processing, convenience, compatibility, mobility, anonymity, and minimal financial risk. Additional benefits includes the high coverage of customers in remote regions, reduced cost related to physical premises and security, fostering high customer awareness and loyalty(Magutu et al., 2010). Real-time transaction or almost instantaneous transactions is another essential aspect for the adoption of digital payment systems. Furthermore, the potential to assist a huge number of users at a same time is a distinct benefit of e-payments. The integration of digital payment system is confirmed watershed moment in the field of microfinance, defining various positive changes in both strategic and operational dimensions. Here's a broad look at the transformational benefits:

- **Extended Reach**: Geographical restraints have lengthy barrier for MFIs. However, with the help of e-payment system MFIs can cover the most remote areas. Without physical presence, MFIs can take up the markets that were not previously accessible(Dalton et al., 2023). Thereby they are making their financial services purely universal by advancing their service domains.
- **Operational Efficiency**: One of the main benefits from blending of digital payment system in microfinance is the phenomenal improvement in operational efficiency. Traditional methods consist of manual interventions and long paper-based processes. E-payment removes this redundancies, swift loan disbursement, allowing instant processing and real-time repayments. This significant boost in efficiency not only minimizes turnaround period but also makes contribution in client satisfaction(Musa & Njeru, 2023).
- **Cost Reductions**: Credible decrease in operational costs is one of the major impacts of electronic transformation in any domain (Wanof, 2023). In microfinance, digital payments curtail costs linked to cash handling, printing, human resources, storage and even transportation. Over time, these provisions can be massive; can lead to higher affordable loan rates.
- **Security & Safety**: Handling cash happen with inherent risks. Multiple challenges can be face by microfinance institutions (MFIs) and their customers when it comes to fraud and mismanagement of cash. The level set by the electronic platforms for security and safety purpose is very hard to meet with physical transactions. Also, secure digital platform operate encryption and other safety measures, further protecting interests of every stakeholders(Okičić et al., 2023).
- **Client Convenience**: Convenience is very important in today's digital era. Digital payments provide this in abundance. Customers no more need to stand in queues, visit branches, or following restrictive banking hours(Cheong & Nasuredin, 2023). They can operate their accounts, apply for loans, and make repayments from their homes.
- **Increases Transparency**: Inbuilt transparencies are there in digital transactions. All transactions leave a proof, making an auditable and clear trail (Refat, 2023). This makes the MFIs be highly responsible and greatly reduces the risk of frauds and other wrongdoings.
- **Data-Driven Insights**: Data is invaluable, in the digital age. Every click, every transaction, provides insights. This data can be used by MFIs for better understandings their customer's behaviors, preferences and needs. Such information can be useful for MFIs in product development, risk assessment and even in creating customized offerings.
- **Financial Inclusion**: E-payments play a paramount role in improving the program of financial inclusion. (Meli et al., 2024) stated that by providing an

accessible and easy mode of transaction, e-payments act as portal, introducing even the hindmost or unbanked individuals to a plenty of financial services. Once introduced to the electronic fold, these peoples will explore more and adopt alternative financial products.

- **Cross-selling opportunities**: With a well-designed e-payment system and abundance of customer data, MFIs can smoothly introduce many other financial products.(Bryson et al., 2015) From saving account to insurance, the opportunities to diversify and cross-sell are immense.
- **Environmental benefit**: The impact on environment is significant, though not immediately. By minimizing the usage of paper, reducing transportation cost (mainly of cash), and not needing physical infrastructure, digital payments take participation in sustainable and greener business model (Dang & Vu, 2020).
- **Integration with Mainstream Banking**: (Sikdar & Kumar, 2016) E-payments seamlessly combine microfinance services with mainstream finance system i.e. traditional banking. E-payments not only make collaboration but also increase the overall cohesion and fluidity in the vast financial ecosystem.
- **Regulatory Compliance**: Consent with financial standards and regulations are non-negotiable. Digital payments, with their electronic trails, make attachment to these rules simpler. Regular reporting, audits, or even immediate monitoring become efficient and feasible(Roy & Sinha, 2014).

The innovative role of digital payments in microfinance sector is undeniable. As the microfinance field continues to expand, the alliance between e-payment systems and microfinance will undoubtedly bring more efficiency, inclusiveness and sustainability in financial world.

9. CONCLUSION

The digital evolution in the financial sector, as witnessed by the fast adoption and growth of electronic payments, makes a remarkable leap forward in making an inclusive financial environment. The integration of microfinance sector with e-payment platforms, as explained in this chapter, gives a clear example of how technology can modify access to significant financial services.

Various traditional constraints were solved by e-payment platforms because of its digital nature. Costs reduce, rise in operational efficiencies and geographical challenges diminish. From internet banking and mobile banking to OR codes and UPI, the array of digital payment methods accessible currently offers numerous customized solutions to meet the different needs of various demographics. Their benefits are extended reach, client convenience, enhanced security, and minimized operational costs are significant and tangible.

However, it is important to balance these advantages with the barriers and concerns these digital systems introduced. The acceptance of e-payment systems requires robust regulatory supervision to ensure data safety, protection of client's interest, and maintain the balance in financial ecosystem. Institution like Reserve Bank of India plays a vital role in formulating this regulatory landscape, establishing a judicious blend of safety and innovation.

The different case studies introduced unique insights into the various opportunities and challenges experienced by nations at different phases of their digital evolution. Countries like Cameroon, India, and Niger state, with distinct socio-economic factors, mentioned common threads towards their digital journey. It became obvious that the growth of the microfinance sector is intrinsically associated with the evolution of electronic payment systems. As innovations happens in technology field, the horizon for microfinance sectors broadens by adopting new tools and methods that can again its aim of financial inclusiveness. The digital payment systems, though transformative, represents just one part in this intricate puzzle. Future innovations, block chain, probably harnessing artificial intelligence, and advance analytics, can again revolutionize this space.

To conclude, the affiliation of e-payments and microfinance sector is symbol of a huge movement towards a higher inclusive, innovative, and efficient financial world. However, these digital payment platforms are not without their barriers and challenges. While the digital transformation offers many advantages, it also proceeds with its portion in pitfalls.

10. RECOMMENDATIONS

- **Financial Literacy Programs**: Lack of digital financial literacy is one of the pivotal challenges affiliated with the adoption of electronic payment system in the microfinance sector. Institutions should arrange the educational programs that aim is to discover digital transactions, by making them more understandable and approachable for the end-users. (Shaikh & Karjaluoto, 2015)Customizes training sessions, seminar, and workshop highlighting the usage and advantages of e-payment platforms should be organized frequently.
- **Infrastructural development in remote areas**: while digital platforms offers the power to cover remote areas, the absence of basic digital infrastructure in these distant areas is adverse factor(Copestake et al., 2016). Collective efforts among microfinance institutions (MFIs), tech firms, and government

can makes things possible for setting up basic infrastructure, such as internet connectivity, to make digital transactions accessible in remote areas.

- **Strengthen Security Protocols**: The risk of cyber-attacks increases with the growing digital transactions, as this goes hand in hand. Microfinance institutions (MFIs) should invest their more funds in robust cyber safety measures to protect client's data and safeguard the integrity of electronic transactions (Raja et al., 2008). Frequent security audits, user authentication protocols, and penetration testing should be done on time.
- **Regulatory Revisions**: In this digital era, where there is fast advancement of technology, it is important that regulatory framework stay adaptable and agile. Constant dialogue among regulatory bodies, microfinance institutions (MFIs) and technology providers will assure the regulations support innovation at time of safeguarding users' interests.
- **Encourage Interactivity**: The potential to transact and interact across numerous digital platforms easily is significant for the boundless adoption of digital payment systems (Shaikh et al., 2017). Making sure that different e-payment platforms can work in collaboration will serve users flexibility and encourage the usage of electronic transactions over traditional.
- **Strengthen Grievance Redressal Systems**: An effective complaint resolution mechanism can build trust in digital payment platforms. (*Reserve Bank of India*, 2022). Microfinance institutions (MFIs) should make sure that the users have a straightforward and clear channel to report issue and raise concerns, with guaranteed timely redressal.
- **Encourage Innovation in E-payment Systems**: To make sure the long-term acceptance and viability of e-payment platforms, constant innovation is needed (Otuonye et al., 2022). Motivation towards research and development may be in the form of tax breaks and grants could encourage technology providers to come up with even more efficient and user-friendly transaction methods.
- **Introduce Rewards for Digital Payments**: To promote the digital transactions methods over traditional ones, microfinance institutions (MFIs) could introduce Rewards. Perhaps in the form of cashback offers, reduced transaction fees, or gift cards that can be redeemed.
- **Holistic User Experience**: On the other side of just transactions, the whole user experience, from starting point of transaction to end step, should be intuitive. Making investment in user experience design and user interface can enhance adoption rates, special focus among those fresh to digital transactions.
- **Collaboration with Tech Startups**: Collaboration between tech startups and microfinance institutions (MFIs) can lead to innovative solutions modified

particularly for microfinance sector(Rastogi et al., 2021). Accelerator or incubator programs concentrating on financial technical solutions for microfinance sector could be a step in this direction.

- **Feedback Loops**: installing systems that is accessible for regular feedback from users. Received feedback can highlights the areas of improvement, user needs, and potential challenges, ensuring that digital payment system evolve in sequence with user expectations(Pengnate & Riggins, 2020).
- **Monitor International Best Practices**: The blending of e-payment platforms in microfinance sector is an international phenomenon. (Abid, 2016)Regular observation and frequent learning from global gold standards can give insights and framework that can be implemented and adapted locally.

The collaboration of e-payment platforms and microfinance sector holds magnificent promise for financial inclusivity, special reference to underserved areas. To perceive the full coverage of this systematic, convergence, security, and user-centric approach is significant. The recommendations mentioned above seek to address the problems and pave the way for a smooth blending of technology into the realm of microfinance.

REFERENCES

Abid, S. (2016). *Electronic Payment System: An Evolution in Indian Banking System*. Academic Press.

Al-Laham, M., Al-Tarawneh, H., & Abdallat, N. (2009). *Development of Electronic Money and Its Impact on the Central Bank Role and Monetary Policy*. Academic Press.

Aldaas, A. (2021). A study on electronic payments and economic growth: Global evidences. *Accounting*, 409–414. doi:10.5267/j.ac.2020.11.010

Benni. (2021). *Digital finance and inclusion in the time of COVID-19*. FAO. doi:10.4060/cb2109en

Bruton, G., Khavul, S., Siegel, D., & Wright, M. (2015). New Financial Alternatives in Seeding Entrepreneurship: Microfinance, Crowdfunding, and Peer–to–Peer Innovations. *Entrepreneurship Theory and Practice*, *39*(1), 9–26. doi:10.1111/etap.12143

Bryson, D., Atwal, G., & Roy Chaudhuri, H., & Dave, K. (2015). Understanding the Antecedents of Intention to Use Mobile Internet Banking in India: Opportunities for Microfinance Institutions: Mobile Internet Banking in India. *Strategic Change, 24*. Advance online publication. doi:10.1002/jsc.2005

Cheong, H. S., & Nasuredin, J. (2023). Relationship Between the Factors and Adoption of E-payment Services among UTHM Students. *Research in Management of Technology and Business, 4*(1), Article 1.

Copestake, J., Johnson, S., Cabello, M., Goodwin-Groen, R., Gravesteijn, R., Humberstone, J., Nino-Zarazua, M., & Titus, M. (2016). Towards a plural history of microfinance. *Canadian Journal of Development Studies. Canadian Journal of Development Studies, 37*(3), 279–297. doi:10.1080/02255189.2016.1197102

Dalton, P. S., Pamuk, H., Ramrattan, R., Uras, B., & van Soest, D. (2023). Electronic Payment Technology and Business Finance: A Randomized, Controlled Trial with Mobile Money. *Management Science*. Advance online publication. doi:10.1287/mnsc.2023.4821

Dang, T. T., & Vu, H. Q. (2020). Fintech in Microfinance: A new direction for Microfinance institutions in Vietnam. *The Journal of Business Economics and Environmental Studies, 10*(3), 13–22. doi:10.13106/jbees.2020.vol10.no3.13

Dayal. (2019). *RBI publishes 'Payment and Settlement Systems in India: Vision 2019 – 2021'* (2687). Reserve Bank of India. www.rbi.org.in

Esperance, M. (2024). *Effect of Cashless Financial Services on Economic Growth in Kigali*. Valley International Journal Digital Library. doi:10.18535/ijsrm/v12i01.em03

Gillon, S. P. (2017). *Indian Microfinance Sector: A Case Study*. Academic Press.

Henry, D., Cooke, S., Buckley, P., Dumagan, J., Gill, G., Pastore, D., LaPorte, S., & Mayer, J. (1999). *Economics and Statistics Administration. Office of Policy Development.*

Hishigsuren, G. (2006). *Information and communication technology and microfinance: Options for Mongolia*. Academic Press.

Hurdawaty, R., & Tukiran, M. (2024). Strategies to Increase the Competitiveness of Micro, Small and Medium Enterprises (MSMEs): A Narrative Literature Review. *South Asian Journal of Social Studies and Economics, 21*(1), 1. Advance online publication. doi:10.9734/sajsse/2024/v21i1768

Jain. (2022). *Influence of behavioural factors on the adoption of digital finance – An empirical study*. Amity University.

Kauffman, R. J., & Riggins, F. J. (2010). Research Directions on the Role and Impact of ICT in Microfinance. *2010 43rd Hawaii International Conference on System Sciences*, 1–10. 10.1109/HICSS.2010.318

Magutu, P., Mwangi, M., Nyaoga, R., Ondimu, G., Kagu, M., Mutai, K., Kilonzo, H., & Nthenya, P. (2010). E-Commerce Products and Services in the Banking Industry: The Adoption and Usage in Commercial Banks in Kenya. *Journal of Electronic Banking Systems*, 1–19. doi:10.5171/2011.678961

Meli, S. D., Kamga, B. F., & Meli, C. N. (2024). Analysis of the Determinants of Mobile Money Adoption and Use: Evidence from Togo with Simple and Multivariate Probit Approaches. *Journal of the Knowledge Economy*. Advance online publication. doi:10.1007/s13132-024-01748-9

MFIN INDIA. (2023). https://mfinindia.org/microfinance/IndustryPortfolio

Musa, S. K., & Njeru, A. W. (2023). Effect of Digital Financial Innovation on the Financial Performance of Small and Medium Enterprises in Nairobi City Centre, Kenya. *International Journal of Social Science and Humanities Research, 1*(1), Article 1. doi:10.61108/ijsshr.v1i1.41

Musa Abdullahi Sakanko, J. D. (2019). The Effect of Electronic Payment Systems on Financial Performance of Microfinance Banks in Niger State. *Jurnal Bisnis Dan Manajemen, 9*(2). doi:10.15408/ess.v9i2.12273

Mwafise, A. M., & Stapleton, L. (2012). Determinants of User Adoption of Mobile Electronic Payment Systems for Microfinance Institutions in Developing Countries: Case Study Cameroon. *IFAC Proceedings Volumes, 45*(10), 38–43. 10.3182/20120611-3-IE-4029.00010

Okičić, J., Jukan, M. K., Okičić, J., & Jukan, M. K. (2023). *Financial inclusion and digital financial literacy: The case of microfinance sector in Bosnia and Herzegovina*. IntechOpen. doi:10.5772/intechopen.1002897

Otuonye, A., Ibe, P., Njoku, D., & Eze, I. (2022). An Innovative Framework for Integrated Loan Management with QR Code Enhancement. *Asian Journal of Computer Science and Technology, 11*(2), 1–10. doi:10.51983/ajcst-2022.11.2.3317

Payment and Settlement Systems Act. (2007). www.rbi.org.in

Pengnate, S., & Riggins, F. J. (2020). The role of emotion in P2P microfinance funding: A sentiment analysis approach. *International Journal of Information Management, 54*, 102138. doi:10.1016/j.ijinfomgt.2020.102138

Raja, J., Dean, A., & Manivannan, S. (2008). Journal of Internet Banking and Commerce E-payments: Problems and Prospects. *Journal of Internet Banking and Commerce, 13*, 1–17.

Rastogi, S., Panse, C., Sharma, A., & Bhimavarapu, V. M. (2021). Unified Payment Interface (UPI): A Digital Innovation and Its Impact on Financial Inclusion and Economic Development. *Universal Journal of Accounting and Finance, 9*(3), 518–530. doi:10.13189/ujaf.2021.090326

Ray, S., Paul, S., & Miglani, S. (2018). *Innovation, efficiency and inclusion: Integration of digital technologies in the Indian microfinance sector. Indian Council for Research on International Economic Relations*. ICRIER.

Refat, M. M. H. (2023). *Adoption of Digital Payment Systems in Microcredit Operations: Challenges & Opportunities in the Context of Bangladesh*. https://www.theseus.fi/handle/10024/816214

Report of the Committee on Financial Inclusion. (2008).

Reserve Bank of India. (2022). https://www.rbi.org.in/commonperson/English/Scripts/FAQs.aspx?Id=3366

Roy, S., & Sinha, D. I. (2014). *Determinants of Customers' Acceptance of Electronic Payment System in Indian Banking Sector – A Study*. Academic Press.

Safari, K., Bisimwa, A., & Buzera, A. M. (2020). Attitudes and intentions toward internet banking in an under developed financial sector. *PSU Research Review, 6*(1), 39–58. doi:10.1108/PRR-03-2020-0009

Shaikh, A. A., Hanafizadeh, P., & Karjaluoto, H. (2017). Mobile Banking and Payment System: A Conceptual Standpoint. *International Journal of E-Business Research, 13*(2), 14–27. doi:10.4018/IJEBR.2017040102

Shaikh, A. A., & Karjaluoto, H. (2015). Mobile banking adoption: A literature review. *Telematics and Informatics, 32*(1), 129–142. doi:10.1016/j.tele.2014.05.003

Sikdar, P., & Kumar, A. (2016). Payment Bank: A Catalyst for Financial Inclusion. *Asia-Pacific Journal of Management Research and Innovation, 12*(3–4), 226–231. doi:10.1177/2319510X17696648

Singh, J., & Singh, M. (2024). Accelerating Financial Inclusion of the Urban Poor: Role of Innovative e-Payment Systems and JAM Trinity in Alleviating Poverty in India. *Global Business Review*. Advance online publication. doi:10.1177/09721509231222609

Sinha, S., Pandey, K. R., & Madan, N. (2018). Fintech and the demand side challenge in financial inclusion. *Enterprise Development & Microfinance*, *29*(1), 94–98. doi:10.3362/1755-1986.17-00016

Song, I., Lui, C., & Vong, J. (2014). Lowering the interest burden for microfinance. *International Journal of Process Management and Benchmarking*, *4*(2), 213. doi:10.1504/IJPMB.2014.060409

Syifa, N., & Tohang, V. (2020). The Use Of E-Wallet System. *2020 International Conference on Information Management and Technology (ICIMTech)*, 342–347. 10.1109/ICIMTech50083.2020.9211213

Wanof, M. I. (2023). Digital Technology Innovation in Improving Financial Access for Low-Income Communities. *Technology and Society Perspectives*, *1*(1), 1. Advance online publication. doi:10.61100/tacit.v1i1.35

Wewege, L., Lee, J., & Thomsett, M. (2020). *Disruptions and Digital Banking Trends*. Academic Press.

Yu, H.-C., Hsi, K.-H., & Kuo, P.-J. (2002). Electronic payment systems: An analysis and comparison of types. *Technology in Society*, *24*(3), 331–347. doi:10.1016/S0160-791X(02)00012-X

Yunus, M. (1999). The Grameen Bank. *Scientific American*, *281*(5), 114–119. doi:10.1038/scientificamerican1199-114

Zainuddin, M., & Yasin, I. M. (2020). Resurgence of an Ancient Idea? A Study on the History of Microfinance. *FIIB Business Review*, *9*(2), 78–84. doi:10.1177/2319714520925933

Chapter 12
Impact of Social Media Influencer Credibility on M-Banking Acceptance:
The Moderating Role of Financial Literacy

Prerna Arora
Amity University, Noida, India

Natasha Sharma
Amity Business School, Amity University, Noida, India

Rupali
https://orcid.org/0000-0003-0527-9365
Amity Business School, Amity University, Noida, India

Anurupa Bagchi Singh
Amity Business School, Amity University, Noida, India

ABSTRACT

Mobile banking is a new form of payment service that aims to acquire the underserved market of prospective mobile banking consumers. Social media influencers are used as a means of disseminating ideas through social media. However, the influence of financial literacy is still not known. This study aims to examine the impact of influencer credentials on mobile banking acceptance. The results demonstrate that influencer reliability has a significant favourable impact on m-banking acceptability as evaluated by attention, interest, desire, and action depicting the cognitive stages of mobile bank acceptance as well as the moderating effect of financial knowledge on this relationship. The results indicate that financial literacy plays a notably positive role in the acceptance of mobile banking. Therefore, it is crucial to scrutinize how financial literacy influences the influencer's credibility on the adoption of mobile banks, providing a nuanced perspective on the intricate relationship between online influence and financial decision-making.

DOI: 10.4018/979-8-3693-1503-3.ch012

INTRODUCTION

The fast-paced changes in the digital realm have revolutionized how people interact with information, decide on purchases, and handle their finances. Social media platforms have gained significant influence, moulding consumer attitudes and actions across different fields (Ullah et al., 2022). In terms of conducting financial transactions, m-banking cannot be considered a tool that has advanced to a degree of worldwide progress and possesses an insufficient rate of adoption and dissemination, especially in developing nations like India. M-banking has eventually revived the core principles of traditional banking and changed customers' perceptions from "nice to have" to "need to have," especially in India where there is a lot of untapped potential (Tiwari et al., 2021). A notable transformation is occurring in the financial sector, driven by the introduction of mobile banking (M-Banking) services (Mallat et al., 2004). Consequently, there is a growing interest among researchers, marketers, and financial institutions in unraveling the complex relationships between social media influencers, their trustworthiness, and the adoption of M-banking (Khasawneh et al., 2018). Understanding these dynamics has become a central focus in this evolving landscape. Social media influencers, individuals with substantial online sway, play a crucial role in molding public sentiment and consumer decisions (Sharma et al., 2022). Mishra (2014) examined the acceptance of m-commerce in India using behavioural psychology that describe customer behaviour and came to the conclusion that if marketers were to encourage favourable emotions towards m-commerce, overall use of m-banking would undoubtedly rise. Today's brands foster these positive emotions by raising awareness by means of endorsements from influencers and leveraging their reputation, which can establish a close bond with followers driving their behavioural decisions. In every industry, adopting technological advancements like Mobile banking (m-banking) has the potential to provide businesses with a competitive edge. M-banking has emerged as a significant phenomenon compared to conventional banking (Wessels & Drennan, 2010). This area of banking services, is projected to reach 1824.7 million US dollars by 2026 (Allied Market Research, 2020), has experienced significant global growth. By 2023, India's digital transaction volume is anticipated to surpass that of China and the United States (KPMG, 2019). Banks are using a variety of media outlets to promote m-banking to acquire the underserved market of prospective mobile banking consumers. Various media platforms, including print, television, and internet-based media such as social media, are used for the same purpose. Social media is extensively used for m-banking promotion because it incorporates the versatility of individual and mass media (Sahoo & S. Pillai, 2017; Shankar et al., 2020; Tam & Oliveira, 2017; Tran & Corner, 2016). Social media influencer marketing is a component of marketing plans that use people as the means of disseminating ideas. The persuasion theory states that audiences view paid advertisements from influencers differently from conventional promotional materials and more as helpful advice from someone who they feel connected to (Han et al. 2021). These influencers are anticipated to be competent to provide the most recent news and details about companies and goods. Thus, influencer credibility holds a major impact on consumers' behavior intention (Sesar et al., 2022). In the long run, such an association could have a significant impact on customers' intentions to accept banking services more readily (Walzhofer et al., 2022). In order to measure m-banking acceptance of individuals we use AIDA model which corresponds to Attention, Interest, Desire and Action. It is crucial to note that due to the complexity of financial products, a foundational understanding of economics is necessary. Introducing financial literacy as a pivotal determinant of individuals' grasp of financial concepts and services, we bring it into the equation as a moderating factor. Therefore, an examination of consumers financial understanding is imperative. The capacity to successfully handle financial resources is referred to as financial literacy. The phrase "financial literacy" is defined in a broad variety of ways. These definitions often suggest that people have the capacity to make choices that will assure their financial security. High financial literacy causes noticeable variations in financial behaviour, according to Sayinzoga (2016). It gives a person the capacity to analyse when buying a financial product and enables him to ignore useless information. From a theoretical standpoint, the authors follow Kiliyanni and Sivaraman (2016) who have proposed four areas of interest as an approach for assessing financial literacy: savings and investment, money management, risk management, and basic knowledge. Based on previous literature, the higher the level of financial literacy of an investor the more easily will be mobile banking be accepted if they perceive the influencer credible. Thus, financial literacy will be studied as a moderating variable between the link between social media influencer credibility and m-banking acceptance.

It is crucial to scrutinize how financial literacy influences the impact of social media influencers on the acceptance of M-Banking, providing a nuanced perspective on the intricate relationship between online influence and financial decision-making. Previous research has investigated the influence of social media on consumer behavior and the determinants of M-banking adoption (Giovanis et al., 2018). However, the detailed exploration of social media influencer credibility and its interplay with financial literacy has been relatively overlooked. By addressing this gap, the authors goal is to provide meaningful insights that can shape marketing strategies, assist financial institutions in refining their services, and furnish policymakers with a nuanced comprehension of the dynamic digital financial landscape. Thus, to illuminate the complex interrelationships among social media, financial literacy, and the acceptance of M-Banking. This endeavor seeks to establish a groundwork for well-informed decision-making in a time where the digital and financial spheres intersect. As we commence this exploration, we anticipate unveiling novel facets of consumer behavior and digital influence that will reverberate throughout academic, industry, and policy landscapes. Building on this the authors put forward the notion that social media influencer credibility influences mobile banking acceptance of consumers. The authors acknowledge the imperative to delve deeper than just the immediate effects of influencer credibility, recognizing the varied levels of financial knowledge among consumers. The chosen title for this investigation, "Influence of Social Media Influencer Trustworthiness on M-Banking Adoption: Examining the Moderating Impact of Financial Literacy," succinctly captures the core of our examination of the intricate connections among social media, financial technology, and consumer decision-making.

Thus, the research objectives are:

1. Social Media Influencer credibility has a direct impact on m-banking acceptance of individuals.
2. There is a moderating effect of financial literacy on the relationship between Social media influencer credibility and m-banking acceptance.

Review of Literature

Social Media Influencer Credibility

The authors have adopted to define influencer marketing according to Martínez-López et al. (2020, p. 579), as follows: "as the use of influential opinion leaders (influencers), celebrity or non-celebrity, with many followers on social platforms, to foster positive attitudinal and behavioral responses in their followers (consumers) regarding the brand's interests by using posts shared on such platforms, and which also allows influencers and followers to participate in the co-creation of the brand image on social media". The significance of influencers in brand awareness and customer influence has grown, but certain aspects remain understudied (Schouten et al., 2020). The effectiveness of influencer marketing initiatives relies heavily on the credibility of the influencers engaged. The theory of influencer credibility encompasses the perceived expertise, attractiveness, and trustworthiness of the influencer (Lee & Kim, 2020). The Source Credibility Model, proposed by (Li & Yin, 2018), suggests that the trustworthiness and expertise of communicators play a significant role in the effectiveness of message delivery to audiences. This study examines the Source Credibility Model, which includes three dimensions: trustworthiness, expertise, and attractiveness.

Trustworthiness is a fundamental aspect of the source credibility model, encompassing honesty, integrity, and trust in a given source. The perceived purpose of a source greatly influences the level of trust or honesty attributed to it by the audience. Source trustworthiness refers to the perception of the message recipient regarding the honesty, sincerity, and truthfulness of the source (Giffin, 1967). It also encompasses the source's reliability, dependability (Ohanian, 1990), integrity, and believability. Trust is a phenomenon that arises when an individual has confidence in their exchange partner. This confidence is based on the belief that the communicator will convey assertions that are considered to be highly valid (Moorman et al., 1993; Munnukka et al., 2016). Trustworthiness is the level of confidence that the listener has in the source of a message (Ohanian, 1990). Munnukka et al. (2016) suggest that endorsers who are perceived as trustworthy are more persuasive due to their product expertise, as supported by Ohanian (1990). McGuire (1985) defines source attractiveness as the perception of physical attributes, likeability, or similarity of the source. The concept of attractiveness encompasses more than just physical attributes, as it also includes personality traits and athletic prowess (Erdogan, 1999). According to Ohanian (1990), the attractiveness dimension of endorsers is associated with elegant, classy, attractive, beautiful, or sexy characteristics. Source expertise is defined as the knowledge and skills possessed by a source that enable them to form opinions, express views, and make claims on a specific topic (McCroskey, 1966). The term "expertise" can also be used to describe the level at which a communicator is seen as a reliable source of accurate information (Munnukka et al., 2016). The expertise of an endorser is characterised by their acquisition of skills, knowledge, and experience in endorsing a brand or product (Van der Waldt et al., 2009). According to Ohanian (1990), source expertise refers to consumers' perception of the endorser as an expert who is qualified, skilled, and possesses proper knowledge. Influencer endorsements are a common way to raise brand exposure, and when combined with an influencer's reputation, this can build a strong bond with a follower that can affect their purchase behaviour. Considering brand awareness is one of the fundamental pillars of loyalty, followers' behaviour is greatly influenced by a source's credibility (Sesar et al., 2022).

M-banking Acceptance

Recent research has examined the key factors that influence the adoption of mobile banking. This has been accomplished through the application of diverse adoption and diffusion theories across multiple areas (Jadil et al., 2021; Sohail and Al-Jabri, 2014; Yu, 2012). The predominant models for m-banking adoption, including TAM 1 & 2, UTAUT 1 & 2, TPB/DTPB, TRA, and IDT, have been successfully tested in different geographical locations and demographic groups. Several studies have incorporated additional theories, such as consumer resistance theory and the task of technology fit (Tran and Corner, 2016). The research on the relationship between social media and mobile banking is limited, and the existing studies do not focus on consumer adoption. This study aims to assess the impact of social media influencer credibility on consumer motivation to adopt mobile banking.

The AIDA model, introduced by St. Elmo Lewis in 1898, was the first model to propose the concept of the 'Hierarchy of Effects' (HOE) in marketing communication (Barry,1987). The acronym AIDA represents the cognitive stages that customers go through as they are motivated to make a purchase. The stages of the consumer decision-making process are Attention, Interest, Desire, and Action (AIDA). The cognitive stages of awareness and interest in consumers occur when they intentionally or unintentionally acquire information about a product. The consumer experiences a desire to make the purchase. According to Lewis, the fourth stage is a mental state that arises as a result of the preceding three stages. During the decision-making process, consumers reach a critical stage where they must determine whether or not to proceed with a purchase.

Attention

The initial stage of the AIDA model involves creating awareness among individuals about products. During this phase, advertisers present their offerings, including products, services, and information regarding product usage. Employing insights from psychological theories of perception and cognition, marketers utilize inventive strategies, including compelling headlines and visually impactful elements, to evoke specific attention. This portion delves into the foundational cognitive processes of attention and assesses the effectiveness of various attention-capturing methods within the current media-saturated environment. Baca et al. (2005) assert that advertisers first establish awareness of products and their benefits within their target market. In their study, Ashcroft and Hoey (2001) assert that awareness plays a crucial role in attracting customers and serves as the initial stage of the communication process. Thus, to understand whether social media influencer credibility has a relationship with the Attention stage for the M-banking acceptance, we propose the following hypothesis:

H1: Social Media influencer Credibility is positively associated with Attention.

Interest

The purpose of advertising a product or service is to generate interest among the intended audience, as this is the primary objective of advertisers (Rowley, 1998; Broeckelmann, 2010). During this phase, marketers utilize the opportunity to furnish pertinent information, accentuating product benefits and features. Drawing from communication theories, this segment examines the significance of narrative structures and informational appeals in fostering interest. It explores how marketers strategically unfold narratives to maintain audience engagement and provoke cognitive interest. The continued purchasing of a specific product indicates consumer interest (Ghirvu, 2013). Thus, to understand whether social media influencer credibility has a relationship with the Interest stage for M-banking acceptance, we propose the following hypothesis:

H2: Social Media Influencer Credibility is positively associated with Interest.

Desire

The third step in the AIDA model pertains to the desire of target customers to purchase a product or service. From an advertising perspective, desire can be defined as the heightened level of consumer interest and longing for a particular product. This section delves into the psychological foundations of desire, exploring emotional appeals and storytelling techniques. It evaluates how marketers strategically position their offerings as solutions that meet not only functional needs but also deeper emotional and aspirational desires. The primary goal of advertisers is to generate desire among consumers by highlighting the features and benefits of their products (Richardson et al., 2014). At this stage, advertisers aim to enhance the visibility of a product among customers (Rowley, 1998). Thus, to understand whether social media influencer credibility has a relationship with the Desire stage for the M-banking acceptance, we propose the following hypothesis:

H3: Social Media Influencer Credibility is positively associated with Desire.

Action

At the fourth level of the AIDA model hierarchy, customers take action by purchasing a product or service. At this stage, customers are willing to make a purchase in order to satisfy their strong desire for a specific product or service. Incentives have the potential to influence customer behaviour and drive purchases. It concentrates on instigating a measurable response from the consumer. Informed by behavioral economics and persuasion theories, this portion meticulously examines the complexities of calls-to-action (CTAs). It evaluates the efficacy of CTAs in transforming consumer interest and desire into tangible actions, shedding light on the behavioral triggers that shape decision-making.Discounted prices are effective in encouraging customers to make purchases (Rawal, 2013). According to Ashcroft and Hoey (2001), action refers to the stage of behaviour that involves the actual act of purchasing. Hoyer and Macinnis (2012) assert that effective advertising generates positive emotions, which in turn result in the actual purchase of the advertised products. Thus, in the acceptance aspect, this stage would mean that consumers are now ready to accept mobile banking.

To understand whether social media influencer credibility has a relationship with the Action stage for M-banking acceptance, we propose the following hypothesis:

H4: Social Media Influencer Credibility is positively associated with Action.

Financial Literacy

Depending on their career, income level, life stage, and other factors, people have varying understandings regarding what financial literacy is (Remund, 2010). Many meanings exist for the phrase "financial literacy." Financial literacy refers to the capacity to effectively manage financial resources (Ateş et al., 2016; Disney & Gathergood, 2013). The knowledge and comprehension of financial ideas, instruments, and practises required to make wise and prudent financial management decisions is referred to as financial literacy. It covers a variety of subjects, including as debt management, budgeting, investing, saving, and comprehending financial products in addition to general financial planning. People who possess a high level of financial literacy are more capable of navigating the intricacies of personal finance and making wise financial choices. Financial literacy has been found to have several benefits for investors. Firstly, it helps investors to disregard irrelevant information (Sabir et al., 2019). Secondly, it enables investors to analyze and make informed decisions when choosing financial product. Lastly, financial literacy also helps to protect investors from engaging in herding behavior (Adil et al., 2021). Access to financing can be significantly influenced by financial literacy (Abdullah and Chong, 2014). The adoption of more sophisticated financial products may be hampered by low financial literacy since buyers may be reluctant to spend money on something they do not completely understand.

Based on prior research, the authors posited that increased credibility of social media influencers may result in greater mobile banking acceptance. However, the effect of financial literacy on the relationship between social media influencer credibility and m-banking acceptance is still not known. Thus, the following hypotheses have been proposed:

H5: Financial Literacy moderates the relationship between Social Media Influencer Credibility and Attention.

H6: Financial Literacy moderates the relationship between Social Media Influencer Credibility and Interest.

H7: Financial Literacy moderates the relationship between Social Media Influencer Credibility and Desire.

H8: Financial Literacy moderates the relationship between Social Media Influencer Credibility and Action.

Figure 1. Proposed conceptual model

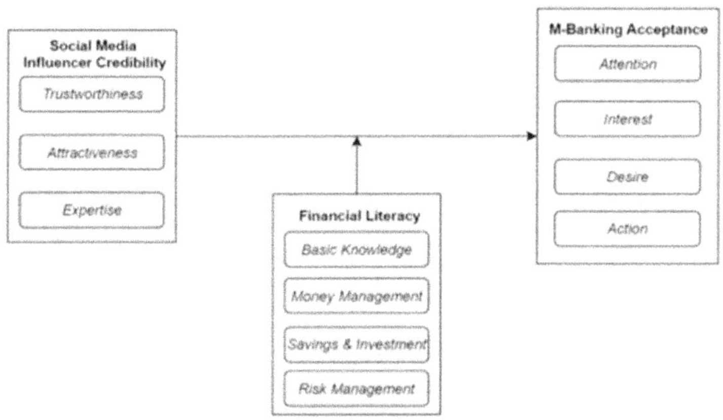

Figure 2. Hypotheses framework

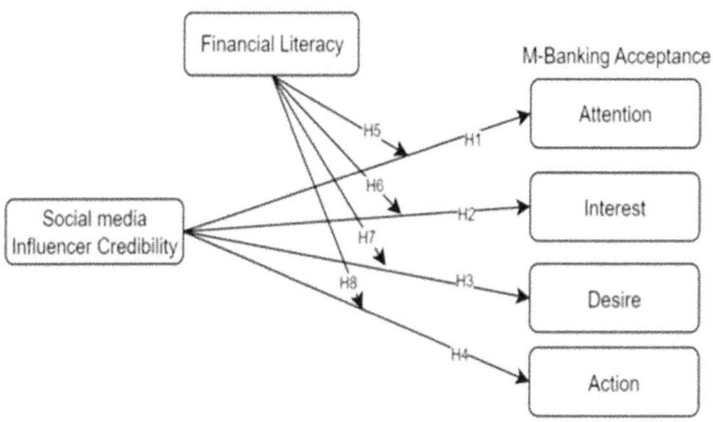

METHODOLOGY

Data Collection and Measurement

A structured questionnaire will be used in the study to analyse the effects of social media influencer credibility and the moderating effect of financial knowledge on the adoption of mobile banking. Each construct is created by modifying the scales from current, pertinent studies in the literature. A five-item scale that was modified from Sesar et al. (2022) was used to assess influencer credibility. We use the AIDA model to gauge m-banking acceptability. According to Sharma et al. (2022), the

Table 1. Descriptive statistics

	Category	Sum	Percentage (%)
Age	18-25	49	16.67%
	26-35	106	36.05%
	36-45	85	28.91%
	Above 45	54	18.37%
Gender	Male	156	53.06%
	Female	138	46.94%
Level of Education	Diploma	23	7.82%
	Graduate	126	42.86%
	Post-Graduate	138	46.94%
	Doctorate	7	2.38%

AIDA model's four statements for each stage (Attention, Interest, Desire, and Action) resulted in a total of 16 statements in this section. Last but not least, we employ a five-item Financial Skills Score based on the total of accurate responses from the U.S. Financial Capability Survey to assess financial literacy (Struckell et al., 2022). The score ranged from 0 to 5 where 1 point for given for every correct answer.

The primary data utilised in this study was gathered by utilising Google Form to distribute the questionnaire online. The data gathering method employed was convenience sampling. The convenience sample approach was previously utilised in research on the adoption of mobile banking conducted in various nations (Zhang et al., 2018). Participation was voluntary and two filter questions were utilized to validate the usage of social media and next to confirm if financial knowledge is acquired through social media influencers. Out of 355 responses received there were 14 respondents who did not used social media and 47 respondents who did not acquire any financial information and knowledge via social media influencers. A total of 294 people were included in the final sample. Smart PLS 4 software was employed for the analysis. Regarding our final sample, we can see that there are 53.06% men and 46.94% women, and that respondents between the ages of 26 and 35 made up the largest age group, with 106 respondents, or 36.05% of respondents. The respondents' level of education might be rated as high as majority of them held a graduate's degree or higher.

RESULTS

Measurement Model

Validity and reliability analyses for the measurement model were evaluated. In order to examine the reliability of the indicators in the suggested model, reliability analysis was carried out. Cronbach's alpha of more than 0.70 is deemed to be a satisfactory dependability value for further study indicating adequate internal consistency across the indicators. According to Hair et al. (2019), three criteria—factor loadings, composite reliability, and average variance extracted (AVE)—were used to evaluate convergent validity. They argued that for good outcomes, the factor loadings ought to

Table 2. Measurement model

Constructs	Items	Outer Loadings	Cronbach's Alpha	Composite Reliability (rho_a)	Composite Reliability (rho_c)	AVE	VIF
Social Media Influencer Credibility	IC1	0.845	0.902	0.904	0.927	0.719	2.441
	IC2	0.864					2.560
	IC3	0.854					2.563
	IC4	0.818					2.114
	IC5	0.857					2.564
Attention	A1	0.819	0.827	0.828	0.885	0.659	1.813
	A2	0.824					1.823
	A3	0.795					1.704
	A4	0.809					1.722
Action	AC1	0.808	0.808	0.813	0.873	0.633	1.674
	AC2	0.795					1.552
	AC3	0.77					1.689
	AC4	0.81					1.808
Desire	D1	0.792	0.839	0.839	0.892	0.674	1.606
	D2	0.841					2.045
	D3	0.827					1.856
	D4	0.825					1.922
Interest	I1	0.817	0.839	0.809	0.875	0.636	1.754
	I2	0.817					1.769
	I3	0.779					1.572
	I4	0.776					1.568

Table 3. Discriminant validity via Fornell-Larcker criterion

	A	AC	D	FL	I	IC
A	**0.812**					
AC	0.733	**0.796**				
D	0.702	0.704	**0.821**			
FL	0.708	0.662	0.7	**1**		
I	0.689	0.694	0.705	0.727	**0.797**	
IC	0.71	0.642	0.686	0.743	0.715	**0.848**

hover above 0.70, the composite reliability should be above 0.70, and the AVE must be greater than 0.50. All of these conditions were satisfied in our study, achieving convergent validity. Furthermore, multicollinearity issues were assessed by taking a look at VIF values as the acceptable value should be less than 5. Thus, no such issues were found.

The discriminant validity of the related components was assessed using the Fornell and Larcker (1981) discriminant validity criterion by comparing the correlation coefficients with square root of AVE. The square root values of AVE in this study (bold diagonal elements) are greater than the off-diagonal parts of the correlation coefficients (Table 3). As a result of it meeting the necessary requirements, discriminant validity was attained.

Structural Model

The following metrics, including "coefficient of determination" (R^2) which depicts variation in one construct explained by another variable, "predictive relevance" (Q2), and "effect sizes" (f^2) to confirm predictive accuracy, were used to measure the structural model further (Table 4). The findings indicated that R^2 values for all variables were 57%, 49%, 55% and 60% which all were in the moderate level. Furthermore, the effect sizes of Influencer Credibility on Attention and Interest were moderate whereas for Action and Desire had a weak effect. Lastly, the fact that the Q2 values were greater than 0 indicates predictive relevance.

Table 5 provides information on the outcomes of the eight hypothesised associations. The findings demonstrate that influencer credibility has a significantly favourable impact on M-Banking acceptability as evaluated by Attention, Interest, Desire, and Action depicting the cognitive stages of m-banking acceptance (β = 0.363, β = 0.366; β = 0.285; β = 0.277; $p<0.05$). Therefore H1, H2, H3, and H4 are supported indicating that influencer credibility is positively associated with all dependent variables (AIDA). Additionally, the effect of financial literacy on consumer

Table 4. Q^2 Predict, R^2 and f^2

Constructs	Q^2 Predict	R^2	f^2
A	0.567	0.576	0.179
AC	0.482	0.495	0.101
D	0.544	0.557	0.141
I	0.592	0.606	0.177

acceptability of mobile banking as defined by the AIDA model was explored. The findings show that financial literacy significantly influenced Interest (β =0.091, $p<0.05$), Desire (β =0.067, $p<0.05$), and Action (β = 0.081, $p<0.05$) supporting the hypotheses H6, H7, and H8. However, financial literacy was not a moderator on the link between influencer credibility and attention (β =0.010, $p>0.05$). Therefore, the study suggests that influencer credibility has a direct influence on mobile banking acceptance and financial literacy plays a moderating role in this relationship.

DISCUSSION

The results indicate that the credibility of influencers plays a notably positive role in the acceptance of mobile banking. This is assessed through Attention, Interest, Desire, and Action, reflecting the cognitive stages of mobile banking acceptance (with coefficients of $\beta = 0.363$, $\beta = 0.366$, $\beta = 0.285$, and $\beta = 0.277$, respectively; all significant at $p < 0.05$). The favorable effect of influencer credibility on the acceptance of mobile banking can be ascribed to its influence on different cognitive

Table 5. Hypotheses testing

	Estimate	Standard Deviation	T Statistics	P Values
H1: IC -> A	0.411	0.060	6.875	0.000*
H2: IC -> I	0.395	0.054	7.381	0.000*
H3: IC -> D	0.374	0.061	6.157	0.000*
H4: IC -> AC	0.338	0.066	5.119	0.000*
H5: FL x IC -> A	0.010	0.029	0.330	0.742
H6: FL x IC -> I	0.091	0.036	2.549	0.011*
H7: FL x IC -> D	0.067	0.033	2.003	0.045*
H8: FL x IC -> AC	0.081	0.037	2.180	0.029*

*significance $p<0.05$

Figure 3. Structural model

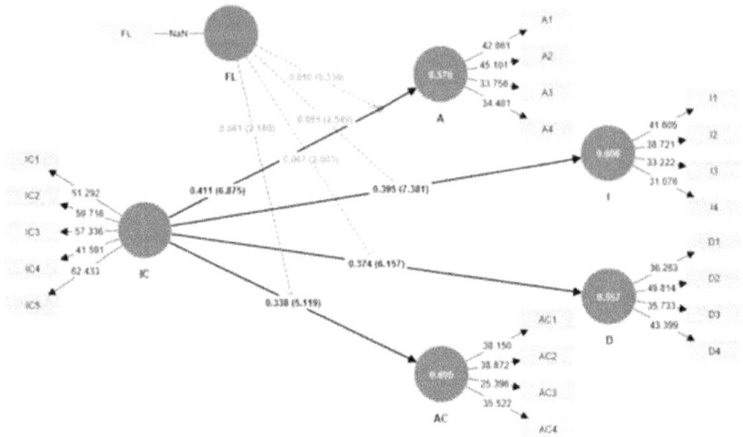

stages. In particular, when individuals encounter influencers regarded as credible, it seizes their attention, cultivating an initial interest in mobile banking (Torbarina et al., 2019). As users explore further, the perceived credibility of influencers maintains their interest and ignites a desire to actively participate in mobile banking services. Moreover, influencers play a role in enhancing the positive perception and appeal of mobile banking, establishing a conducive atmosphere for users to initiate actions. This advancement through the cognitive stages of Attention, Interest, Desire, and Action underscores the pivotal role of influencer credibility in molding users' attitudes and acceptance of mobile banking (Fetter et al., 2023; Harkins & Athineos, 2023; Lee & Kim, 2020; Saini & Bansal, 2023). Furthermore, the results indicate a significant impact of financial literacy on Interest ($\beta = 0.091$, $p < 0.05$), Desire ($\beta = 0.067$, $p < 0.05$), and Action ($\beta = 0.081$, $p < 0.05$), thereby providing support for hypotheses H6, H7, and H8, which depicts that Individuals possessing advanced financial literacy are more likely to grasp the financial content conveyed by influencers effectively. This understanding can serve as a moderating factor in the connection between influencer credibility and interest. Those with higher financial literacy are predisposed to express interest in content that aligns with their comprehensive understanding of financial concepts (Mottola, 2013). Individuals with advanced financial literacy possess the skills to make well-informed decisions regarding financial affairs. When influencers share financial information, those with higher financial literacy are likely to engage in a more discerning evaluation, thereby acting as a moderating factor in the association between influencer credibility and desire. The capacity for informed decision-making may result in a heightened desire for credible and trustworthy financial advice (Fetter et al., 2023). Their ability to comprehend and evaluate financial information serves as a moderating influence on the correlation between influencer credibility and subsequent actions. Individuals with greater financial literacy are more likely to take decisive steps after conducting a thorough assessment of both the influencer's credibility and the financial advice provided (Nykiforuk et al., 2023). And lastly, H5 was rejected, financial literacy might not function as a robust moderator as it may not inherently tackle the nuanced emotional aspects that underpin attention in the domain of social media influencer marketing. Social media attention is influenced by a range of psychological and sociocultural factors, and financial literacy may not exert a significant influence on these elements. Users are often attracted to influencers for reasons such as entertainment value, lifestyle, or personal connection, rather than being driven primarily by financial knowledge.

Implications

The impact of social media influencer credibility on the acceptance of mobile banking is profound. Influencers with credibility serve as trustworthy guides, simplifying the user adoption journey by sharing positive experiences and alleviating concerns. This credibility has the potential to amplify awareness and spark interest in mobile banking services. Conversely, if influencers lack authenticity or support unreliable platforms, trust can be compromised, impeding the widespread adoption of mobile banking. For businesses in the mobile banking sector, the key lies in the careful selection of influencers. It's essential to choose individuals whose values align seamlessly with the security and reliability aspects of their services. This strategic influencer collaboration not only enhances credibility but also maximizes positive impacts, fostering greater acceptance of mobile banking among users. Understanding how social media influencer credibility affects mobile banking acceptance allows businesses to strategically choose influencers with a genuine and trustworthy image. This can enhance the effectiveness of marketing campaigns related to mobile banking services.

Recognizing the moderating role of financial literacy helps tailor communication strategies. Businesses can design content that suits the comprehension levels of their target audience, thereby increasing the likelihood of acceptance. Financially literate consumers may make more informed decisions regarding mobile banking based on influencer endorsements. This insight can guide businesses in designing campaigns that resonate with the financial knowledge of their audience. Consumers are likely to trust influencers who align with their financial literacy levels. This emphasizes the importance of credibility in influencer marketing for mobile banking services. Insights from this research may contribute to the development of guidelines or best practices for influencer marketing in the financial sector, ensuring responsible and transparent practices.

Limitations and Future Research Directions

This study, although it offers significant and practical insights into the role of social media on mobile banking in a developing nation, is constrained by certain limitations. The current investigation is a cross-sectional study. In the future, researchers can employ longitudinal data to evaluate the efficacy of the research paradigm. Longitudinal evidence is helpful in discerning the interplay between various elements. The sample consisted of an urban population characterized by a high level of technological acceptance. Chatbot services are not widely embraced by the rural populace, thus necessitating a study to comprehend the level of acceptance towards chatbots. This study examines financial literacy as a moderator. However, future studies have the opportunity to uncover additional moderators, such as user involvement, user knowledge, and personal qualities that may influence users' adoption of mobile banking. The conventional characteristics of service quality, tangibility and empathy, are assessed in terms of understandability and interactivity. Nevertheless, these measures have constraints. Subsequent investigations should prioritize the exploration of alternative measures for tangibility and empathy within the domains of understandability and interaction. The presence of subjective limitations leads to the applicability of the AIDA model. The impact of social media can also be analyzed through the cognitive, emotional, and conative stages of consumer behavior. This would enhance the validity of the idea on the behavioral usage patterns in social media study. Conducting an ethnographic study is advised to comprehend the influential function of social media in shaping the behavior of millennial consumers.

The study suggests that social media might be a valuable tool for users who are already using mobile banking. The study demonstrates the impact of social media on customers during various stages of mobile banking adoption. Additional investigation can be conducted to comprehend the impact of social media on individuals who are now utilizing mobile banking services. Exploring this domain in future research is crucial due to the increasing adoption of mobile banking services. It is imperative to investigate client expectations, identify emerging potential for additional services, and address informational requirements.

REFERENCES

Abdullah, M. A., & Chong, R. (2014). Financial literacy: An exploratory review of the literature and future research. *J. Emerg. Econ. Islamic Res.*, *2*(3), 32–41. doi:10.24191/jeeir.v2i3.9631

Adil, M., Singh, Y., & Ansari, M. S. (2021). How financial literacy moderate the association between behaviour biases and investment decision? *Asian Journal of Accounting Research*, *7*(1), 17–30. doi:10.1108/AJAR-09-2020-0086

Ashcroft, L., & Hoey, C. (2001). PR, marketing and the Internet: Implications for information professionals. *Library Management*, *22*(1/2), 68–74. doi:10.1108/01435120110358952

Ateş, S., Coskun, A., Sahin, M., & Demircan, M. (2016). Impact of Financial Literacy on the Behavioral Biases of Individual Stock Investors: Evidence from Borsa Istanbul. *Business and Economics Research Journal*, *7*(3), 1–1. doi:10.20409/berj.2016321805

Baca, E. E., Holguin, J. Jr, & Stratemeyer, A. W. (2005). Direct-to-consumer advertising and young consumers: Building brand value. *Journal of Consumer Marketing*, *22*(7), 379–387. doi:10.1108/07363760510631110

Barry, T. E. (1987). The development of the hierarchy of effects: An historical perspective. *Current issues and Research in Advertising, 10*(1-2), 251-295.

Broeckelmann, P. (2010). Exploring consumers' reactions towards innovative mobile services. *Qualitative Market Research*, *13*(4), 414–429. doi:10.1108/13522751011078827

Disney, R., & Gathergood, J. (2013). Financial literacy and consumer credit portfolios. *Journal of Banking & Finance*, *37*(7), 2246–2254. doi:10.1016/j.jbankfin.2013.01.013

Erdogan, B. Z. (1999). Celebrity endorsement: A literature review. *Journal of Marketing Management*, *15*(4), 291–314. doi:10.1362/026725799784870379

Fetter, S., Coyne, P., Monk, S., & Woodruff, S. (2023). An Exploration of Social Media Users' Desires to Become Social Media Influencers. *Media Watch*, *14*(2). doi:10.1177/09760911231159690

Ghirvu, A. I. (2013). The AIDA model for advergames. *The USV Annals of Economics and Public Administration*, *13*(1 (17)), 90–98.

Giffin, K. (1967). The contribution of studies of source credibility to a theory of interpersonal trust in the communication process. *Psychological Bulletin*, *68*(2), 104–120. doi:10.1037/h0024833 PMID:6065581

Giovanis, A., Assimakopoulos, C., & Sarmaniotis, C. (2018). Adoption of mobile self-service retail banking technologies: The role of technology, social, channel and personal factors. *International Journal of Retail & Distribution Management*, *47*(9), 894–914. doi:10.1108/IJRDM-05-2018-0089

Hair, J. F., Risher, J. J., Sarstedt, M., & Ringle, C. M. (2019b). When to use and how to report the results of PLS-SEM. *European Business Review*, *31*(1), 2–24. doi:10.1108/EBR-11-2018-0203

Han, H., Yi, J., Jun, S., & Ahn, S. (2021). How do followers infer the motives behind an influencer's advertising disclosures? *Asia Pacific Journal of Marketing and Logistics*, *33*(5), 1159–1174. doi:10.1108/APJML-06-2019-0397

Harkins, D., & Athineos, C. (2023). Inspiring action through social media. *International Journal of Science and Technology Research Archive*, *5*. doi:10.53771/ijstra.2023.5.1.0076

Hoyer, W. D., MacInnis, D. J., & Pieters, R. (2012). *Consumer behavior*. Cengage Learning.

Jadil, Y., Rana, N. P., & Dwivedi, Y. K. (2021). A meta-analysis of the UTAUT model in the mobile banking literature: The moderating role of sample size and culture. *Journal of Business Research*, *132*, 354–372. doi:10.1016/j.jbusres.2021.04.052

Khasawneh, M. H. A., Hujran, O., & Abdrabbo, T. (2018). A quantitative examination of the factors that influence users' perceptions of trust towards using mobile banking services. *International Journal of Internet Marketing and Advertising*, *12*(2), 181–207. doi:10.1504/IJIMA.2018.090957

Kiliyanni, A. L., & Sivaraman, S. (2016). The perception-reality gap in financial literacy: Evidence from the most literate state in India. *International Review of Economics Education*, *23*, 47–64. doi:10.1016/j.iree.2016.07.001

KPMG. (2019, August). *Fintech in India—Powering mobile payments*. https://assets.kpmg/content/dam/kpmg/in/ pdf/2019/08/Fintech-in-India%E2% 80%93 Poweringmobile-payments.pdf

Lee, S., & Kim, E. (2020). Influencer marketing on Instagram: How sponsorship disclosure, influencer credibility, and brand credibility impact the effectiveness of Instagram promotional post. *Journal of Global Fashion Marketing, 11*(3), 232–249. doi:10.1080/20932685.2020.1752766

Lee, Y., & Kim, K. H. (2020). De-motivating employees' negative communication behaviors on anonymous social media: The role of public relations. *Public Relations Review, 46*(4), 101955. doi:10.1016/j.pubrev.2020.101955

Li, Z., & Yin, Y. (2018). Attractiveness, expertise and closeness: The effect of source credibility of the first lady as political endorser on social media in China. *Global Media and China, 3*(4), 297–315. doi:10.1177/2059436418819228

Mallat, N., Rossi, M., & Tuunainen, V. K. (2004). Mobile banking services. *Communications of the ACM, 47*(5), 42–46. doi:10.1145/986213.986236

Martínez-López, F. J., Anaya-Sánchez, R., Esteban-Millat, I., Torrez-Meruvia, H., D'Alessandro, S., & Miles, M. (2020). Influencer marketing: Brand control, commercial orientation and post credibility. *Journal of Marketing Management, 36*(17-18), 1805–1831. doi:10.1080/0267257X.2020.1806906

Martínez-López, F. J., Anaya-Sánchez, R., Giordano, M. F., & Lopez-Lopez, D. (2020). Behind influencer marketing: Key marketing decisions and their effects on followers' responses. *Journal of Marketing Management, 36*(7-8), 579–607. doi:10.1080/0267257X.2020.1738525

McCroskey, J. C. (1966). *Scales for the measurement of ethos*. Academic Press.

McGuire, W. J. (1985). Attitudes and attitude change. In G. Lindzey & E. Aronson (Eds.), *The Handbook of Social Psychology* (2nd ed., pp. 262–276). Erlbaum.

McGuire, W. J. (1986). The myth of massive media impact: Savagings and salvagings. *Public Communication and Behavior, 1*, 173-257.

Mishra, S. (2014). Adoption of M-Commerce in India: Applying Theory of Planned Behaviour Model. *Journal of Internet Banking and Commerce, 19*(1), 1-17.

Moorman, C., Deshpande, R., & Zaltman, G. (1993). Factors affecting trust in market research relationships. *Journal of Marketing, 57*(1), 81–101. doi:10.1177/002224299305700106

Mottola, G. (2013). In Our Best Interest: Women, Financial Literacy, and Credit Card Behavior. *Numeracy, 6*(2). Advance online publication. doi:10.5038/1936-4660.6.2.4

Munnukka, J., Karjaluoto, H., Mahlamäki, T., & Hokkanen, V. (2017). Effects of social media on consumers' sports brand experiences and loyalty. In *Creating marketing magic and innovative future marketing trends: Proceedings of the 2016 Academy of Marketing Science (AMS) annual conference* (pp. 1051-1064). Springer International Publishing.

Nykiforuk, C., Belon, A., de Leeuw, E., Harris, P., Allen-Scott, L., Atkey, K., Glenn, N., Hyshka, E., Jaques, K., Kongats, K., Montesanti, S., Nieuwendyk, L., Pabayo, R., Springett, J., & Yashadhana, A. (2023). An action-oriented public health framework to reduce financial strain and promote financial wellbeing in high-income countries. *International Journal for Equity in Health, 22*(1), 66. Advance online publication. doi:10.1186/s12939-023-01877-8 PMID:37055742

Ohanian, R. (1990). Construction and Validation of a Scale to Measure Celebrity Endorsers' Perceived Expertise, Trustworthiness, and Attractiveness. *Journal of Advertising, 19*(3), 39–52. doi:10.1080/00913367.1990.10673191

Rawal, A., Collishaw, S., Thapar, A., & Rice, F. (2013). 'The risks of playing it safe': A prospective longitudinal study of response to reward in the adolescent offspring of depressed parents. *Psychological Medicine, 43*(1), 27–38. doi:10.1017/S0033291712001158 PMID:22617461

Richardson, A., Ganz, O., Stalgaitis, C., Abrams, D., & Vallone, D. (2014). Noncombustible tobacco product advertising: How companies are selling the new face of tobacco. *Nicotine & Tobacco Research: Official Journal of the Society for Research on Nicotine and Tobacco, 16*(5), 606–614. doi:10.1093/ntr/ntt200 PMID:24379146

Rowley, J. (1998). Promotion and marketing communications in the information marketplace. *Library Review, 47*(8), 383–387. doi:10.1108/00242539810239543

Sabir, S. A., Mohammad, H. B., & Shahar, H. B. K. (2019). The Role of Overconfidence and Past Investment Experience in Herding Behaviour with a Moderating Effect of Financial Literacy: Evidence from Pakistan Stock Exchange. *Asian Economic and Financial Review, 9*(4), 480–490. doi:10.18488/journal.aefr.2019.94.480.490

Sahoo, D., & Pillai, S., S. (. (2017). Role of mobile banking servicescape on customer attitude and engagement: An empirical investigation in India. *International Journal of Bank Marketing, 35*(7), 1115–1132. doi:10.1108/IJBM-09-2015-0144

Saini, S., & Bansal, R. (2023). *Power of Social Media Influencer Credibility on the Influence of Brand Attitude*. doi:10.4018/978-1-6684-8898-0.ch010

Sayinzoga, A., Bulte, E. H., & Lensink, R. (2016). Financial literacy and financial behaviour: Experimental evidence from rural Rwanda. *Economic Journal (London), 126*(594), 1571–1599. doi:10.1111/ecoj.12217

Schouten, A. P., Janssen, L., & Verspaget, M. (2020). Celebrity vs. Influencer endorsements in advertising: The role of identification, credibility, and Product-Endorser fit. *International Journal of Advertising*, *39*(2), 258–281. doi:10.1080/02650487.2019.1634898

Sesar, V., Martinčević, I., & Boguszewicz-Kreft, M. (2022). Relationship between advertising disclosure, influencer credibility and purchase intention. *Journal of Risk and Financial Management*, *15*(7), 276. doi:10.3390/jrfm15070276

Shankar, A., Jebarajakirthy, C., & Ashaduzzaman, M. (2020). How do electronic word of mouth practices contribute to mobile banking adoption? *Journal of Retailing and Consumer Services*, *52*, 101920. doi:10.1016/j.jretconser.2019.101920

Sharma, M., Banerjee, S., & Paul, J. (2022). Role of social media on mobile banking adoption among consumers. *Technological Forecasting and Social Change, 180*, 121720. doi:10.1016/j.techfore.2022.121720

Sohail, M. S., & Al-Jabri, I. M. (2014). Attitudes towards mobile banking: Are there any differences between users and non-users? *Behaviour & Information Technology*, *33*(4), 335–344. doi:10.1080/0144929X.2013.763861

Struckell, E. M., Patel, P. C., Ojha, D., & Oghazi, P. (2022). Financial literacy and self employment – The moderating effect of gender and race. *Journal of Business Research*, *139*, 639–653. doi:10.1016/j.jbusres.2021.10.003

Tam, C., & Oliveira, T. (2017). Literature review of mobile banking and individual performance. *International Journal of Bank Marketing*, *35*(7), 1044–1067. doi:10.1108/IJBM-09-2015-0143

Tiwari, P., Tiwari, S. K., & Gupta, A. (2021). Examining the Impact of Customers' Awareness, Risk and Trust in M-Banking Adoption. *FIIB Business Review, 10*(4), 413–423.

Torbarina, M., Jelenc, L., & Brkljačić, I. (2019). Faces engage social media influencers' followers (SSRN *Scholarly Paper 3961288*). https://papers.ssrn.com/abstract=3961288

Tran, H. T. T., & Corner, J. (2016). The impact of communication channels on mobile banking adoption. *International Journal of Bank Marketing*, *34*(1), 78–109. doi:10.1108/IJBM-06-2014-0073

Ullah, S., Kiani, U. S., Raza, B., & Mustafa, A. (2022). Consumers' Intention to Adopt m-payment/m-banking: The Role of Their Financial Skills and Digital Literacy. *Frontiers in Psychology*, *13*, 873708. doi:10.3389/fpsyg.2022.873708 PMID:35572297

Van der Waldt, D. L. R., Van Loggerenberg, M., & Wehmeyer, L. (2009). Celebrity endorsements versus created spokespersons in advertising: A survey among students. *Suid-Afrikaanse Tydskrif vir Ekonomiese en Bestuurswetenskappe*, *12*(1), 100–114. doi:10.4102/sajems.v12i1.263

Walzhofer, N., Riekeberg, M., & Follert, F. (2022). From White Collar to Influencer Marketing? How Banks Can Reach Young Customers. *International Journal of Financial Studies*, *10*(3), 79. doi:10.3390/ijfs10030079

Wessels, L., & Drennan, J. (2010). An investigation of consumer acceptance of M-banking. *International Journal of Bank Marketing*, *28*(7), 547–568. doi:10.1108/02652321011085194

Yu, C. S. (2012). Factors affecting individuals to adopt mobile banking: Empirical evidence from the UTAUT model. *Journal of Electronic Commerce Research*, *13*(2), 104.

Zhang, T., Lu, C., & Kizildag, M. (2018). Banking "on-the-go": Examining consumers' adoption of mobile banking services. *International Journal of Quality and Service Sciences*, *10*(3), 279–295. doi:10.1108/IJQSS-07-2017-0067

Chapter 13
Digital Lending Dilemma:
How BNPL Impacts Consumers' Propensity Towards Debt

Renu Singh
Amity University, Noida, India

Ekta Kasana
https://orcid.org/0000-0002-4429-1677
Amity University, Noida, India

ABSTRACT

Digital lending has emerged as a disruptive force in the financial industry's ever-changing landscape, transforming the way customers access and manage credit. BNPL products have grown in popularity, particularly among the younger generation, because to their ease of use, flexibility, and seamless integration into online purchasing experiences. Consumers can use these services to break their payments into smaller, interest-free installments, providing an alternative to standard credit products and payment methods. However, the potential costs to consumers have not been quantified. The study results suggest that BNPL consumers face financial charges that are on par with credit card fees and are vulnerable to unfavorable risks due to loopholes in customer protection. Customers face varying expenses both before and after they go into default on BNPL repayments, with the annual percentage rate (APR) ranging from 0% to 36%.

DOI: 10.4018/979-8-3693-1503-3.ch013

INTRODUCTION

The concept of loan is as old as civilization itself, but the way it is done has changed dramatically in the last decade. Traditional lending institutions, such as banks and credit unions, have been challenged by creative financial technology (FinTech) firms that have introduced a variety of digital lending choices. Peer-to-peer lending, online personal loans, and, most notably, BNPL services are among these choices.

Consumers can use BNPL services to make purchases, generally on e-commerce sites, and defer payment by dividing the entire cost into many, smaller installments. In contrast to standard credit cards, BNPL solutions often offer interest-free payback as long as clients make timely payments. The simplicity, openness, and ability to spread the financial load of a purchase over time make BNPL an appealing alternative to credit cards or traditional loans.

While BNPL services have grown in popularity, there have been some concerns raised regarding their possible impact on consumer debt habits. According to critics, these services may encourage impulsive purchasing and lead to users incurring more debt than they can safely manage. Proponents of BNPL options, on the other hand, believe that they provide greater financial freedom and enable individuals avoid the typically onerous interest rates associated with regular credit cards.

The seamless integration of BNPL services into the online purchasing experience has contributed to their success. Customers can choose to pay with BNPL with just a few clicks during the checkout process, rapidly reducing a large expense into affordable installments. Furthermore, the absence of interest costs when payments are made on time has made BNPL an enticing choice for those who do not want to incur further debt through interest.

The growing presence of BNPL providers, who frequently collaborate with e-commerce platforms and brick-and-mortar stores, has broadened the reach of these services, making them available to a broader range of consumers. Notably, BNPL services are especially appealing to younger groups, who are more likely to embrace digital financial solutions and frequently prefer the convenience of installment payments over traditional credit cards.

Pay Later Purchases

The BNPL system is an example of the digitization of a formerly paper-based payment method. Credit card and layaway systems were originally the sole BNPL options, but digital invoicing services account for the vast majority of the industry's revenue today. These programmes have a long history of making already vulnerable persons even more so. Every other user now claims to utilize invoice services during the checkout process, and this trend is expected to continue as digital in-voice services become the major payment method in e-commerce.

As the acronym suggests, “buy now, pay later” (BNPL) refers to digital services that allow customers to make immediate purchases without worrying about making immediate payments. Instead, the service immediately pays the merchant and charges the client depending on the installment plan. These services are similar to traditional banks in that they lend money to consumers and collect payments at a later date. Assuming prompt payment and no usage of the extended payment schedule, they are often offered at no additional cost. Both interest revenues (from customers who postpone payments) and merchant fees provide the bulk of the corporations’ bottom lines. Interest costs are calculated on a sliding scale based on the total purchase amount and payment schedule you choose. Direct payments, post-purchase payments, and partial payments are all options. Two types of payments may be made after a purchase has been made: a “pay within n number of days” payment that is interest-free if made on time but incurs a cost if the payment is delayed, and a “pay at the end of the following month” payment that comes with an immediate late fee. Additional interest and a small administration charge are added to the split payment installment. Instantaneous access to credit is provided by digital invoice services, and there are fewer restrictions to be qualified for credit with digital invoice services than with other BNPL choices. Most online bill pay systems now utilize what’s called a “soft credit inquiry,” which, unlike a “hard credit inquiry,” does not affect the user’s credit rating. However, if a user accrues debt due to persistently late payments to the service, this would reflect negatively on the user’s credit score. Because of the increased potential for credit and fraud associated with online transactions, digital invoicing systems bear the brunt of these dangers.

The popularity of “Buy Now Pay Later” (BNPL) applications and other forms of alternative finance has skyrocketed in recent years. Regular data from the Bank of England’s consumer credit report showed a 14.5% drop in credit card borrowing at the start of 2021, setting a new record low (Bank of England, 2021; Key, 2021). Credit alternatives provided by online BNPL services like Klarna and Qliro have been cited as a cause for the decline in millennials’ use of credit cards (Key, 2021). Sixty-two percent of BNPL customers believe BNPL might replace their credit card, according to a new study by the Motley Fool (Backman, 2021). BNPL alternatives are growing in popularity at online checkouts, for instance, where buyers may make a purchase right away and subsequently pay off their balance in 30 days with no interest (Klarna, n.d.-b; Webster & Rees, 2021).

Many consumers see credit card debt to be a helpful financial resource. The product has the potential to help customers accept who they are, bring about positive changes in their lives, and triumph over hardship. Credit debt may be helpful in budgeting if it is recognized as such and paid back on time (ING, 2020a). Even though many modern youths might disagree, this was not always the case. In 2018, Kredinor, Norway's largest debt collection company, processed 1,4 million debt collection cases and 700,000 overdue notice cases. Those between the ages of 18 and 25 and 26 and 34 were found to have the highest debt and collection rate increases. Those findings are detailed in Dinero (2019). One reason why more and more young people are dependent on credit is the proliferation of online shopping, which can be financed quickly and easily (Dinero, 2019; Kredinor, 2018). Bankruptcy and family debt have been on the rise in recent years, especially among the young adult population, and experts attribute this to the widespread availability of 0% APR credit cards and an increasing dependence on credit for purchases (Bauer et al., 2021). Consumers' decisions regarding how much debt to take on are influenced by several psychological and societal factors in addition to age (Frigerio et al., 2020). Personal issues such as weak self-control and lack of financial understanding have been cited in previous research as reasons for increased credit card debt. Customers that exhibit these characteristics are at a higher risk of amassing excessive debt, according to previous research (Brougham et al., 2011; Frigerio et al., 2020; Gathergood, 2012; Majamaa et al., 2019). (Brougham et al., 2011; Frigerio et al., 2020; Gathergood, 2012; Majamaa et al., 2019).

Few studies have examined how BNPL and other nontraditional approaches to credit card repayment affect customers' propensity to incur debt. This motivates us to investigate the following:

Statement of the Issue

- How does offering the option to "buy now, pay later" influence consumers' tendency to incur debt?
- To what extent does young consumers and customers with low levels of self-control and/or financial literacy face a greater risk of consumer debt while using online BNPL as opposed to more traditional ways of payment (such as credit cards)?

LITERATURE REVIEW

We have reviewed the available literature extensively to learn more about the effects of various payment mechanisms on consumers' propensity to take on debt. Beginning with an overview of BNPL and its history as a consumer payment method, we present the concept. Next, we examine how prior studies have shown consumers' propensity to take on debt. After that, we relate their results to the BNPL application. Thus, we have a more thorough understanding of the topic we want to study and how

Table 1. Literature review and findings

Authors	Title	Year	Findings
Johannes C. Bauer, Vicki G. Morwitz, and Liane Nagengast	Customer demand for credit to purchase experiences rises when companies provide promotional interest-free financing.	2021	This is the first study to investigate the effects of interest-free financing offers on buyer decisions. Five trials reveal that when the offer of financing is phrased in such a way that the lack of interest is stressed, buyers are more ready to use credit to acquire experience items rather than material products. For example, customers are more likely to take out loans for solely experience purchases (such as trips) or mixed shopping baskets that give primarily experienced benefits (if the experiencing components of the products are emphasised, such as a bike). The findings suggest that interest-free signals mitigate consumers' debt aversion to discretionary experiences through mediation and moderation.
Rufina Gafeeva, Hoelzl, Erik, and Roschk, Holger.	Where else may you use your credit card? Payment transparency may be compromised by the proliferation of payment methods.	2018	The amount of money you can see leaving your account is determined by how you pay (cash vs. credit card, for example). The use of smart cards, also known as flexible cards, which integrate payment with other functions (such as loyalty programmes, identification, and data storage), is increasing. People are predicted to have a less trustworthy recollection of their previous financial outlays when more payment methods become available. The usefulness of utilising cash, a single-purpose card, and a multi-purpose card in recalling recent transactions is compared using field research. When compared to cash, using a single- or multi-function card results in lower recall accuracy. Furthermore, it is the user's distinctive behaviour, not the card's variety, that produces a bigger recall error: the recall error increases as the frequency of usage of the non-payment functions increases.
Anderloni L.; Bacchiocchi E.; Vandone D.	Household financial vulnerability: An empirical analysis	2012	The study looks into household financial distress using survey data. According to the empirical investigation, households at the median level of the financial vulnerability index already demonstrate certain critical symptoms of financial vulnerability, such as difficulty getting to the end of the month or an inability to meet unexpected expenses. Three conclusions should be highlighted in terms of the factors of the financial vulnerability index. First, debt servicing is associated to financial vulnerability, and the effect is larger for households with unsecured debt, such as consumer credit. Second, impulsive people are more likely to be financially vulnerable because they may adopt impatient, short-sighted behaviour patterns that make it harder for them to completely understand the ramifications of their financial and spending actions. Third, a greater degree of education aids in the reduction of financial insecurity.
Arisandy Y.; Dasril Y.B.; Salahudin S.N.B.; Muslim M.A.; Adnan A.; Wen G.K.	Buy now pay later services on generation z: exploratory data analysis using machine learning	2023	A novel approach to installment loans is the buy now, pay later (BNPL) business model. It enables clients to take ownership of their item immediately, with or without a down payment. Furthermore, the bulk of BNPL loans are structured so that four installments are required. This form of financing, however, comes with its own set of dangers and obstacles. This article investigates the risk of BNPL as a product for Generation Z consumers. The data utilised is secondary data provided by Kaggle in csv format (loan data.csv), and it contains 159,584 postpaid customer records and 28 attributes that were analysed using descriptive and exploratory data analysis (EDA). According to the findings, the majority of pay later consumers are married, and millennials (52.10%) are the most likely to use pay later services. Generation Z has the highest percentage of loan default, which is approximately 34.16%, with the time employee being approximately 0-8 months (35.8%). Furthermore, the unemployed generation Z has the greatest default percentage of 32.16%, according to the findings.

Authors	Title	Year	Findings
Behera C.K.; Dadra R.	Understanding young consumers' attitude formation for new-age fintech credit products: an SOR framework perspective	2023	This study intends to address a gap in the literature by investigating young consumers' attitudes towards FCP in the context of BNPL. The study investigated the stimulus (affordability, flexibility, and structural assurance) and organism (perceived usefulness and trust) aspects that affect attitude formation towards FCP among young customers using a stimulus-organism-response paradigm using SmartPLS. The findings indicate that price, flexibility, structural assurance, and perceived usefulness all have a role in shaping consumers' opinions towards FCP. The study's findings can help to understand young consumers' preferences and expectations towards FCP and can help fintech companies build and sell FCP that satisfy consumer needs.
Cook J.; Davies K.; Farrugia D.; Threadgold S.; Coffey J.; Senior K.; Haro A.; Shannon B.	Buy now pay later services as a way to pay: credit consumption and the depoliticization of debt	2023	This study examines the located landscape of BNPL service marketing and branding through an examination of their websites and apps, a walking ethnography of a large retail centre, and interviews with BNPL consumers. The findings show that BNPL services foster a "structure of feeling" that is reminiscent of digitally intimate online environments, and that they distinguish themselves from other more "serious" financial services by providing a sense of pleasure and amusement. According to the study, this helps them market themselves as a "way to pay" rather than a type of credit, and it constitutes a significant new step in the depoliticization of debt.
Fook L.A.; McNeill L.	Click to buy: The impact of retail credit on over-consumption in the online environment	2020	This study investigates the impact of a set of impulse-enabling financial tools (buy-now-pay-later (BNPL) credit schemes) on young adult female consumers' impulse buying tendency in an online fashion shopping scenario. The research adds a consumer viewpoint on the impact of BNPL on unsustainable spending behaviour in the online retail scenario, which is currently lacking in the literature, by taking into account customers' impulse buying tendencies in such a setting. Findings show that BNPL users have a larger online impulse buying tendency than non-BNPL users, and a clear correlation between online impulse buying tendency and sales conversion tool sensitivity is established, favouring overconsumption in this scenario.
Guttman-Kenney B.; Firth C.; Gathergood J.	Buy now, pay later (BNPL) …on your credit card	2023	Consumers charging BNPL transactions to their credit cards are documented in the BNPL research utilising UK credit card transaction data. Charging BNPL to credit cards is especially common among younger consumers and those living in the poorest areas. Charging 0% interest and amortising BNPL debt to credit cards – where normal interest rates are 20% and amortisation schedules are decades long – calls into question these consumers' ability to pay for BNPL. This raises the regulatory issue of whether customers should be permitted to refinance their unsecured debt.
Hoang V.H.; Nguyen P.M.; Luu T.M.N.; Vu T.M.H.	Determinants of Intention to Borrow Consumer Credit in Vietnam: Application and Extension of Technology Acceptance Model	2021	The goal of this study is to examine the determinants of Vietnamese people's intention to borrow consumer credit using the Technology Acceptance Model (TAM) and extending it with several variables extracted and adapted from the existing literature, such as anxiety, perceived trust, and perceived financial costs. A questionnaire survey was distributed to 602 consumers in Vietnam's major cities. The link between intention determinants to borrow has been investigated using structural equation modelling (SEM) approaches. According to the findings, perceived utility moderates the effect of subjective standards on the propensity to borrow consumer credit. At the same time, subjective norms have a direct impact on borrowing intentions. Notably, anxiety, perceived trust, perceived financial cost, and reported ease of use have no effect on borrowing intention. Meanwhile, education level is verified to have a moderate influence on Vietnamese people's propensity to borrow consumer credit.

Authors	Title	Year	Findings
Joe Boden and Robert Wilken	Comparison of the benefits and drawbacks of accepting credit card and mobile payment transactions on the time and effort it takes to transact with customers.	2020	The existing payment mechanism literature largely compares cash to credit cards, with the latter hailed for its "reduced pain of paying," or lack of unfavourable impacts. This study then explains why customers' willingness to pay (WTP) is higher when they use credit cards. The current study expands on the existing body of work by include mobile technology as a payment option. It emphasises the relevance of convenience as a motivator for consumers to increase their WTP for mobile payment. These findings add to the current research on the approaches customers employ while utilising various payment systems, and they provide nation administrators with a variety of payment channel options.
Johnson D.; Rodwell J.; Hendry T.	Analyzing the impacts of financial services regulation to make the case that buy-now-pay-later regulation is failing	2021	Fee-based Buy-Now-Pay-Later (BNPL) programmes are becoming increasingly popular in many industrialised countries, including Australia. There appears to be relatively little regulatory coverage of fee-based BNPL across a number of regulatory approaches. This review evaluates the regulatory outcomes of fee-based BNPL using a results-oriented, behaviorally informed market failure methodology. The review argues that the consequences of fee-based BNPL regulation in Australia reveal numerous types of regulatory failure. The regulatory failure is mostly due to regulatory capture on a broad scale, as well as a lack of consumer protections. Consumers may require special consideration and protection since understanding the rising complexity and financial knowledge at the heart of many fintech services may be beyond the consumer's capability or obligation.
Lisa McNeill, Lauren Ah Fook	When it comes to online shopping, the use of retail credit may lead to excessive spending.	2020	Because of the group's proclivity for identity and lifestyle adjustments, young people frequently consume "non-essential" items such as apparel and accessories. This study investigates how various buy-now-pay-later (BNPL) credit schemes influence the proclivity of young adult female customers to make impulsive purchases while shopping for apparel online. This study addresses a gap in the literature by providing a consumer's perspective on the effect of BNPL on wasteful consumption patterns, taking into account customers' proclivity for impulsive purchases in the context of online shopping. The findings suggest that those who use BNPL are more likely than those who do not to make impulsive purchases online, and that there is a direct association between this behaviour and susceptibility to sales conversion techniques.
Lupșa-Tătaru D.A.; Nichifor E.; Dovleac L.; Chițu I.B.; Todor R.D.; Brătucu G.	Buy Now Pay Later—A Fad or a Reality? A Perspective on Electronic Commerce	2023	For their extremely demanding needs, Millennials and Generation Z use online shopping for a holistic experience and purchase more expensive or higher-quality products with buy now pay later payment methods. The authors sought to gain a better grasp of this issue by identifying associated knowledge domains and identifying the sort of economy that will represent a growing market share for the method of domestic e-commerce payments. To explain the market share of 23 economies globally, the methodology used computer-assisted review, descriptive statistics, and linear regression. Student credit card use, myopic consumer law, and purchasing habits. Dark financial triangles and other relevant topics were identified.

Authors	Title	Year	Findings
Marron D.	Debt, consumption and freedom: Social scientific representations of consumer credit in Anglo-America	2015	The research investigates a variety of social scientific representations of credit and debt in the United States and the United Kingdom, as well as how these have been organised around the issue of freedom. On the one hand, credit is seen as productive, encapsulating and protecting liberal values such as human autonomy and self-determination. Debt, on the other hand, is characterised as consumptive, ensnaring the individual, subverting her or his will, and undermining the ability to self-determine. The Puritan ethic, which portrays indebtedness as contrary to the values of individual freedom and autonomy, captures the classic cultural injunction against consumer borrowing; however, it is demonstrated here how the meanings attached to credit and debt have always been ambiguous in practise.
Powell R.; Do A.; Gengatharen D.; Yong J.; Gengatharen R.	The relationship between responsible financial behaviours and financial wellbeing: The case of buy-now-pay-later	2023	Buy-now-pay-later (BNPL) is a rapidly expanding payment innovation in Australia. Regulators and consumer groups have raised worry about BNPL's financial vulnerabilities. Because BNPL is not regulated under consumer credit law, financial regulators and consumer groups have advised BNPL users to engage in a variety of responsible financial practises to ensure their financial well-being. Using a survey of BNPL users and structural equation modelling, this study found a link between most of these recommended financially responsible behaviours and financial wellbeing, and that the financial behaviours of younger users (those under the age of 25) put them at a higher risk of financial distress.
Raj V.A.; Jasrotia S.S.; Rai S.S.	Intensifying materialism through buy-now pay-later (BNPL): examining the dark sides	2023	The purpose of this study is to look into how consumerism influences BNPL use as well as impulsive and compulsive buying. Furthermore, the authors investigate whether BNPL use and impulsive buying act as a buffer between materialism and compulsive buying. The findings demonstrate that materialism influences BNPL use and increases the proclivity for impulse purchases, resulting in compulsive buying behaviour. However, BNPL use has no direct effect on compulsive buying. It was discovered that BNPL use and impulsive purchase mitigate the association between materialism and compulsive shopping.
Relja R.; Ward P.; Zhao A.L.	Understanding the psychological determinants of buy-now-pay-later (BNPL) in the UK: a user perspective	2023	This study investigates the psychological factors of buy-now-pay-later (BNPL) use in the United Kingdom and assesses the effectiveness of existing payment frameworks. Findings: While positive sentiments regarding BNPL predominate, additional psychological variables are visible to varying degrees. Transparency and transaction convenience are less appealing, but psychological distance and ownership of borrowed money are more noticeable. BNPL users comprehend temporality in ways that go beyond its present conceptualizations. Because some users interpret BNPL as a "savings" product, payment format conceptualizations may be incorrect. Those that are optimistic highlight BNPL's advantages in terms of consumption and budget management. However, the risk of unexpected consequences exists for all users.
Tan G.K.S.	Buy what you want, today! Platform ecologies of 'buy now, pay later' services in Singapore	2022	The growing acceptance of fintech-driven solutions has changed financial markets and retail consumer behaviour. This study investigates the rising 'buy-now-pay-later' (BNPL) phenomena as a novel, platform-driven financial innovation to better understand how this digitally mediated economic arrangement has given rise to new financial subjects and subjectivities. This article demonstrates how automated risk assessment and debt collection technologies are used to regulate borrowers and keep them digitally tied to their loans, where creditworthiness is continuously evaluated based on user transaction and payback data. The strategic use of affect in framing BNPL services to meet immediate materialist consumption obscures the underlying nature of BNPL as debt, while the targeting of young people with no credit history via opaque credit and risk management practises generates new indebted subjects.

customers react to various payment methods. Finally, we want to create a positive social impact by investigating the many consumer traits used by earlier scholars to characterise demographics who are seen as more at-risk when it comes to obtaining credit and then engaging in risky financial behaviour.

being overburdened by debt. We've narrowed our attention to three factors because of the breadth and depth of this topic: (1) youth, (2) self-discipline, and (3) financial savvy. Recent writings on BNPL and the subject of consumer credit and over-indebtedness all make frequent reference to these three ideas Gathergood (2012); ING (2020b); Johnson (2020), 2021; Majamaa et al. (2019); and Brougham, et al.

What Is BNPL?

Point-of-sale (POS) financing, or BNPL, allows customers to make immediate purchases and spread out their payments over 30 days with no interest. Many BNPL providers, Klarna included, provide their clients the option of paying off the debt early, making payments, or extending the due date by using the provider's app or customer site (Klarna, n.d.-b). Typically, the big BNPL suppliers provide a variety of alternatives, but the merchant must pay a commission on each option purchased. The user will not be charged any interest for using the larger credit limit. Customers who don't pay by the specified deadline will be charged late fees. People are more inclined to buy things large and little when there are no surprises in the fine print (Johnson et al., 2021; Visser, 2021). Figure 1 displays the processes a customer takes to make a repayment to the BNPL provider, as described by the research of Xing et al (2019).

Figure 1. How BNPL customers repay the provider
(Source: Author)

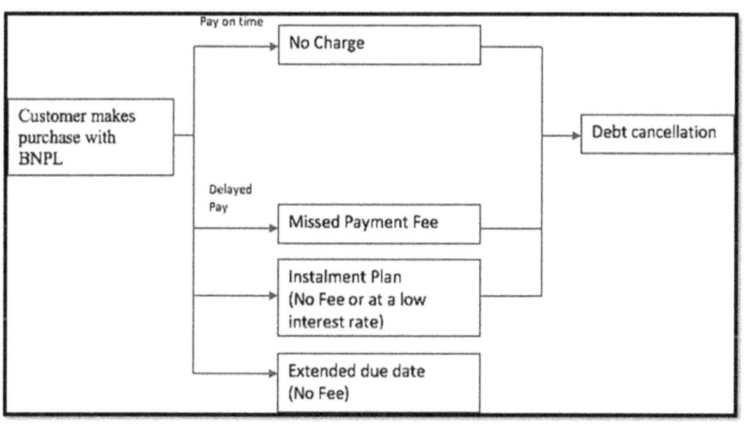

Customers put great importance on avoiding having to pay interest when purchasing credit. Previous research has revealed that many consumers experience anxiety while completing a transaction with a credit card (Eckel et al., 2007; Greenberg & Hershfield, 2016). However, recent research by Bauer et al. (2021) suggests that highlighting the interest-free feature of the credit financing option helps attenuate negative feelings. In this way, the unease caused by the financing option's debt is lessened. The importance of interest-free financing has increased in recent years due to the rising expectations of today's customers. In today's world, consumers need and expect a streamlined, no-hassle, and cost-free shopping experience (Bauer et al., 2021).

It's not that BNPL is a unique concept per se; rather, it's fundamental to the traditional understanding of the consumer credit system. However, e-Business, like BNPL, focuses on online commerce and mobile payments, while traditional credit business relies on credit card usage (Xing et al., 2019). In these up-to-date versions of online BNPL systems, consumers and the third party agree that the third party will acquire the credit sale from the merchant. After then, the buyer is obligated to pay the seller the entire purchase price, either immediately or in installments (Johnson et al., 2021). Customers applying for loans from BNPL companies may expect little to no scrutiny of their credit histories. Lesser amounts of credit may be easily obtained by consumers who desire a "clean" credit score or who are refused loans due to poor credit history. Credit limits are often based on the total amount of a customer's purchase (Visser, 2021).

The Customer Lifecycle: BNPL

Today's e-Businesses accept BNPL payments online, as Xing et al. (2019) showed. The first step in purchasing from an e-Business retailer is for customers to utilize their smart devices or computers to do it. In addition to accepting traditional payment methods like debit and credit cards, many retailers now accept payments using one or more BNPLs.

With a previously used BNPL payment method (like Klarna), the consumer needs just click "purchase" to complete the transaction; their details will already be stored in the BNPL system. If a buyer is making their first purchase with BNPL, they will have the opportunity to open a financing account directly from the online store's checkout page (Klarna, n.d.-a). Klarna can get your credit authorized in minutes (Klarna, n.d.-a; Visser, 2021). Instead of applying for a credit card at a bank, you may use BNPL in a fraction of the time. When a BNPL supplier is selected, they will provide money to the online business owner. Ultimately, clients will reimburse the BNPL provider in the following weeks (Xing et al., 2019). The primary actions of this process are shown in Figure 2.

Figure 2. BNPL customer journey

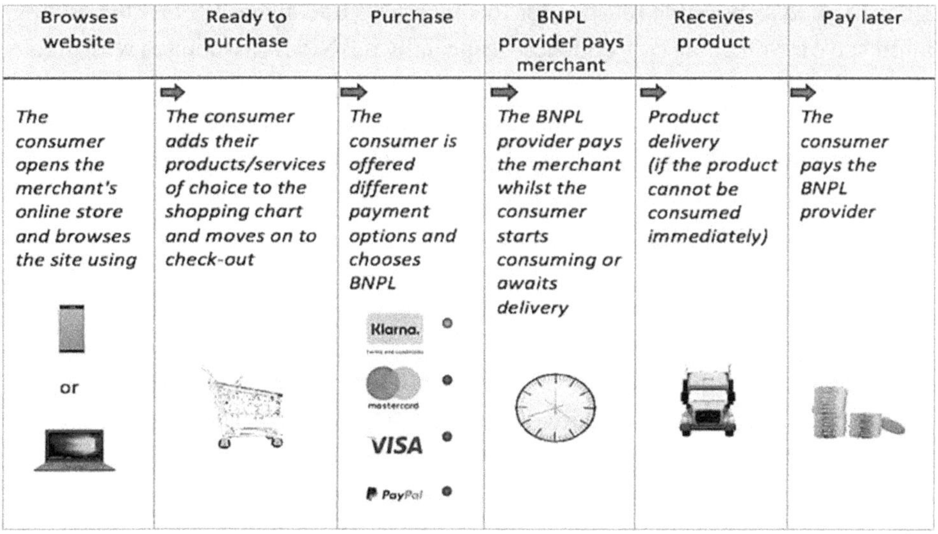

Growth of The BNPL Market

In recent years, BNPL's consumer base has exploded. In 2015, several fintech firms joined the market as payment platforms, forming relationships with big online retailers to provide credit to customers (Capco, 2020; Xing et al., 2019). Since accepting its first payment in 2005, Klarna has grown into Europe's largest independent BNPL operator, with a current market value of around €26 billion. Klarna is available in most major regions of the world, where it services over 250,000 shops (Visser, 2021). A study named "Worldpay 2020: EMEA BNPL Payment Schemes" predicted that by 2025, roughly 11% of eCommerce spending in the area will be done using BNPL payment schemes (Worldpay, 2020). Statistics from Kaleido insight indicate that the BNPL market in Europe will grow to €300bn by 2025, accounting for almost 30% of overall eCommerce expenditure in that year (Visser, 2021).

After already seeing significant growth before the COVID-19 pandemic, the BNPL market saw even greater gains and price increases throughout the outbreak. This is because the pandemic is directly related to the meteoric rise of online shopping and other types of electronic payment (Bullock, 2020). We've been less active than normal because of the pandemic, and that's led to more purchases made over the internet (ING, 2020b). According to data compiled by the Motley Fool, 55% of American consumers would have used BNPL payment methods by March 2021, up from 37% in July 2020. (Backman, 2021). The study also found that the number of customers who used BNPL services increased year over year by 64 percent. Increased online shopping, income loss, and the need to put money aside for unexpected expenses have all been cited as possible reasons for this increase (Backman, 2021). Our findings might have far-reaching consequences, especially if BNPL is associated with greater debt-taking among the most financially vulnerable consumers.

Determinants impacting the Propensity Towards Debt

1. The Ache of Billing

While we do offer consumers fast, flexible, simple, and interest-free credit choices anytime they make an online purchase, consumers still loathe spending money. This anguish was first explained by Zellermayer (1996), who coined the term "pain of paying" to characterize the negative emotions felt by buyers throughout the payment process (Zellermayer, 1996). Because most customers are "loss averse," meaning they equate the possibility of financial failure with negative feelings. Consumers may respond by decreasing their expenditures or forgoing purchases entirely. To restate, the more we feel the "pain of paying," the less likely we are to enjoy the purchasing process or to purchase anything at all (Prelec & Loewenstein, 1998). One possible solution to this "pain" is to pay for the item(s) using a credit card or to wait some time before using them (Ariely & Kreisler, 2018).

It is the pain felt while making a purchase that helps consumers self-regulate their spending (Prelec & Loewenstein, 1998). It is critical to monitor the effects of new payment methods on consumers' spending habits and restraint. A recent survey conducted by Capco found that 44% of respondents had spent more money than they had intended because of BNPL (Webster & Rees, 2021). We should all take a cue from our caveman ancestors and attempt to avoid making difficult financial decisions that may be detrimental to our bank balances. Nonetheless, with the "assistance" of several monetary services, we experience quick alleviation. This implies there is a risk that we will eventually make matters worse for ourselves (Ariely & Kreisler, 2018). When assessing the benefits of taking on debt, it's important to remember that there are a variety of things that might increase the stress caused by monthly payments. After surveying the state of the art in marketing research, we've settled on two major ideas that influence the consumer's level of unease throughout the payment process: (1) the transparency of the payment method (and the debt that is created), and (2) the availability of the payment method itself.

2. The Openness of the Payment System

How a customer feels about using a certain method of payment depends on the significance the consumer assigns to that method about the purchase itself (Prelec

& Loewenstein, 1998). Knowing and being at ease with the act of parting with money strengthens the mental coupling that happens as a consequence of payment. In light of these findings, Soman (2003) defines payment transparency as "the salience of parting with money" (Soman, 2003). For instance, if we use a financial service that simplifies the payment process, this will make it more difficult for us to track where our money is going (Ariely & Kreisler, 2018). For the great majority of BNPL choices, the checkout process is simple and just "one click away." It has been discovered that the value of a single transaction is diminished when paid for using a credit card rather than cash. The disparity in spending habits, however, is predicted to narrow if the significance of the transaction itself is emphasized (Raghubir & Srivastava, 2002). This is especially true for mobile payments, where the underlying payment system is sometimes not even visible to the buyer (Soman, 2003). Both Pisani and Atalay (2018) and Gafeeva et al. (2018) conclude that the complexity of mobile payments makes them less trustworthy than credit cards. So, customers feel more at ease utilizing their mobile devices for purchases (Gafeeva et al., 2018; Pisani & Atalay, 2018). As a result, customers are more willing to spend more money on less obvious payment options since the "pain of payment" is lessened. If this is the case, then we propose that BNPL is not as transparent as other forms of credit (e.g., credit cards).

3. The Simplicity of the Transaction Technique

It has been noted by Xing et al. (2019) that the convenience of online BNPL schemes is a major perk for participants (PYMNTS.com & PayPal, 2020; Xing et al., 2019). What people call "ease of use" or "convenience" refers to how they imagine using a certain piece of technology. This is why clients place a premium on simplicity when evaluating new forms of technology, such as payment systems (Taylor & Todd, 1995). Teo et al. (2015) discovered that consumers' evaluations of a transaction's ease depended on their estimations of how much work was involved in completing the payment (Teo et al., 2015). If clients are provided a payment option that is both easy and familiar, it stands to reason that they will be more likely to make a purchase.

Due to the convenience of using a credit card to make transactions over the phone, more people are incurring debt. The importance of mobile applications to BNPL schemes makes this topic especially timely (Johnson et al., 2021). Customers who are more comfortable using mobile devices, such as the young, are likely to feel this effect more strongly (Boden et al., 2020; Wilska, 2003). Service companies offering BNPL solutions often guarantee "smooth" processes and speedy refunds to their clientele. Registration of payment information is offered via most BNPL providers and may help alleviate the "painful" feelings associated with completing a purchase. Customers have a lot of control over their BNPL experience since BNPL providers provide them with a variety of options in the form of customer portals and apps. The BNPL payment process seems to have been designed to minimize disruptions for customers. Following these assumptions, we provide our second hypothesis:

H2 proposes that if consumers are given less onerous ways to repay their debts, they will be more willing to take on debt (BNPL compared to credit cards).

4. Vulnerable Group Consumer Profiles

We can now presume that the discomfort one feels while accumulating debt varies with the chosen method of repayment since we have found various elements that influence this experience. Similarly, we do not presume that everyone has the same level of discomfort while using a certain payment method. According to Thomas et al. (2011), previous research on the unpleasantness of making a payment failed to take into account the fact that customers' experiences of this phenomenon varied widely (Thomas et al., 2011). In light of Bauer et al(2021) .'s suggestion, we want to learn more about how different types of clients respond to interest-free financing. Since there are many easy-to-access consumer debt solutions like BNPL, we also want to have a good social impact by assisting in the identification of the kind of customers most at risk for the negative repercussions of excessive spendings, such as over-indebtedness (Bauer et al., 2021).

A Special Focus on Vulnerable Consumers

This literature review found that when describing groups that are vulnerable and at a higher risk of over-indebtedness, researchers have primarily focused on socio-demographic and economic characteristics, such as low-income individuals, younger individuals, single parents, and large-size families (Bridges & Disney, 2004; Brown et al., 2005; Jiang & Dunn, 2013; Patel et al., 2012). Recent interdisciplinary studies have emphasized the importance of customers' perspectives in determining their debt decisions and the likelihood of their being overindebted, among other psychological factors (Frigerio et al., 2020). Scientists have shown that self-discipline and knowledge of personal finance are two of the most crucial characteristics (Brougham et al., 2011; Frigerio et al., 2020; Gathergood, 2012; Majamaa et al., 2019). We'll be looking closely at how age, lack of financial discipline, and lack of financial literacy relate to a desire to take out a loan with BNPL.

Age

According to Houle (2014), the high prevalence of financial issues among persons in their twenties is a direct result of the fact that many of them anticipate making ends meet completely through the usage of credit (Houle, 2014). Researchers Majamaa et al. (2019) and Oksanen et al. (2015) found that those under the age of 30 are more likely to have financial troubles. Those between the ages of 19 and 24 are most vulnerable, while those between the ages of 25 and 29 are also very susceptible. For example, (Majamaa et al., 2019; Oksanen et al., 2015). Once a person reaches the age of 18, they are no longer considered a juvenile and is instead classified as a young adult. It is the time of year when the vast majority of high school seniors leave their high school behind and enter college (Oksanen et al., 2015). In light of their propensity for making spur-of-the-moment purchases, millennials are a significant target audience for BNPL solutions, as found by Johnson et al (2021). Reference: (Johnson et al., 2021). This suggests that a significant chunk of BNPL's advertising budget is designated to reach out to the younger market.

This age group is particularly vulnerable due to low income (due to probable recent move out of home), little financial literacy, and easy access to fast payment mechanisms (Brougham et al., 2011; Majamaa et al., 2019).

It might be simpler for students to engage in dangerous borrowing when their financial identities don't match up with their real financial conditions (Brougham et al., 2011). And, compared to people of all ages, millennials are far more likely to use credit to pay for discretionary items (Majamaa et al., 2019). Millennials and Gen Zers may be more eager to take on debt since they will likely not be around to see the full repercussions of their spending habits (Lo & Harvey, 2011). Modern adolescents are setting themselves up for future financial hardship due to their attitudes and behaviors around debt (Majamaa et al., 2019). The growing flood of consumer debt among young people has harmed the mental and physical health of many individuals. Some of the psychological effects include increased levels of financial anxiety, stress, and unhappiness, as well as diminished self-assessments of general health. Since young people are the major users of modern credit payment systems, an increase in such problems might foreshadow future troubles with BNPL usage (Johnson et al., 2021).

Self-Control

"The mental process that allows people to halt the activity of thoughts and emotions, so letting behavior to change from moment to moment," write Inzlicht et al. (2014) to define self-control (Inzlicht et al., 2014). Consumption wants in the present may be quite different from consumption desires in the future, and this difference can lead to a conflict known as self-control (Hoch & Loewenstein, 1991). Achtziger et al. found that those who can't defer pleasure and whose inability to deal with negative emotions leads to compensatory behaviors like buying are more likely to run into money problems (2015). That was the conclusion reached by researchers

(Achtziger et al., 2015). Meier and Sprenger found a correlation between the need for rapid pleasure and the use of credit (2010). Meier and Sprenger (2010).

According to studies conducted by Fook and McNeill, consumers who use BNPL solutions are more likely to make spontaneous purchases while shopping online (2020). Consumers who have access to BNPL solutions are more likely to make subsequent purchases, which is another sign that BNPL may promote excessive spending in this setting (Fook & McNeill, 2020). An individual's risk-taking tendencies are shaped by their combination of impulsivity and capacity for self-control (Duckworth & Kern, 2011; Frigerio et al., 2020). Pirog and Roberts (2007) claim that strong emotions often accompany the impulse to make a purchase. These emotions might be positive, like glee over a new purchase, or negative, like dread over a bill that finally arrived (Pirog & Roberts, 2007). Poor consumers, as described by Gathergood (2012), use a disproportionate quantity of easy-access credit products and may benefit from reduced access to credit if they were unable to amass so much debt (Gathergood, 2012). Our fourth hypothesis is as follows:

The discomfort of making payments mediates the influence of the inclination to acquire debt on consumers' levels of self-control, thus those with lower levels of self-control will feel less pain when making payments and will be more likely to take on debt.

Learning How to Manage Money

In the financial world, "financially literate" refers to consumers who not only know the basics but also have the analytical skills to decipher complex financial data (Gathergood, 2012). Indicators of this concept have been sought in the past via studies of consumers' perspectives, behaviors, and knowledge in relation to monetary matters (INFE, 2011; Potrich et al., 2015). Previous research has shown that consumers with lower levels of financial literacy have a higher debt-to-income ratio and face more debt repayment issues (Disney & Gathergood, 2013; Frigerio et al., 2020; Lusardi & Tufano, 2015; Robb, 2011). According to research conducted by Gathergood (2012), customers who lacked financial literacy were more likely to miss credit card payments and had a higher total debt burden (Gathergood, 2012). Customers struggle to make head or tail of the many fintech offerings owing to a lack of financial literacy and the complex nature of these products.

The reason for this is that many customer subsets find it financially unfeasible to make use of fintech services like BNPL (Johnson et al., 2021). In ING's most recent poll, 57% of the respondents (aged 18-34) didn't know if BNPL meant "taking on debt" or "deferring a payment" (ING, 2020a). A consumer's financial situation is less stressful when making a postponed payment rather than an immediate one since the purchase is not seen as a debt (ING, 2020b). Since all overdue payments are counted as debt, this data shows a serious deficiency in knowledge of BNPL, especially among the younger age groups (ING, 2020b).

RESULTS AND CONCLUSION

The results of our research point to an association between BNPL and a greater propensity to incur debt, especially among young individuals and consumers who lack financial literacy (i.e., customers who are more sensitive to incurring adverse financial concerns) (Brougham et al., 2011; Frigerio et al., 2020; Gathergood, 2012; Majamaa et al., 2019).

Regardless of whether or not such interventions are advantageous in the larger scheme of things (say, the interventions happening in California), regulators may undertake assessments of fintech regulation. can take preventative measures, such as enacting rules that promote long-term financial approaches to service delivery.

- Whereas the socially beneficial aspects of that fintech may account for any net good results, in contrast, this may be an exception due to the fintech's unique character rather than the regulatory framework.
- The negative effects of BNPL and consumer debt have far-reaching consequences.
- Unless authorities make adjustments, the harm to consumers will only increase. short-term, there is a glimmer of optimism that, after evaluating the effects on relatively
- Some businesses may take advantage of these vulnerabilities.
- An ever-present issue concerning consumers' exposure to financial services and fintech goods issue that requires careful oversight because one of the defining features is Debt.

If BNPL is used creatively in the realm of payment methods, it need not be harmful to society. Indeed, BNPL may often make responsible consumerism more successful and ensure that payment alternatives in the consumer market are varied (i.e., catered to the demands of various kinds of consumers) and innovative.

Discussion

Debt is inflexible because it "is a direct and immediate obligation for which there is no grace period" (from which to make payments). A demand for repayment that is "fixed" regardless of whether or not the underlying asset is worth anything.

Debt is dangerous because of its rigidity, especially in bad economic times, but the interest rate on a credit card is a prime illustration of this. When it comes to mortgages in particular, the lender is usually the one who has to absorb the loss when the value of a property lowers. properties, which might cause a family's whole financial stability to crumble. permissible under any legal need for the debtor to make set periodic payments to the creditor, irrespective of the debtor's circumstances or market conditions. In addition, as has been said before, BNPL debt and payments disproportionately impact the young. Credit crises are dangerous because they may damage several sectors of the economy. The consequences of debt may be devastating, including poverty, unemployment, and health problems. Domestic unrest, all of which harm the purchaser. Consequently, regulatory measures will probably be required.

The only way to fix regulatory shortcomings is by government regulation or involvement. Changes like this have the potential to address some of the problems with the regulatory framework that have been discussed above. through "market" forces, as when, for example, markets gradually birth institutions and methods (like data producers or certification bodies) that alleviate the effects of knowledge inequality, despite the need for Prices and flaws that would not exist if the asymmetric knowledge issue did not exist.

However, regulators address market failure with initiative and care because of the significant incentives for regulatory evasion and manipulation. People's inability to see what's in their own best interests calls for regulatory actions, such as requiring changes to manufacturing practices and/or product characteristics; asymmetrical knowledge calls for similar strategies, with the addition of Vendors being required to provide certain sorts of information with their wares, and product or service. There is mounting evidence of consumer damage in several countries at this stage, but the opportunity cost has to be included in any analysis of BNPL's impact on consumers.

REFERENCES

Achtziger, A., Hubert, M., Kenning, P., Raab, G., & Reisch, L. (2015). Debt out of control: The links between self-control, compulsive buying, and real debts. *Journal of Economic Psychology*, *49*, 141–149. doi:10.1016/j.joep.2015.04.003

Ah Fook, L., & McNeill, L. (2020). Click to buy: The impact of retail credit on over-consumption in the online environment. *Sustainability (Basel)*, *12*(18), 7322. doi:10.3390/su12187322

Anderloni, L., Bacchiocchi, E., & Vandone, D. (2012). Household financial vulnerability: An empirical analysis. *Research in Economics*, *66*(3), 284–296. doi:10.1016/j.rie.2012.03.001

Ariely, D., & Kreisler, J. (2018). *Small change: Money mishaps and how to avoid them*. Pan Macmillan.

Arisandy, T., Dasril, Y. B., Salahudin, S. N. B., Muslim, M. A., Adnan, A., & Wen, G. K. (2023). Buy Now Pay Later Services on Generation Z: Exploratory Data Analysis Using Machine Learning. *Journal of Theoretical and Applied Information Technology*, *101*(11), 4194–4204.

Backman, M. (2021). *Study: Buy Now, Pay Later Services Continue Explosive Growth*. The Motley Fool. https://www.fool.com/the-ascent/research/buy- now-pay-later-statistics/

Bank of England. (2021). *Money and Credit—January 2021*. https://www.bankofengland.co.uk/statistics/money-and- credit/2021/January-2021

Bauer, J. C., Morwitz, V. G., & Nagengast, L. (2021). Interest-Free Financing Promotions Increase Consumers' Demand for Credit for Experiential Goods. *Journal of the Association for Consumer Research*, *6*(1), 54–66. doi:10.1086/710250

Behera, C. K., & Dadra, R. (2023). Understanding young consumers' attitude formation for new-age fintech credit products: An SOR framework perspective. *Journal of Financial Services Marketing*, 1–15. doi:10.1057/s41264-023-00247-3

Boden, J., Maier, E., & Wilken, R. (2020). The effect of credit card versus mobile payment on convenience and consumers' willingness to pay. *Journal of Retailing and Consumer Services*, *52*, 101910. Advance online publication. doi:10.1016/j.jretconser.2019.101910

Bridges, S., & Disney, R. (2004). Use of credit and arrears on debt among low-income families in the United Kingdom. *Fiscal Studies*, *25*(1), 1–25. doi:10.1111/j.1475-5890.2004.tb00094.x

Brougham, R. R., Jacobs-Lawson, J. M., Hershey, D. A., & Trujillo, K. M. (2011). Who pays your debt? This is an important question for understanding compulsive buying among American college students. *International Journal of Consumer Studies*, *35*(1), 79–85. doi:10.1111/j.1470-6431.2010.00923.x

Bullock, M. (2020). *Panic, Pandemic and Payment Preferences*. Speech at the Morgan Stanley Disruption Evolved Webcast.

CAPCO. (2020). *The era of buy now pay later*. Available at: https://assets.ey.com/content/dam/ey-sites/ey-com/en_in/topics/media-and-entertainment/ficci-ey-m-and-e-report-2019-era-of-consumer-art.pdf

Cater, L. (2021). *Payment giant Klarna faces scrutiny over buy now, pay later practices*. https://www.politico.eu/article/klarna-payment-firm-scrutiny-buy-now-pay-later-business/

Cook, J., Davies, K., Farrugia, D., Threadgold, S., Coffey, J., Senior, K., Haro, A., & Shannon, B. (2023). Buy now pay later services as a way to pay: Credit consumption and the depoliticization of debt. *Consumption Markets & Culture*, *26*(4), 1–13. doi:10.1080/10253866.2023.2219606

Dinero. (2019). *Inkassogjelden øker blant unge* [Debt collection is increasing among the younger]. https://dinero.no/inkassogjelden-oker-blant-unge/

Disney, R., & Gathergood, J. (2013). Financial literacy and consumer credit portfolios. *Journal of Banking & Finance*, *37*(7), 2246–2254. doi:10.1016/j.jbankfin.2013.01.013

Duckworth, A. L., & Kern, M. L. (2011). A meta-analysis of the convergent validity of self-control measures. *Journal of Research in Personality*, *45*(3), 259–268. doi:10.1016/j.jrp.2011.02.004 PMID:21643479

Fook, L. A., & McNeill, L. (2020). Click to buy: The impact of retail credit on over-consumption in the online environment. *Sustainability (Basel)*, *12*(18), 7322. Advance online publication. doi:10.3390/su12187322

Frigerio, M., Ottaviani, C., & Vandone, D. (2020). A meta-analytic investigation of consumer over-indebtedness: The role of impulsivity. *International Journal of Consumer Studies*, *44*(4), 328–342. doi:10.1111/ijcs.12570

Gafeeva, R., Hoelzl, E., & Roschk, H. (2018). What else can your payment card do? The multifunctionality of payment modes can reduce payment transparency. *Marketing Letters*, *29*(1), 61–72. doi:10.1007/s11002-017-9445-2

Gathergood, J. (2012). Self-control, financial literacy, and consumer over-indebtedness. *Journal of Economic Psychology*, *33*(3), 590–602. doi:10.1016/j.joep.2011.11.006

Guttman-Kenney, B., Firth, C., & Gathergood, J. (2023). Buy now, pay later (BNPL)... on your credit card. *Journal of Behavioral and Experimental Finance*, *37*, 100788. doi:10.1016/j.jbef.2023.100788

Hoang, V. H., & Nguyen, P. M., Luu, T. M. N., & Vu, T. M. H. (2021). Determinants of intention to borrow consumer credit in Vietnam: Application and extension of technology acceptance model. *The Journal of Asian Finance. Economics and Business*, *8*(4), 885–895.

Hoch, S. J., & Loewenstein, G. F. (1991). Time-inconsistent preferences and consumer self-control. *The Journal of Consumer Research*, *17*(4), 492–506. doi:10.1086/208573

Houle, J. N. (2014). A generation indebted: Young adult debt across three cohorts. *Social Problems*, *61*(12), 448–465.

INFE. (2011). Measuring financial literacy: Questionnaire and guidance notes for conducting an internationally comparable survey of financial literacy. *Periodical Measuring Financial Literacy: Questionnaire and Guidance Notes for conducting an Internationally Comparable Survey of Financial Literacy*.

Johnson, D., Rodwell, J., & Hendry, T. (2021). Analyzing the Impacts of Financial Services Regulation to Make the Case That Buy-Now-Pay-Later Regulation Is Failing. *Sustainability (Basel)*, *13*(4), 1992. doi:10.3390/su13041992

Johnson, R. R. (2004). Persuasive Technology. *Using Computers to Change What We Think and Do.*, *18*, 251.

Key, A. (2021). *Credit cards: Why young people are turned off by paying on plastic: Millennials and Gen Z blame negative connotations for their aversion*. Inews. https://inews.co.uk/inews-lifestyle/money/credit-cards-young-people-millennials-plastic-836713

Klarna, A. B. (2020). *Årsredovisning* 2019. https://www.klarna.com/assets/2020/04/Klarna_Bank_AB_ publ_Annual_Report_2019_SV.pdf

Majamaa, K., Lehtinen, A. R., & Rantala, K. (2019). Debt judgments as a reflection of consumption-related debt problems. *Journal of Consumer Policy*, *42*(2), 223–244. doi:10.1007/s10603-018-9402-3

Marron, D. (2015). Debt, consumption and freedom: Social scientific representations of consumer credit in Anglo-America. *History of the Human Sciences*, *28*(4), 25–43. doi:10.1177/0952695115599314

McNeill Meier, S., & Sprenger, C. (2010). Present-biased preferences and credit card borrowing. *American Economic Journal. Applied Economics*, *2*(1), 193–201. doi:10.1257/app.2.1.193

Oksanen, A., Aaltonen, M., & Rantala, K. (2015). Social determinants of debt problems in a Nordic welfare state: A Finnish register-based study. *Journal of Consumer Policy*, *38*(3), 229–246. doi:10.1007/s10603-015-9294-4

Pirog, S., & Roberts, J. (2007). Personality and credit card misuse among college students: The mediating role of impulsiveness. *Journal of Marketing Theory and Practice*, *15*(1), 65–77. doi:10.2753/MTP1069-6679150105

Pisani, F., & Atalay, S. (2018). *Cashless Payments, Pain of Paying and the Role of Attachment*. ACR European Advances.

Powell, R., Do, A., Gengatharen, D., Yong, J., & Gengatharen, R. (2023). The relationship between responsible financial behaviours and financial wellbeing: The case of buy-now-pay-later. *Accounting and Finance*, *63*(4), 4431–4451. doi:10.1111/acfi.13100

Prelec, D., & Loewenstein, G. (1998). The red and the black: Mental accounting of savings and debt. *Marketing Science*, *17*(1), 4–28. doi:10.1287/mksc.17.1.4

PYMNTS.com & PayPal. (2020). *Buy now, pay later: Millennials and the shifting dynamics of online credit*. https://assets.ctfassets.net/7rifqg28wcbd/51nEg86tuS5X6Ln0k7mQp2/df8 d2305bf8b19e0430c00f22dbd7e5f/PYMNTS_-

Raj, V. A., Jasrotia, S. S., & Rai, S. S. (2023). Intensifying materialism through buy-now pay-later (BNPL): Examining the dark sides. *International Journal of Bank Marketing*.

Relja, R., Ward, P., & Zhao, A. L. (2023). Understanding the psychological determinants of buy-now-pay-later (BNPL) in the UK: A user perspective. *International Journal of Bank Marketing*.

Soman, D. (2003). The effect of payment transparency on consumption: Quasi- experiments from the field. *Marketing Letters*, *14*(3), 173–183. doi:10.1023/A:1027444717586

Tan, G. K. S. (2022). Buy what you want, today! Platform ecologies of 'buy now, pay later'services in Singapore. *Transactions of the Institute of British Geographers*, *47*(4), 912–926. doi:10.1111/tran.12539

Taylor, S., & Todd, P. A. (1995). Understanding information technology usage: A test of competing models. *Information Systems Research*, *6*(2), 144–176. doi:10.1287/isre.6.2.144

Teo, A. C., Tan, G. W. H., Ooi, K. B., Hew, T. S., & Yew, K. T. (2015). The effects of convenience and speed in m-payment. *Industrial Management & Data Systems*, *115*(2), 311–331. doi:10.1108/IMDS-08-2014-0231

Thomas, M., Desai, K. K., & Seenivasan, S. (2011). How Credit Card Payments Increase Unhealthy Food Purchases: Visceral Regulation of Vices. *The Journal of Consumer Research*, *38*(1), 126–139. doi:10.1086/657331

Visser, B. (2021). *A deep-dive into Europe's fast-growing BNPL market*. https://www.linkedin.com/pulse/deep-dive-europes-fast-growing-bnpl- market-Bart-visser/

Worldpay. (2020). *Global Payments Report: The pathways of people and payments*. http://offers.worldpayglobal.com/rs/850-JOA-856/images/GPR-2020.pdf?mkt_tok=eyJpIjoiWm1SalpEUXhOelEyWkdZeiIsInQiOiJXbX

Xing, Y., Chen, H., & Zhuang, X. (2019). Australian Online BNPL Services Research: Building Gain Value Model of Individual Credit Background. *Proceedings of the 2019 International Conference on Information Technology and Computer Communications*, 45–51. 10.1145/3355402.3355410

Zellermayer, O. (1996). *The Pain of Paying*. PhD Dissertation.

Compilation of References

Abd-Alrazaq, A. A., Alajlani, M., Ali, N., Denecke, K., Bewick, B. M., & Househ, M. (2021). Perceptions and opinions of patients about mental health chatbots: Scoping review. *Journal of Medical Internet Research*, *23*(1), e17828. doi:10.2196/17828 PMID:33439133

Abdu, A., Zhai, Z., Algabri, R., Abdo, H. A., Hamad, K., & Al-antari, M. A. (2022). Deep learning-based software defect prediction via semantic key features of source code—Systematic survey. *Mathematics*, *10*(17), 3120. doi:10.3390/math10173120

Abdullah, M. A., & Chong, R. (2014). Financial literacy: An exploratory review of the literature and future research. *J. Emerg. Econ. Islamic Res.*, *2*(3), 32–41. doi:10.24191/jeeir.v2i3.9631

Abdulquadri, A., Mogaji, E., Kieu, T. A., & Nguyen, N. P. (2021). Digital transformation in financial services provision: A Nigerian perspective to the adoption of chatbot. *Journal of Enterprising Communities: People and Places in the Global Economy*, *15*(2), 258–281. doi:10.1108/JEC-06-2020-0126

Abid, S. (2016). *Electronic Payment System: An Evolution in Indian Banking System*. Academic Press.

About CMA. (n.d.). Capital Market Authority, Sultanate of Oman.

Achtziger, A., Hubert, M., Kenning, P., Raab, G., & Reisch, L. (2015). Debt out of control: The links between self-control, compulsive buying, and real debts. *Journal of Economic Psychology*, *49*, 141–149. doi:10.1016/j.joep.2015.04.003

Adamopoulou, E., & Moussiades, L. (2020). An Overview of Chatbot Technology. In IFIP Advances in Information and Communication Technology: Vol. 584 IFIP. Springer International Publishing. doi:10.1007/978-3-030-49186-4_31

Adel, A. (2022). Future of industry 5.0 in society: Human-centric solutions, challenges and prospective research areas. *Journal of Cloud Computing (Heidelberg, Germany)*, *11*(1), 1–15. doi:10.1186/s13677-022-00314-5 PMID:36101900

Adelaar, T., Chang, S., Lancendorfer, K. M., Lee, B., & Morimoto, M. (2003). Effects of media formats on emotions and impulse buying intent. *Journal of Information Technology*, *18*(4), 247–266. doi:10.1080/0268396032000150799

Adil, M., Singh, Y., & Ansari, M. S. (2021). How financial literacy moderate the association between behaviour biases and investment decision? *Asian Journal of Accounting Research*, *7*(1), 17–30. doi:10.1108/AJAR-09-2020-0086

Agarwal, A., Singhal, C., & Thomas, R. (2021). *AI-powered decision making for the bank of the future*. McKinsey & Company. https://www. mckinsey. com/~/media/mckinsey/industries/financial% 20services/our% 20insights/ai% 20powered% 20decision% 20making% 20for% 20the% 20bank% 20of% 20the% 20future/ai-powered-decision-making-forthe-bank-of-the-future. pdf

Agarwal, R., & Wadhwa, M. (2020). Review of State-of-the-Art Design Techniques for Chatbots. *SN Computer Science*, *1*(5), 246. doi:10.1007/s42979-020-00255-3

Ah Fook, L., & McNeill, L. (2020). Click to buy: The impact of retail credit on over-consumption in the online environment. *Sustainability (Basel)*, *12*(18), 7322. doi:10.3390/su12187322

Ahiabenu, K. (2022). A comparative study of the design frameworks of the Ghanaian and Nigerian central banks' digital currencies (CBDC). *FinTech*, *1*(3), 235–249. doi:10.3390/fintech1030019

Ahmed, F. (2022). Ethical aspects of artificial intelligence in banking. *Journal of Research in Economics and Finance Management*, *1*(2), 55–63. doi:10.56596/jrefm.v1i2.7

Ai, C. (n.d.). *The New wave of customer and employee experiences.* Deloitte Digital.

Aizawa, A. (2000, July). The feature quantity: an information theoretic perspective of tfidf-like measures. In *Proceedings of the 23rd annual international ACM SIGIR conference on Research and development in information retrieval* (pp. 104-111). 10.1145/345508.345556

Ajzen, I. (1991). The theory of planned behavior. *Organizational Behavior and Human Decision Processes*, *50*(2), 179–211. doi:10.1016/0749-5978(91)90020-T

Akbar, M. M., & Parvez, N. (2009). Impact of Service Quality, Trust, and Customer Satisfaction on Customers Loyalty. *ABAC Journal*, *29*(1), 1. http://www.assumptionjournal.au.edu/index.php/abacjournal/article/view/526

Akıl, S., & Ungan, M. C. (2021). E-Commerce logistics service quality. *Journal of Electronic Commerce in Organizations*, *20*(1), 1–19. doi:10.4018/JECO.292473

Alam, A. (2021). Possibilities and Apprehensions in the Landscape of Artificial Intelligence in Education. *2021 International Conference on Computational Intelligence and Computing Applications, ICCICA 2021.* 10.1109/ICCICA52458.2021.9697272

Al-Blooshi, L., & Nobanee, H. (2020). Applications of Artificial Intelligence in Financial Management Decisions: A Mini-Review. *Consumer Financial Fraud eJournal.*

Aldaas, A. (2021). A study on electronic payments and economic growth: Global evidences. *Accounting*, 409–414. doi:10.5267/j.ac.2020.11.010

Al-Laham, M., Al-Tarawneh, H., & Abdallat, N. (2009). *Development of Electronic Money and Its Impact on the Central Bank Role and Monetary Policy.* Academic Press.

Allen, F., & Santomero, A. M. (1997). The theory of financial intermediation. *Journal of Banking & Finance*, *21*(11-12), 1461–1485. doi:10.1016/S0378-4266(97)00032-0

Alshubiri, F., Jamil, S.A. & Elheddad, M. (2019). The impact of ICT on financial development: Empirical evidence from the Gulf Cooperation Council countries. *International Journal of Engineering Business Management, 11*.

Alzeaideen, K. (2019). Credit risk management and business intelligence approach of the banking sector in Jordan. *Cogent Business & Management*, *6*(1), 1675455. doi:10.1080/23311975.2019.1675455

Ameen, N., Hosany, S., & Tarhini, A. (2021). Consumer interaction with cutting-edge technologies: Implications for future research. *Computers in Human Behavior*, *120*, 106761. doi:10.1016/j.chb.2021.106761

An Interactive Machine-Learning-Based Electronic Fraud and Abuse Detection System in Healthcare Insurance. (2015). Faculty of Engineering and Natural Sciences, Sabanci University.

Analytics, C. (2020). *Key Factors Driving the Growth of Conversational AI in Retail*. Uniphore. https://www.uniphore.com/key-factors-driving-the-growth-of-conversational-ai-in-retail/

Anderloni, L., Bacchiocchi, E., & Vandone, D. (2012). Household financial vulnerability: An empirical analysis. *Research in Economics*, *66*(3), 284–296. doi:10.1016/j.rie.2012.03.001

Andonova, V. (2006). Mobile phones, the Internet and the institutional environment. *Telecommunications Policy*, *30*(1), 29–45. doi:10.1016/j.telpol.2005.06.015

Andreou, P. C., & Anyfantaki, S. (2021). Financial literacy and its influence on internet banking behavior. *European Management Journal*, *39*(5), 658–674. doi:10.1016/j.emj.2020.12.001

Ariely, D., & Kreisler, J. (2018). *Small change: Money mishaps and how to avoid them*. Pan Macmillan.

Arisandy, T., Dasril, Y. B., Salahudin, S. N. B., Muslim, M. A., Adnan, A., & Wen, G. K. (2023). Buy Now Pay Later Services on Generation Z: Exploratory Data Analysis Using Machine Learning. *Journal of Theoretical and Applied Information Technology*, *101*(11), 4194–4204.

Arsić, M. (2020). Impact of digitalisation on economic growth, productivity and employment. *Economic Themes*, *58*(4), 431–457. doi:10.2478/ethemes-2020-0025

Artificial Intelligence-Based Fraud Detection in Insurance. (2019). Niccolo. https://emerj.com/

Ashcroft, L., & Hoey, C. (2001). PR, marketing and the Internet: Implications for information professionals. *Library Management*, *22*(1/2), 68–74. doi:10.1108/01435120110358952

Ashfaq, M., Yun, J., Yu, S., & Loureiro, S. M. C. (2020). I, Chatbot: Modeling the determinants of users' satisfaction and continuance intention of AI-powered service agents. *Telematics and Informatics*, *54*, 101473. doi:10.1016/j.tele.2020.101473

Ashta, A., & Herrmann, H. (2021). Artificial intelligence and fintech: An overview of opportunities and risks for banking, investments, and microfinance. *Strategic Change*, *30*(3), 211–222. doi:10.1002/jsc.2404

Asongu, S. A., & Nwachukwu, J. C. (2019). ICT, financial sector development and financial access. *Journal of the Knowledge Economy*, *10*(2), 465–490. doi:10.1007/s13132-017-0477-x

Ateş, S., Coskun, A., Sahin, M., & Demircan, M. (2016). Impact of Financial Literacy on the Behavioral Biases of Individual Stock Investors: Evidence from Borsa Istanbul. *Business and Economics Research Journal*, *7*(3), 1–1. doi:10.20409/berj.2016321805

Avis, E. (2015). The Rise of Digital Challengers. *Independent Banker, 65*(11), 28–30. http://search.ebscohost.com/login.aspx?direct=true%7B&%7Ddb=bth%7B&%7DAN=111109565%7B&%7Dsite=ehost-live

Babin, R., Smith, D., & Shah, H. (2022). Central bank digital currency: Advising the financial services industry. *Journal of Information Technology Teaching Cases.*

Baca, E. E., Holguin, J. Jr, & Stratemeyer, A. W. (2005). Direct-to-consumer advertising and young consumers: Building brand value. *Journal of Consumer Marketing*, *22*(7), 379–387. doi:10.1108/07363760510631110

Backman, M. (2021). *Study: Buy Now, Pay Later Services Continue Explosive Growth.* The Motley Fool. https://www.fool.com/the-ascent/research/buy- now-pay-later-statistics/

Bajracharya, A., Harvey, B., & Rawat, D. B. (2023, March). Recent Advances in Cybersecurity and Fraud Detection in Financial Services: A Survey. In *2023 IEEE 13th Annual Computing and Communication Workshop and Conference (CCWC)* (pp. 368-374). IEEE. 10.1109/CCWC57344.2023.10099355

Ballard, J., & Butler, P. (2011). Personalised learning: Developing a Vygotskian framework for e-learning. *International Journal of Technology, Knowledge and Society*, *7*(2), 21–36. doi:10.18848/1832-3669/CGP/v07i02/56198

Banerjee, A., Karlan, D., & Zinman, J. (2015). Six randomized evaluations of microcredit: Introduction and further steps. *American Economic Journal. Applied Economics*, *7*(1), 1–21. doi:10.1257/app.20140287

Bank of England. (2021). *Money and Credit—January 2021.* https://www.bankofengland.co.uk/statistics/money-and- credit/2021/January-2021

Barry, T. E. (1987). The development of the hierarchy of effects: An historical perspective. *Current issues and Research in Advertising, 10*(1-2), 251-295.

Bashir, I., & Madhavaiah, C. (2014). Revisiting Technology Acceptance Model (TAM) at the Individual Internet Banking Adoption Level. *Metamorphosis*, *13*(1), 42–56. doi:10.1177/0972622520140107

Basiri, M. E., Nemati, S., Abdar, M., Cambria, E., & Acharya, U. R. (2021). ABCDM: An attention-based bidirectional CNN-RNN deep model for sentiment analysis. *Future Generation Computer Systems*, *115*, 279–294. doi:10.1016/j.future.2020.08.005

Bauer, J. C., Morwitz, V. G., & Nagengast, L. (2021). Interest-Free Financing Promotions Increase Consumers' Demand for Credit for Experiential Goods. *Journal of the Association for Consumer Research*, *6*(1), 54–66. doi:10.1086/710250

Baur-Yazbeck, S., Frickenstein, J., & Medine, D. (2019). Cyber Security in Financial Sector Development. *CGAP Background Documents, 5*(2).

Bayar, Y., Gavriletea, M. D., & Păun, D. (2021). Impact of mobile phones and internet use on financial inclusion: Empirical evidence from the EU post-communist countries. *Technological and Economic Development of Economy*, *27*(3), 722–741. doi:10.3846/tede.2021.14508

Bearman, M., Ryan, J., & Ajjawi, R. (2022). Discourses of artificial intelligence in higher education: A critical literature review. *Higher Education*, *86*(2), 369–385. doi:10.1007/s10734-022-00937-2

Beck, T. (2003). Stock markets, banks, and economic development: theory and evidence. *EIB papers, 8*(1), 37-54.

Behera, C. K., & Dadra, R. (2023). Understanding young consumers' attitude formation for new-age fintech credit products: An SOR framework perspective. *Journal of Financial Services Marketing*, 1–15. doi:10.1057/s41264-023-00247-3

Benni. (2021). *Digital finance and inclusion in the time of COVID-19*. FAO. doi:10.4060/cb2109en

Bernacki, M. L., Greene, M. J., & Lobczowski, N. G. (2021). A Systematic Review of Research on Personalized Learning: Personalized by Whom, to What, How, and for What Purpose(s)? *Educational Psychology Review*, *33*(4), 1675–1715. doi:10.1007/s10648-021-09615-8

Bjerg, O., & Nielsen, R. H. (2018). *Who Should Make Kroner? A Review of Danmarks Nationalbank's Analysis of CBDC.* CBS Working Paper.

Bludnik, I. (2023). *Central bank digital currency and the cashless economy: The African experience*. Academic Press.

Boden, J., Maier, E., & Wilken, R. (2020). The effect of credit card versus mobile payment on convenience and consumers' willingness to pay. *Journal of Retailing and Consumer Services*, *52*, 101910. Advance online publication. doi:10.1016/j.jretconser.2019.101910

Bousrih, J. (2023). The impact of digitalization on the banking sector: Evidence from fintech countries. *Asian Economic and Financial Review*, *13*(4), 269–278. doi:10.55493/5002.v13i4.4769

Brandtzaeg, P. B., & Følstad, A. (2017). Why people use chatbots. Lecture Notes in Computer Science (Including Subseries Lecture Notes in Artificial Intelligence and Lecture Notes in Bioinformatics), 10673 LNCS, 377–392. doi:10.1007/978-3-319-70284-1_30

Braveen Kumar. (2016). *How Conversational Commerce Is Forever Changing the Way We Shop*. Shopify. https://www.shopify.in/blog/113660229-how-conversational-commerce-is-forever-changing-the-way-we-shop

Brennen, J. S., & Kreiss, D. (2016). Digitalization. The international encyclopedia of communication theory and philosophy, 1-11.

Brenner, L., & Meyll, T. (2020). Robo-advisors: A substitute for human financial advice? *Journal of Behavioral and Experimental Finance*, *25*, 100275. doi:10.1016/j.jbef.2020.100275

Bridges, S., & Disney, R. (2004). Use of credit and arrears on debt among low-income families in the United Kingdom. *Fiscal Studies*, *25*(1), 1–25. doi:10.1111/j.1475-5890.2004.tb00094.x

Broeckelmann, P. (2010). Exploring consumers' reactions towards innovative mobile services. *Qualitative Market Research*, *13*(4), 414–429. doi:10.1108/13522751011078827

Brougham, R. R., Jacobs-Lawson, J. M., Hershey, D. A., & Trujillo, K. M. (2011). Who pays your debt? This is an important question for understanding compulsive buying among American college students. *International Journal of Consumer Studies*, *35*(1), 79–85. doi:10.1111/j.1470-6431.2010.00923.x

Bruton, G., Khavul, S., Siegel, D., & Wright, M. (2015). New Financial Alternatives in Seeding Entrepreneurship: Microfinance, Crowdfunding, and Peer–to–Peer Innovations. *Entrepreneurship Theory and Practice*, *39*(1), 9–26. doi:10.1111/etap.12143

Bryson, D., Atwal, G., & Roy Chaudhuri, H., & Dave, K. (2015). Understanding the Antecedents of Intention to Use Mobile Internet Banking in India: Opportunities for Microfinance Institutions: Mobile Internet Banking in India. *Strategic Change*, *24*. Advance online publication. doi:10.1002/jsc.2005

Bullock, M. (2020). *Panic, Pandemic and Payment Preferences*. Speech at the Morgan Stanley Disruption Evolved Webcast.

Burgt, J. V. D. (2020). Explainable AI in banking. *Journal of Digital Banking*, *4*(4), 344–350.

Business Insider Intelligence. (2016). *80% of Businesses Want Chatbots By 2020*. https://www.businessinsider.com/80-of-businesses-want-chatbots-by-2020-2016-12?r=DE&IR=T

Business, F. (2019). *F8 2019: Making It Easier for Businesses to Connect with Customers on Messenger*. https://www.facebook.com/business/news/f8-2019-making-it-easier-for-businesses-to-connect-with-customers-on-messenger

Butcher, A. (2004). International students in New Zealand: Needs and responses. *International Education Journal, 5*(4).

Camara, N., Dos Santos, E., Grippa, F., Sebastian, J., Soto, F., & Varela, C. (2018). *Central bank digital currencies: An assessment of their adoption in Latin America*. BBVA Researh Working Paper (No. 18/13).

CAPCO. (2020). *The era of buy now pay later*. Available at: https://assets.ey.com/content/dam/ey-sites/ey-com/en_in/topics/media-and-entertainment/ficci-ey-m-and-e-report-2019-era-of-consumer-art.pdf

Cappiello, A. (2020). The technological disruption of the insurance industry: A review. *International Journal of Business and Social Science*, *11*(1), 1–11. doi:10.30845/ijbss.v11n1a1

Cater, L. (2021). *Payment giant Klarna faces scrutiny over buy now, pay later practices*. https://www.politico.eu/article/klarna-payment-firm-scrutiny-buy-now-pay-later-business/

Chadha, P., Gera, R., Khera, G. S., & Sharma, M. (2024). Challenges of Artificial Intelligence Adoption for Financial Inclusion. In Artificial Intelligence, Fintech, and Financial Inclusion (pp. 135-160). CRC Press.

Chaipidech, P., Srisawasdi, N., Kajornmanee, T., & Chaipah, K. (2022). A personalized learning system-supported professional training model for teachers' TPACK development. *Computers and Education: Artificial Intelligence*, *3*, 100064. Advance online publication. doi:10.1016/j.caeai.2022.100064

Chambers-Jones, C. (2021). AI, big data, quantum computing, and financial exclusion: Tempering enthusiasm and offering a human-centric approach to policy. FinTech. *Artificial Intelligence and Law*, 193–210.

Charlton, G. (2013). *Consumers Prefer Live Chat For Customer Service: Stats*. Econsultancy. https://econsultancy.com/blog/63867-consumers-prefer-live-chat-for-customer-service-stats#i.1nockyz1cffd8a

Chassignol, M., Khoroshavin, A., Klimova, A., & Bilyatdinova, A. (2018). U. (2018). Artificial Intelligence trends in education: A narrative overview. *Procedia Computer Science*, *136*, 16–24. doi:10.1016/j.procs.2018.08.233

Cheng, Y., & Jiang, H. (2020). How Do AI-driven Chatbots Impact User Experience? Examining Gratifications, Perceived Privacy Risk, Satisfaction, Loyalty, and Continued Use. *Journal of Broadcasting & Electronic Media*, *64*(4), 592–614. doi:10.1080/08838151.2020.1834296

Chen, J. S., Le, T. T. Y., & Florence, D. (2021). Usability and responsiveness of artificial intelligence chatbot on online customer experience in e-retailing. *International Journal of Retail & Distribution Management*, *49*(11), 1512–1531. doi:10.1108/IJRDM-08-2020-0312

Chen, J., Lim, C. P., Tan, K. H., Govindan, K., & Kumar, A. (2021). Artificial intelligence-based human-centric decision support framework: An application to predictive maintenance in asset management under pandemic environments. *Annals of Operations Research*, 1–24. doi:10.1007/s10479-021-04373-w PMID:34785834

Chen, L., Chen, P., & Lin, Z. (2020). Artificial Intelligence in Education: A Review. *IEEE Access : Practical Innovations, Open Solutions*, *8*, 75264–75278. doi:10.1109/ACCESS.2020.2988510

Chen, Q., Gong, Y., Lu, Y., & Tang, J. (2022). Classifying and measuring the service quality of AI chatbot in frontline service. *Journal of Business Research*, *145*, 552–568. doi:10.1016/j.jbusres.2022.02.088

Chen, X., Xie, H., Zou, D., & Hwang, G. J. (2020). Application and theory gaps during the rise of Artificial Intelligence in Education. *Computers and Education: Artificial Intelligence*, *1*, 100002. Advance online publication. doi:10.1016/j.caeai.2020.100002

Chen, X., Zou, D., Xie, H., & Cheng, G. (2022). Two decades of artificial intelligence in education. *Journal of Educational Technology & Society*, *25*(1).

Cheong, H. S., & Nasuredin, J. (2023). Relationship Between the Factors and Adoption of E-payment Services among UTHM Students. *Research in Management of Technology and Business, 4*(1), Article 1.

Chhillar, N., & Arora, S. (2022). Personal Financial Management Behavior Using Digital Platforms And Its Domains. *Journal of Financial Management. Markets and Institutions*, *10*(02), 2250009. doi:10.1142/S2282717X22500098

Chibba, M. (2009). Financial inclusion, poverty reduction and the Millennium Development Goals. *European Journal of Development Research*, *21*(2), 213–230. doi:10.1057/ejdr.2008.17

Chichekian, T., & Benteux, B. (2022). The potential of learning with (and not from) artificial intelligence in education. *Frontiers in Artificial Intelligence*, *5*, 903051. Advance online publication. doi:10.3389/frai.2022.903051 PMID:36177366

Chien, M. S., Cheng, C. Y., & Kurniawati, M. A. (2020). The non-linear relationship between ICT diffusion and financial development. *Telecommunications Policy*, *44*(9), 102023. doi:10.1016/j.telpol.2020.102023

Chisadza, C., & Biyase, M. (2023). Financial development and income inequality: Evidence from advanced, emerging and developing economies. *Annals of Financial Economics*, *18*(01), 2241002. doi:10.1142/S2010495222410020

Chiu, C. Y. (1992). *Artificial intelligence and its applications to capital budgeting decisions under uncertainty*. Auburn University.

Choi, E. P. H., Lee, J. J., Ho, M.-H., Kwok, J. Y. Y., & Lok, K. Y. W. (2023). Chatting or cheating? The impacts of ChatGPT and other artificial intelligence language models on nurse education. *Nurse Education Today*, *125*, 105796. doi:10.1016/j.nedt.2023.105796 PMID:36934624

Cho, J., & Lee, G. (2019). A chatbot system for construction daily report information management. In *ISARC. Proceedings of the International Symposium on Automation and Robotics in Construction* (Vol. 36, pp. 429-437). IAARC Publications. 10.22260/ISARC2019/0058

Choubey, A., & Sharma, M. (2021, May). Implementation of robotics and its impact on sustainable banking: A futuristic study. *Journal of Physics: Conference Series*, *1911*(1), 012013. doi:10.1088/1742-6596/1911/1/012013

Chou, E. Y., & Hsu, W. C. (2021). Conversational Service Experiences in Chatbots: A Perspective on Cognitive Load. *Management Review*, *40*, 111–130.

Chowdhury, E. K., & Chowdhury, R. (2023). Role of financial inclusion in human development: Evidence from Bangladesh, India and Pakistan. *Journal of the Knowledge Economy*, 1–26. doi:10.1007/s13132-023-01366-x

Clarke, M. (2012). Policies and perceptions of insurance law. Oxford University Press.

Clarke, M. (1990). the control of insurance fraud, a comparative view. *British Journal of Criminology*, *30*(1).

Comes, Y., Trindade, J. de S., Shimizu, H. E., Hamann, E. M., Bargioni, F., Ramirez, L., Sanchez, M. N., & Santos, L. M. P. (2016). Evaluation of user satisfaction and service responsiveness in municipalities enrolled in the Mais Médicos (More Doctors) Program. *Ciencia & Saude Coletiva*, *21*, 2749–2759. doi:10.1590/1413-81232015219.16202016 PMID:27653060

Cook, J., Davies, K., Farrugia, D., Threadgold, S., Coffey, J., Senior, K., Haro, A., & Shannon, B. (2023). Buy now pay later services as a way to pay: Credit consumption and the depoliticization of debt. *Consumption Markets & Culture*, *26*(4), 1–13. doi:10.1080/10253866.2023.2219606

Copestake, J., Johnson, S., Cabello, M., Goodwin-Groen, R., Gravesteijn, R., Humberstone, J., Nino-Zarazua, M., & Titus, M. (2016). Towards a plural history of microfinance. *Canadian Journal of Development Studies. Canadian Journal of Development Studies*, *37*(3), 279–297. doi:10.1080/02255189.2016.1197102

Cox, A. M. (2021). Exploring the impact of Artificial Intelligence and robots on higher education through literature-based design fictions. *International Journal of Educational Technology in Higher Education*, *18*(1), 1–19. doi:10.1186/s41239-020-00237-8

Cox, A. M., Pinfield, S., & Rutter, S. (2019). The intelligent library: Thought leaders' views on the likely impact of artificial intelligence on academic libraries. *Library Hi Tech*, *37*(3), 418–435. doi:10.1108/LHT-08-2018-0105

Crawford, J., Cowling, M., & Allen, K.-A. (2023). Leadership is needed for ethical ChatGPT: Character, assessment, and learning using artificial intelligence (AI). *Journal of University Teaching & Learning Practice*, *20*(3). Advance online publication. doi:10.53761/1.20.3.02

Crompton, H., & Burke, D. (2023). Artificial intelligence in higher education: The state of the field. *International Journal of Educational Technology in Higher Education*, *20*(1), 1–22. doi:10.1186/s41239-023-00392-8

Crowe, D., LaPierre, M., & Kebritchi, M. (2017). Knowledge Based Artificial Augmentation Intelligence Technology: Next Step in Academic Instructional Tools for Distance Learning. *TechTrends*, *61*(5), 494–506. doi:10.1007/s11528-017-0210-4

Curtis, R. G., Bartel, B., Ferguson, T., Blake, H. T., Northcott, C., Virgara, R., & Maher, C. A. (2021). Improving User Experience of Virtual Health Assistants: Scoping Review. *J Med Internet Res*, *23*(12), e31737. doi:10.2196/31737

Cydni. (2016, April 18). *Insurance fraud - definition, examples, cases, processes*. Legal Dictionary. https://legaldictionary.net/insurance-fraud/

Dabla-Norris, E., Ji, Y., Townsend, R., & Unsal, F. (2015). Identifying constraints to financial inclusion and their impact on GDP and inequality: A structural framework for policy (IMF Working Paper No. 15/22). doi:10.5089/9781498381598.001

Dale, R. (2016). The return of the chatbots. *Natural Language Engineering*, *22*(5), 811–817. doi:10.1017/S1351324916000243

Dalton, P. S., Pamuk, H., Ramrattan, R., Uras, B., & van Soest, D. (2023). Electronic Payment Technology and Business Finance: A Randomized, Controlled Trial with Mobile Money. *Management Science*. Advance online publication. doi:10.1287/mnsc.2023.4821

Dang, T. T., & Vu, H. Q. (2020). Fintech in Microfinance: A new direction for Microfinance institutions in Vietnam. *The Journal of Business Economics and Environmental Studies*, *10*(3), 13–22. doi:10.13106/jbees.2020.vol10.no3.13

Data misrepresentation detection for insurance underwriting fraud prevention. (2022, May 5). ScienceDirect. https://doi.org/ doi:10.1016/j.dss.2022.113798

Daud, S. N. M., & Ahmad, A. H. (2023). Financial inclusion, economic growth and the role of digital technology. *Finance Research Letters*, *53*, 103602. doi:10.1016/j.frl.2022.103602

Davenport, T. H., & Dyché, J. (2013). Big data in big companies. *International Institute for Analytics*, *3*, 1–31.

Dayal. (2019). *RBI publishes 'Payment and Settlement Systems in India: Vision 2019 – 2021'* (2687). Reserve Bank of India. www.rbi.org.in

de Cosmo, L. M., Piper, L., & Di Vittorio, A. (2021). The role of attitude toward chatbots and privacy concern on the relationship between attitude toward mobile advertising and behavioral intent to use chatbots. *Italian Journal of Marketing*, *2021*(1-2), 83–102. doi:10.1007/s43039-021-00020-1

DeLone, W. H., & McLean, E. R. (2003). The DeLone and McLean model of information systems success: A ten-year update. *Journal of Management Information Systems*, *19*(4), 9–30. doi:10.1080/07421222.2003.11045748

Demirguc-Kunt, A., Klapper, L., & Randall, D. (2013). *The global Findex database* (No. 8). Note.

Demirgüç-Kunt, A., Klapper, L., Singer, D., & Ansar, S. (2022). *The Global Findex Database 2021: Financial inclusion, digital payments, and resilience in the age of COVID-19*. World Bank Publications. doi:10.1596/978-1-4648-1897-4

Deng, J., Russakovsky, O., Krause, J., Bernstein, M. S., Berg, A., & Fei-Fei, L. (2014, April). Scalable multi-label annotation. In *Proceedings of the SIGCHI Conference on Human Factors in Computing Systems* (pp. 3099-3102). 10.1145/2556288.2557011

Detecting insurance claims fraud using machine learning techniques. (2022). https://managementevents.com/

Dinero. (2019). *Inkassogjelden øker blant unge* [Debt collection is increasing among the younger]. https://dinero.no/inkassogjelden-oker-blant-unge/

Dirksen, N., & Takahashi, S. (2020). *Artificial intelligence in Japan 2020. Actors, Market, Opportunities and Digital Solutions in a Newly Transformed World.* Netherlands Enterprise Agency.

Disney, R., & Gathergood, J. (2013). Financial literacy and consumer credit portfolios. *Journal of Banking & Finance*, *37*(7), 2246–2254. doi:10.1016/j.jbankfin.2013.01.013

Druzhkov, P. N., & Kustikova, V. D. (2016). A survey of deep learning methods and software tools for image classification and object detection. *Pattern Recognition and Image Analysis*, *26*(1), 9–15. doi:10.1134/S1054661816010065

Duckworth, A. L., & Kern, M. L. (2011). A meta-analysis of the convergent validity of self-control measures. *Journal of Research in Personality*, *45*(3), 259–268. doi:10.1016/j.jrp.2011.02.004 PMID:21643479

Duho, K. C. T., Abankwah, S. A., Azu, G., Agbozo, D. A., Duho, V. S., & Atigodey, J. S. (2022). Central Bank Digital Currency in Ghana, the e-Cedi: Disruptions, Opportunities and Risks. Dataking Policy Brief, 6.

Dutsinma, F. L. I., Pal, D., Funilkul, S., & Chan, J. H. (2022). A Systematic Review of Voice Assistant Usability: An ISO 9241–11 Approach. *SN Computer Science*, *3*(4), 1–23. doi:10.1007/s42979-022-01172-3 PMID:35531568

Dwivedi, R., Alrasheedi, M., Dwivedi, P., & Starešinić, B. (2022). Leveraging financial inclusion through technology-enabled services innovation: A case of economic development in India. *International Journal of E-Services and Mobile Applications*, *14*(1), 1–13. doi:10.4018/IJESMA.289633

Dzomira, S. (2014). Electronic fraud (cyber fraud) risk in the banking industry, Zimbabwe. *Risk Governance and Control: Financial Markets and Institutions*, *4*(2), 16–26. doi:10.22495/rgcv4i2art2

Edwards, S. (2021). *Central Bank Digital Currencies and The Emerging Markets: The Currency Substitution Challenge (No. w29489).* National Bureau of Economic Research. doi:10.3386/w29489

Ejemeyovwi, J. O., Osabuohien, E. S., & Bowale, E. I. (2021). ICT adoption, innovation and financial development in a digital world: Empirical analysis from Africa. *Transnational Corporations Review*, *13*(1), 16–31. doi:10.1080/19186444.2020.1851124

Elahi, M., Beheshti, A., & Goluguri, S. R. (2021). Recommender systems: Challenges and opportunities in the age of big data and artificial intelligence. *Data Science and Its Applications*, 15-39.

Elevating customer experience excellence in the next normal | McKinsey. (n.d.). Retrieved August 5, 2021, from https://www.mckinsey.com/business-functions/operations/our-insights/elevating-customer-experience-excellence-in-the-next-normal# doi:10.1111/j.1540-5414.2006.00108.x

Enholm, I. M., Papagiannidis, E., Mikalef, P., & Krogstie, J. (2022). Artificial intelligence and business value: A literature review. *Information Systems Frontiers*, *24*(5), 1709–1734. doi:10.1007/s10796-021-10186-w

Erdogan, B. Z. (1999). Celebrity endorsement: A literature review. *Journal of Marketing Management*, *15*(4), 291–314. doi:10.1362/026725799784870379

Eren, B. A. (2021). Determinants of customer satisfaction in chatbot use: Evidence from a banking application in Turkey. *International Journal of Bank Marketing*, *39*(2), 294–311. doi:10.1108/IJBM-02-2020-0056

Esperance, M. (2024). *Effect of Cashless Financial Services on Economic Growth in Kigali*. Valley International Journal Digital Library. doi:10.18535/ijsrm/v12i01.em03

Feinman, J. M. (2017). Insurance Fraud, Agency, and Opportunism: False Swearing in Insurance Claims. *Agency, and Opportunism: False Swearing in Insurance Claims*.

Fetter, S., Coyne, P., Monk, S., & Woodruff, S. (2023). An Exploration of Social Media Users' Desires to Become Social Media Influencers. *Media Watch*, *14*(2). doi:10.1177/09760911231159690

Feyen, E., Frost, J., Gambacorta, L., Natarajan, H., & Saal, M. (2021). *Fintech and the digital transformation of financial services: implications for market structure and public policy*. BIS Papers.

Forcadell, F. J., Aracil, E., & Úbeda, F. (2020). The impact of corporate sustainability and digitalization on international banks' performance. *Global Policy*, *11*(S1), 18–27. doi:10.1111/1758-5899.12761

Fornell, C. (2007). *The satisfied customer: Winners and losers in the battle for buyer preference*. Macmillan.

FosterK.BlakstadS.GaziS.BosM. (2021). Digital currencies and CBDC impacts on least developed countries (LDCs). The Dialogue on Global Digital Finance Governance Paper Series. doi:10.2139/ssrn.3871301

Frigerio, M., Ottaviani, C., & Vandone, D. (2020). A meta-analytic investigation of consumer over-indebtedness: The role of impulsivity. *International Journal of Consumer Studies*, *44*(4), 328–342. doi:10.1111/ijcs.12570

Fritz-Morgenthal, S. G., Hein, B., & Papenbrock, J. (2021). Financial Risk Management and Explainable, Trustworthy, Responsible AI. *Frontiers in Artificial Intelligence*, 5. PMID:35295866

Furini, M., Gaggi, O., Mirri, S., Montangero, M., Pelle, E., Poggi, F., & Prandi, C. (2022). U. (2022). Digital twins and artificial intelligence: As pillars of personalized learning models. *Communications of the ACM*, *65*(4), 98–104. doi:10.1145/3478281

G20 Policy Recommendations for Advancing Financial Inclusion and Productivity Gains through Digital Public Infrastructure. (2023). *Global Partnership for Financial Inclusion*. Advance online publication. doi:10.1596/40421

Gafeeva, R., Hoelzl, E., & Roschk, H. (2018). What else can your payment card do? The multifunctionality of payment modes can reduce payment transparency. *Marketing Letters*, *29*(1), 61–72. doi:10.1007/s11002-017-9445-2

Gallego-Losada, M., Montero-Navarro, A., García-Abajo, E., & Losada, R. G. (2023). Digital financial inclusion. Visualizing the academic literature. *Research in International Business and Finance*, *64*, 101862. doi:10.1016/j.ribaf.2022.101862

Gao, J., Zhang, L., Zhao, F., & Zhai, Y. (2019, March). Research on software defect classification. In *2019 IEEE 3rd Information Technology, Networking, Electronic and Automation Control Conference (ITNEC)* (pp. 748-754). IEEE.

Gathergood, J. (2012). Self-control, financial literacy, and consumer over- indebtedness. *Journal of Economic Psychology*, *33*(3), 590–602. doi:10.1016/j.joep.2011.11.006

Gefen & Straub. (2003). Managing User Trust in B2C e-Services. *E-Service Journal, 2*(2), 7. doi:10.2979/esj.2003.2.2.7

Geng, Z., & He, G. (2021). Digital financial inclusion and sustainable employment: Evidence from countries along the belt and road. *Borsa Istanbul Review*, *21*(3), 307–316. doi:10.1016/j.bir.2021.04.004

George, G., Haas, M. R., & Pentland, A. (2014). Big data and management. *Academy of Management Journal*, *57*(2), 321–326. doi:10.5465/amj.2014.4002

Ghirvu, A. I. (2013). The AIDA model for advergames. *The USV Annals of Economics and Public Administration*, *13*(1 (17)), 90–98.

Giffin, K. (1967). The contribution of studies of source credibility to a theory of interpersonal trust in the communication process. *Psychological Bulletin*, *68*(2), 104–120. doi:10.1037/h0024833 PMID:6065581

Gillon, S. P. (2017). *Indian Microfinance Sector: A Case Study*. Academic Press.

Giovanis, A., Assimakopoulos, C., & Sarmaniotis, C. (2018). Adoption of mobile self-service retail banking technologies: The role of technology, social, channel and personal factors. *International Journal of Retail & Distribution Management*, *47*(9), 894–914. doi:10.1108/IJRDM-05-2018-0089

Giudici, P. (2018). Fintech risk management: A research challenge for artificial intelligence in finance. *Frontiers in Artificial Intelligence*, *1*, 1. doi:10.3389/frai.2018.00001 PMID:33733089

Gnewuch, U., Morana, S., Adam, M., & Maedche, A. (2017). This is the author ' s version of a work that was published in the following source Please note : Copyright is owned by the author and / or the publisher. Commercial use is not allowed. Institute of Information Systems and Marketing (IISM) The psychop. *Thirty Eighth International Conference on Information Systems.*

Go, E., & Sundar, S. S. (2019). Humanizing chatbots: The effects of visual, identity and conversational cues on humanness perceptions. *Computers in Human Behavior*, *97*, 304–316. doi:10.1016/j.chb.2019.01.020

Goel, R. K., & Hsieh, E. W. (2002). Internet growth and economic theory. *NETNOMICS: Economic Research and Electronic Networking*, *4*(2), 221–225. doi:10.1023/A:1021225514442

Gomber, P., Kauffman, R. J., Parker, C., & Weber, B. W. (2018). On the fintech revolution: Interpreting the forces of innovation, disruption, and transformation in financial services. *Journal of Management Information Systems*, *35*(1), 220–265. doi:10.1080/07421222.2018.1440766

Goutam, R. K. (2015). Importance of cyber security. *International Journal of Computer Applications*, *111*(7). https://en.unesco.org/unesco_science_report/sdg9

Graves, A., Mohamed, A. R., & Hinton, G. (2013, May). *Speech recognition with deep recurrent neural networks. In 2013 IEEE international conference on acoustics, speech and signal processing*. Ieee.

Griesser, J. W. (1991, January). Expert systems capital budgeting. In *1991 IEEE/ACM International Conference on Developing and Managing Expert System Programs* (pp. 249-250). IEEE Computer Society. 10.1109/DMESP.1991.171725

Group, U. M. (2018, October 5). *What are the consequences of insurance fraud?* Cataño Insurance Brokers. https://catanoinsures.com/insurance-fraud-consequences/

Gubareva, R. (2020). Virtual Assistants for Learning: A Systematic Literature Review. *Proceedings of the 12th International Conference on Computer Supported Education (CSEDU 2020)*. 10.5220/0009417600970103

Guttman-Kenney, B., Firth, C., & Gathergood, J. (2023). Buy now, pay later (BNPL)... on your credit card. *Journal of Behavioral and Experimental Finance*, *37*, 100788. doi:10.1016/j.jbef.2023.100788

Habibi, F., & Zabardast, M. A. (2020). Digitalization, education and economic growth: A comparative analysis of Middle East and OECD countries. *Technology in Society*, *63*, 101370. doi:10.1016/j.techsoc.2020.101370

Hagberg, J., Sundstrom, M., & Egels-Zandén, N. (2016). The digitalization of retailing: An exploratory framework. *International Journal of Retail & Distribution Management*, *44*(7), 694–712. doi:10.1108/IJRDM-09-2015-0140

Hair, J. F. Jr, Howard, M. C., & Nitzl, C. (2020). Assessing measurement model quality in PLS-SEM using confirmatory composite analysis. *Journal of Business Research*, *109*, 101–110. doi:10.1016/j.jbusres.2019.11.069

Hair, J. F., Risher, J. J., Sarstedt, M., & Ringle, C. M. (2019). When to use and how to report the results of PLS-SEM. *European Business Review*, *31*(1), 2–24. doi:10.1108/EBR-11-2018-0203

Han, H., Yi, J., Jun, S., & Ahn, S. (2021). How do followers infer the motives behind an influencer's advertising disclosures? *Asia Pacific Journal of Marketing and Logistics*, *33*(5), 1159–1174. doi:10.1108/APJML-06-2019-0397

Hanif, A. (2021). Towards Explainable Artificial Intelligence in Banking and Financial Services. *arXiv preprint arXiv:2112.08441*.

Hari, H., Iyer, R., & Sampat, B. (2022). Customer Brand Engagement through Chatbots on Bank Websites– Examining the Antecedents and Consequences. *International Journal of Human-Computer Interaction*, *38*(13), 1212–1227. doi:10.1080/10447318.2021.1988487

Harkins, D., & Athineos, C. (2023). Inspiring action through social media. *International Journal of Science and Technology Research Archive, 5*. doi:10.53771/ijstra.2023.5.1.0076

He, M. D., Leckow, M. R. B., Haksar, M. V., Griffoli, M. T. M., Jenkinson, N., Kashima, M. M., Khiaonarong, T., Rochon, M. C., & Tourpe, H. (2017). *Fintech and financial services: Initial considerations*. International Monetary Fund.

Henry, D., Cooke, S., Buckley, P., Dumagan, J., Gill, G., Pastore, D., LaPorte, S., & Mayer, J. (1999). *Economics and Statistics Administration. Office of Policy Development.*

Hishigsuren, G. (2006). *Information and communication technology and microfinance: Options for Mongolia*. Academic Press.

Hoang, V. H., & Nguyen, P. M., Luu, T. M. N., & Vu, T. M. H. (2021). Determinants of intention to borrow consumer credit in Vietnam: Application and extension of technology acceptance model. *The Journal of Asian Finance. Economics and Business*, *8*(4), 885–895.

Hoch, S. J., & Loewenstein, G. F. (1991). Time-inconsistent preferences and consumer self-control. *The Journal of Consumer Research*, *17*(4), 492–506. doi:10.1086/208573

Hodson, D. (2021). The politics of FinTech: Technology, regulation, and disruption in UK and German retail banking. *Public Administration*, *99*(4), 859–872. doi:10.1111/padm.12731

Holmes, W., & Tuomi, I. (2022). State of the art and practice in AI in education. *European Journal of Education*, *57*(4), 542–570. doi:10.1111/ejed.12533

Hornik, K., Stinchcombe, M., & White, H. (1989). Multilayer feedforward networks are universal approximators. *Neural Networks*, *2*(5), 359–366. doi:10.1016/0893-6080(89)90020-8

Horobet, A., Mnohoghitnei, I., Zlatea, E. M. L., & Belascu, L. (2022). The interplay between digitalization, education, and financial development: A european case study. *Journal of Risk and Financial Management*, *15*(3), 135. doi:10.3390/jrfm15030135

Horzyk, A., Magierski, S., & Miklaszewski, G. (2009). An Intelligent Internet Shop-Assistant Recognizing a Customer Personality for Improving Man-Machine Interactions. *Recent Advances in Intelligent Information Systems*, 13–26.

Houle, J. N. (2014). A generation indebted: Young adult debt across three cohorts. *Social Problems, 61*(12), 448–465.

How does the insurance sector benefit from artificial intelligence applications? (n.d.). Samar Al-Mashata. https://www.alarabiya.net

How, M. L., Cheah, S. M., Khor, A. C., & Chan, Y. J. (2020). Artificial intelligence-enhanced predictive insights for advancing financial inclusion: A human-centric ai-thinking approach. *Big Data and Cognitive Computing, 4*(2), 8. doi:10.3390/bdcc4020008

Hoyer, W. D., MacInnis, D. J., & Pieters, R. (2012). *Consumer behavior*. Cengage Learning.

Huang, W., Gu, X., Lin, L., Alharthi, M., & Usman, M. (2023). Do financial inclusion and income inequality matter for human capital? Evidence from sub-Saharan economies. *Borsa Istanbul Review, 23*(1), 22–33. doi:10.1016/j.bir.2022.09.002

Hu, B., & Wu, Y. (2023). Unlocking Causal Relationships in Commercial Banking Risk Management: An Examination of Explainable AI Integration with Multi-Factor Risk Models. *Journal of Financial Risk Management, 12*(3), 262–274. doi:10.4236/jfrm.2023.123014

Hurdawaty, R., & Tukiran, M. (2024). Strategies to Increase the Competitiveness of Micro, Small and Medium Enterprises (MSMEs): A Narrative Literature Review. *South Asian Journal of Social Studies and Economics, 21*(1), 1. Advance online publication. doi:10.9734/sajsse/2024/v21i1768

Hutson, J., & Plate, D. (2023). *Human-AI Collaboration for Smart Education: Reframing Applied Learning to Support Metacognition*. IntechOpen.

Iddrisu, A.G. & Chen, B. (2022). Economic growth through digitalization in Africa: does financial sector development play a mediating role? *International Journal of Emerging Markets*.

Imai, K. S., Gaiha, R., Thapa, G., & Annim, S. K. (2012). Microfinance and poverty—A macro perspective. *World Development, 40*(8), 1675–1689. doi:10.1016/j.worlddev.2012.04.013

INFE. (2011). Measuring financial literacy: Questionnaire and guidance notes for conducting an internationally comparable survey of financial literacy. *Periodical Measuring Financial Literacy: Questionnaire and Guidance Notes for conducting an Internationally Comparable Survey of Financial Literacy*.

Insurance fraud report 2022: Real Time Data, a crucial asset in fraud fighting. (2022, March 17). Business Wire. https://www.businesswire.com/news/home/20220317005223/en/Insurance-Fraud-Report-2022-Real-Time-Data-A-Crucial-Asset-In-Fraud-Fighting

Insurance Fraud Taskforce final report. (2016, January 21). GOV.UK. https://www.gov.uk/government/publications/insurance-fraud-taskforce-final-report

Ismail, A., & Yunan, Y. M. (2016). Service quality as a predictor of customer satisfaction and customer loyalty. *LogForum, 12*(4), 269–283. doi:10.17270/J.LOG.2016.4.7

Jadil, Y., Rana, N. P., & Dwivedi, Y. K. (2021). A meta-analysis of the UTAUT model in the mobile banking literature: The moderating role of sample size and culture. *Journal of Business Research, 132*, 354–372. doi:10.1016/j.jbusres.2021.04.052

Jain, M., Kumar, P., Kota, R., & Patel, S. N. (2018). Evaluating and informing the design of chatbots. *DIS 2018 - Proceedings of the 2018 Designing Interactive Systems Conference*, 895–906. 10.1145/3196709.3196735

Jain. (2022). *Influence of behavioural factors on the adoption of digital finance – An empirical study*. Amity University.

Jain, R. (2023). Role of artificial intelligence in banking and finance. *Journal of Management and Science, 13*(3), 1–4. doi:10.26524/jms.13.27

Jappelli, R., & Marconi, N. (1997). Recommendations and prejudices in the realm of foundation engineering in Italy: A historical review. In Geotechnical engineering for the preservation of monuments and historic sites (pp. 191-214).

Jenneboer, L., Herrando, C., & Constantinides, E. (2022). The impact of chatbots on customer loyalty: A systematic literature review. *Journal of Theoretical and Applied Electronic Commerce Research, 17*(1), 212–229. doi:10.3390/jtaer17010011

Jepsen, M., & Drahokoupil, J. (2017). The digital economy and its implications for labour. 2. The consequences of digitalisation for the labour market. *Transfer: European Review of Labour and Research, 23*(3), 249–252. doi:10.1177/1024258917714659

Johnson, K., Li, Y., Phan, H., Singer, J., & Trinh, H. (2012). The Innovative Success that is Apple, Inc. Theses, Dissertations and Capstones. https://mds.marshall.edu/etd/418

Johnson, M., & Nádas, R. (2009). Marking essays on screen: An investigation into the reliability of marking extended subjective texts. *Wiley Online Library*. doi:10.1111/j.1467-8535.2009.00979.x

Johnson, D., Rodwell, J., & Hendry, T. (2021). Analyzing the Impacts of Financial Services Regulation to Make the Case That Buy-Now-Pay-Later Regulation Is Failing. *Sustainability (Basel), 13*(4), 1992. doi:10.3390/su13041992

Johnson, R. R. (2004). Persuasive Technology. *Using Computers to Change What We Think and Do., 18*, 251.

Jolly, J. (2023, August 29). *Top 7 Reasons to Transform Insurance Underwriting with AI*. Saxon. https://saxon.ai/blogs/top-7-reasons-to-transform-insurance-underwriting-with-ai/#:~:text=In%20this%20case%2C%20using%20AI,predictive%20analytics%20models%20and%20algorithms

Jorayeva, M., Akbulut, A., Catal, C., & Mishra, A. (2022). Deep learning-based defect prediction for mobile applications. *Sensors (Basel), 22*(13), 4734. doi:10.3390/s22134734 PMID:35808230

Kaczorowska-Spychalska, D. (2019). How chatbots influence marketing. *Management, 23*(1), 251–270. doi:10.2478/manment-2019-0015

Kagan, J. (n.d.). *Insurance*. Investopedia. https://www.investopedia.com/terms/i/insurance.asp

Kandpal, V., & Khalaf, O. I. (2020). Artificial intelligence and SHGs: enabling financial inclusion in India. In *Deep Learning Strategies for Security Enhancement in Wireless Sensor Networks* (pp. 291–303). IGI Global. doi:10.4018/978-1-7998-5068-7.ch015

Kasey Panetta. (2016). *Artificial intelligence, machine learning, and smart things promise an intelligent future*. Gartner. https://www.gartner.com/smarterwithgartner/gartners-top-10-technology-trends-2017/

Kauffman, R. J., & Riggins, F. J. (2010). Research Directions on the Role and Impact of ICT in Microfinance. *2010 43rd Hawaii International Conference on System Sciences*, 1–10. 10.1109/HICSS.2010.318

Kaur, R., Sandhu, R. S., Gera, A., Kaur, T., & Gera, P. (2020). Intelligent voice bots for digital banking. In *Smart Systems and IoT: Innovations in Computing: Proceeding of SSIC 2019* (pp. 401-408). Springer Singapore.

Kaur, S., Kaur, H., & Singh, N. (2020). A study on digitalization and technology environment and its impact on banks. *Globus-An International Journal of Management and IT*, *11*(2), 17–20. doi:10.46360/globus.mgt.120201004

Key, A. (2021). *Credit cards: Why young people are turned off by paying on plastic: Millennials and Gen Z blame negative connotations for their aversion*. Inews. https://inews.co.uk/inews-lifestyle/money/credit-cards-young-people-millennials-plastic-836713

Khan, F., Siddiqui, M. A., & Imtiaz, S. (2022). Role of financial literacy in achieving financial inclusion: A review, synthesis and research agenda. *Cogent Business & Management*, *9*(1), 2034236. doi:10.1080/23311975.2022.2034236

Khan, T., & Mollah, A. F. (2019). AUTNT-A component level dataset for text non-text classification and benchmarking with novel script invariant feature descriptors and D-CNN. *Multimedia Tools and Applications*, *78*(22), 32159–32186. doi:10.1007/s11042-019-08028-8

Khasawneh, M. H. A., Hujran, O., & Abdrabbo, T. (2018). A quantitative examination of the factors that influence users' perceptions of trust towards using mobile banking services. *International Journal of Internet Marketing and Advertising*, *12*(2), 181–207. doi:10.1504/IJIMA.2018.090957

Kiliyanni, A. L., & Sivaraman, S. (2016). The perception-reality gap in financial literacy: Evidence from the most literate state in India. *International Review of Economics Education*, *23*, 47–64. doi:10.1016/j.iree.2016.07.001

Killingland, M., & Dahl, L. B. (2018). Central bank digital currencies–fad or the future? a framework for country level assessment of central bank digital currencies (Master's thesis).

Kim, D., Kang, H. G., Bae, K., & Jeon, S. (2021). An artificial intelligence-enabled industry classification and its interpretation. *Internet Research*, *32*(2), 406–424. doi:10.1108/INTR-05-2020-0299

Kim, J. (2023). Leading teachers' perspective on teacher-AI collaboration in education. *Education and Information Technologies*. Advance online publication. doi:10.1007/s10639-023-12109-5

Kim, M., & Chang, B. (2020). The Effect of Service Quality on the Reuse Intention of a Chatbot: Focusing on User Satisfaction, Reliability, and Immersion. *International JOURNAL OF CONTENTS*, *16*(4), 1–15.

Klarna, A. B. (2020). *Årsredovisning* 2019. https://www.klarna.com/assets/2020/04/Klarna_Bank_AB_ publ_Annual_Report_2019_SV.pdf

KPMG. (2019, August). *Fintech in India—Powering mobile payments*. https://assets.kpmg/content/dam/kpmg/in/ pdf/2019/08/Fintech-in-India%E2% 80%93 Poweringmobile-payments.pdf

Kreijns, K., Xu, K., & Weidlich, J. (2021). Social presence: Conceptualization and measurement. *Educational Psychology Review*, *34*(1), 139–170. doi:10.1007/s10648-021-09623-8 PMID:34177204

Krishnaraj Arul, O., & Megargel, A. (2023). Human-centred artificial intelligence in the banking sector. *Journal of Digital Banking*, *7*(3), 266–279.

Krizhevsky, A., Sutskever, I., & Hinton, G. E. (2017). ImageNet classification with deep convolutional neural networks. *Communications of the ACM*, *60*(6), 84–90. doi:10.1145/3065386

Kuchciak, I., & Wiktorowicz, J. (2021). Empowering financial education by banks—Social media as a modern channel. *Journal of Risk and Financial Management*, *14*(3), 118. doi:10.3390/jrfm14030118

Kulkarni, L., & Ghosh, A. (2021). Gender disparity in the digitalization of financial services: Challenges and promises for women's financial inclusion in India. *Gender, Technology and Development*, *25*(2), 233–250. doi:10.1080/09718524.2021.1911022

Kumah, S. P. (2024). Cryptocurrency and African fiat currencies: A peaceful coexistence? *Economic Notes*, *53*(1), e12229. doi:10.1111/ecno.12229

Kumar, S., Mahadev, R. G., Kamal, P., & Aggarwal, A. (2024). Original Research Article An optimized deep learning-based fault-tolerant mechanism for energy efficient data transmission in IoT. *Journal of Autonomous Intelligence*, *7*(4). Advance online publication. doi:10.32629/jai.v7i4.1380

Kutnjak, A., Pihiri, I., & Furjan, M. T. (2019, May). Digital transformation case studies across industries–literature review. In *2019 42nd International Convention on Information and Communication Technology, Electronics and Microelectronics (MIPRO)* (pp. 1293-1298). IEEE. 10.23919/MIPRO.2019.8756911

Kuzmina, O. Y., Konovalova, M. E., & Chulova, E. S. (2020). Transformation of the banking system as a way to minimize information asymmetry. In Digital Age: Chances, Challenges and Future 7 (pp. 12-18). Springer International Publishing. doi:10.1007/978-3-030-27015-5_2

Labhard, V. & Lehtimäki, J. (2022). *Digitalisation, institutions and governance, and growth: Mechanisms and evidence*. Academic Press.

Laboure, M. (2021a). Corporate Bank Research: The Future of Payments: Series 2 – Part II. When Digital Currencies become Mainstream. Available from: https://research.db.com/Research/Article?rid=82185081-9b23-4f5a-8fd7-a454a9ee7b75-604&kid=RP0001&documentType=R&wt_cc1=IND-3015026-0000

Laboure, & Müller, Heinz, Singh, & Köhling. (2021b). Cryptocurrencies and CBDC: The Route Ahead. *Global Policy*. Advance online publication. doi:10.1111/1758-5899.13017

Land, R., Beetham, H., Sharpe, R., DeNoyelles, A., Zydney, J., Chen, B., Sendall, P., Shaw, R., Round, K., Larkin, J., Barczyk, C. C., Duncan, D. G., Abes, E. S., Jones, S. R., McEwen, M. K., Boon, S., Sinclair, C., Borup, J., West, R. E., ... Tu, C.-H. (2013). Social Presence and Cognitive Engagement in Online Learning Environments. *Language Learning & Technology*, *10*(1), 1–22. doi:10.1111/j.1467-8527.2008.00397_1.x

Lappeman, J., Marlie, S., Johnson, T., & Poggenpoel, S. (2023). Trust and digital privacy: Willingness to disclose personal information to banking chatbot services. *Journal of Financial Services Marketing*, *28*(2), 337–357. doi:10.1057/s41264-022-00154-z

LeCun, Y., Bottou, L., Bengio, Y., & Haffner, P. (1998). Gradient-based learning applied to document recognition. *Proceedings of the IEEE*, *86*(11), 2278–2324. doi:10.1109/5.726791

Lee, E. (2020). *Central bank digital currencies*. Economic Diplomacy Initiative, Harvard Kennedy School, Belter Centre.

Lee, J. J., & Hammer, J. (2011). Gamification in Education: What, How, Why Bother? *Academic Exchange Quarterly, 15*(2), 146.

Lee, D., & Yeo, S. (2022). Developing an AI-based chatbot for practicing responsive teaching in mathematics. *Computers & Education*, *191*, 104646. doi:10.1016/j.compedu.2022.104646

Lee, M. K., & Park, H. (2019). Exploring factors influencing usage intention of chatbot-chatbot in financial service. *Journal of Korean Society for Quality Management*, *47*(4), 755–765.

Lee, S., & Kim, E. (2020). Influencer marketing on Instagram: How sponsorship disclosure, influencer credibility, and brand credibility impact the effectiveness of Instagram promotional post. *Journal of Global Fashion Marketing*, *11*(3), 232–249. doi:10.1080/20932685.2020.1752766

Lee, Y., & Kim, K. H. (2020). De-motivating employees' negative communication behaviors on anonymous social media: The role of public relations. *Public Relations Review*, *46*(4), 101955. doi:10.1016/j.pubrev.2020.101955

Leoste, J., Jõgi, L., Õun, T., Pastor, L., San Martín López, J., & Grauberg, I. (2021). Perceptions about the Future of Integrating Emerging Technologies into Higher Education—The Case of Robotics with Artificial Intelligence. *Computers*, *10*(9), 110. doi:10.3390/computers10090110

Lessig, L. (2013). "Institutional corruption" defined. *The Journal of Law, Medicine & Ethics*, *41*(3), 553–555. doi:10.1111/jlme.12063 PMID:24088144

Letheren, K., & Glavas, C. (2017). Embracing the bots: How direct to consumer advertising is about to change forever. *QUT Business School*, 11–13. https://eprints.qut.edu.au/107945/

Liao, Q. V., Davis, M., Geyer, W., Muller, M., & Shami, N. S. (2016). What can you do? Studying social-agent orientation and agent proactive interactions with an agent for employees. *DIS 2016 - Proceedings of the 2016 ACM Conference on Designing Interactive Systems: Fuse*, 264–275. 10.1145/2901790.2901842

Li, C., Pan, R., Xin, H., & Deng, Z. (2020). Research on Artificial Intelligence Customer Service on Consumer Attitude and Its Impact during Online Shopping. *Journal of Physics: Conference Series*, *1575*(1), 012192. doi:10.1088/1742-6596/1575/1/012192

Li, F., Lu, H., Hou, M., Cui, K., & Darbandi, M. (2021). Customer satisfaction with bank services: The role of cloud services, security, e-learning and service quality. *Technology in Society*, *64*, 101487. doi:10.1016/j.techsoc.2020.101487

Li, L., Lee, K. Y., Emokpae, E., & Yang, S. B. (2021). What makes you continuously use chatbot services? Evidence from chinese online travel agencies. *Electronic Markets*, *31*(3), 1–25. doi:10.1007/s12525-020-00454-z PMID:35603227

Liu, J., Abhishek, V., & Li, B. (2017). *The impact of mobile channel adoption on customeromni-channel banking behaviour.* Available at SSRN 2912691.

Liu, P., Qiu, X., & Huang, X. (2016). Recurrent neural network for text classification with multi-task learning. *arXiv preprint arXiv:1605.05101.*

Li, Z., & Yin, Y. (2018). Attractiveness, expertise and closeness: The effect of source credibility of the first lady as political endorser on social media in China. *Global Media and China*, *3*(4), 297–315. doi:10.1177/2059436418819228

Lopes, F., Agnelo, J., Teixeira, C. A., Laranjeiro, N., & Bernardino, J. (2020). Automating orthogonal defect classification using machine learning algorithms. *Future Generation Computer Systems*, *102*, 932–947. doi:10.1016/j.future.2019.09.009

Lucarelli, B. (2011). *The economics of financial turbulence: alternative theories of money and finance*. Edward Elgar Publishing. doi:10.4337/9781849808798

Lucia, P., Schmid, B. F., Wolfgang, M., & Müller, J. P. (2003). Editorial: Software Agents. *Electronic Markets*, *13*(1), 1–2. doi:10.1080/1019678032000062195

Lui, A., & Lamb, G. W. (2018). Artificial intelligence and augmented intelligence collaboration: Regaining trust and confidence in the financial sector. *Information & Communications Technology Law*, *27*(3), 267–283. doi:10.1080/13600834.2018.1488659

Lund, B. D., Omame, I., Tijani, S., & Agbaji, D. (2020). Perceptions toward Artificial Intelligence among Academic Library Employees and Alignment with the Diffusion of Innovations' Adopter Categories. *College & Research Libraries*, *81*(5), 865. doi:10.5860/crl.81.5.865

Lund, B. D., Wang, T., Mannuru, N. R., Nie, B., Shimray, S., & Wang, Z. (2023). ChatGPT and a new academic reality: Artificial Intelligence-written research papers and the ethics of the large language models in scholarly publishing. *Journal of the Association for Information Science and Technology*, *74*(5), 570–581. doi:10.1002/asi.24750

Ma, W., Adesope, O. O., Nesbit, J. C., & Liu, Q. (2014). *Intelligent Tutoring Systems and Learning Outcomes: A Meta-Analysis*. doi:10.1037/a0037123.supp

Machine Learning Techniques for Detecting Insurance Claims Fraud. (2023). Aarathi Jaikrishnan. https://experionglobal.com/

Magutu, P., Mwangi, M., Nyaoga, R., Ondimu, G., Kagu, M., Mutai, K., Kilonzo, H., & Nthenya, P. (2010). E-Commerce Products and Services in the Banking Industry: The Adoption and Usage in Commercial Banks in Kenya. *Journal of Electronic Banking Systems*, 1–19. doi:10.5171/2011.678961

Majamaa, K., Lehtinen, A. R., & Rantala, K. (2019). Debt judgments as a reflection of consumption-related debt problems. *Journal of Consumer Policy*, *42*(2), 223–244. doi:10.1007/s10603-018-9402-3

Mallat, N., Rossi, M., & Tuunainen, V. K. (2004). Mobile banking services. *Communications of the ACM*, *47*(5), 42–46. doi:10.1145/986213.986236

Mallinson, D. J. (2021). Policy innovation adoption across the diffusion life course. *Policy Studies Journal: the Journal of the Policy Studies Organization*, *49*(2), 335–358. doi:10.1111/psj.12406

Marani, M., Soltani, M., Bahadori, M., Soleimani, M., & Moshayedi, A. (2023). The role of biometric in banking: A review. *EAI Endorsed Transactions on AI and Robotics, 2*(1).

MarottaG.AuC. D. (2022). Budgeting in the Age of Artificial Intelligence–New Opportunities and Challenges. Available at SSRN 4168230. doi:10.2139/ssrn.4168230

Marron, D. (2015). Debt, consumption and freedom: Social scientific representations of consumer credit in Anglo-America. *History of the Human Sciences*, *28*(4), 25–43. doi:10.1177/0952695115599314

Martínez-López, F. J., Anaya-Sánchez, R., Esteban-Millat, I., Torrez-Meruvia, H., D'Alessandro, S., & Miles, M. (2020). Influencer marketing: Brand control, commercial orientation and post credibility. *Journal of Marketing Management*, *36*(17-18), 1805–1831. doi:10.1080/0267257X.2020.1806906

Martínez-López, F. J., Anaya-Sánchez, R., Giordano, M. F., & Lopez-Lopez, D. (2020). Behind influencer marketing: Key marketing decisions and their effects on followers' responses. *Journal of Marketing Management*, *36*(7-8), 579–607. doi:10.1080/0267257X.2020.1738525

Maseke, B. F. (2024). The Transformative Power of Artificial Intelligence in Banking Client Service. *South Asian Journal of Social Studies and Economics*, *21*(3), 93–105. doi:10.9734/sajsse/2024/v21i3787

Matadeen, J., & Seetanah, B. (2015). Stock market development and economic growth: Evidence from Mauritius. *Journal of Developing Areas*, *49*(6), 25–36. doi:10.1353/jda.2015.0120

McCroskey, J. C. (1966). *Scales for the measurement of ethos*. Academic Press.

McGuire, W. J. (1986). The myth of massive media impact: Savagings and salvagings. *Public Communication and Behavior, 1*, 173-257.

McGuire, W. J. (1985). Attitudes and attitude change. In G. Lindzey & E. Aronson (Eds.), *The Handbook of Social Psychology* (2nd ed., pp. 262–276). Erlbaum.

McLean, G., & Wilson, A. (2016). Evolving the online customer experience … is there a role for online customer support? *Computers in Human Behavior*, *60*, 602–610. doi:10.1016/j.chb.2016.02.084

McNeill Meier, S., & Sprenger, C. (2010). Present-biased preferences and credit card borrowing. *American Economic Journal. Applied Economics*, *2*(1), 193–201. doi:10.1257/app.2.1.193

McTear, M., Callejas, Z., & Griol, D. (2016). The conversational interface: Past and. *The Conversational Interface: Talking to Smart Devices.*

Medhi Thies, I., Menon, N., Magapu, S., Subramony, M., & O'Neill, J. (2017). How do you want your chatbot? An exploratory Wizard-of-Oz study with young, Urban Indians. Lecture Notes in Computer Science (Including Subseries Lecture Notes in Artificial Intelligence and Lecture Notes in Bioinformatics), 10513 LNCS, 441–459. doi:10.1007/978-3-319-67744-6_28

Meli, S. D., Kamga, B. F., & Meli, C. N. (2024). Analysis of the Determinants of Mobile Money Adoption and Use: Evidence from Togo with Simple and Multivariate Probit Approaches. *Journal of the Knowledge Economy*. Advance online publication. doi:10.1007/s13132-024-01748-9

Meuter, M. L., Bitner, M. J., Ostrom, A. L., & Brown, S. W. (2005). Choosing among alternative service delivery modes: An investigation of customer trial of self-service technologies. *Journal of Marketing*, *69*(2), 61–83. doi:10.1509/jmkg.69.2.61.60759

MFIN INDIA. (2023). https://mfinindia.org/microfinance/IndustryPortfolio

Mhlanga, D. (2020). Industry 4.0 in finance: The impact of artificial intelligence (ai) on digital financial inclusion. *International Journal of Financial Studies*, *8*(3), 45. doi:10.3390/ijfs8030045

Mhlanga, D. (2022). Human-centered artificial intelligence: The superlative approach to achieve sustainable development goals in the fourth industrial revolution. *Sustainability (Basel)*, *14*(13), 7804. doi:10.3390/su14137804

Mhlanga, D. (2023). Artificial Intelligence (AI) Solutions for Financial Inclusion of the Excluded: What Are the Challenges? In *Economic Inclusion in Post-Independence Africa: An Inclusive Approach to Economic Development* (pp. 257–272). Springer Nature Switzerland. doi:10.1007/978-3-031-31431-5_14

Mialou, A., Amidzic, G., & Massara, A. (2017). Assessing countries' financial inclusion standing–a new composite index. *Journal of Banking and Financial Economics*, *2*(8), 105–126. doi:10.7172/2353-6845.jbfe.2017.2.5

Miao, Y., Gowayyed, M., & Metze, F. (2015, December). EESEN: End-to-end speech recognition using deep RNN models and WFST-based decoding. In 2015 IEEE workshop on automatic speech recognition and understanding (ASRU) (pp. 167-174). IEEE.

Michiels, E. (2017). Modelling Chatbots with a cognitive system allows for a differentiating user experience. *CEUR Workshop Proceedings*, *2027*, 70–78.

Mikolov, T., Karafiát, M., Burget, L., Cernocký, J., & Khudanpur, S. (2010, September). Recurrent neural network based language model. *Interspeech*, *2*(3), 1045–1048. doi:10.21437/Interspeech.2010-343

Mishra, S. (2014). Adoption of M-Commerce in India: Applying Theory of Planned Behaviour Model. *Journal of Internet Banking and Commerce, 19*(1), 1-17.

Modwey, H. H. F., & Abd Elgabar, E. E. (2022). Using sentiment analysis technology to analyze bank customers' textual comments. *Humanities and Natural Sciences Journal.*

Mohamed, M. (2013). *Countering fraud in the insurance industry: A case study of Malaysia.* Academic Press.

Moorman, C., Deshpande, R., & Zaltman, G. (1993). Factors affecting trust in market research relationships. *Journal of Marketing*, *57*(1), 81–101. doi:10.1177/002224299305700106

Mottola, G. (2013). In Our Best Interest: Women, Financial Literacy, and Credit Card Behavior. *Numeracy*, *6*(2). Advance online publication. doi:10.5038/1936-4660.6.2.4

Muhammad Bitar, M. (2016). *The Role of Criminal Legislation in Fraud Prevention.* Naif University for Security Sciences.

Munnukka, J., Karjaluoto, H., Mahlamäki, T., & Hokkanen, V. (2017). Effects of social media on consumers' sports brand experiences and loyalty. In *Creating marketing magic and innovative future marketing trends: Proceedings of the 2016 Academy of Marketing Science (AMS) annual conference* (pp. 1051-1064). Springer International Publishing.

Musa Abdullahi Sakanko, J. D. (2019). The Effect of Electronic Payment Systems on Financial Performance of Microfinance Banks in Niger State. *Jurnal Bisnis Dan Manajemen, 9*(2). doi:10.15408/ess.v9i2.12273

Musa, S. K., & Njeru, A. W. (2023). Effect of Digital Financial Innovation on the Financial Performance of Small and Medium Enterprises in Nairobi City Centre, Kenya. *International Journal of Social Science and Humanities Research, 1*(1), Article 1. doi:10.61108/ijsshr.v1i1.41

Mwafise, A. M., & Stapleton, L. (2012). Determinants of User Adoption of Mobile Electronic Payment Systems for Microfinance Institutions in Developing Countries: Case Study Cameroon. *IFAC Proceedings Volumes, 45*(10), 38–43. 10.3182/20120611-3-IE-4029.00010

Myovella, G., Karacuka, M., & Haucap, J. (2020). Digitalization and economic growth: A comparative analysis of Sub-Saharan Africa and OECD economies. *Telecommunications Policy, 44*(2), 101856. doi:10.1016/j.telpol.2019.101856

Nagwani, N. K., & Suri, J. S. (2023). An artificial intelligence framework on software bug triaging, technological evolution, and future challenges: A review. *International Journal of Information Management Data Insights, 3*(1), 100153. Advance online publication. doi:10.1016/j.jjimei.2022.100153

Náñez Alonso, S. L., Echarte Fernández, M. Á., Sanz Bas, D., & Kaczmarek, J. (2020). Reasons Fostering or Discouraging the Implementation of Central Bank-Backed Digital Currency. *A Review. Economies, 8*(2), 41. doi:10.3390/economies8020041

Nassar, M., Salah, K., ur Rehman, M. H., & Svetinovic, D. (2020). Blockchain for explainable and trustworthy artificial intelligence. *Wiley Interdisciplinary Reviews. Data Mining and Knowledge Discovery, 10*(1), e1340. doi:10.1002/widm.1340

Ng, A. W., & Kwok, B. K. (2017). Emergence of Fintech and cybersecurity in a global financial centre: Strategic approach by a regulator. *Journal of Financial Regulation and Compliance, 25*(4), 422–434. doi:10.1108/JFRC-01-2017-0013

Nguyen, D. M., Chiu, Y. T. H., & Le, H. D. (2021). Determinants of continuance intention towards banks' chatbot services in Vietnam: A necessity for sustainable development. *Sustainability (Basel), 13*(14), 7625. doi:10.3390/su13147625

Nguyen, T. M., & Malik, A. (2022). Impact of knowledge sharing on employees' service quality: The moderating role of artificial intelligence. *International Marketing Review, 39*(3), 482–508. doi:10.1108/IMR-02-2021-0078

Nicole & Benton. (2017). Evaluating Quality of Chatbots and Intelligent Conversational Agents. *Arxiv.Org.*

Niemand, T., Rigtering, J. P. C., Kallmünzer, A., Kraus, S., & Matijas, S. (2017). Entrepreneurial orientation and digitalization in the financial service industry: A contingency approach. In *Proceedings of the 25th European Conference on Information Systems (ECIS), Guimarães, Portugal, 2017* (pp. 1081-1096). Academic Press.

Niemi, H. (1995). Insurance fraud. *Eur. J. on Crim. Pol'y & Rsch., 3*, 48.

Nordheim, C. B., Følstad, A., & Bjørkli, C. A. (2019). An initial model of trust in chatbots for customer service—Findings from a questionnaire study. *Interacting with Computers, 31*(3), 317–335. doi:10.1093/iwc/iwz022

Noreen, U., Shafique, A., Ahmed, Z., & Ashfaq, M. (2023). Banking 4.0: Artificial intelligence (AI) in banking industry & consumer's perspective. *Sustainability (Basel), 15*(4), 3682. doi:10.3390/su15043682

Nye, B. D. (2015). Intelligent tutoring systems by and for the developing world: A review of trends and approaches for educational technology in a global context. *International Journal of Artificial Intelligence in Education, 25*(2), 177–203. doi:10.1007/s40593-014-0028-6

Nykiforuk, C., Belon, A., de Leeuw, E., Harris, P., Allen-Scott, L., Atkey, K., Glenn, N., Hyshka, E., Jaques, K., Kongats, K., Montesanti, S., Nieuwendyk, L., Pabayo, R., Springett, J., & Yashadhana, A. (2023). An action-oriented public health framework to reduce financial strain and promote financial wellbeing in high-income countries. *International Journal for Equity in Health, 22*(1), 66. Advance online publication. doi:10.1186/s12939-023-01877-8 PMID:37055742

O'Neill, R., & Russell, A. M. T. (2019). Stop! Grammar time: University students' perceptions of the automated feedback program Grammarly. *Australasian Journal of Educational Technology, 35*(1), 42–56. doi:10.14742/ajet.3795

OECD. (2018). *Maintaining competitive conditions in the era of digitalisation.* https://www.oecd.org/g20/Maintaining-competitive-conditions-in-era-of-digitalisation-OECD.pdf

Oh, E. Y., & Zhang, S. (2020). *Central bank digital currency and in-formal economy*. Working Papers in Economics & Finance, 2020-11.

Ohanian, R. (1990). Construction and Validation of a Scale to Measure Celebrity Endorsers' Perceived Expertise, Trustworthiness, and Attractiveness. *Journal of Advertising, 19*(3), 39–52. doi:10.1080/00913367.1990.10673191

Okičić, J., Jukan, M. K., Okičić, J., & Jukan, M. K. (2023). *Financial inclusion and digital financial literacy: The case of microfinance sector in Bosnia and Herzegovina*. IntechOpen. doi:10.5772/intechopen.1002897

Oksanen, A., Aaltonen, M., & Rantala, K. (2015). Social determinants of debt problems in a Nordic welfare state: A Finnish register-based study. *Journal of Consumer Policy, 38*(3), 229–246. doi:10.1007/s10603-015-9294-4

OpenAI. (2023). https://openai.com/chatgpt

Otuonye, A., Ibe, P., Njoku, D., & Eze, I. (2022). An Innovative Framework for Integrated Loan Management with QR Code Enhancement. *Asian Journal of Computer Science and Technology, 11*(2), 1–10. doi:10.51983/ajcst-2022.11.2.3317

Owusu-Agyei, S., Okafor, G., Chijoke-Mgbame, A. M., Ohalehi, P., & Hasan, F. (2020). Internet adoption and financial development in sub-Saharan Africa. *Technological Forecasting and Social Change, 161*, 120293. doi:10.1016/j.techfore.2020.120293

Oxford Analytica. (2021). *Digital currencies mark a tectonic shift for banking*. Expert Briefings. doi:10.1108/OXAN-DB263446

Ozili, P. K. (2023b). A survey of central bank digital currency adoption in African countries. The Fourth Industrial Revolution in Africa: Exploring the Development Implications of Smart Technologies in Africa.

Ozili, P. K. (2024a). 100 Quotes about central bank digital currencies. Academic Press.

Ozili, P. K. (2018). Impact of digital finance on financial inclusion and stability. *Borsa Istanbul Review*, *18*(4), 329–340. doi:10.1016/j.bir.2017.12.003

Ozili, P. K. (2021, October). Financial inclusion research around the world: A review. *The Forum for Social Economics*, *50*(4), 457–479. doi:10.1080/07360932.2020.1715238

Ozili, P. K. (2022a). Central bank digital currency in Nigeria: opportunities and risks. In *The new digital era: digitalisation, emerging risks, and opportunities* (pp. 125–133). Emerald Publishing Limited. doi:10.1108/S1569-37592022000109A008

Ozili, P. K. (2022b). Can central bank digital currency increase financial inclusion? Arguments for and against. In *Big Data Analytics in the Insurance Market* (pp. 241–249). Emerald Publishing Limited. doi:10.1108/978-1-80262-637-720221013

Ozili, P. K. (2023a). Central bank digital currency research around the World: A review of literature. *Journal of Money Laundering Control*, *26*(2), 215–226. doi:10.1108/JMLC-11-2021-0126

Ozili, P. K. (2024b). Central bank digital currency and the monetary policy and financial stability implications. In *Digital Currency Assets and Challenges to Financial System Stability* (pp. 52–62). IGI Global.

Ozturk, I., & Ullah, S. (2022). Does digital financial inclusion matter for economic growth and environmental sustainability in OBRI economies? An empirical analysis. *Resources, Conservation and Recycling*, *185*, 106489. doi:10.1016/j.resconrec.2022.106489

Pagano, A., & Marengo, A. (2021). Training Time Optimization through Adaptive Learning Strategy. *2021 International Conference on Innovation and Intelligence for Informatics, Computing, and Technologies, 3ICT 2021*, 563–567. 10.1109/3ICT53449.2021.9582096

Pal, A., De', R., & Herath, T. (2020). The role of mobile payment technology in sustainable and human-centric development: Evidence from the post-demonetization period in India. *Information Systems Frontiers*, *22*(3), 607–631. doi:10.1007/s10796-020-09982-7

Parasuraman, A., Zeithaml, V. A., & Berry, L. L. (1985). A conceptual model of service quality and its implications for future research. *Journal of Marketing*, *49*(4), 41–50. doi:10.1177/002224298504900403

Park, C. Y., & Mercado, R. (2015). Financial inclusion, poverty, and income inequality in developing Asia. Asian Development Bank Economics Working Paper Series, (426).

Park, C. Y., & Mercado, R. Jr. (2018). Financial inclusion, poverty, and income inequality. *The Singapore Economic Review*, *63*(01), 185–206. doi:10.1142/S0217590818410059

Patel, S. (2023, May 23). *Top Benefits & Use Cases of AI in Insurance Industry*. REVE Chat. https://www.revechat.com/blog/insuranceai/#:~:text=Insurers%20can%20rely%20on%20AI,them%20based%20on%20customer%20needs

Patel, N., & Trivedi, S. (2020). Leveraging Predictive Modeling, Machine Learning Personalization, NLP Customer Support, and AI Chatbots to Increase Customer Loyalty. *Empirical Quests for Management Essences*, *3*(3), 1–24.

Payment and Settlement Systems Act. (2007). www.rbi.org.in

Pearson, A. (2019). Personalisation the artificial intelligence way. *Journal of Digital and Social Media Marketing*, *7*(3), 245–269.

Penelitian, J., Pembelajaran, P., Nurmayanti, N., Stkip, S., & Banten, S. (2023). The Effectiveness Of Using Quillbot In Improving Writing For Students Of English Education Study Program. *Jurnal Teknologi Pendidikan : Jurnal Penelitian Dan Pengembangan Pembelajaran*, *8*(1), 32–40. doi:10.33394/jtp.v8i1.6392

Pengnate, S., & Riggins, F. J. (2020). The role of emotion in P2P microfinance funding: A sentiment analysis approach. *International Journal of Information Management*, *54*, 102138. doi:10.1016/j.ijinfomgt.2020.102138

Pereira, M. J., Coheur, L., Fialho, P., & Ribeiro, R. (2019). Chatbots' greetings to human-computer communication. *CEUR Workshop Proceedings, 2390*(1994), 61–66.

Pereira, J., & Díaz, Ó. (2018). Chatbot dimensions that matter: Lessons from the trenches. In Web Engineering: 18th International Conference, ICWE 2018, Cáceres, Spain, June 5-8, 2018 [Springer International Publishing.]. *Proceedings*, *18*, 129–135.

Perez-Saiz, H., & Sharma, P. (2019). *FinTech in Sub-Saharan African Countries: A Game Changer*. International Monetary Fund.

Picard, P. (2000). *Insurance fraud: theory. Handbook of Insurance*. Kluwer.

Pirog, S., & Roberts, J. (2007). Personality and credit card misuse among college students: The mediating role of impulsiveness. *Journal of Marketing Theory and Practice*, *15*(1), 65–77. doi:10.2753/MTP1069-6679150105

Pisani, F., & Atalay, S. (2018). *Cashless Payments, Pain of Paying and the Role of Attachment*. ACR European Advances.

Pokrivcakova, S. (2019). Preparing teachers for the application of AI-powered technologies in foreign language education. *Journal of Language and Cultural Education*, *7*(3), 135–153. doi:10.2478/jolace-2019-0025

Powell, R., Do, A., Gengatharen, D., Yong, J., & Gengatharen, R. (2023). The relationship between responsible financial behaviours and financial wellbeing: The case of buy-now-pay-later. *Accounting and Finance*, *63*(4), 4431–4451. doi:10.1111/acfi.13100

Pratama, Y. D. (2021). The investigation of using grammarly as online grammar checker in the process of writing. *English Ideas. Journal of English Language Education*, *1*(2).

Prelec, D., & Loewenstein, G. (1998). The red and the black: Mental accounting of savings and debt. *Marketing Science*, *17*(1), 4–28. doi:10.1287/mksc.17.1.4

Priyadarshini, D., & Kar, S. (2021). Central Bank Digital Currency (CBDC): Critical Issues and the Indian Perspective. IEG Working Paper No. 44.

Przegalinska, A., Ciechanowski, L., Stroz, A., Gloor, P., & Mazurek, G. (2019). In bot we trust: A new methodology of chatbot performance measures. *Business Horizons*, *62*(6), 785–797. doi:10.1016/j.bushor.2019.08.005

PYMNTS.com & PayPal. (2020). *Buy now, pay later: Millennials and the shifting dynamics of online credit*. https://assets.ctfassets.net/7rifqg28wcbd/51nEg86tuS5X6Ln0k7mQp2/df8d2305bf8b19e0430c00f22dbd7e5f/PYMNTS_-

Rabbani, M. R., Sarea, A., Khan, S., & Abdullah, Y. (2022). Ethical concerns in artificial intelligence (AI): The role of RegTech and Islamic finance. In *Artificial Intelligence for Sustainable Finance and Sustainable Technology: Proceedings of ICGER 2021 1* (pp. 381-390). Springer International Publishing.

Rabbianty, E. N., Azizah, S., & Virdyna, N. K. (2023). AI in academic writing: Assessing current usage and future implications. *INSANIA : Jurnal Pemikiran Alternatif Kependidikan*, *28*(1a), 14–35. doi:10.24090/insania.v28i1a.9278

Rahman, A. M., Mamun, A. A., & Islam, A. (2017). Programming challenges of chatbot: Current and future prospective. *2017 IEEE Region 10 Humanitarian Technology Conference (R10-HTC)*, 75–78. doi:10.1109/R10-HTC.2017.8288910

Raja, J., Dean, A., & Manivannan, S. (2008). Journal of Internet Banking and Commerce E-payments: Problems and Prospects. *Journal of Internet Banking and Commerce*, *13*, 1–17.

Raj, V. A., Jasrotia, S. S., & Rai, S. S. (2023). Intensifying materialism through buy-now pay-later (BNPL): Examining the dark sides. *International Journal of Bank Marketing*.

RaneN.ChoudharyS.RaneJ. (2023). Explainable Artificial Intelligence (XAI) approaches for transparency and accountability in financial decision-making. *Available at* SSRN 4640316. doi:10.2139/ssrn.4640316

Rao, K., Sak, H., & Prabhavalkar, R. (2017, December). Exploring architectures, data and units for streaming end-to-end speech recognition with rnn-transducer. In 2017 IEEE Automatic Speech Recognition and Understanding Workshop (ASRU) (pp. 193-199). IEEE. doi:10.1109/ASRU.2017.8268935

Rapp, A., Curti, L., & Boldi, A. (2021). The human side of human-chatbot interaction: A systematic literature review of ten years of research on text-based chatbots. *International Journal of Human-Computer Studies*, *151*, 102630. doi:10.1016/j.ijhcs.2021.102630

Rashmi, R., & Nirmal, R. V. (2021). A study on the implementation and the impact of artificial intelligence in banking processes. *Asian Journal of Management*, *12*(1), 47–54.

Rastogi, S., Panse, C., Sharma, A., & Bhimavarapu, V. M. (2021). Unified Payment Interface (UPI): A Digital Innovation and Its Impact on Financial Inclusion and Economic Development. *Universal Journal of Accounting and Finance*, *9*(3), 518–530. doi:10.13189/ujaf.2021.090326

Rawal, A., Collishaw, S., Thapar, A., & Rice, F. (2013). 'The risks of playing it safe': A prospective longitudinal study of response to reward in the adolescent offspring of depressed parents. *Psychological Medicine*, *43*(1), 27–38. doi:10.1017/S0033291712001158 PMID:22617461

Rawlusyk, P. E. (2018). Assessment in Higher Education and Student Learning. *Journal of Instructional Pedagogies*, *21*, 1.

Ray, S., Paul, S., & Miglani, S. (2018). *Innovation, efficiency and inclusion: Integration of digital technologies in the Indian microfinance sector. Indian Council for Research on International Economic Relations*. ICRIER.

RBI. (2020). National Strategy for Financial Inclusion (NSFI): 2019-2024. Retrieved 11/10/2023, 2023, from Reserve Bank of India - Press Releases (rbi.org.in)

Reddy, T. (2017). *How chatbots can help reduce customer service costs by 30% - Watson Blog*. Ibm.Com. https://www.ibm.com/blogs/watson/2017/10/how-chatbots-reduce-customer-service-costs-by-30-percent/

Refat, M. M. H. (2023). *Adoption of Digital Payment Systems in Microcredit Operations: Challenges & Opportunities in the Context of Bangladesh*. https://www.theseus.fi/handle/10024/816214

Rehman, A. U., Malik, A. K., Raza, B., & Ali, W. (2019). A hybrid CNN-LSTM model for improving accuracy of movie reviews sentiment analysis. *Multimedia Tools and Applications*, *78*(18), 26597–26613. doi:10.1007/s11042-019-07788-7

Relja, R., Ward, P., & Zhao, A. L. (2023). Understanding the psychological determinants of buy-now-pay-later (BNPL) in the UK: A user perspective. *International Journal of Bank Marketing*.

Report of the Committee on Financial Inclusion. (2008).

Reserve Bank of India. (2022). https://www.rbi.org.in/commonperson/English/Scripts/FAQs.aspx?Id=3366

Richardson, A., Ganz, O., Stalgaitis, C., Abrams, D., & Vallone, D. (2014). Noncombustible tobacco product advertising: How companies are selling the new face of tobacco. *Nicotine & Tobacco Research: Official Journal of the Society for Research on Nicotine and Tobacco*, *16*(5), 606–614. doi:10.1093/ntr/ntt200 PMID:24379146

Rifkin, J. (2001). *The Age of Access: The New Culture of Hypercapitalism, Where all of Life is a Paid-For Experience. 2*, 320. https://www.amazon.com/The-Age-Access-Hypercapitalism-Experience/dp/1585420824

Rimavicius, T., & Gelzinis, A. 2017. A comparison of the deep learning methods for solving seafloor image classification task. In *Information and Software Technologies: 23rd International Conference, ICIST 2017, Druskininkai, Lithuania, October 12–14, 2017, Proceedings* (pp. 442-453). Springer International Publishing. 10.1007/978-3-319-67642-5_37

Rios-Campos, C., Viteri, J., Batalla, E., Castro, J., Núñez, J., Calderón, E., Nicacio, F., & Tello, M. (2023). Generative Artificial Intelligence. *South Florida Journal of Development*, *4*(6), 2305–2320. doi:10.46932/sfjdv4n6-008

Rizky, M., & Hariasih, M. (2023). Consumer Loyalty: Brand Perception, Trust, Product Quality, and the Mediating Role of Customer Satisfaction. *Academia Open*, *9*(2). Advance online publication. doi:10.21070/acopen.9.2024.5562

Rochon, L. P. (1999). *Credit, money, and production: an alternative post-Keynesian approach.* Edward Elgar Publishing. doi:10.4337/9781781959596

Rogha, M. (2023). Explain To Decide: A Human-Centric Review on the Role of Explainable Artificial Intelligence in AI-assisted Decision Making. *arXiv preprint arXiv:2312.11507.*

Rotaru, I. (n.d.). *How do insurance companies use AI in 2023? Benefits and examples.* Chatfuel. https://chatfuel.com/blog/ai-insurance

Rousseau, P. L., & Wachtel, P. (2000). Equity markets and growth: Cross-country evidence on timing and outcomes, 1980–1995. *Journal of Banking & Finance*, *24*(12), 1933–1957. doi:10.1016/S0378-4266(99)00123-5

Rowley, J. (1998). Promotion and marketing communications in the information marketplace. *Library Review*, *47*(8), 383–387. doi:10.1108/00242539810239543

Roy, S., & Sinha, D. I. (2014). *Determinants of Customers' Acceptance of Electronic Payment System in Indian Banking Sector – A Study.* Academic Press.

Ruane, E., Farrell, S., & Ventresque, A. (2021). User Perception of Text-Based Chatbot Personality. Lecture Notes in Computer Science (Including Subseries Lecture Notes in Artificial Intelligence and Lecture Notes in Bioinformatics), 12604 LNCS(February), 32–47. doi:10.1007/978-3-030-68288-0_3

Ruan, Y., & Mezei, J. (2022). When do AI chatbots lead to higher customer satisfaction than human frontline employees in online shopping assistance? Considering product attribute type. *Journal of Retailing and Consumer Services*, *68*, 103059. doi:10.1016/j.jretconser.2022.103059

Rusli, A., Young, J. C., & Iswari, N. M. S. (2020, July). Identifying fake news in Indonesian via supervised binary text classification. In *2020 IEEE International Conference on Industry 4.0, Artificial Intelligence, and Communications Technology (IAICT)* (pp. 86-90). IEEE. 10.1109/IAICT50021.2020.9172020

Rus, V., D'Mello, S., Hu, X., & Graesser, A. C. (2013). Recent advances in conversational intelligent tutoring systems. *AI Magazine*, *34*(3), 42–54. doi:10.1609/aimag.v34i3.2485

Rzepka, C., Berger, B., & Hess, T. (2022). Voice assistant vs. Chatbot–examining the fit between conversational agents' interaction modalities and information search tasks. *Information Systems Frontiers*, *24*(3), 839–856. doi:10.1007/s10796-021-10226-5

Sabir, S. A., Mohammad, H. B., & Shahar, H. B. K. (2019). The Role of Overconfidence and Past Investment Experience in Herding Behaviour with a Moderating Effect of Financial Literacy: Evidence from Pakistan Stock Exchange. *Asian Economic and Financial Review*, *9*(4), 480–490. doi:10.18488/journal.aefr.2019.94.480.490

Safari, K., Bisimwa, A., & Buzera, A. M. (2020). Attitudes and intentions toward internet banking in an under developed financial sector. *PSU Research Review*, *6*(1), 39–58. doi:10.1108/PRR-03-2020-0009

Saha, S., & Shaw, P. (2019). Revisiting industrialisation and innovation in India: roadmap for SDG 9. *2030 Agenda and India: Moving from Quantity to Quality: Exploring Convergence and Transcendence*, 41-64.

Sahoo, D., & Pillai, S., S. (. (2017). Role of mobile banking servicescape on customer attitude and engagement: An empirical investigation in India. *International Journal of Bank Marketing*, *35*(7), 1115–1132. doi:10.1108/IJBM-09-2015-0144

Saini, S., & Bansal, R. (2023). *Power of Social Media Influencer Credibility on the Influence of Brand Attitude*. doi:10.4018/978-1-6684-8898-0.ch010

Samans, R. (2021). Financing human-centred COVID-19 recovery and decisive climate action worldwide: International cooperation's twenty-first century moment of truth (No. 40). ILO Working Paper.

Sannon, S., Stoll, B., DiFranzo, D., Jung, M., & Bazarova, N. N. (2018, October). How personification and interactivity influence stress-related disclosures to conversational agents. In *Companion of the 2018 ACM conference on computer supported cooperative work and social computing* (pp. 285-288). ACM.

Santa Barletta, V., Cassano, F., Marengo, A., Pagano, A., Pange, J., & Piccinno, A. (2022). Switching learning methods during the pandemic: A quasi-experimental study on a master course. *Mdpi.ComVS Barletta, F Cassano, A Marengo, A Pagano, J Pange, A PiccinnoApplied Sciences, 2022•mdpi. Applied Sciences (Basel, Switzerland)*, *12*(17), 8438. Advance online publication. doi:10.3390/app12178438

Sanusi, I. T., Oyelere, S. S., & Omidiora, J. O. (2022). Exploring teachers' preconceptions of teaching machine learning in high school: A preliminary insight from Africa. *Computers and Education Open*, *3*, 100072. doi:10.1016/j.caeo.2021.100072

Sarstedt, M., Hair, J. F., Pick, M., Liengaard, B. D., Radomir, L., & Ringle, C. M. (2022). Progress in partial least squares structural equation modeling use in marketing research in the last decade. *Psychology &amp. Psychology and Marketing*, *39*(5), 1035–1064. doi:10.1002/mar.21640

Sarwar, M. A., Saima, M., & Gul, A. (2024). The Role of Artificial Intelligence in Shaping the Future of Education at Higher Secondary Level. *Journal of Education and Social Studies*, *5*(1), 34–45. doi:10.52223/jess.2024.5104

Sashi, C. M. (2012). Customer engagement, buyer-seller relationships, and social media. *Management Decision*, *50*(2), 253–272. doi:10.1108/00251741211203551

Sayinzoga, A., Bulte, E. H., & Lensink, R. (2016). Financial literacy and financial behaviour: Experimental evidence from rural Rwanda. *Economic Journal (London)*, *126*(594), 1571–1599. doi:10.1111/ecoj.12217

Schouten, A. P., Janssen, L., & Verspaget, M. (2020). Celebrity vs. Influencer endorsements in advertising: The role of identification, credibility, and Product-Endorser fit. *International Journal of Advertising*, *39*(2), 258–281. doi:10.1080/02650487.2019.1634898

Schumaker, R. P., Ginsburg, M., Chen, H., & Liu, Y. (2007). An evaluation of the chat and knowledge delivery components of a low-level dialog system:The AZ-ALICE experiment. *Decision Support Systems*, *42*(4), 2236–2246. doi:10.1016/j.dss.2006.07.001

Seldon, A., & Abidoye, O. (2018). *The fourth education revolution*. Academic Press.

Seounmi Youn and Ronald J. Faber. (2000). *Impulse Buying: Its Relation to Personality Traits and Cues*. The Association for Consumer Research. https://www.acrwebsite.org/volumes/8383/volumes/v27/NA-27/full

Sesar, V., Martinčević, I., & Boguszewicz-Kreft, M. (2022). Relationship between advertising disclosure, influencer credibility and purchase intention. *Journal of Risk and Financial Management*, *15*(7), 276. doi:10.3390/jrfm15070276

Sethi, D., & Acharya, D. (2018). Financial inclusion and economic growth linkage: Some cross country evidence. *Journal of Financial Economic Policy*, *10*(3), 369–385. doi:10.1108/JFEP-11-2016-0073

Shaikh, A. A., Hanafizadeh, P., & Karjaluoto, H. (2017). Mobile Banking and Payment System: A Conceptual Standpoint. *International Journal of E-Business Research*, *13*(2), 14–27. doi:10.4018/IJEBR.2017040102

Shaikh, A. A., & Karjaluoto, H. (2015). Mobile banking adoption: A literature review. *Telematics and Informatics*, *32*(1), 129–142. doi:10.1016/j.tele.2014.05.003

Shankar, A., Jebarajakirthy, C., & Ashaduzzaman, M. (2020). How do electronic word of mouth practices contribute to mobile banking adoption? *Journal of Retailing and Consumer Services*, *52*, 101920. doi:10.1016/j.jretconser.2019.101920

Sharif, M. H. U., & Mohammed, M. A. (2022). A literature review of financial losses statistics for cyber security and future trend. *World Journal of Advanced Research and Reviews*, *15*(1), 138–156. doi:10.30574/wjarr.2022.15.1.0573

Sharma, M., Banerjee, S., & Paul, J. (2022). Role of social media on mobile banking adoption among consumers. *Technological Forecasting and Social Change*, *180*, 121720. doi:10.1016/j.techfore.2022.121720

Shemshack, A., & Spector, J. M. (2020). A systematic literature review of personalized learning terms. *Smart Learning Environments*, *7*(1), 33. Advance online publication. doi:10.1186/s40561-020-00140-9

Shi, M., Wang, K., & Li, C. (2019, June). A C-LSTM with word embedding model for news text classification. In *2019 IEEE/ACIS 18th International Conference on Computer and Information Science (ICIS)* (pp. 253-257). IEEE. 10.1109/ICIS46139.2019.8940289

Shneiderman, B. (2020). Bridging the gap between ethics and practice: Guidelines for reliable, safe, and trustworthy human-centered AI systems. *ACM Transactions on Interactive Intelligent Systems*, *10*(4), 1–31. doi:10.1145/3419764

Sibanda, W., Ndiweni, E., Boulkeroua, M., Echchabi, A., & Ndlovu, T. (2020). Digital technology disruption on bank business models. *International Journal of Business Performance Management*, *21*(1-2), 184–213. doi:10.1504/IJBPM.2020.106121

Sikdar, P., & Kumar, A. (2016). Payment Bank: A Catalyst for Financial Inclusion. *Asia-Pacific Journal of Management Research and Innovation*, *12*(3–4), 226–231. doi:10.1177/2319510X17696648

Singh, J., & Singh, M. (2024). Accelerating Financial Inclusion of the Urban Poor: Role of Innovative e-Payment Systems and JAM Trinity in Alleviating Poverty in India. *Global Business Review*. Advance online publication. doi:10.1177/09721509231222609

Singh, M., Adebayo, S. O., Saini, M., & Singh, J. (2021). Indian government E-learning initiatives in response to COVID-19 crisis: A case study on online learning in Indian higher education system. *Education and Information Technologies*, *26*(6), 7569–7607. doi:10.1007/s10639-021-10585-1 PMID:34177350

Sinha, S., Pandey, K. R., & Madan, N. (2018). Fintech and the demand side challenge in financial inclusion. *Enterprise Development & Microfinance*, *29*(1), 94–98. doi:10.3362/1755-1986.17-00016

Sivadas, E., & Baker-Prewitt, J. L. (2000). An examination of the relationship between service quality, customer satisfaction, and store loyalty. *International Journal of Retail & Distribution Management*, *28*(2), 73–82. doi:10.1108/09590550010315223

Skjuve, M., Følstad, A., Fostervold, K. I., & Brandtzaeg, P. B. (2021). My chatbot companion-a study of human-chatbot relationships. *International Journal of Human-Computer Studies*, *149*, 102601. doi:10.1016/j.ijhcs.2021.102601

Slade, S., & Prinsloo, P. (2013). Learning Analytics: Ethical Issues and Dilemmas. doi:10.1177/0002764213479366

Soares, A. M., Camacho, C., & Elmashhara, M. G. (2022, April). Understanding the impact of chatbots on purchase intention. In *World Conference on Information Systems and Technologies* (pp. 462-472). Cham: Springer International Publishing. 10.1007/978-3-031-04829-6_41

Sobrino-García, I. (2021). Artificial intelligence risks and challenges in the Spanish public administration: An exploratory analysis through expert judgements. *Administrative Sciences, 11*(3), 102. doi:10.3390/admsci11030102

Sohail, M. S., & Al-Jabri, I. M. (2014). Attitudes towards mobile banking: Are there any differences between users and non-users? *Behaviour & Information Technology, 33*(4), 335–344. doi:10.1080/0144929X.2013.763861

Solomon, E. M., & van Klyton, A. (2020). The impact of digital technology usage on economic growth in Africa. *Utilities Policy, 67*, 101104. doi:10.1016/j.jup.2020.101104 PMID:32904493

Soman, D. (2003). The effect of payment transparency on consumption: Quasi- experiments from the field. *Marketing Letters, 14*(3), 173–183. doi:10.1023/A:1027444717586

Song, I., Lui, C., & Vong, J. (2014). Lowering the interest burden for microfinance. *International Journal of Process Management and Benchmarking, 4*(2), 213. doi:10.1504/IJPMB.2014.060409

Sørensen, K. B. (2012). The Self-Leading Customer: A new human-centred financial service. *Proceedings of the 2nd Innovation for Financial Services Summit.*

Srivastava, S. K., Singh, S. K., & Suri, J. S. (2020). A healthcare text classification system and its performance evaluation: A source of better intelligence by characterizing healthcare text. In *Cognitive informatics, computer modelling, and cognitive science* (pp. 319–369). Academic Press. doi:10.1016/B978-0-12-819445-4.00016-3

Stiglitz, J. E., & Greenwald, B. C. (2015). *Creating a learning society: A new approach to growth, development, and social progress*. Columbia University Press. doi:10.7312/stig17549

Stone, M., Aravopoulou, E., Ekinci, Y., Evans, G., Hobbs, M., Labib, A., Laughlin, P., Machtynger, J., & Machtynger, L. (2020). Artificial intelligence (AI) in strategic marketing decision-making: A research agenda. *The Bottom Line (New York, N.Y.), 33*(2), 183–200. doi:10.1108/BL-03-2020-0022

Struckell, E. M., Patel, P. C., Ojha, D., & Oghazi, P. (2022). Financial literacy and self employment – The moderating effect of gender and race. *Journal of Business Research, 139*, 639–653. doi:10.1016/j.jbusres.2021.10.003

Subudhi, S. R. I. H. A. R. I. (2019). Banking on artificial intelligence: Opportunities & challenges for banks in India. *International Journal of Research in Commerce, Economics and Management, 9*(7).

Suhel, S. F., Shukla, V. K., Vyas, S., & Mishra, V. P. (2020, June). Conversation to automation in banking through chatbot using artificial machine intelligence language. In *2020 8th international conference on reliability, infocom technologies and optimization (trends and future directions) (ICRITO)* (pp. 611-618). IEEE. 10.1109/ICRITO48877.2020.9197825

Sujith, A. V. L. N., Qureshi, N. I., Dornadula, V. H. R., Rath, A., Prakash, K. B., & Singh, S. K. (2022). A comparative analysis of business machine learning in making effective financial decisions using structural equation model (SEM). *Journal of Food Quality*, *2022*, 1–7. doi:10.1155/2022/6382839

Sundar, S. S., & Marathe, S. S. (2010). Personalization versus customization: The importance of agency, privacy, and power usage. *Human Communication Research*, *36*(3), 298–322. doi:10.1111/j.1468-2958.2010.01377.x

Suresh, A., & Rani, N. J. (2020). Role of Artificial Intelligence (AI) in the Indian Banking Scenario. *Journal of Information Technology and Economic Development*, *11*(2).

Sutton, H. (2019). Minimize online cheating through proctoring, consequences. *Recruiting & Retaining Adult Learners*, *21*(5), 1–5. doi:10.1002/nsr.30434

Swaid, S. I., & Wigand, R. T. (2007). Key dimensions of e-commerce service quality and its relationships to satisfaction and loyalty. *BLED 2007 Proceedings*, 29.

Syifa, N., & Tohang, V. (2020). The Use Of E-Wallet System. *2020 International Conference on Information Management and Technology (ICIMTech)*, 342–347. 10.1109/ICIMTech50083.2020.9211213

Tajeddini, K., Rasoolimanesh, S. M., Gamage, T. C., & Martin, E. (2021). Exploring the visitors' decision-making process for Airbnb and hotel accommodations using value-attitude-behavior and theory of planned behavior. *International Journal of Hospitality Management*, *96*, 102950. doi:10.1016/j.ijhm.2021.102950

Talking the Talk: The Beginner's Guide to Designing a Chatbot Conversation. (2017). Hubspot. https://blog.hubspot.com/marketing/beginners-guide-to-designing-a-chatbot-conversation

Tam, C., & Oliveira, T. (2017). Literature review of mobile banking and individual performance. *International Journal of Bank Marketing*, *35*(7), 1044–1067. doi:10.1108/IJBM-09-2015-0143

Tan, G. K. S. (2022). Buy what you want, today! Platform ecologies of 'buy now, pay later' services in Singapore. *Transactions of the Institute of British Geographers*, *47*(4), 912–926. doi:10.1111/tran.12539

Tang, Y. C. (2009). An approach to budget allocation for an aerospace company—Fuzzy analytic hierarchy process and artificial neural network. *Neurocomputing*, *72*(16-18), 3477–3489. doi:10.1016/j.neucom.2009.03.020

Tatineni, S. (2022). Customer Authentication in Mobile Banking-MLOps Practices and AI-Driven Biometric Authentication Systems. *Journal of Economics & Management Research.* doi. org/(3). doi:10.47363/JESMR/2022

Tay, L. Y., Tai, H. T., & Tan, G. S. (2022). Digital financial inclusion: A gateway to sustainable development. *Heliyon*, *8*(6), e09766. doi:10.1016/j.heliyon.2022.e09766 PMID:35785228

Taylor, S., & Todd, P. A. (1995). Understanding information technology usage: A test of competing models. *Information Systems Research*, *6*(2), 144–176. doi:10.1287/isre.6.2.144

Teo, A. C., Tan, G. W. H., Ooi, K. B., Hew, T. S., & Yew, K. T. (2015). The effects of convenience and speed in m-payment. *Industrial Management & Data Systems*, *115*(2), 311–331. doi:10.1108/IMDS-08-2014-0231

Thomas, M., Desai, K. K., & Seenivasan, S. (2011). How Credit Card Payments Increase Unhealthy Food Purchases: Visceral Regulation of Vices. *The Journal of Consumer Research*, *38*(1), 126–139. doi:10.1086/657331

Thomaz, F., Salge, C., Karahanna, E., & Hulland, J. (2020). Learning from the Dark Web: Leveraging conversational agents in the era of hyper-privacy to enhance marketing. *Journal of the Academy of Marketing Science*, *48*(1), 43–63. doi:10.1007/s11747-019-00704-3

Ting Yan Chan, W., & Hong Leung, C. (2021). Mind the Gap: Discrepancy Between Customer Expectation and Perception on Commercial Chatbots Usage. *Asian Journal of Empirical Research*, *11*(1), 1–10. doi:10.18488/journal.1007.2021.111.1.10

Tiwari, P., Tiwari, S. K., & Gupta, A. (2021). Examining the Impact of Customers' Awareness, Risk and Trust in M-Banking Adoption. *FIIB Business Review, 10*(4), 413–423.

Toader, D. C., Boca, G., Toader, R., Măcelaru, M., Toader, C., Ighian, D., & Rădulescu, A. T. (2020). The effect of social presence and chatbot errors on trust. *Sustainability (Basel)*, *12*(1), 1–24. doi:10.3390/su12010256

Todor, R. D. (2016). Blending traditional and digital marketing. *Bulletin of the Transilvania University of Brasov, Series I: Engineering Sciences, 9*(1), 51–56. http://ezproxy.leedsbeckett.ac.uk/login?url=http://search.ebscohost.com/login.aspx?direct=true&db=a9h&AN=116699220&site=eds-live&scope=site

Torbarina, M., Jelenc, L., & Brkljačić, I. (2019). Faces engage social media influencers' followers (SSRN *Scholarly Paper 3961288*). https://papers.ssrn.com/abstract=3961288

Tran, H. T. T., & Corner, J. (2016). The impact of communication channels on mobile banking adoption. *International Journal of Bank Marketing*, *34*(1), 78–109. doi:10.1108/IJBM-06-2014-0073

Tresierra, A. E., & Reyes, S. D. (2018). Effects of institutional quality and the development of the banking system on corporate debt. *Journal of Economics, Finance and Administrative Science*, *23*(44), 113–124. doi:10.1108/JEFAS-03-2017-0053

Tripathi, R., & Tripathi, S. (2023). Identifying Fraud Detection Techniques Using Text Analytics Processing. *Adhyayan: A Journal of Management Sciences, 13*(1), 5-8.

TsvetkovaM.García-GavilanesR.FloridiL.YasseriT. (2016). *Even Good Bots Fight. December.* http://arxiv.org/abs/1609.04285

Tyagi, R. (2023). Empowering the unbanked: A revolution in financial inclusion through artificial intelligence. *International Journal of Research in Engineering. Science and Management*, *6*(10), 4–12.

Úbeda, F., Mendez, A., & Forcadell, F. J. (2023). The sustainable practices of multinational banks as drivers of financial inclusion in developing countries. *Finance Research Letters*, *51*, 103278. doi:10.1016/j.frl.2022.103278

UK. (2018). *How Chatbots Can Redefine Your Sales Process.* https://www.salesforce.com/uk/blog/2018/09/how-chatbots-can-redefine-your-sales-process.html

Ullah, S., Ali, K., Shah, S. A., & Ehsan, M. (2022). Environmental concerns of financial inclusion and economic policy uncertainty in the era of globalization: Evidence from low & high globalized OECD economies. *Environmental Science and Pollution Research International*, *29*(24), 36773–36787. doi:10.1007/s11356-022-18758-2 PMID:35064882

Ullah, S., Kiani, U. S., Raza, B., & Mustafa, A. (2022). Consumers' Intention to Adopt m-payment/m-banking: The Role of Their Financial Skills and Digital Literacy. *Frontiers in Psychology*, *13*, 873708. doi:10.3389/fpsyg.2022.873708 PMID:35572297

Umamaheswari, S., & Valarmathi, A. (2023). Role of Artificial Intelligence in The Banking Sector. *Journal of Survey in Fisheries Sciences*, *10*(4S), 2841–2849.

Um, T., Kim, T., & Chung, N. (2020). How does an intelligence chatbot affect customers compared with self-service technology for sustainable services? *Sustainability (Basel)*, *12*(12), 5119. Advance online publication. doi:10.3390/su12125119

United Nations. (2021). The Imperative of Financial Inclusion. Retrieved on from 11/10/2023, Financial Inclusion | United Nations | UNSGSA Queen Máxima.

Valle-Cruz, D., Fernandez-Cortez, V., & Gil-Garcia, J. R. (2022). From E-budgeting to smart budgeting: Exploring the potential of artificial intelligence in government decision-making for resource allocation. *Government Information Quarterly*, *39*(2), 101644. doi:10.1016/j.giq.2021.101644

Van den Broeck, E., Zarouali, B., & Poels, K. (2019). Chatbot advertising effectiveness: When does the message get through? *Computers in Human Behavior*, *98*, 150–157. doi:10.1016/j.chb.2019.04.009

Van der Waldt, D. L. R., Van Loggerenberg, M., & Wehmeyer, L. (2009). Celebrity endorsements versus created spokespersons in advertising: A survey among students. *Suid-Afrikaanse Tydskrif vir Ekonomiese en Bestuurswetenskappe*, *12*(1), 100–114. doi:10.4102/sajems.v12i1.263

van Dis, E. A. M., Bollen, J., Zuidema, W., van Rooij, R., & Bockting, C. L. (2023). ChatGPT: Five priorities for research. *Nature*, *614*(7947), 224–226. doi:10.1038/d41586-023-00288-7 PMID:36737653

Vandewaetere, M., & Clarebout, G. (2014). Advanced technologies for personalized learning, instruction, and performance. Handbook of Research on Educational Communications and Technology: Fourth Edition, 425–437. https://doi.org/ doi:10.1007/978-1-4614-3185-5_34/COVER

Varghese, A., Agyeman-Badu, G., & Cawley, M. (2020). Deep learning in automated text classification: A case study using toxicological abstracts. *Environment Systems & Decisions, 40*(4), 465–479. doi:10.1007/s10669-020-09763-2

Varsha, P. (2023). How can we manage biases in artificial intelligence systems – A systematic literature review. *International Journal of Information Management Data Insights, 3*(1), 100165. https://doi.org/. 2023.100165 doi:10.1016 /j.jjimei

VARTEQ Inc. (2023, July 11). *AI in Credit Scoring: Enhancing Loan Approvals and Financial Inclusion through Advanced Algorithms.* https://www.linkedin.com/pulse/ai-credit-scoring-enhancing-loan-approvals-financial-inclusion

Venkatesh, V., & Zhang, X. (2020). Unified theory of acceptance and use of technology. Encyclopedia of Education and Information Technologies, 13(1), 1750–1750. doi:10.1007/978-3-030-10576-1_300692

Venkatesh, V., & Davis, F. D. (2000). A theoretical extension of the technology acceptance model: Four longitudinal field studies. *Management Science, 46*(2), 186–204. doi:10.1287/mnsc.46.2.186.11926

Verbik, L., & Lasanowski, V. (2007). International Student Mobility: Patterns and Trends. *World Education News and Reviews, 20*(10), 1–16.

Viaene, S., & Dedene, G. (2004). Insurance fraud: Issues and challenges. *The Geneva Papers on Risk and Insurance-Issues and Practice, 29*, 313-333.

Visser, B. (2021). *A deep-dive into Europe's fast-growing BNPL market.* https://www.linkedin.com/pulse/deep-dive-europes-fast-growing-bnpl- market-Bart-visser/

Vučinić, M., & Luburić, R. (2022). Fintech, risk-based thinking and cyber risk. *Journal of Central Banking Theory and Practice, 11*(2), 27–53. doi:10.2478/jcbtp-2022-0012

Vuppalapaty, P. (2021). *The Need for Agility in Capital Budgeting of Intelligent Automations for Knowledge and Service Work.* Temple University.

Walkington, C., & Bernacki, M. L. (2020). Appraising research on personalized learning: Definitions, theoretical alignment, advancements, and future directions. doi:10.1080/15391523.2020.1747757

Walzhofer, N., Riekeberg, M., & Follert, F. (2022). From White Collar to Influencer Marketing? How Banks Can Reach Young Customers. *International Journal of Financial Studies, 10*(3), 79. doi:10.3390/ijfs10030079

Wang, H., & Gao, S. (2024). The future of the international financial system: The emerging CBDC network and its impact on regulation. *Regulation & Governance*, *18*(1), 288–306. doi:10.1111/rego.12520

Wang, H., Tlili, A., Huang, R., Cai, Z., Li, M., Cheng, Z., Yang, D., Li, M., Zhu, X., & Fei, C. (2023). Examining the applications of intelligent tutoring systems in real educational contexts: A systematic literature review from the social experiment perspective. *Education and Information Technologies*, *28*(7), 9113–9148. Advance online publication. doi:10.1007/s10639-022-11555-x PMID:36643383

Wang, H., & Yuan, L. (2022). Software engineering defect detection and classification system based on artificial intelligence. *Nonlinear Engineering*, *11*(1), 380–386. doi:10.1515/nleng-2022-0042

Wang, P., & Yip, C. K. (1992). Alternative approaches to money and growth. *Journal of Money, Credit and Banking*, *24*(4), 553–562. doi:10.2307/1992811

Wang, T., & Kolen, M. J. (2001). Evaluating comparability in computerized adaptive testing: Issues, criteria and an example. *Journal of Educational Measurement*, *38*(1), 19–49. doi:10.1111/j.1745-3984.2001.tb01115.x

Wanof, M. I. (2023). Digital Technology Innovation in Improving Financial Access for Low-Income Communities. *Technology and Society Perspectives*, *1*(1), 1. Advance online publication. doi:10.61100/tacit.v1i1.35

Ward, O., & Rochemont, S. (2019). *Understanding Central Bank Digital Currencies (CBDC)*. Institute and Faculty of Actuaries.

Weinberg, C. (2017). *How Messenger and "M" Are Shifting Gears*. The Information. https://www.theinformation.com/articles/how-messenger-and-m-are-shifting-gears

Wessels, L., & Drennan, J. (2010). An investigation of consumer acceptance of M-banking. *International Journal of Bank Marketing*, *28*(7), 547–568. doi:10.1108/02652321011085194

Wewege, L., Lee, J., & Thomsett, M. (2020). *Disruptions and Digital Banking Trends*. Academic Press.

Wilson, F. (2023). *INSURTECH market size to reach USD 166.4 billion by 2030*. Retrieved from https://www.acumenresearchandconsulting.com/press-releases/insurtech-market

Wood, E. A., Ange, B. L., & Miller, D. D. (2021). Are We Ready to Integrate Artificial Intelligence Literacy into Medical School Curriculum: Students and Faculty Survey. *Journal of Medical Education and Curricular Development*, *8*. doi:10.1177/23821205211024078 PMID:34250242

World Bank (2021b). The Global Findex Database 2021 Financial Inclusion, Digital Payments, and Resilience in the Age of COVID-19. Retrieved 13/10/2023, from 9781464818974 (1).pdf

World Bank. (2021a). The Drive for Financial Inclusion: Lessons of World Bank Group Experience. Retrieved 11/10/2023, 2023, from ap_driveforfinancialinclusion.pdf (worldbankgroup.org).

World bank. (2022a). Financial inclusion is a key enabler to reducing poverty and boosting prosperity.Retrieved 13/10/2023, from Financial Inclusion Overview (worldbank.org).

World Bank. (2022b). COVID-19 Drives Global Surge in use of Digital Payments. Retrieved 11/10/2023, 2023, from COVID-19 Drives Global Surge in use of Digital Payments (worldbank.org).

Worldpay. (2020). *Global Payments Report: The pathways of people and payments*. http://offers.worldpayglobal.com/rs/850-JOA-856/images/GPR-2020.pdf?mkt_tok=eyJpIjoiWm1SalpEUXhOelEyWkdZeiIsInQiOiJXbX

Xiao, Y., Keung, J., Bennin, K. E., & Mi, Q. (2019). Improving bug localization with word embedding and enhanced convolutional neural networks. *Information and Software Technology*, *105*, 17–29. doi:10.1016/j.infsof.2018.08.002

Xing, Y., Chen, H., & Zhuang, X. (2019). Australian Online BNPL Services Research: Building Gain Value Model of Individual Credit Background. *Proceedings of the 2019 International Conference on Information Technology and Computer Communications*, 45–51. 10.1145/3355402.3355410

Yan, L., Zheng, Y., & Cao, J. (2018). Few-shot learning for short text classification. *Multimedia Tools and Applications*, *77*(22), 29799–29810. doi:10.1007/s11042-018-5772-4

Yasir, A., Ahmad, A., Abbas, S., Inairat, M., Al-Kassem, A. H., & Rasool, A. (2022, February). How Artificial Intelligence Is Promoting Financial Inclusion? A Study On Barriers Of Financial Inclusion. In *2022 International Conference on Business Analytics for Technology and Security (ICBATS)* (pp. 1-6). IEEE. 10.1109/ICBATS54253.2022.9759038

Yeh, H. C., Yu, M. C., Liu, C. H., & Huang, C. I. (2023). Robo-advisor based on unified theory of acceptance and use of technology. *Asia Pacific Journal of Marketing and Logistics*, *35*(4), 962–979. doi:10.1108/APJML-07-2021-0493

Yoon, J. W., Andrews, J. E., & Ward, H. L. (2022). Perceptions on adopting artificial intelligence and related technologies in libraries: Public and academic librarians in North America. *Library Hi Tech*, *40*(6), 1893–1915. doi:10.1108/LHT-07-2021-0229

Yu, C. S. (2012). Factors affecting individuals to adopt mobile banking: Empirical evidence from the UTAUT model. *Journal of Electronic Commerce Research*, *13*(2), 104.

Yüce, E. (2022). The Immediate Reactions of EFL Learners towards Total Digitalization at Higher Education during the Covid-19 Pandemic. *Journal of Theoretical Educational Science*, *15*(1), 1–15. doi:10.30831/akukeg.939836

Yu, H.-C., Hsi, K.-H., & Kuo, P.-J. (2002). Electronic payment systems: An analysis and comparison of types. *Technology in Society*, *24*(3), 331–347. doi:10.1016/S0160-791X(02)00012-X

Yun, J., & Park, J. (2022). The Effects of Chatbot Service Recovery With Emotion Words on Customer Satisfaction, Repurchase Intention, and Positive Word-Of-Mouth. *Frontiers in Psychology*, *13*, 922503. doi:10.3389/fpsyg.2022.922503 PMID:35712132

Yunus, M. (1999). The Grameen Bank. *Scientific American*, *281*(5), 114–119. doi:10.1038/scientificamerican1199-114

Zainuddin, M., & Yasin, I. M. (2020). Resurgence of an Ancient Idea? A Study on the History of Microfinance. *FIIB Business Review*, *9*(2), 78–84. doi:10.1177/2319714520925933

Zawacki Richter, O., Marín Juarros, V. I., Bond, M., & Gouverneur, F. (2019). Systematic review of research on artificial intelligence applications in higher education: where are the educators? *International Journal of Educational Technology in Higher Education, 16*, 6. doi:10.1186/s41239-019-0171-0

Zeb, A., Ullah, R., & Karim, R. (2024). Exploring the role of ChatGPT in higher education: Opportunities, challenges and ethical considerations. *The International Journal of Information and Learning Technology*, *41*(1), 99–111. doi:10.1108/IJILT-04-2023-0046

Zeleznikow, J. (2021). Using artificial intelligence to provide intelligent dispute resolution support. *Group Decision and Negotiation*, *30*(4), 789–812. doi:10.1007/s10726-021-09734-1 PMID:33867681

Zellermayer, O. (1996). *The Pain of Paying*. PhD Dissertation.

Zhang, Q., & Posso, A. (2019). Thinking inside the box: A closer look at financial inclusion and household income. *The Journal of Development Studies*, *55*(7), 1616–1631. doi:10.1080/00220388.2017.1380798

Zhang, T., Lu, C., & Kizildag, M. (2018). Banking "on-the-go": Examining consumers' adoption of mobile banking services. *International Journal of Quality and Service Sciences*, *10*(3), 279–295. doi:10.1108/IJQSS-07-2017-0067

Zhou, P., Liu, J., Liu, X., Yang, Z., & Grundy, J. (2019). Is deep learning better than traditional approaches in tag recommendation for software information sites? *Information and Software Technology*, *109*, 1–13. doi:10.1016/j.infsof.2019.01.002

Zumstein, D., & Hundertmark, S. (2018). Chatbots: An interactive technology for personalized communication and transaction. *IADIS International Journal on Www/Internet, 15*(1), 96–109.

About the Contributors

Debora A. is an Assistant Professor in the Department of Business and Management. She has four years of experience in academia. She has published research articles in Scopus listed journals.

Rachit Agarwal is working as an Assistant Professor at University School of Business, Chandigarh University, Mohali. He is having more than 6 years of work experience in teaching and research. His areas of interest are financial analysis, investment behavior analysis and behavioral study. He has published various papers in national and international journals including Scopus and ABDC listed journals. He has also organized many workshops and Faculty Development Programme on Research Methodology and on different statistical tools.

Alankrita Aggarwal is an academician and researcher in the field of computer science and engineering. She did Ph.D from IKGPTU, Kapurthala, Punjab (India) and done BE & M.Tech in Computer Science and Engineering from MDU, Rohtak, Haryana (India) having experience of around 18 years. She is working as Associate Professor in Department of Computer Science and Engineering, Chandigarh University, Gharuan, Mohali Punjab,India .Research interests are in the field of risk management and Generative adverserial networks. She has served as Session Chair at numerous international conferences, organized and attended various Workshops, FDPs and presented papers in various Conferences on National/International Platforms. She also written two books,12 book chapters and published around 40 papers in reputed journals and in national/international conferences. Also published 5 patents (2 Indian and 3 Australian). She is also a member of IEEE Under Delhi Section and Region R10 –Asia and Pacific Membership Number: 977724535,Life Member of Indian Society of Technical Education (ISTE) vide membership number: LM49112, Member of International Association of Engineers (IAENG), Hong Kong vide membership number: 10897.

Santosh Satyanarayan Baheti is an Assistant Professor in the Department of Business and Management. He has worked in corporate prior to joining academia. He has published research articles in Scopus and ABDC listed journals.

Shruti Bansal is pursuing Doctorate of Philosophy in Commerce from M.M.H. College, Ghaziabad affiliated to Chaudhary Charan Singh University, Meerut, Uttar Pradesh, India. She holds the UGC NTA NET qualification (2021) in the field of Management. With over 6 years of dedicated experience in the field of research, her intellectual journey is marked by a profound commitment to exploring the intricate intersection of finance and human resource management. Her areas of interest are financial analysis, investment behavior analysis and behavioral study. She has a rich publishing history with multiple research papers and chapters in Scopus, ABDC listed journals and UGC-listed national and international journals. She has also presented extensively at national and international conferences such as in IIM Indore, IIM Jammu and many more. Her brief biography summarizes her academic affiliation, qualifications, and notable contributions to Finance and Management domain research.

Ekta Kasana is a Research Scholar at Amity College of Commerce and Finance, Amity University, Noida, Uttar Pradesh. Her area of research is finance and economics. She has published papers in Scopus and Web of Science indexed journals. She qualified the UGC JRF examination in 2020. She obtained her undergraduate degree from Kalindi College, University of Delhi, in 2015 and postgraduate degree from the Amity College of Commerce and Finance.

Rupali is a full-time research scholar pursuing her doctorate degree in the field of management from Amity Business School, Amity University Uttar Pradesh. Her area of research includes Human resource management, Organisational behavior and Diversity and Inclusion.

Renu Singh is a FinTech Consultant and Trainer with 6+ years of experience in teaching, training, and research. She is currently working as a consultant with National Stock Exchange(NSE) and a Faculty cum Trainer with London Institute of Banking and Finance (LIBF UK). Her expertise includes Open APIs, Blockchain, Artificial Intelligence, Digital Payments, and Data Analytics. She has designed curricula for Fintech certifications and degree programs in collaboration with National Stock Exchange(NSE) and various EdTech consultancy firms. She has also been associated as a Asst. Professor Fintech and Finance with Christ University, Symbiosis Centre for Information Technology(SCIT), Narsee Monjee Institute of

Management Sciences(NMIMS). She has presented and published her research work at various international conferences in FinTech and won best research paper awards.

Dippi Verma is Assistant Professor at CHRIST University Bangalore. She has published research papers in different peer reviewed journals. She has more than 10 years of experience in Academics.

Index

T

W

www.ingramcontent.com/pod-product-compliance
Lightning Source LLC
LaVergne TN
LVHW080635011026
849160LV00014B/1229

* 9 7 9 8 3 6 9 3 4 8 1 9 2 *